Shojo Beat

STROBE EDGE

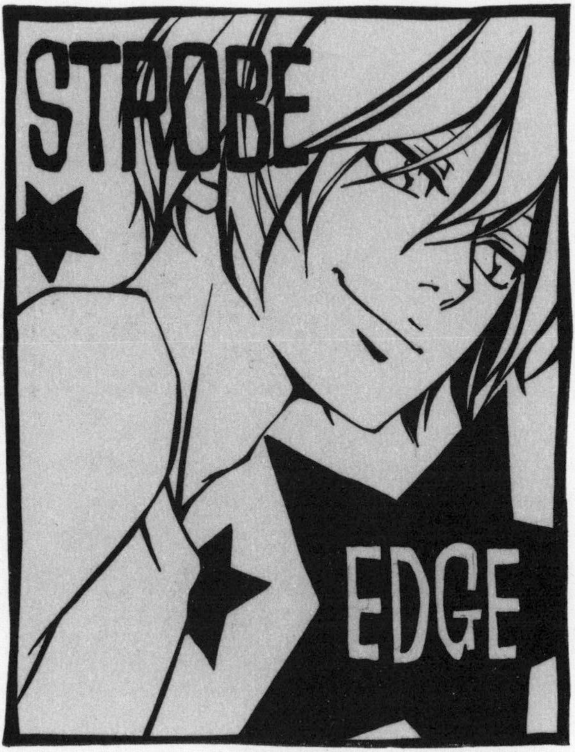
STROBE
EDGE

Vol. 10

Story & Art by
Io Sakisaka

STROBE EDGE

Volume 10
CONTENTS

Story Thus Far

Ninako is a down-to-earth high school girl who's in love for the first time—with Ren, the most popular boy in her grade. She tells him her feelings, but he turns her down and asks if they can still be friends. In the meantime, Ren's friend from middle school, Ando, confesses his love for Ninako, but she turns him down.

Now in their second year, Ninako, Ren and Ando are all in the same homeroom. Ando's ex-girlfriend, Mao, enters their school. She tells Ninako why Ren and Ando are not as close as they used to be. Ninako tries to give up on her love for Ren because she fears that the two boys could become even more distant. Not knowing any of this, Ren finally acknowledges his feelings for Ninako and decides to tell her. Right before he does, however, Ando gets hurt protecting Ninako from some thugs. Partly because of that, Ninako turns Ren down when he confesses his feelings for her. But after school one day, Ren catches Ninako sitting at his desk…!

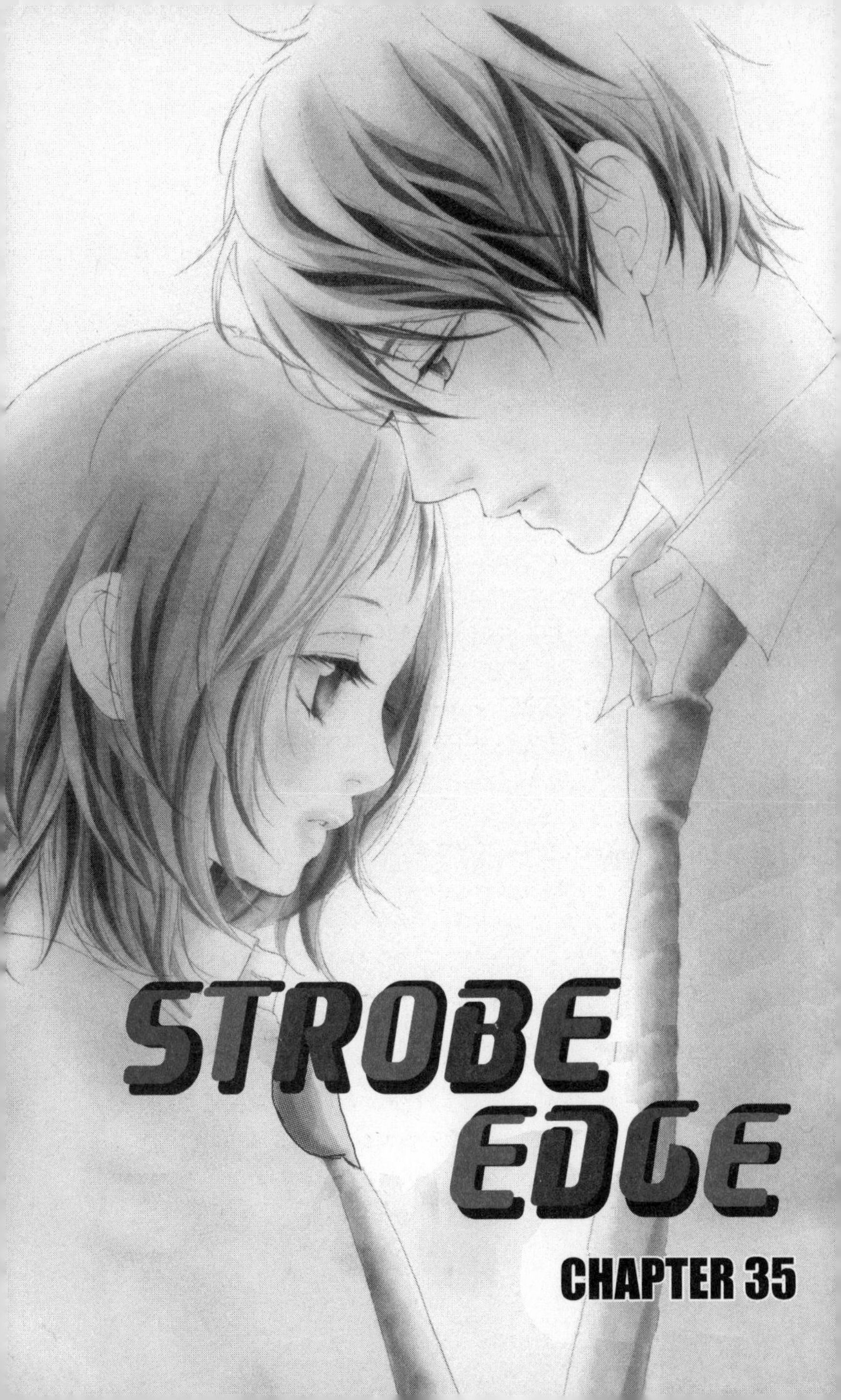
STROBE
EDGE
CHAPTER 35

GREETINGS ★

Hello! This is Io Sakisaka. Thank you so much for picking up a copy of
Strobe Edge 10!!

Well, we've made it to the last volume. It feels like it's taken a long
time to get here, but it also feels like time just flew by.

In looking back on this series, I can honestly tell anyone who asks that
I had a lot of fun doing it. It was a fulfilling experience! I did so many
things for the first time. During the course of it, I felt confused and
anxious (and I was sometimes almost crushed by worry), but there was
always excitement somewhere in my heart too. Naturally there were a
lot of sad and difficult times, but all the happy and fun experiences
more than made up for it!

I wonder what lies ahead? The reason I can feel this anticipation and
excitement is thanks to all of you who are reading this right now.
Thank you so very much!

As you'll see, *Strobe Edge* 10 is packed with even more gratitude than
usual! If it leaves you feeling even a bit warm inside when you're done
reading, then I'll be very happy indeed. Please stick with us to the end!

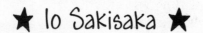 ★ Io Sakisaka ★

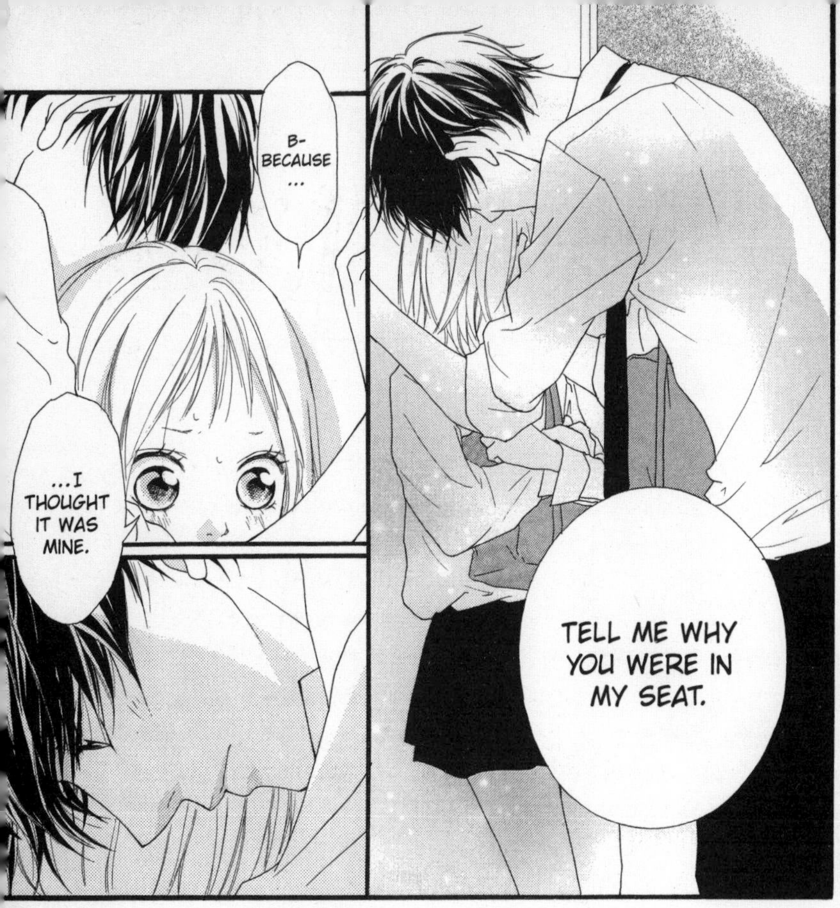
TELL ME WHY YOU WERE IN MY SEAT.
B- BECAUSE ...
...I THOUGHT IT WAS MINE.

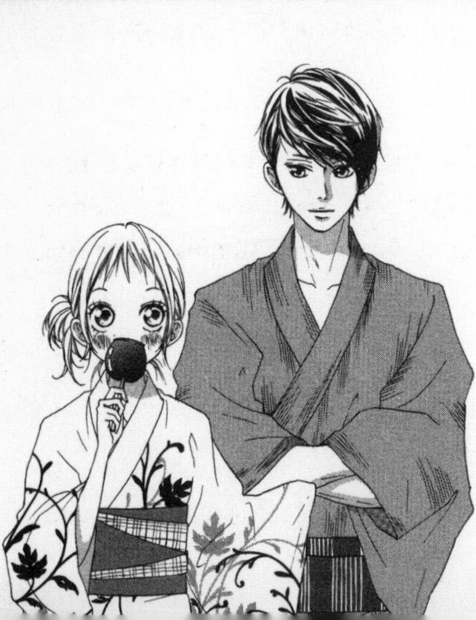

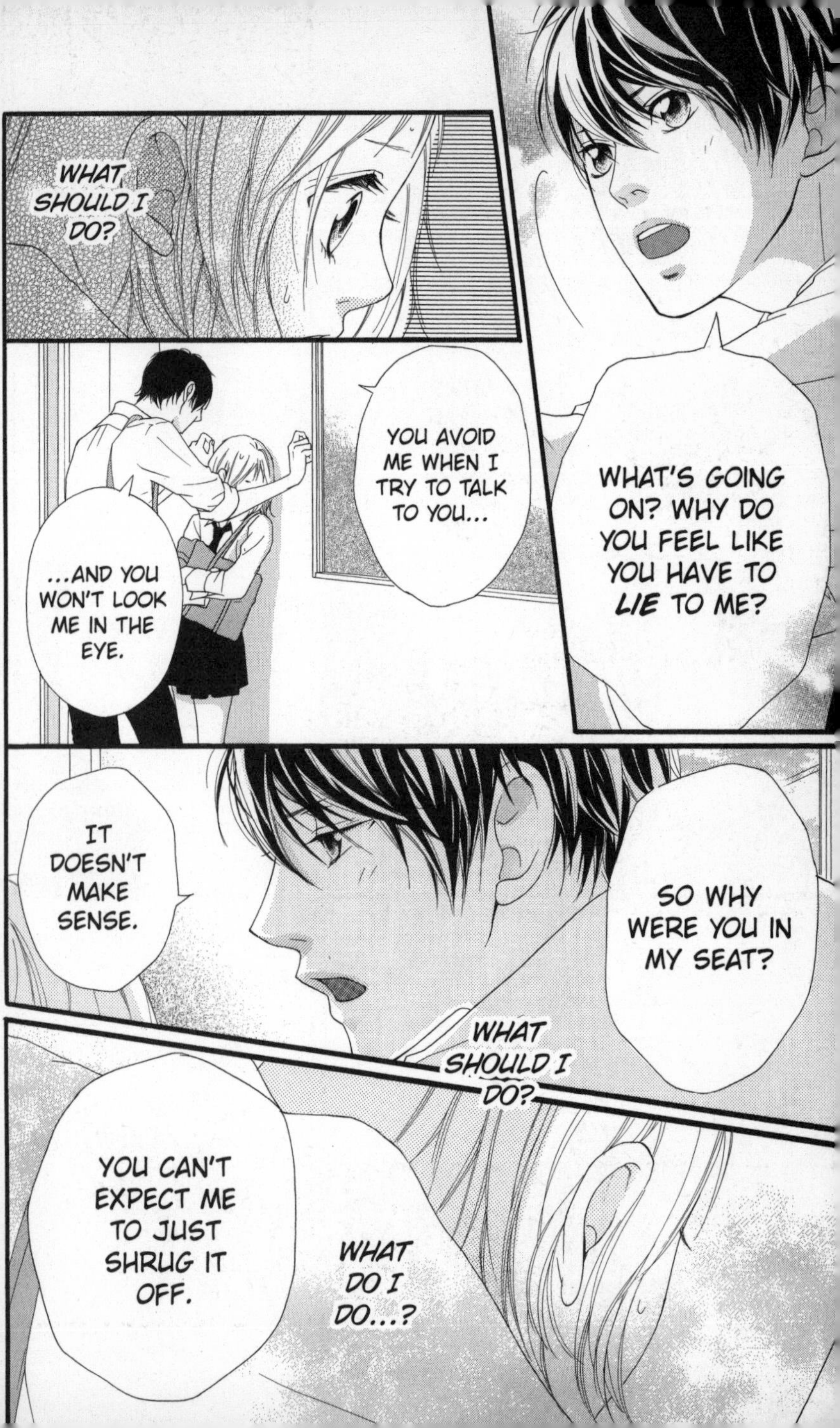
WHAT'S GOING ON? WHY DO YOU FEEL LIKE YOU HAVE TO *LIE* TO ME?
WHAT SHOULD I DO?
YOU AVOID ME WHEN I TRY TO TALK TO YOU...
...AND YOU WON'T LOOK ME IN THE EYE.
SO WHY WERE YOU IN MY SEAT?
IT DOESN'T MAKE SENSE.
WHAT SHOULD I DO?
WHAT DO I DO...?
YOU CAN'T EXPECT ME TO JUST SHRUG IT OFF.

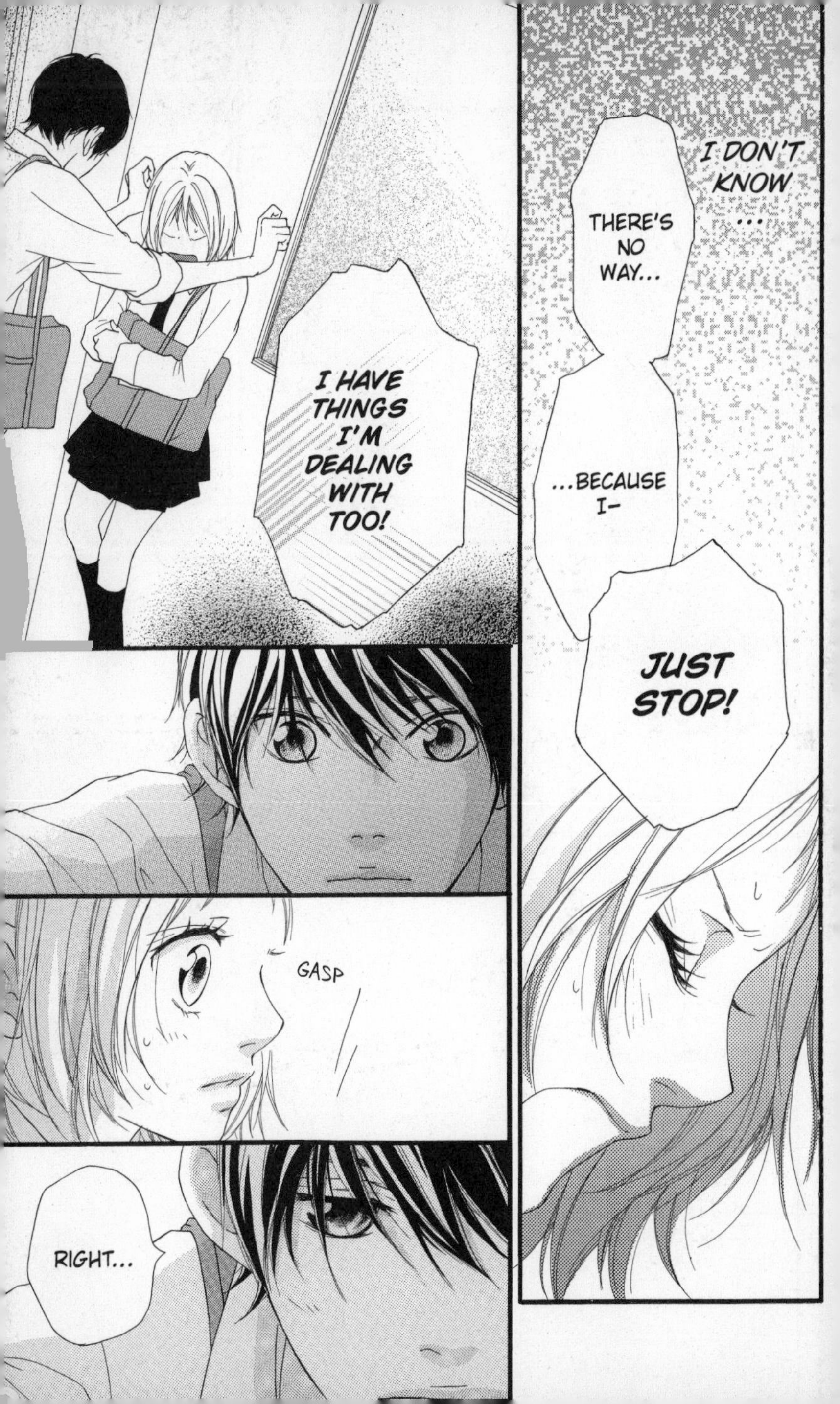
I DON'T KNOW ...
THERE'S NO WAY...
...BECAUSE I-
JUST STOP!
I HAVE THINGS I'M DEALING WITH TOO!
GASP
RIGHT...

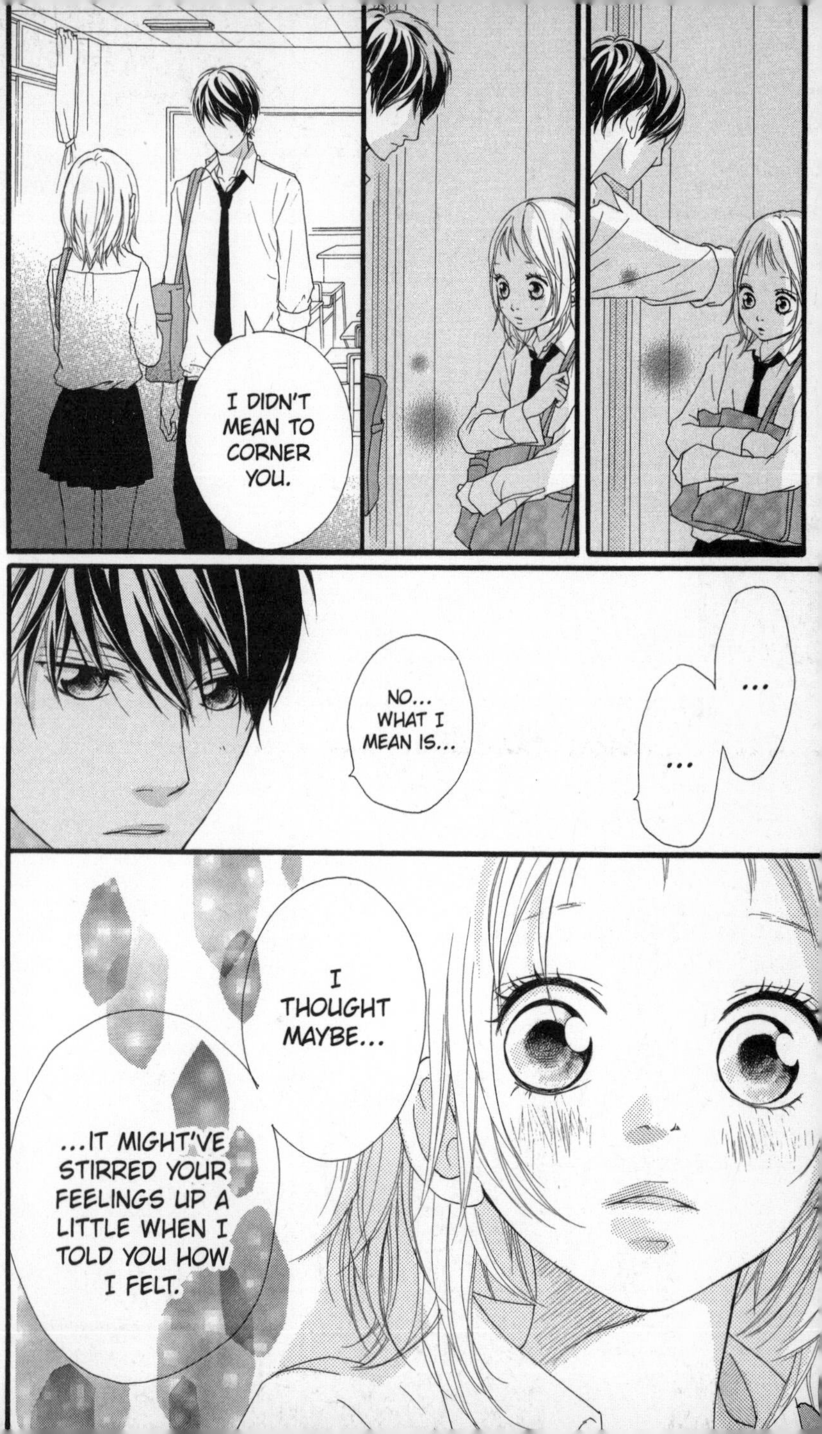

I DIDN'T MEAN TO CORNER YOU.
...
...
NO... WHAT I MEAN IS...
I THOUGHT MAYBE...
...IT MIGHT'VE STIRRED YOUR FEELINGS UP A LITTLE WHEN I TOLD YOU HOW I FELT.

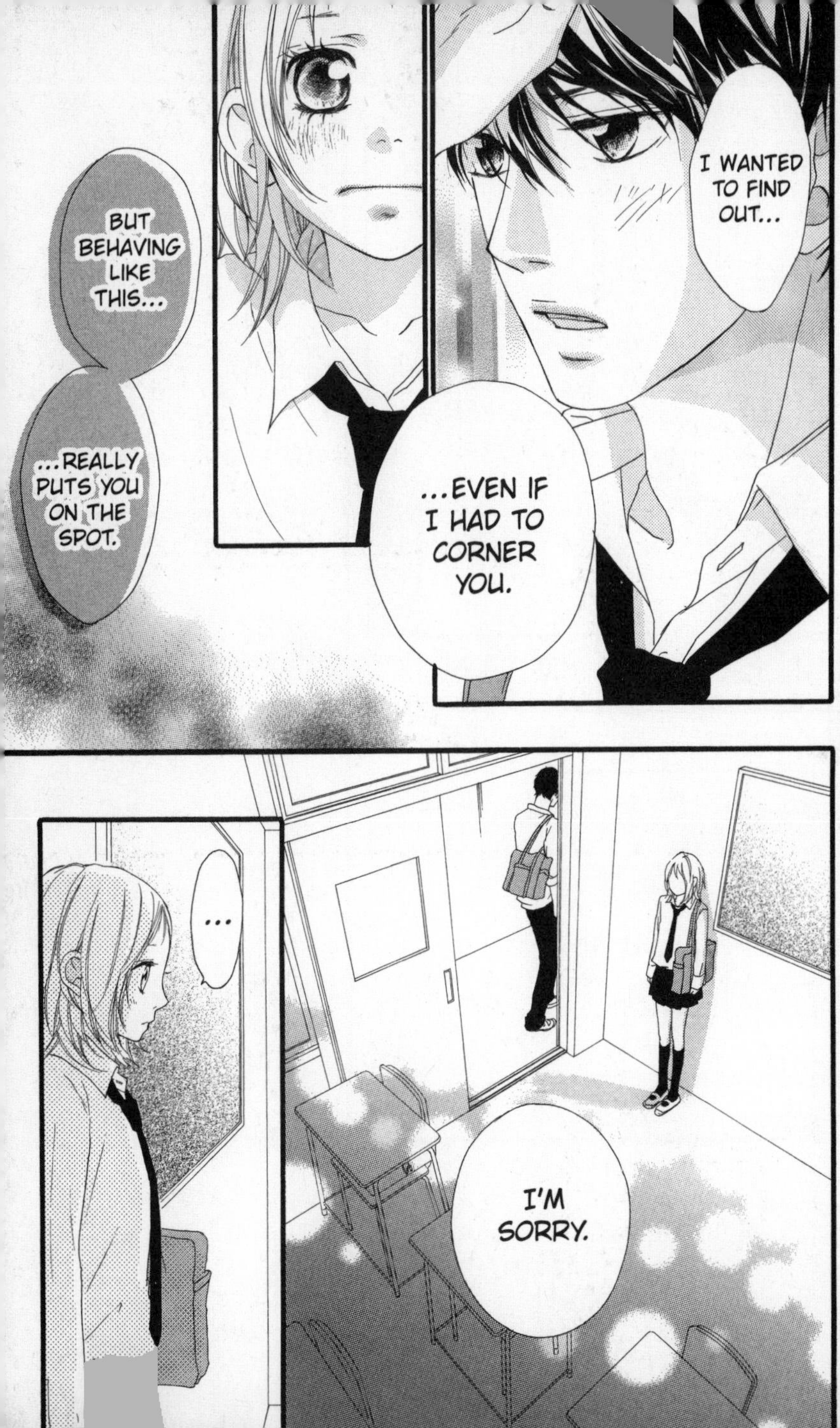
I WANTED TO FIND OUT...
...EVEN IF I HAD TO CORNER YOU.
BUT BEHAVING LIKE THIS...
...REALLY PUTS YOU ON THE SPOT.
I'M SORRY.
...

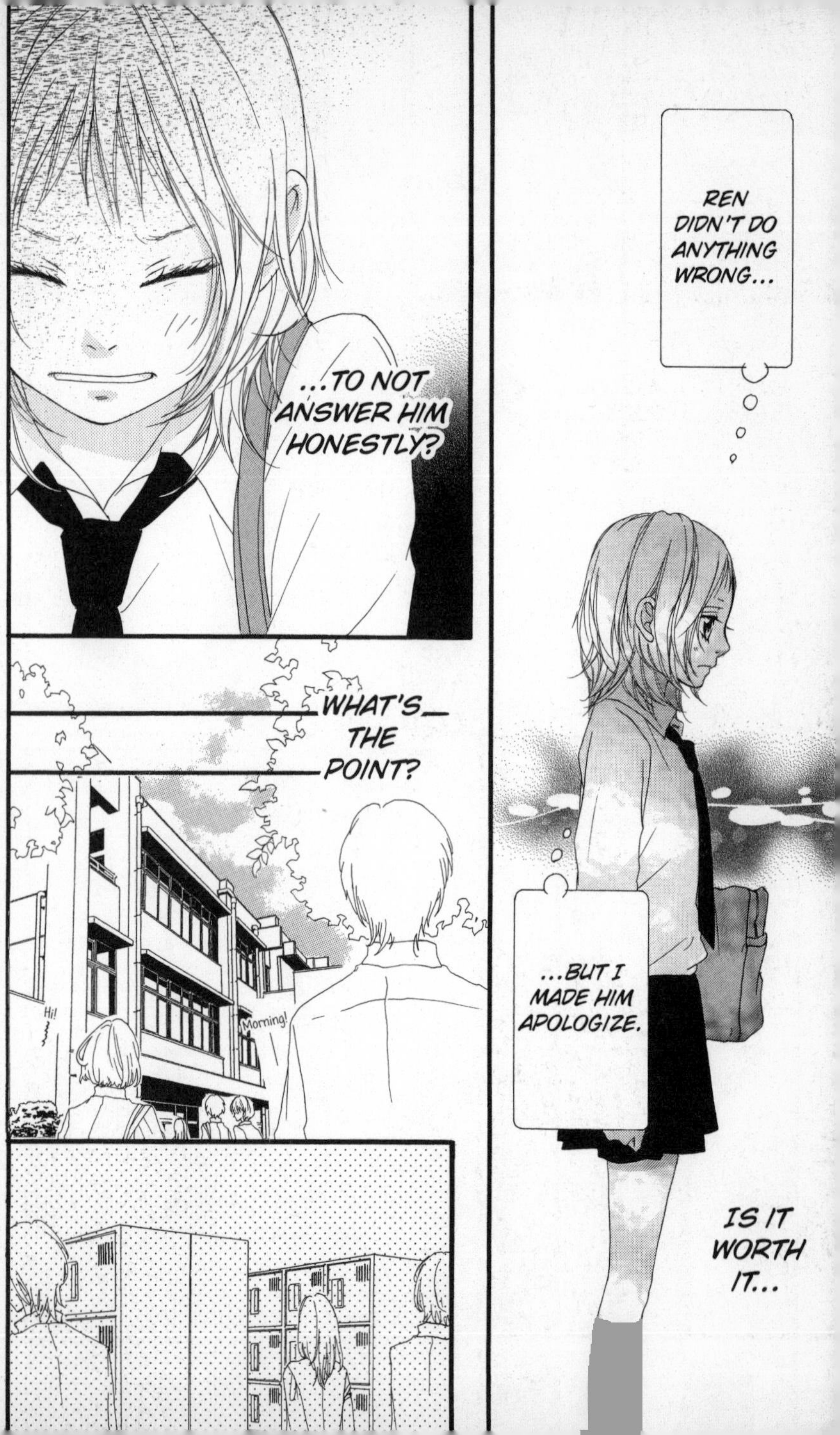
REN DIDN'T DO ANYTHING WRONG...
...BUT I MADE HIM APOLOGIZE.
IS IT WORTH IT...
...TO NOT ANSWER HIM HONESTLY?
WHAT'S THE POINT?
Morning!
Hi!

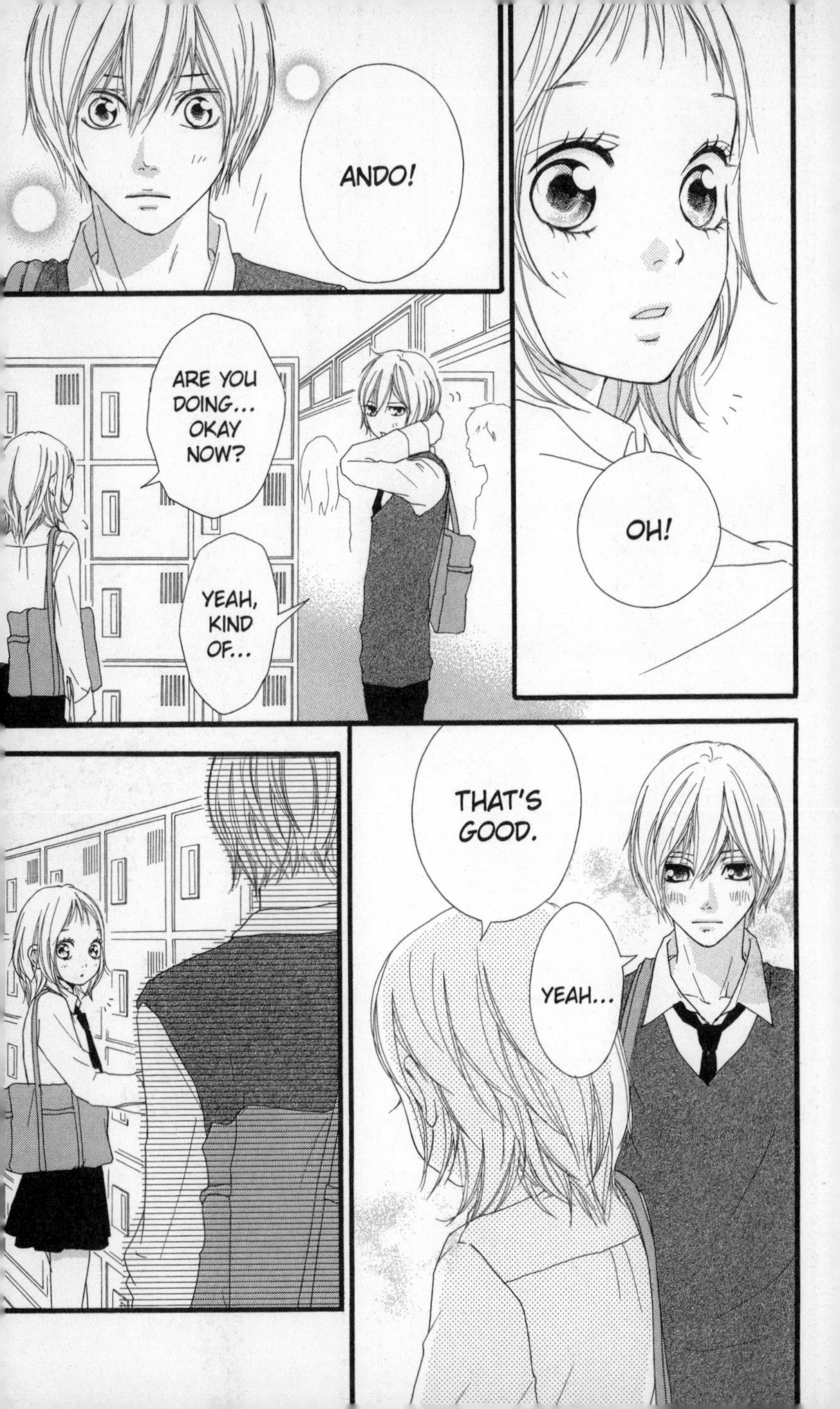
OH!
ANDO!
ARE YOU DOING... OKAY NOW?
YEAH, KIND OF...
THAT'S GOOD.
YEAH...

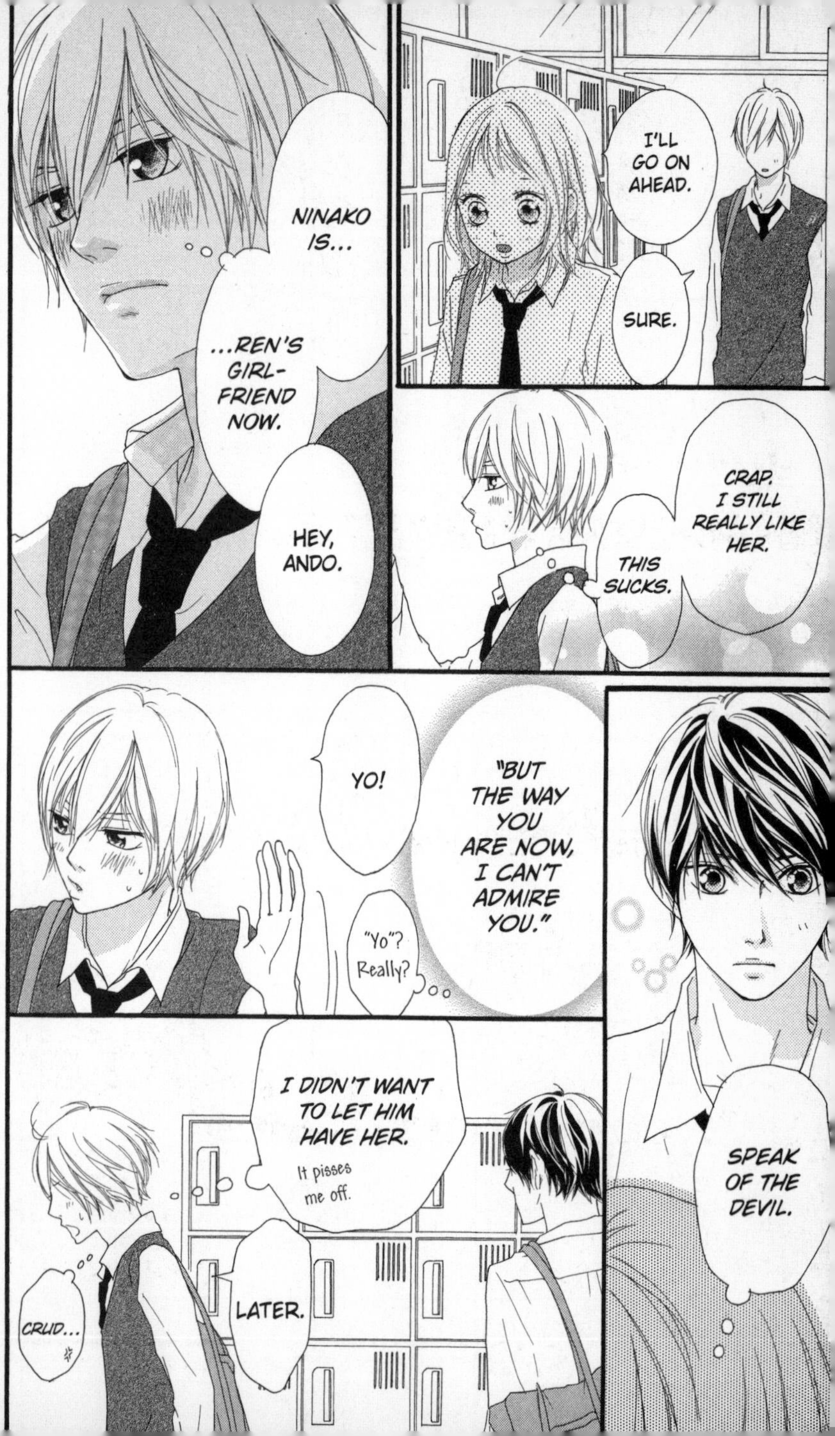

I'LL GO ON AHEAD.
SURE.
CRAP. I STILL REALLY LIKE HER.
THIS SUCKS.
NINAKO IS...
...REN'S GIRL-FRIEND NOW.
HEY, ANDO.
SPEAK OF THE DEVIL.
"BUT THE WAY YOU ARE NOW, I CAN'T ADMIRE YOU."
YO!
"Yo"? Really?
I DIDN'T WANT TO LET HIM HAVE HER.
It pisses me off.
LATER.
CRUD...

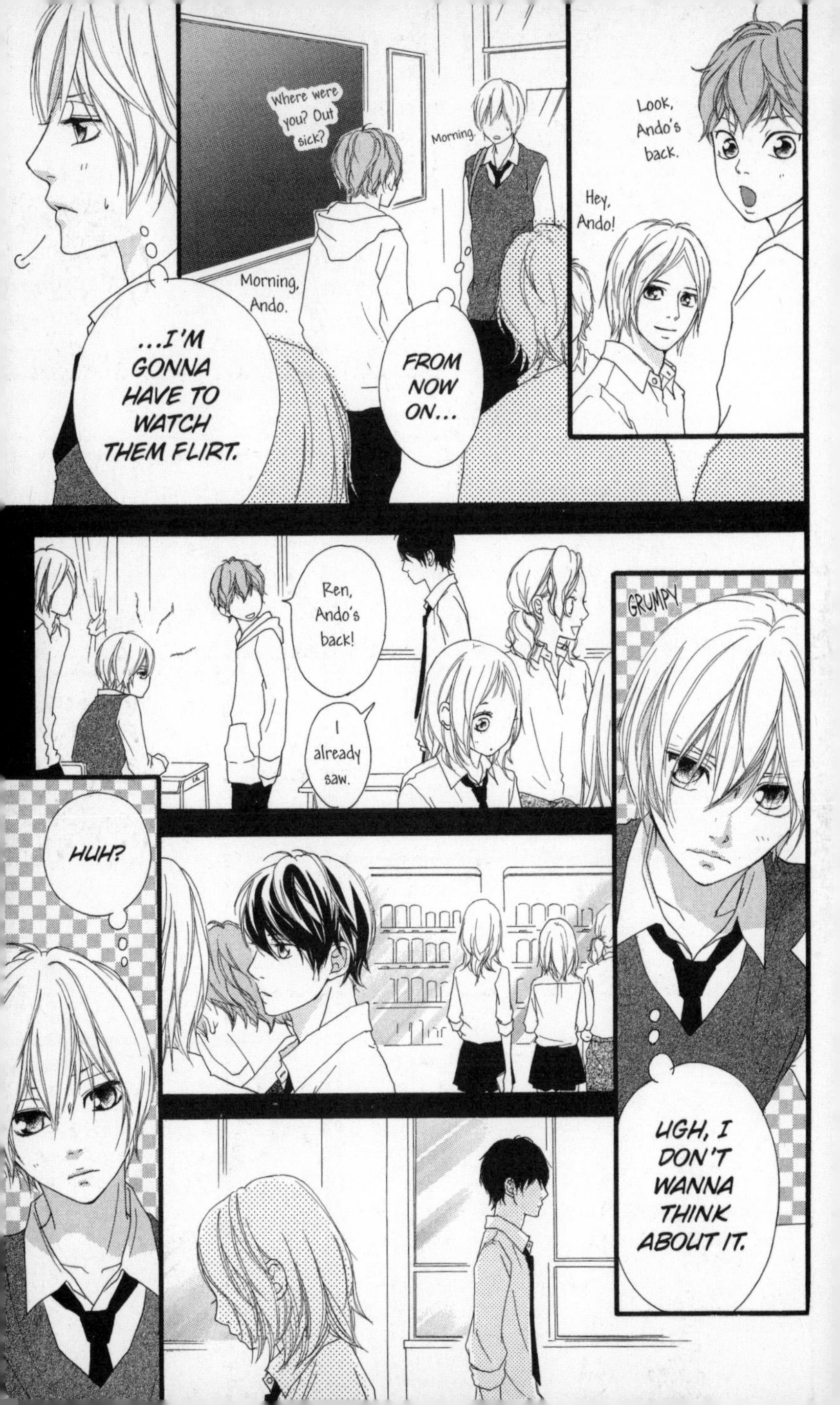
Look, Ando's back.
Hey, Ando!
Morning.
Where were you? Out sick?
Morning, Ando.
FROM NOW ON...
...I'M GONNA HAVE TO WATCH THEM FLIRT.
GRUMPY
UGH, I DON'T WANNA THINK ABOUT IT.
Ren, Ando's back!
I already saw.
HUH?

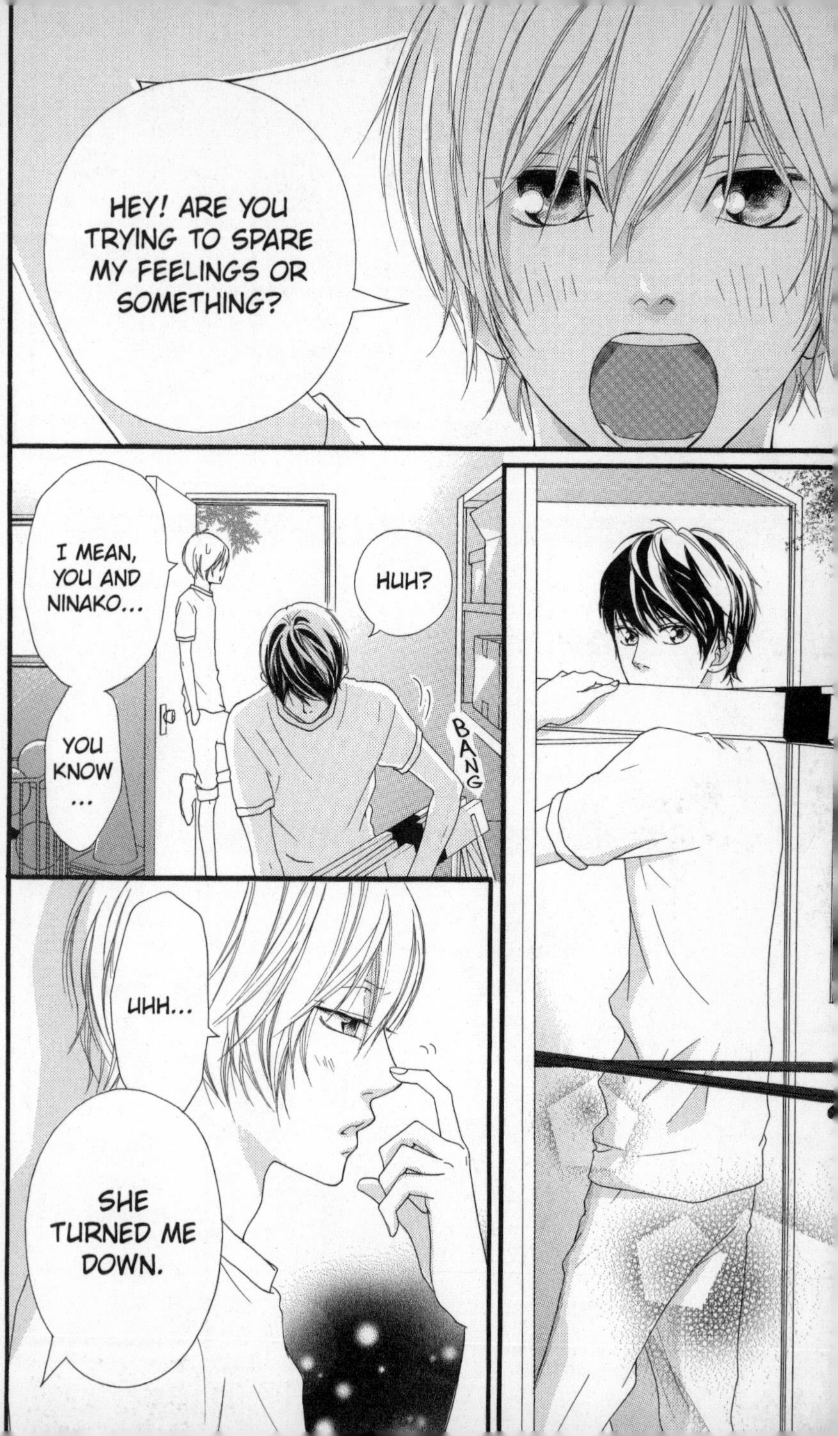
HEY! ARE YOU TRYING TO SPARE MY FEELINGS OR SOMETHING?
BANG
HUH?
I MEAN, YOU AND NINAKO...
YOU KNOW ...
UHH...
SHE TURNED ME DOWN.

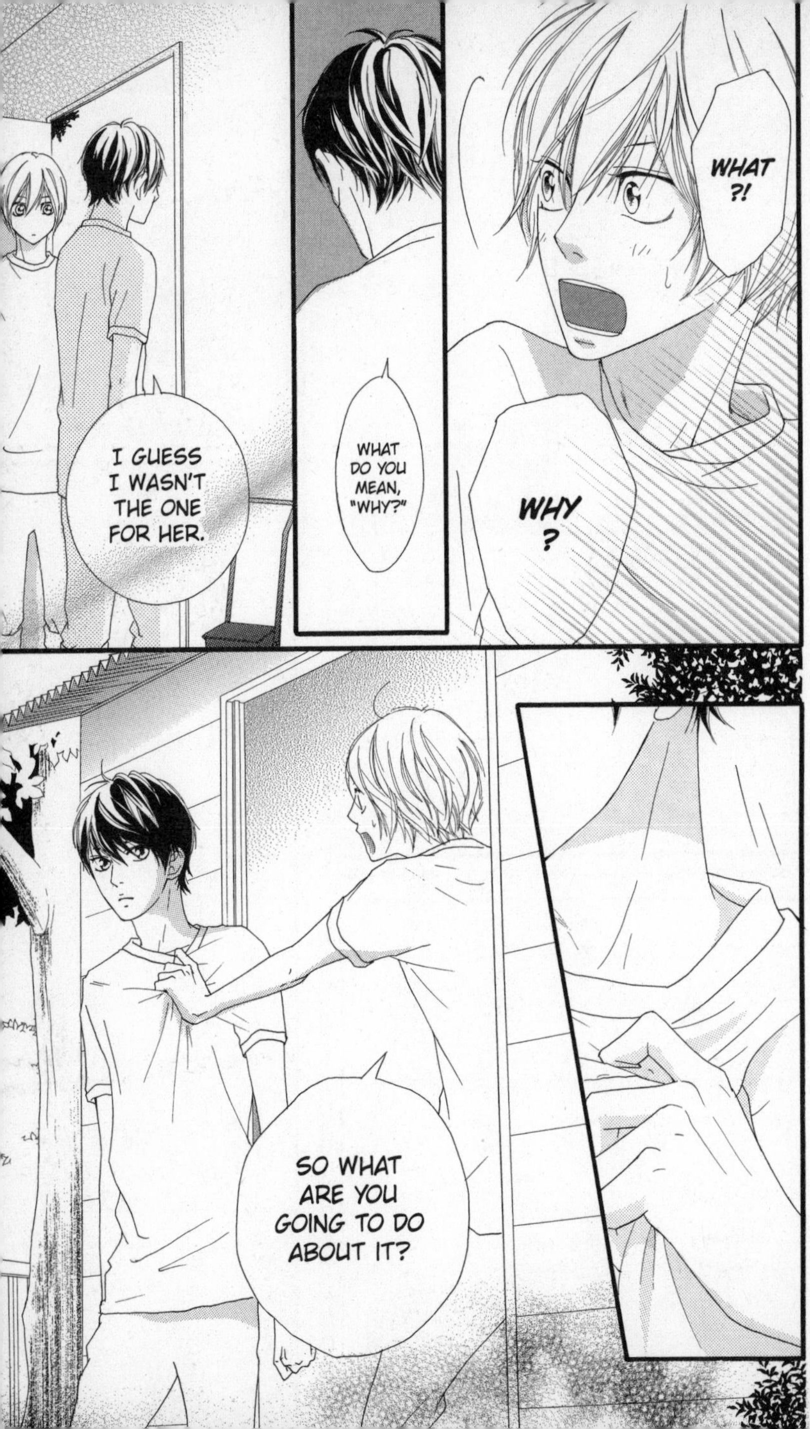
WHAT ?!
WHY ?
WHAT DO YOU MEAN, "WHY?"
I GUESS I WASN'T THE ONE FOR HER.
SO WHAT ARE YOU GOING TO DO ABOUT IT?

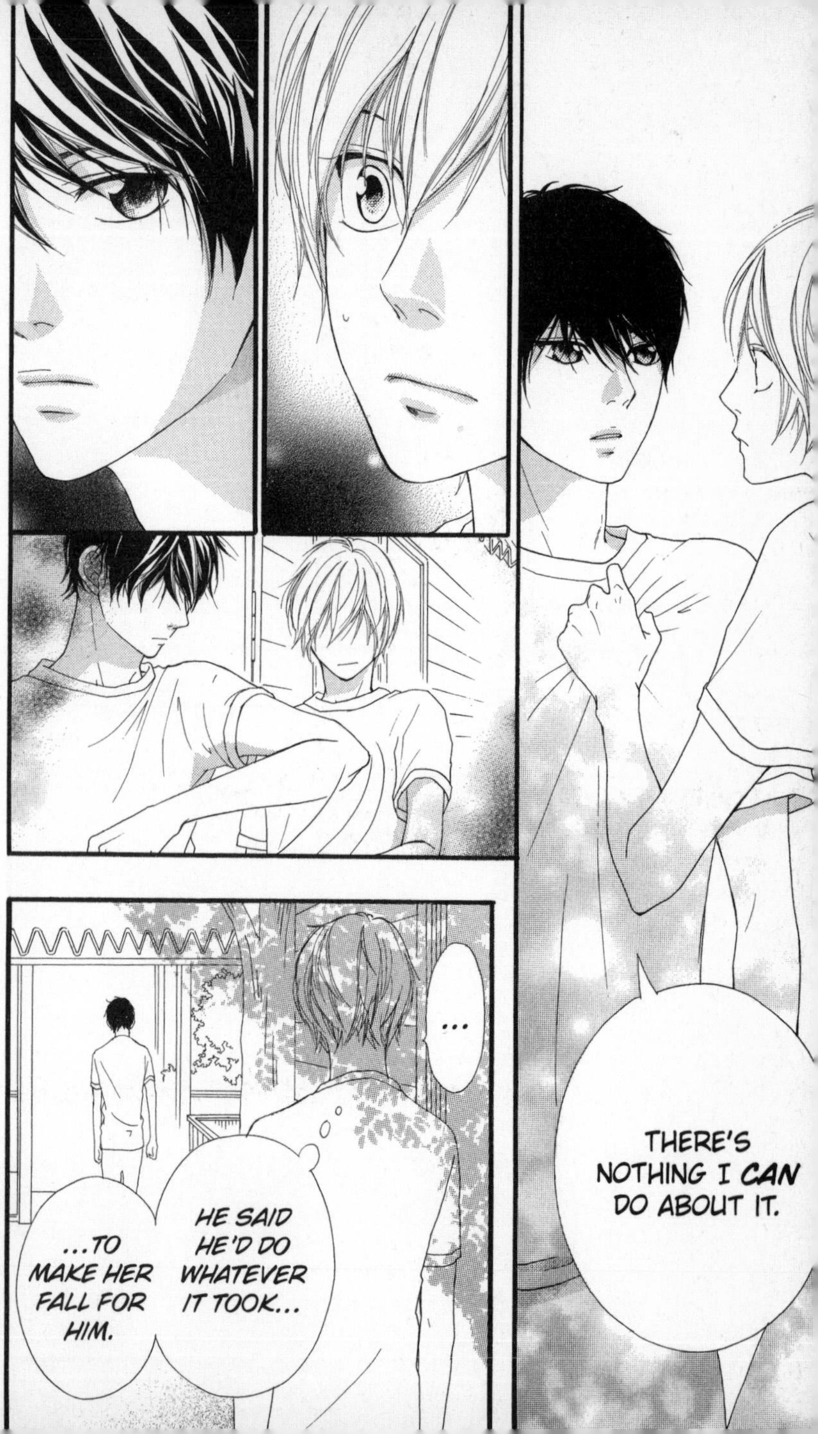
THERE'S NOTHING I CAN DO ABOUT IT.
...
HE SAID HE'D DO WHATEVER IT TOOK...
...TO MAKE HER FALL FOR HIM.

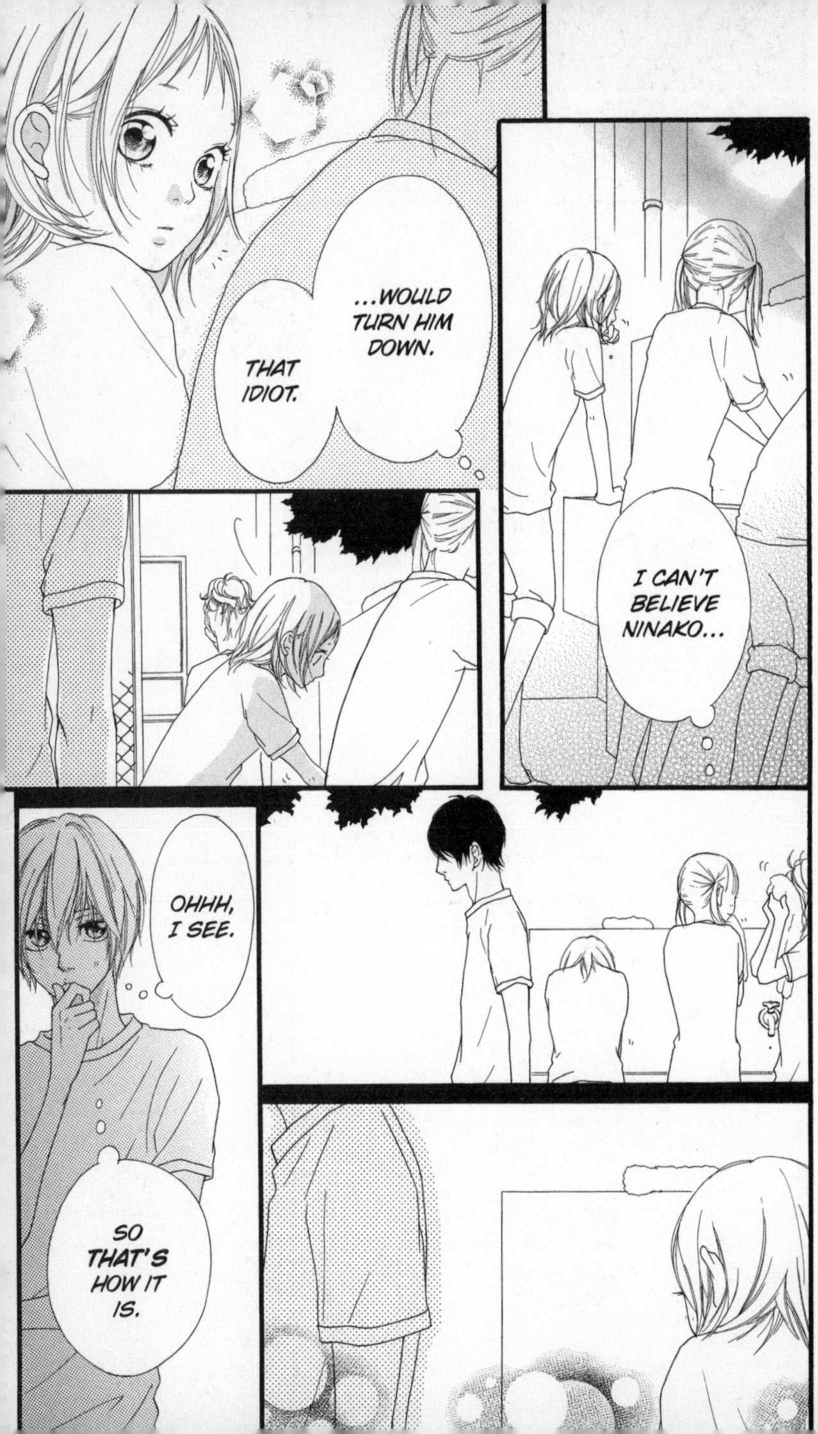
I CAN'T BELIEVE NINAKO...
...WOULD TURN HIM DOWN.
THAT IDIOT.
OHHH, I SEE.
SO THAT'S HOW IT IS.

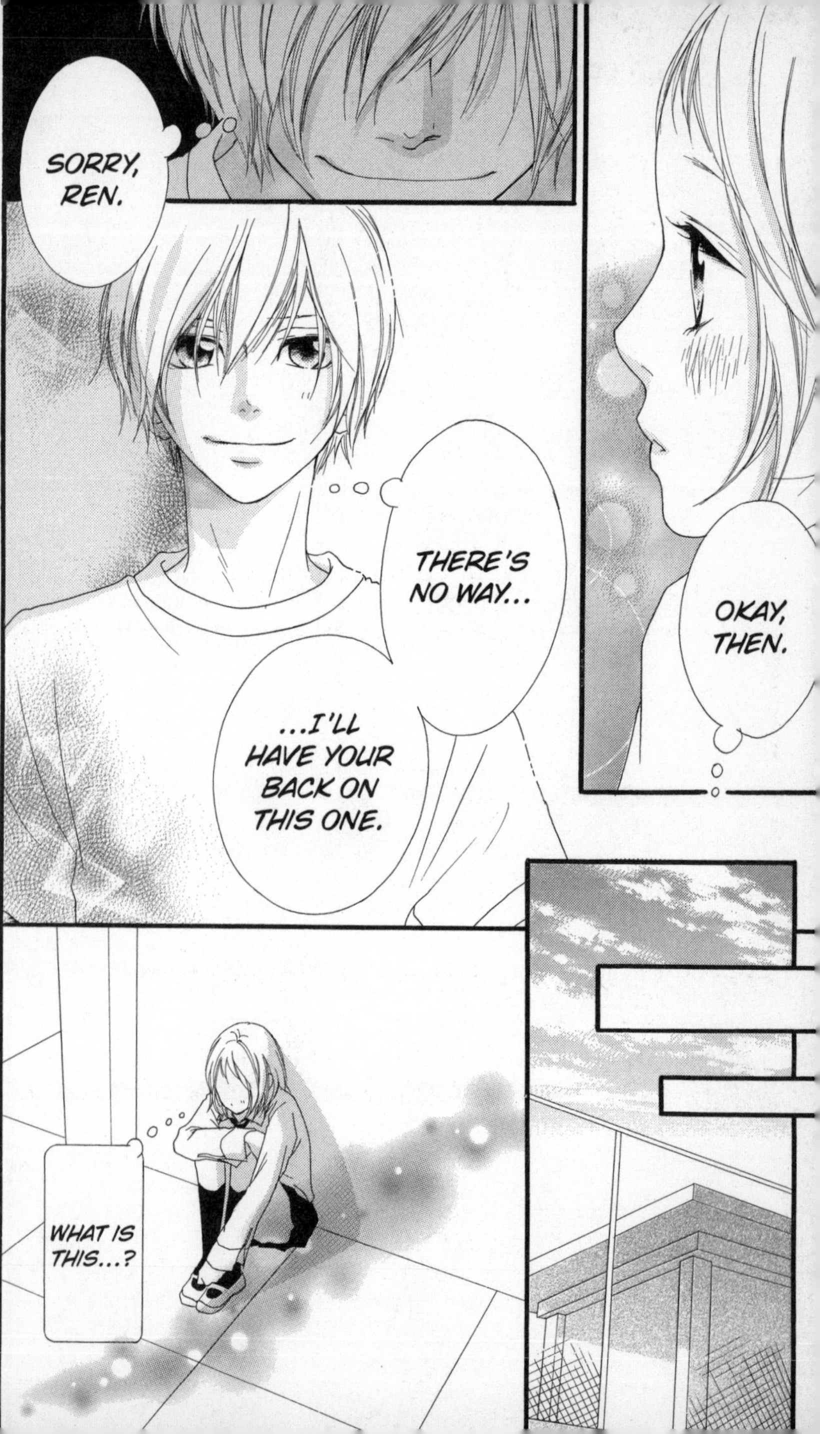
OKAY, THEN.
SORRY, REN.
THERE'S NO WAY...
...I'LL HAVE YOUR BACK ON THIS ONE.
WHAT IS THIS...?

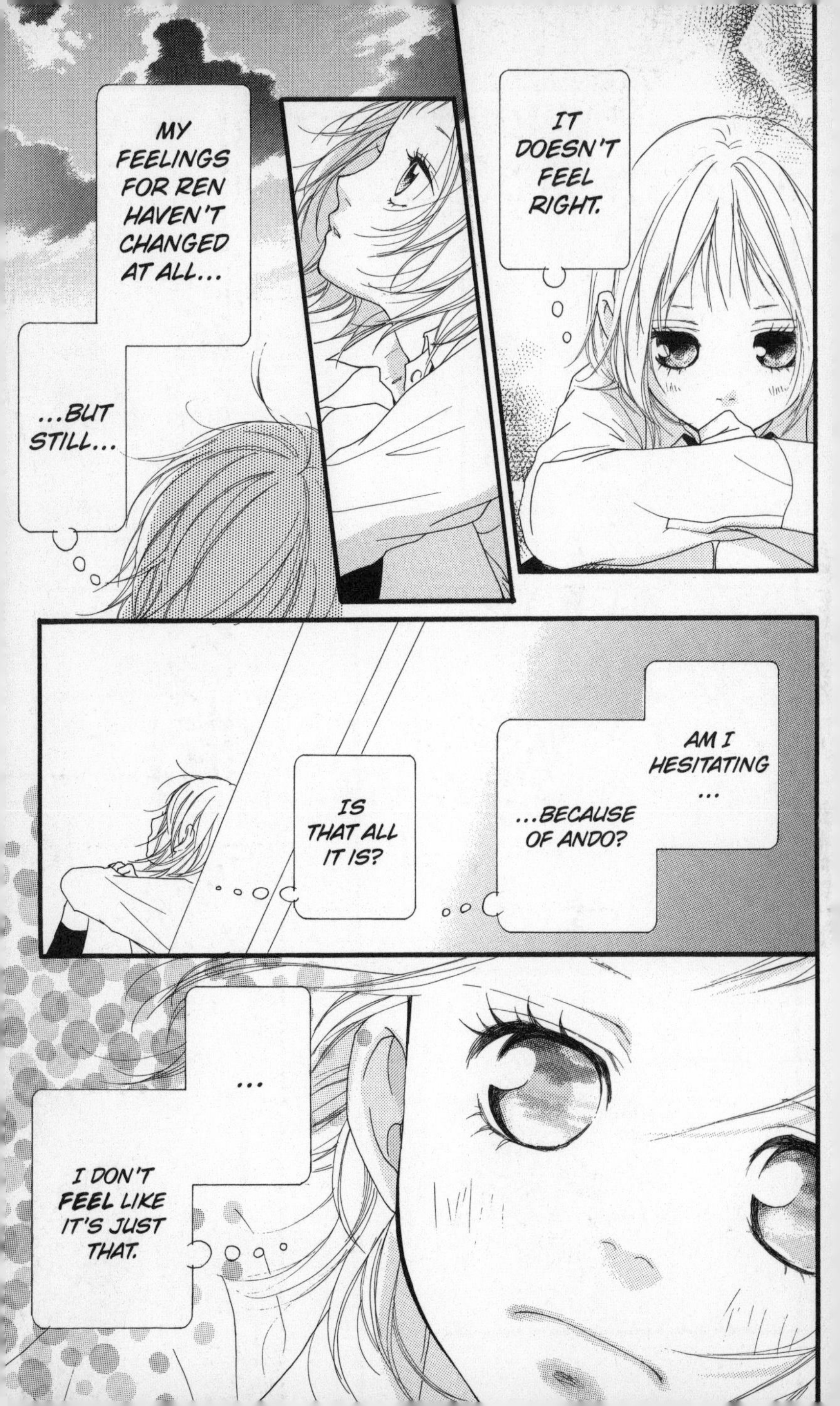
IT DOESN'T FEEL RIGHT.
MY FEELINGS FOR REN HAVEN'T CHANGED AT ALL...
...BUT STILL...
AM I HESITATING ...
...BECAUSE OF ANDO?
IS THAT ALL IT IS?
...
I DON'T FEEL LIKE IT'S JUST THAT.

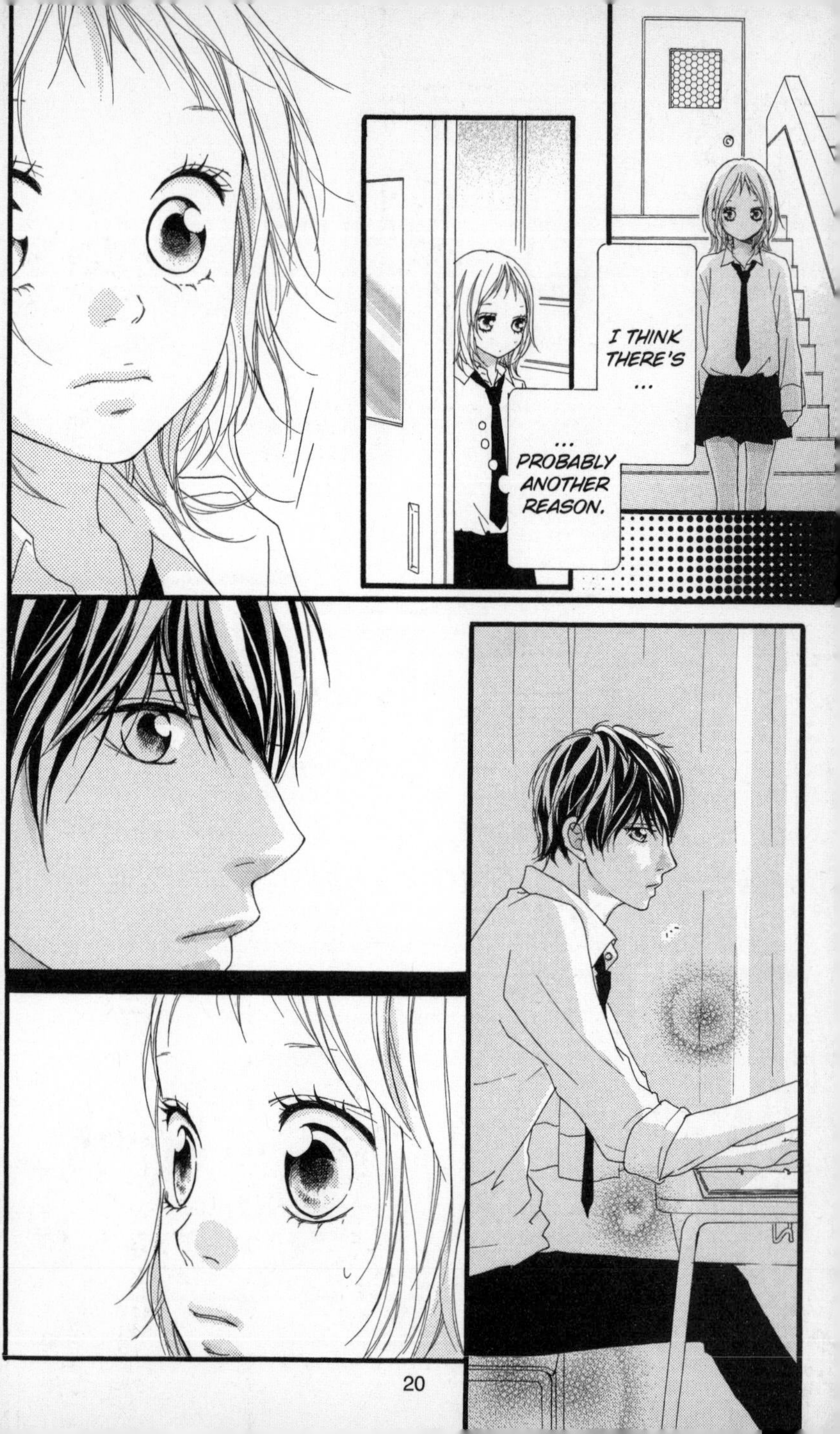
I THINK THERE'S ...
... PROBABLY ANOTHER REASON.
...

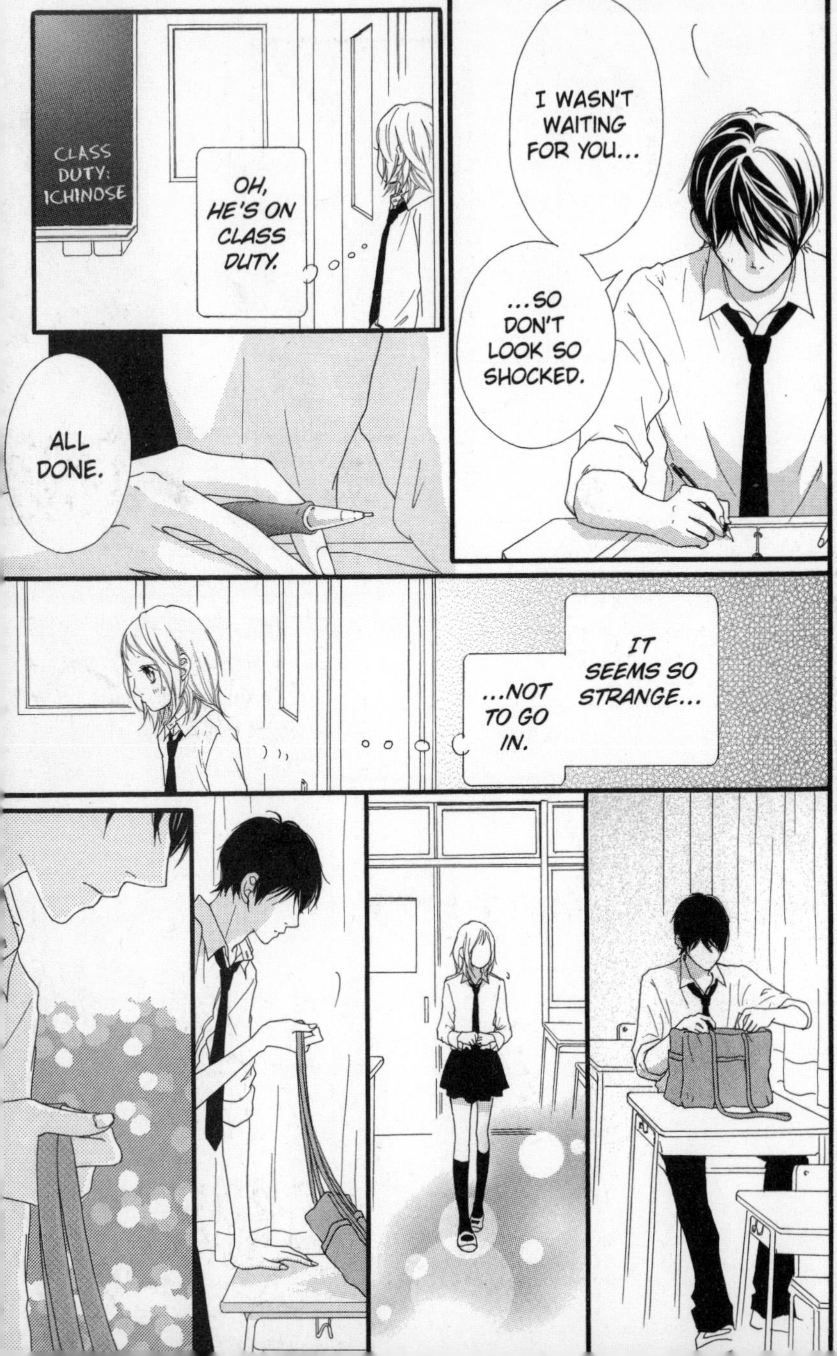
I WASN'T WAITING FOR YOU...
...SO DON'T LOOK SO SHOCKED.
CLASS DUTY: ICHINOSE
OH, HE'S ON CLASS DUTY.
ALL DONE.
IT SEEMS SO STRANGE...
...NOT TO GO IN.

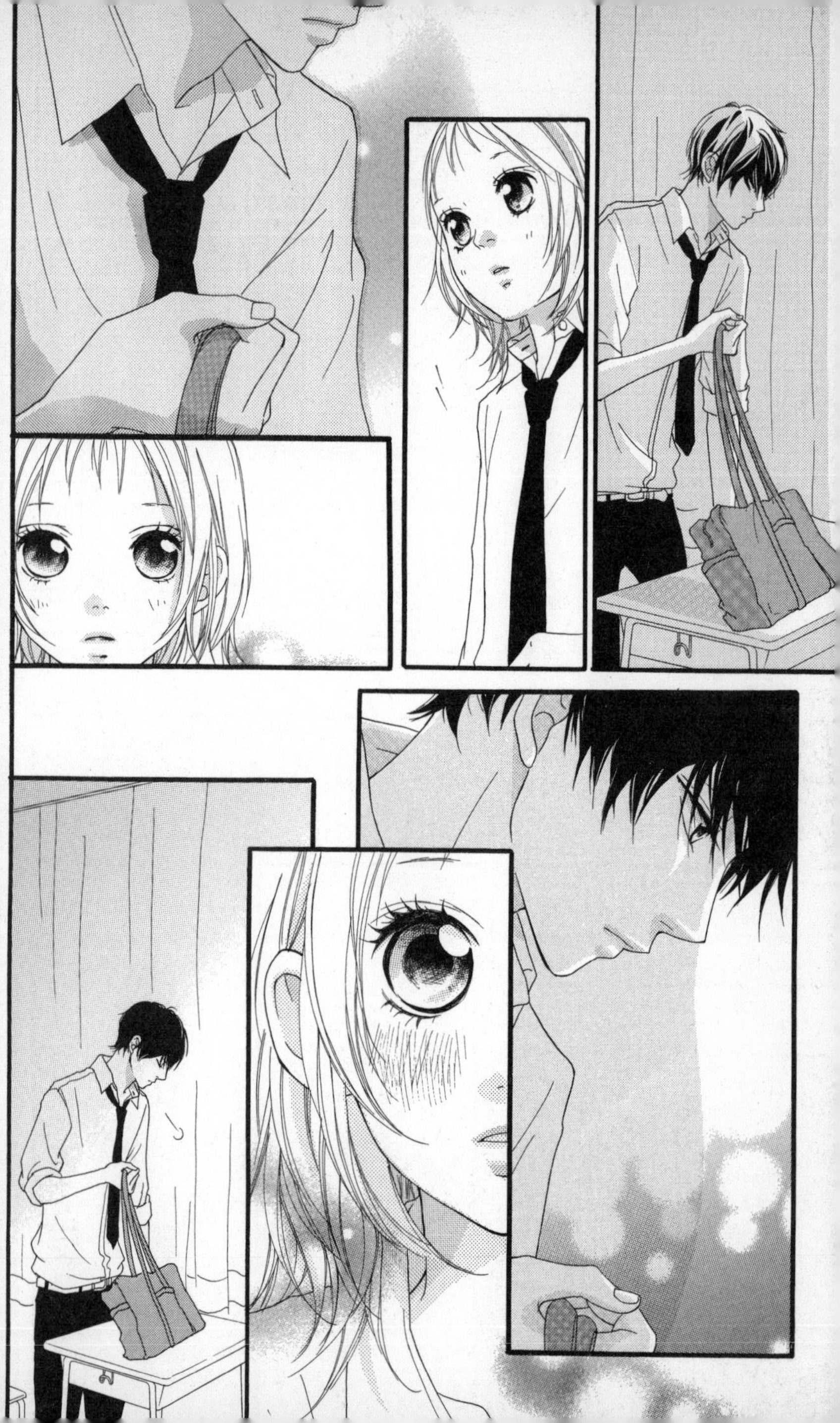

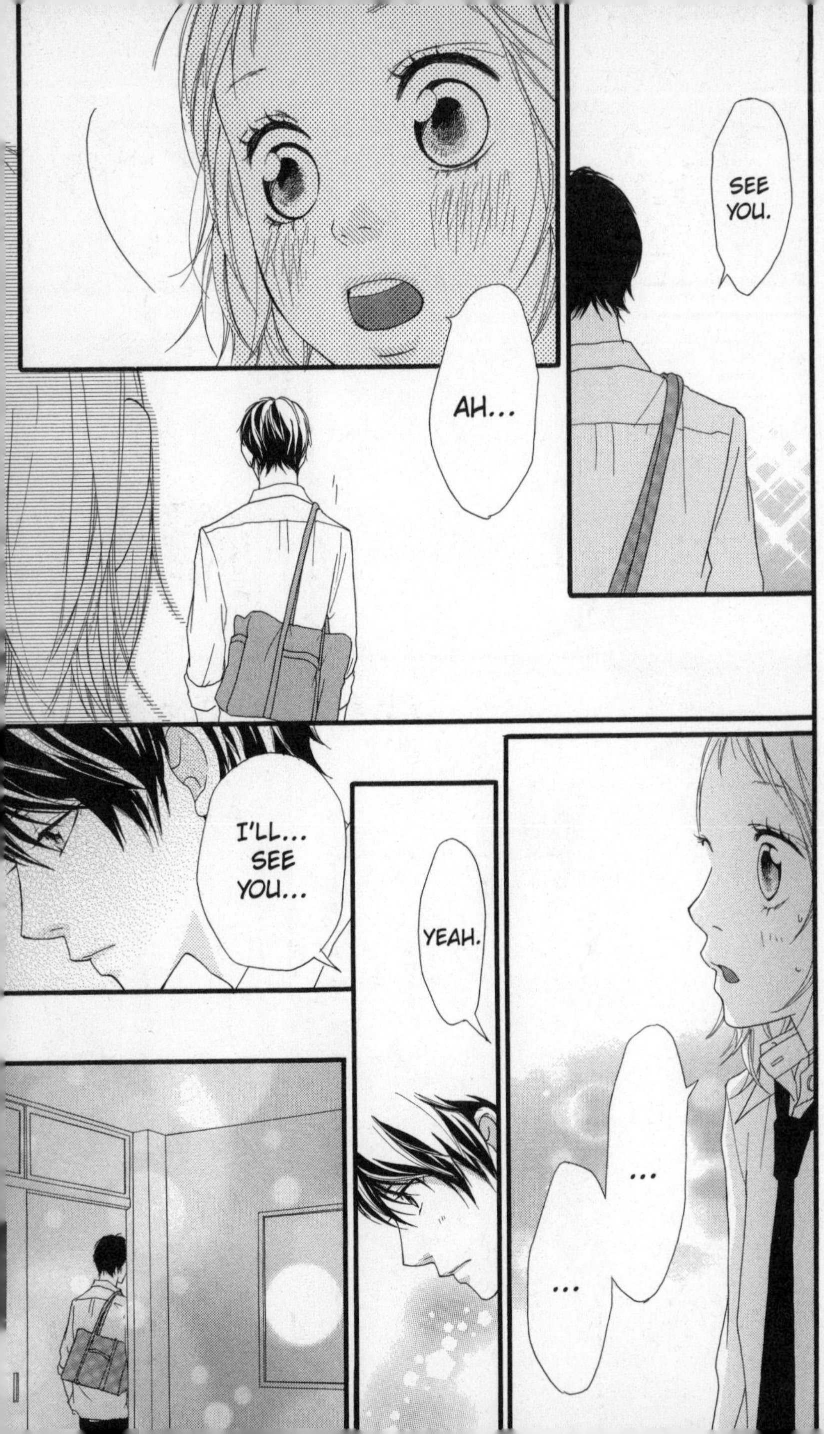
SEE YOU.
AH...
...
...
YEAH.
I'LL... SEE YOU...

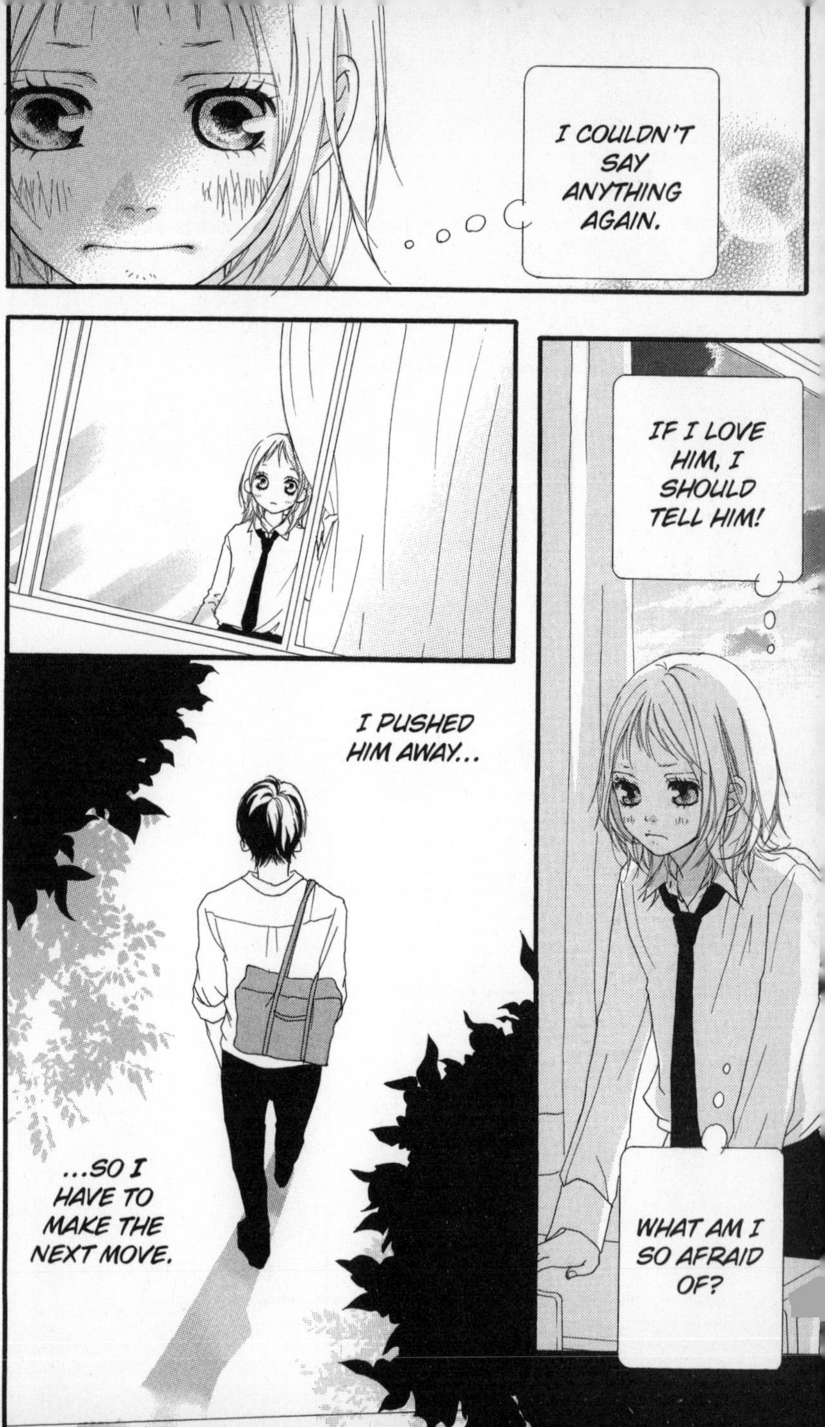
I COULDN'T SAY ANYTHING AGAIN.
IF I LOVE HIM, I SHOULD TELL HIM!
WHAT AM I SO AFRAID OF?
I PUSHED HIM AWAY...
...SO I HAVE TO MAKE THE NEXT MOVE.

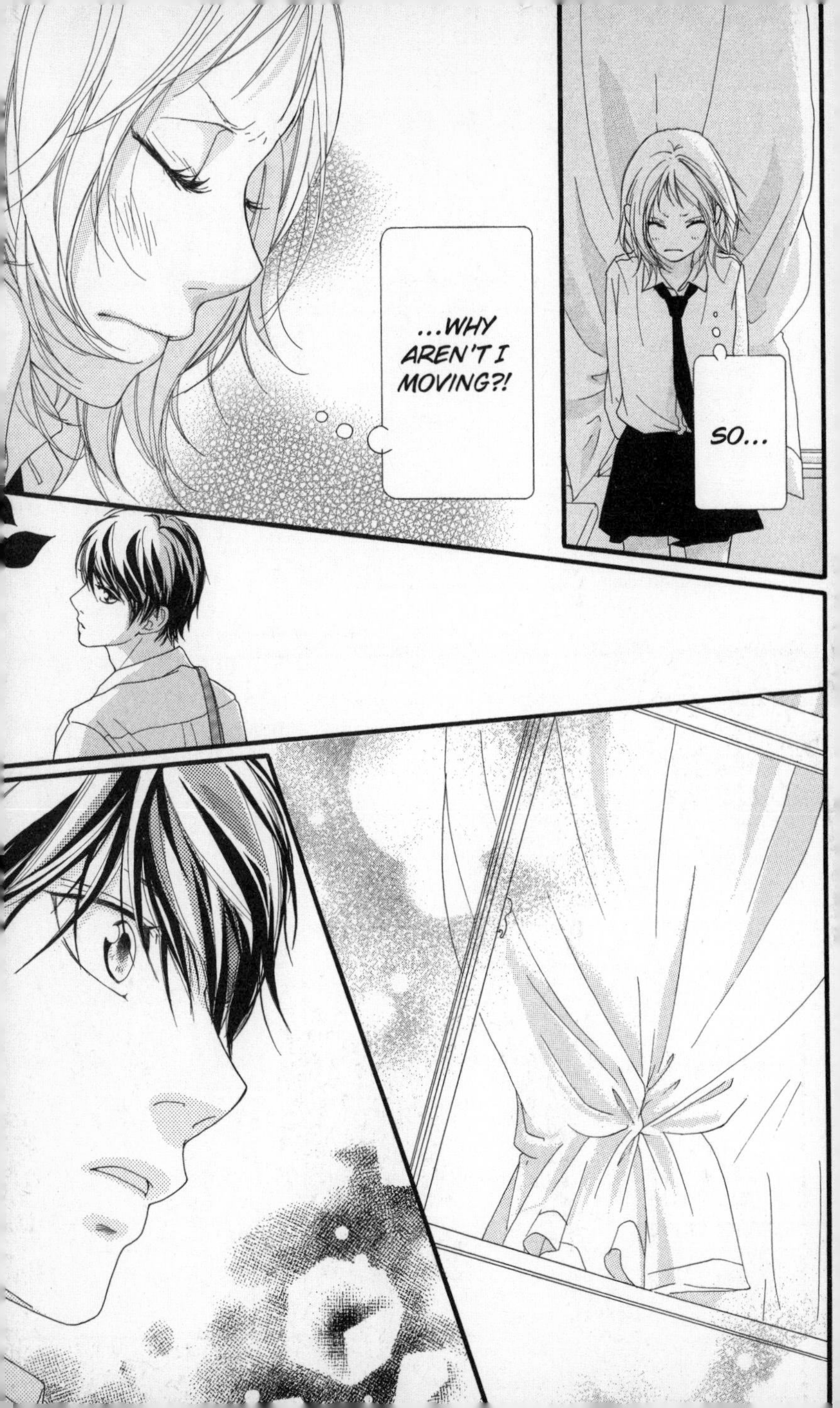
SO...
...WHY AREN'T I MOVING?!

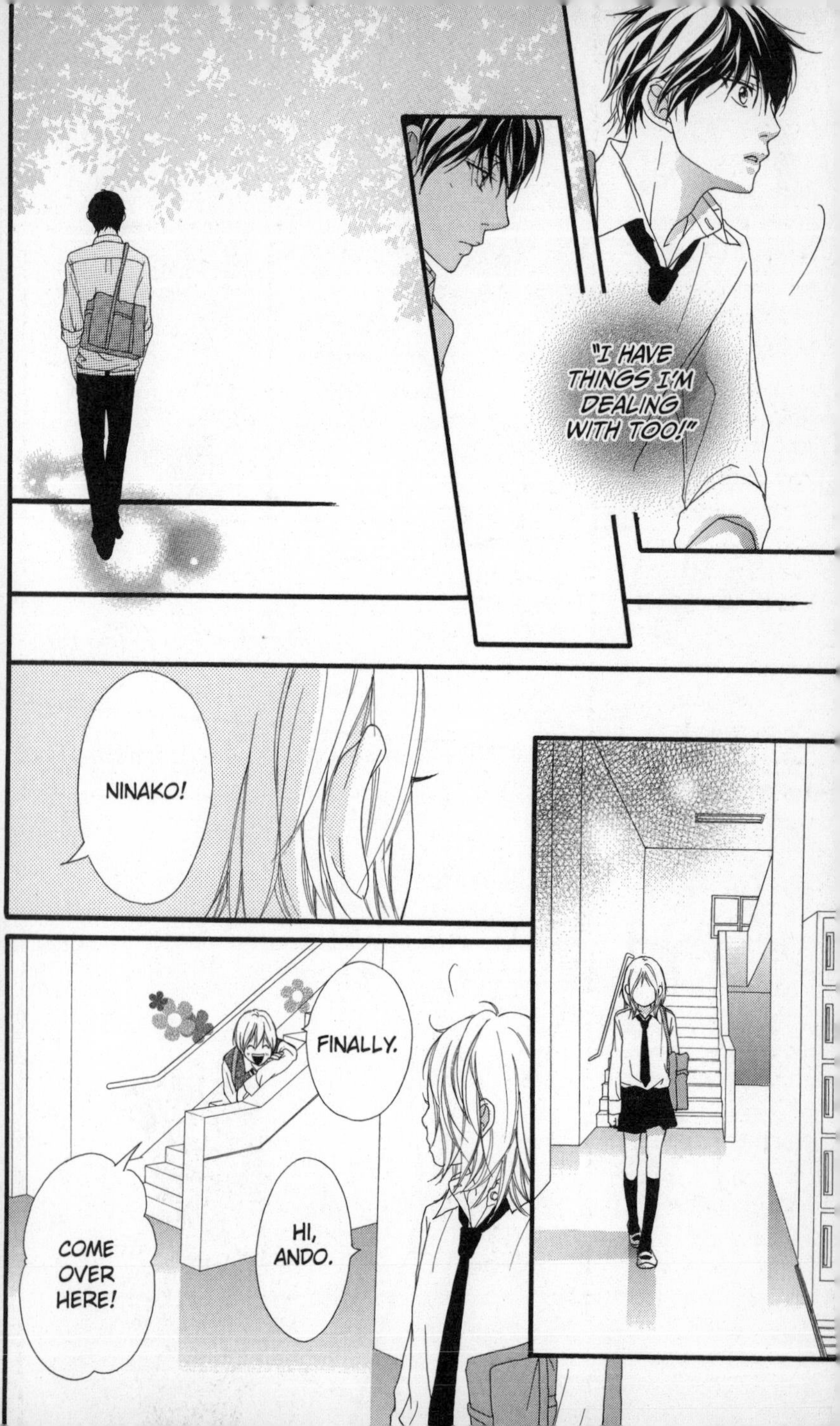
"I HAVE THINGS I'M DEALING WITH TOO!"
NINAKO!
FINALLY.
HI, ANDO.
COME OVER HERE!

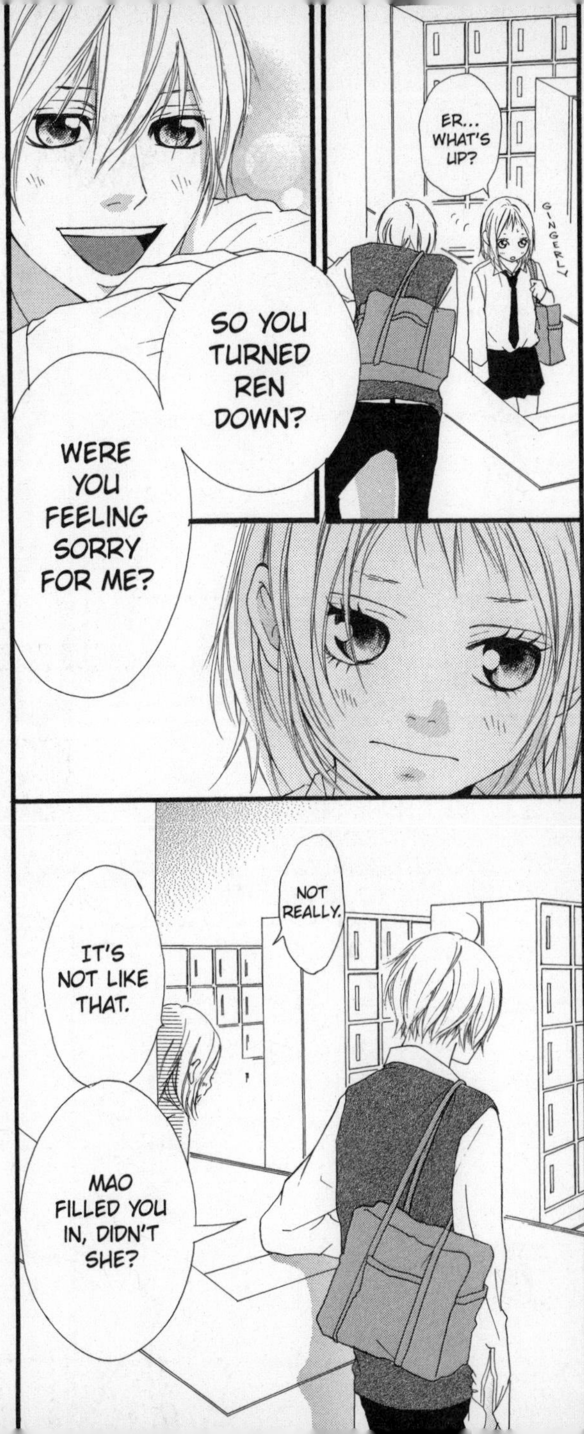
ER... WHAT'S UP?
GINGERLY
SO YOU TURNED REN DOWN?
WERE YOU FEELING SORRY FOR ME?
NOT REALLY.
IT'S NOT LIKE THAT.
MAO FILLED YOU IN, DIDN'T SHE?

As far as I remember, I haven't been sick with a fever or anything for the entire time I've been working on this series—three and a half years! That's amazing!

I was so impressed by how well I was taking care of myself until I realized that, of course, the amount of time I spend inside by myself means I don't have any opportunities to come into contact with a cold virus. So it's not that remarkable, and it has nothing to do with how well I take care of myself. It's just how things are.

Actually, when I think about it, I did have a fever a couple of times. If I'd been taking proper care of myself, I probably wouldn't have gotten that sick. And really, getting a cold when I'm never outside probably means I'm not taking care of myself at all...

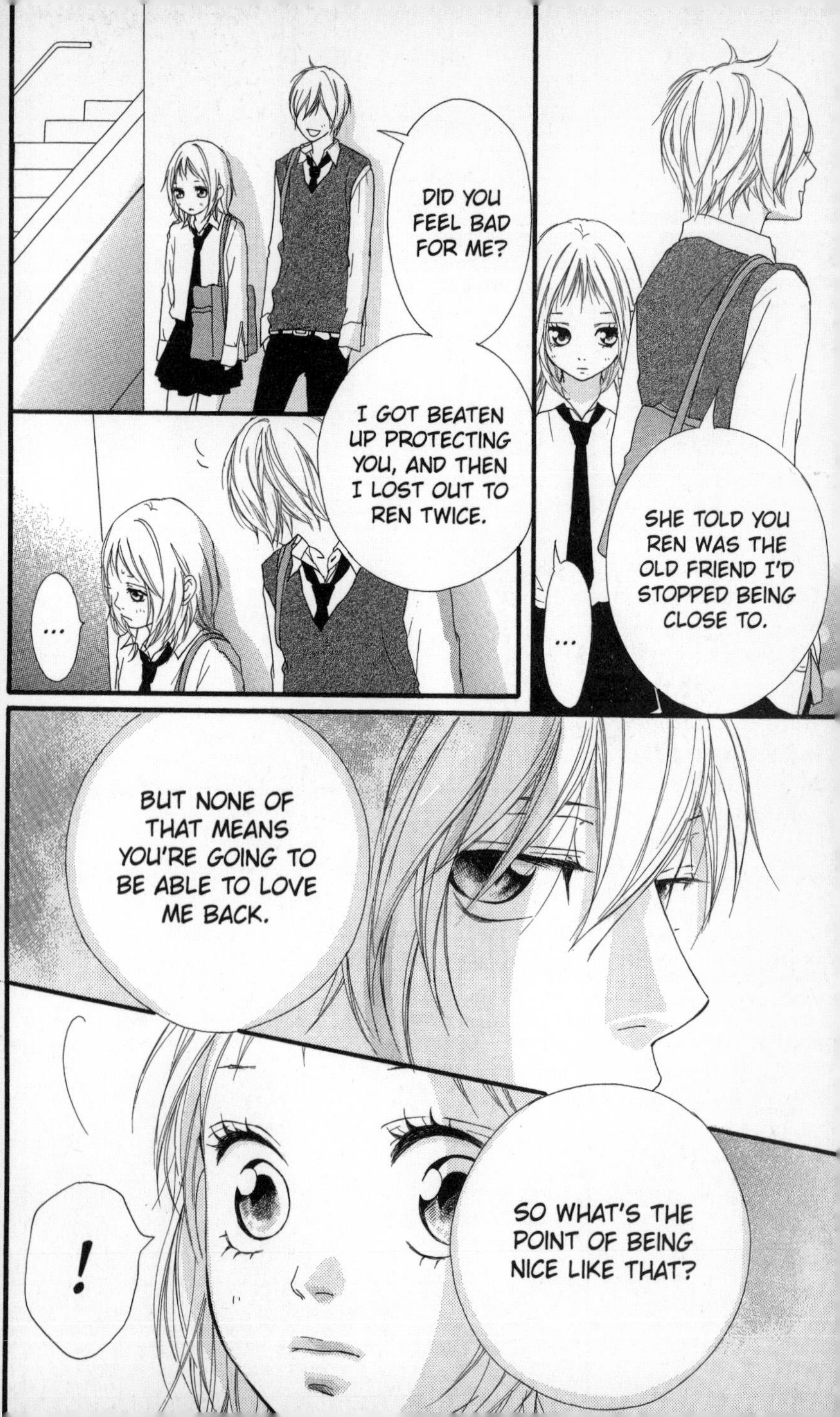

SHE TOLD YOU REN WAS THE OLD FRIEND I'D STOPPED BEING CLOSE TO.
...
DID YOU FEEL BAD FOR ME?
I GOT BEATEN UP PROTECTING YOU, AND THEN I LOST OUT TO REN TWICE.
...
BUT NONE OF THAT MEANS YOU'RE GOING TO BE ABLE TO LOVE ME BACK.
SO WHAT'S THE POINT OF BEING NICE LIKE THAT?
!

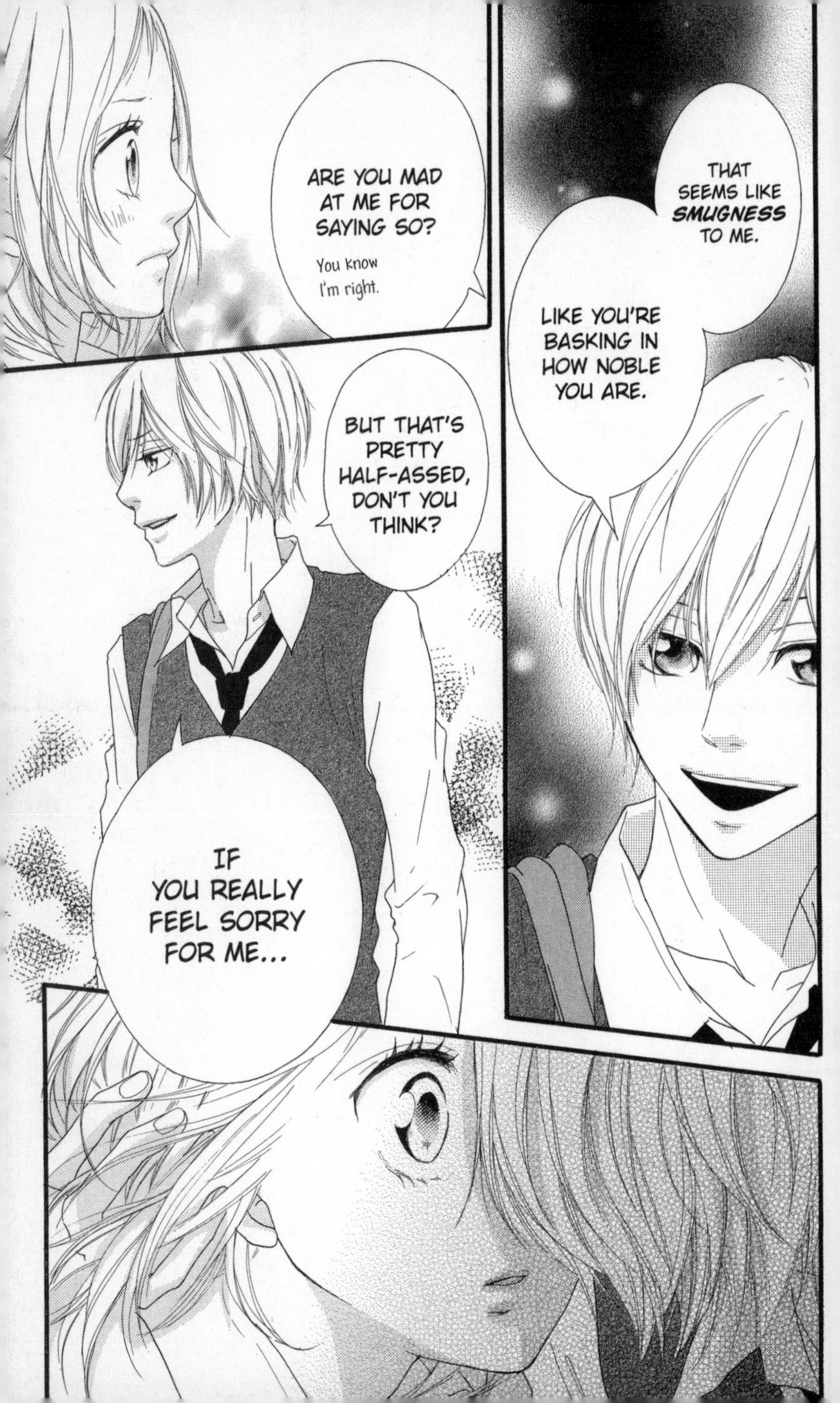
THAT SEEMS LIKE SMUGNESS TO ME.
LIKE YOU'RE BASKING IN HOW NOBLE YOU ARE.
ARE YOU MAD AT ME FOR SAYING SO?
You know I'm right.
BUT THAT'S PRETTY HALF-ASSED, DON'T YOU THINK?
IF YOU REALLY FEEL SORRY FOR ME...

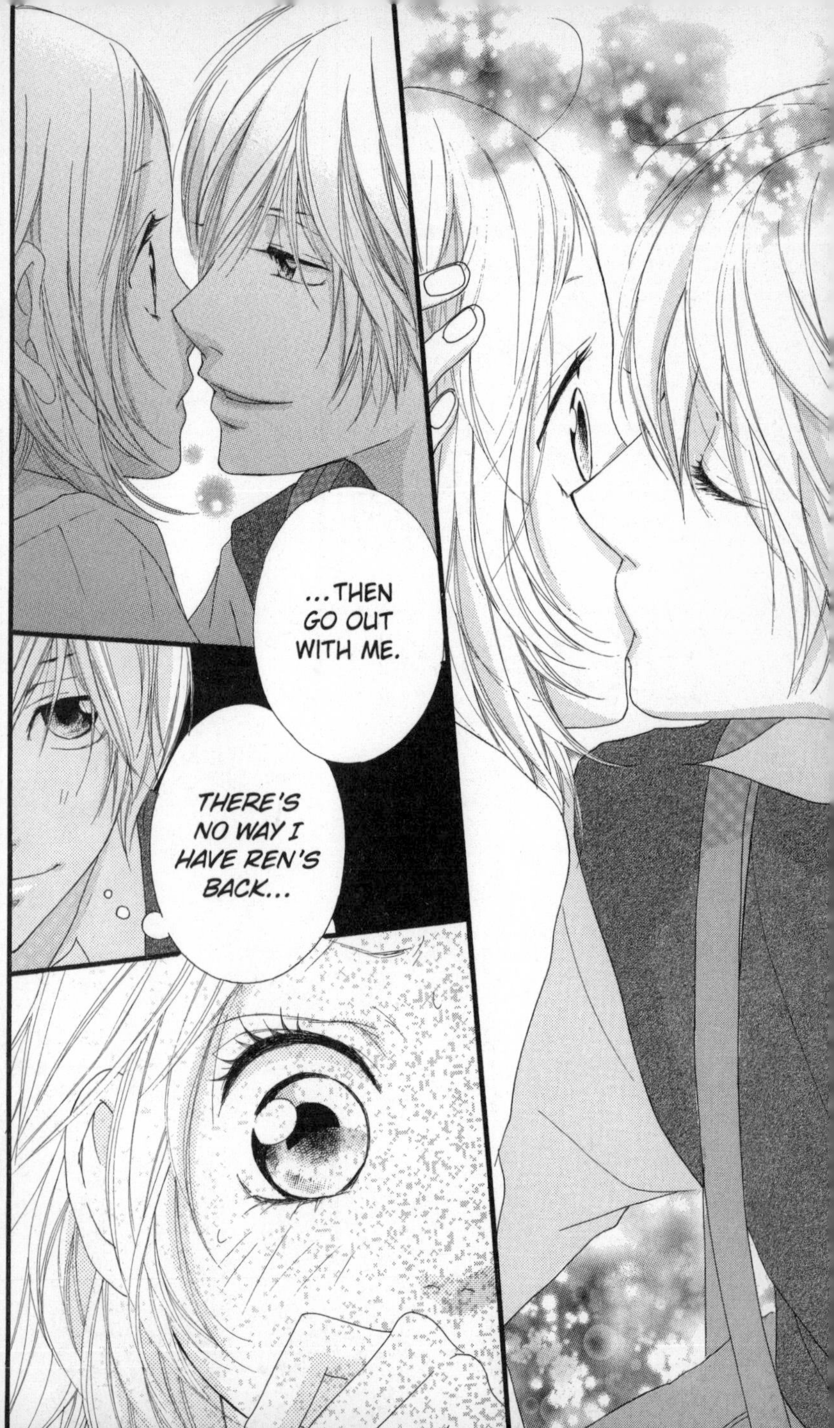
...THEN GO OUT WITH ME.
THERE'S NO WAY I HAVE REN'S BACK...

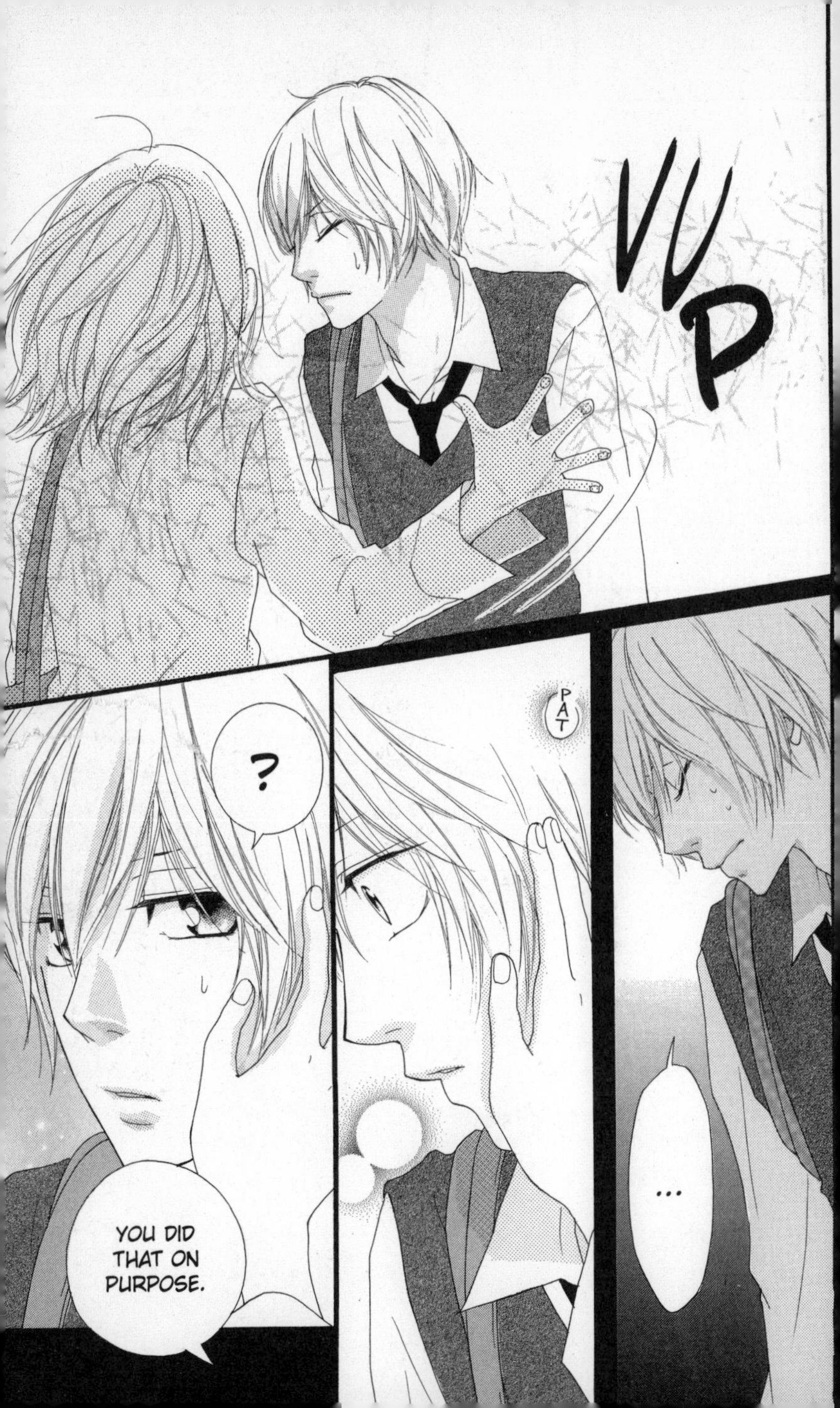
VUP
...
PAT
?
YOU DID THAT ON PURPOSE.

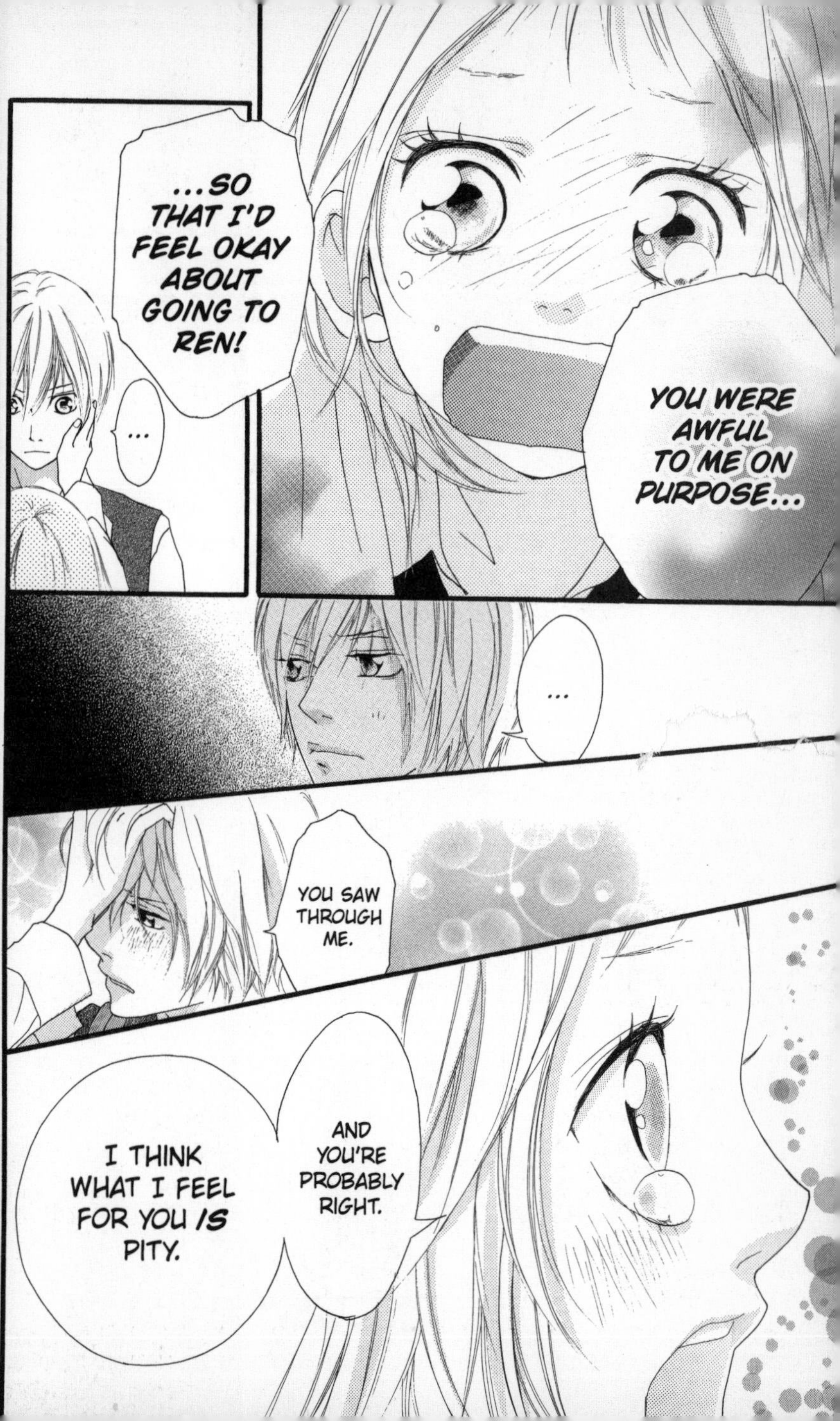
YOU WERE AWFUL TO ME ON PURPOSE...
...SO THAT I'D FEEL OKAY ABOUT GOING TO REN!
...
...
YOU SAW THROUGH ME.
AND YOU'RE PROBABLY RIGHT.
I THINK WHAT I FEEL FOR YOU *IS* PITY.

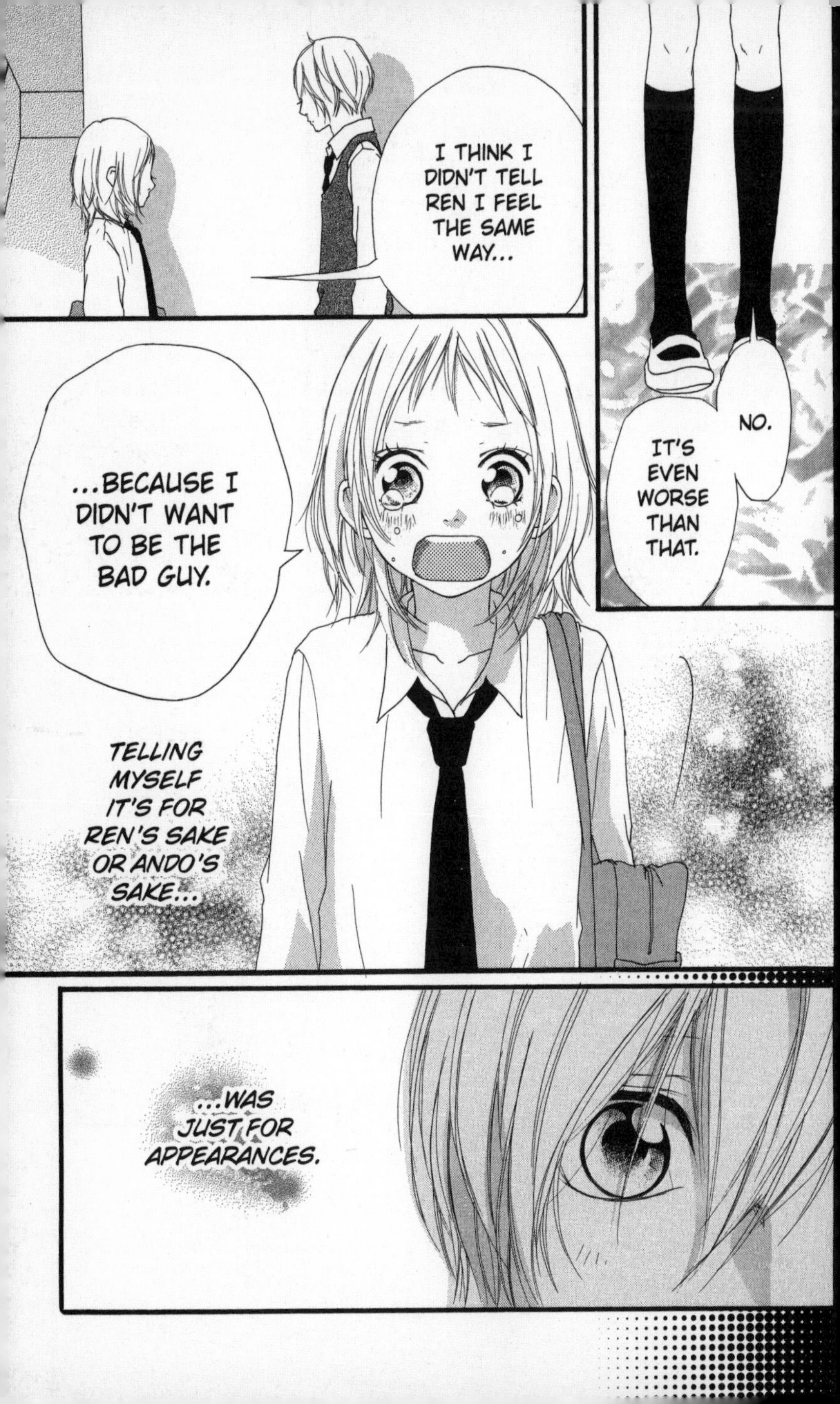
NO.
IT'S EVEN WORSE THAN THAT.
I THINK I DIDN'T TELL REN I FEEL THE SAME WAY...
...BECAUSE I DIDN'T WANT TO BE THE BAD GUY.
TELLING MYSELF IT'S FOR REN'S SAKE OR ANDO'S SAKE...
...WAS JUST FOR APPEARANCES.

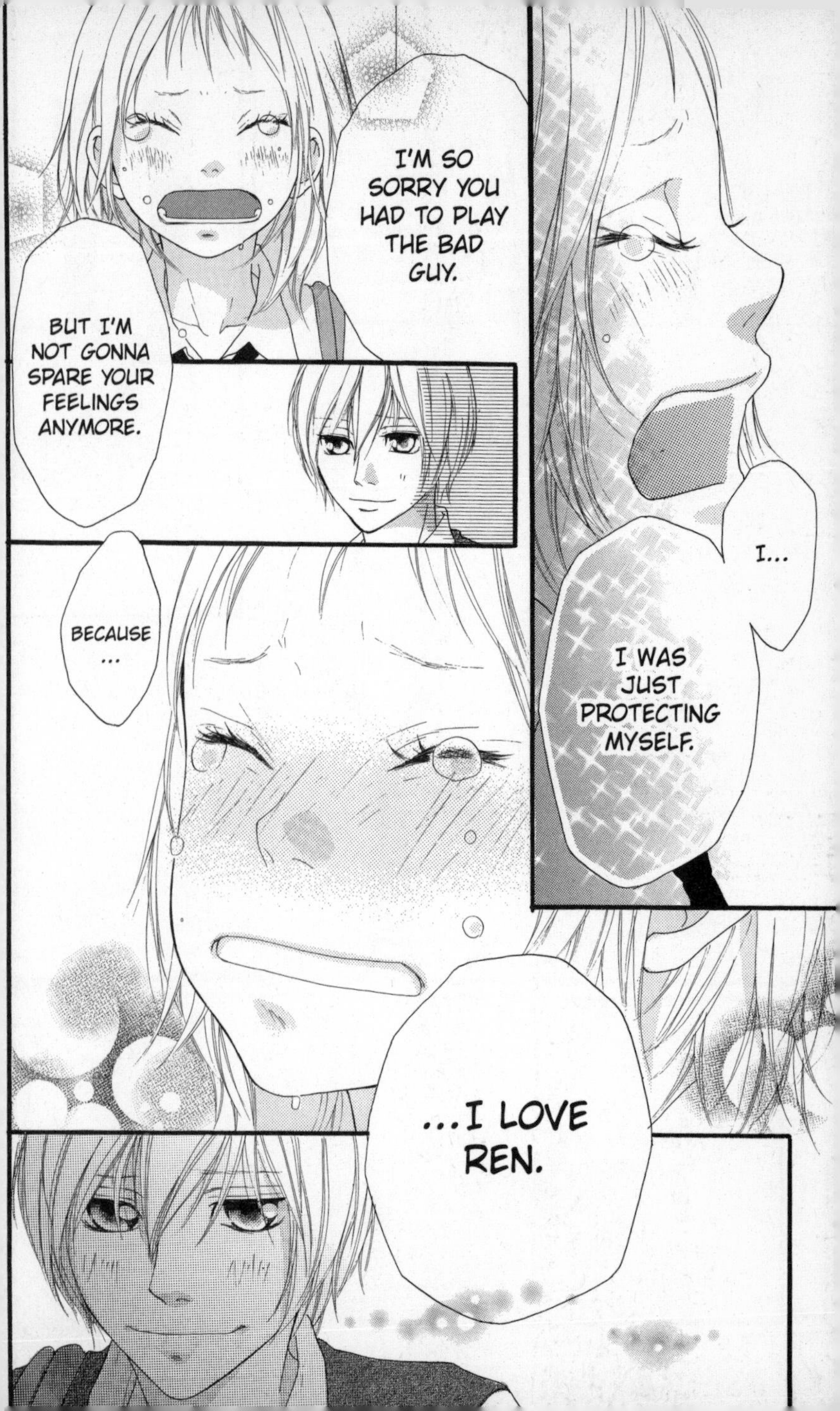
I...
I WAS JUST PROTECTING MYSELF.
I'M SO SORRY YOU HAD TO PLAY THE BAD GUY.
BUT I'M NOT GONNA SPARE YOUR FEELINGS ANYMORE.
BECAUSE ...
...I LOVE REN.

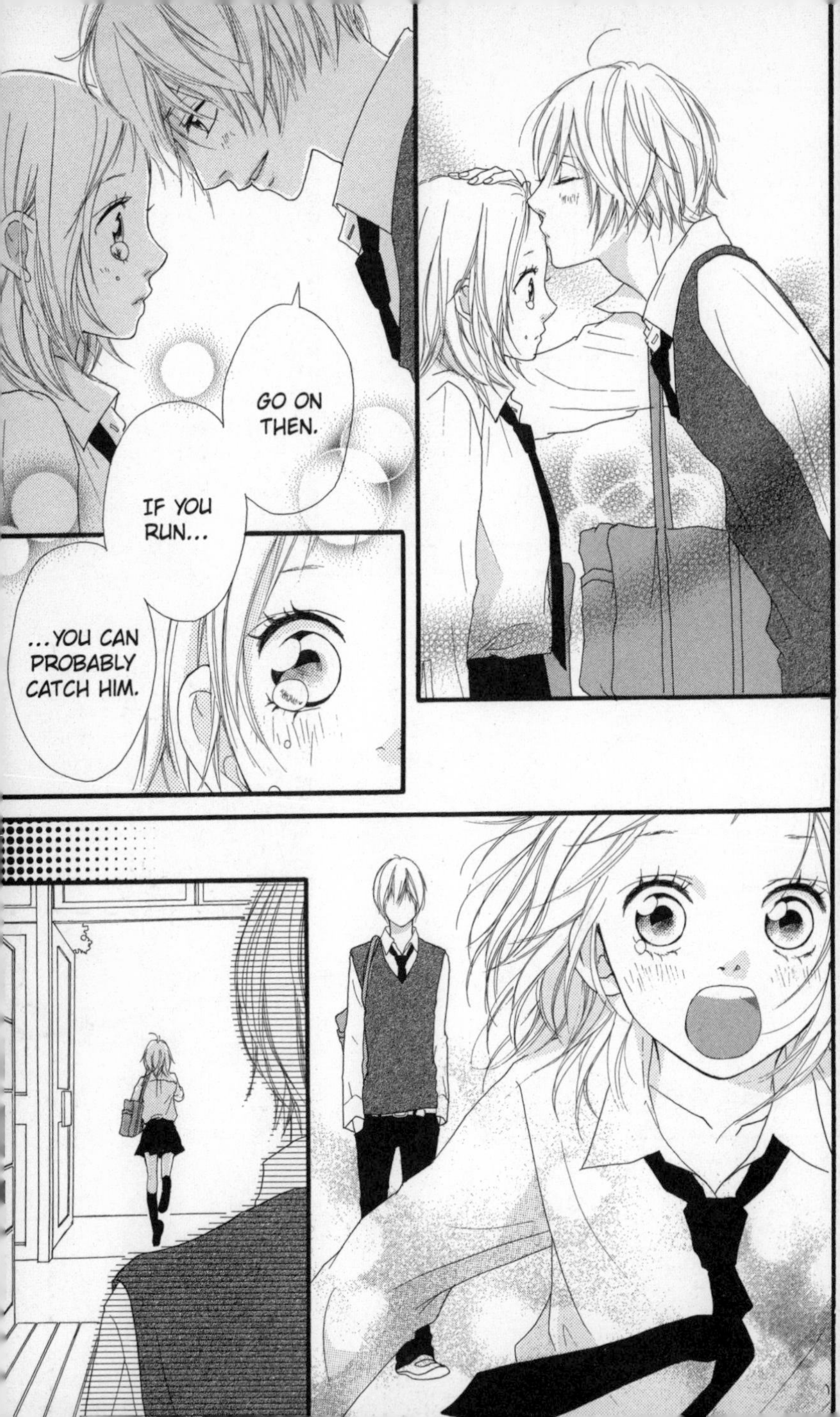
GO ON THEN.
IF YOU RUN...
...YOU CAN PROBABLY CATCH HIM.

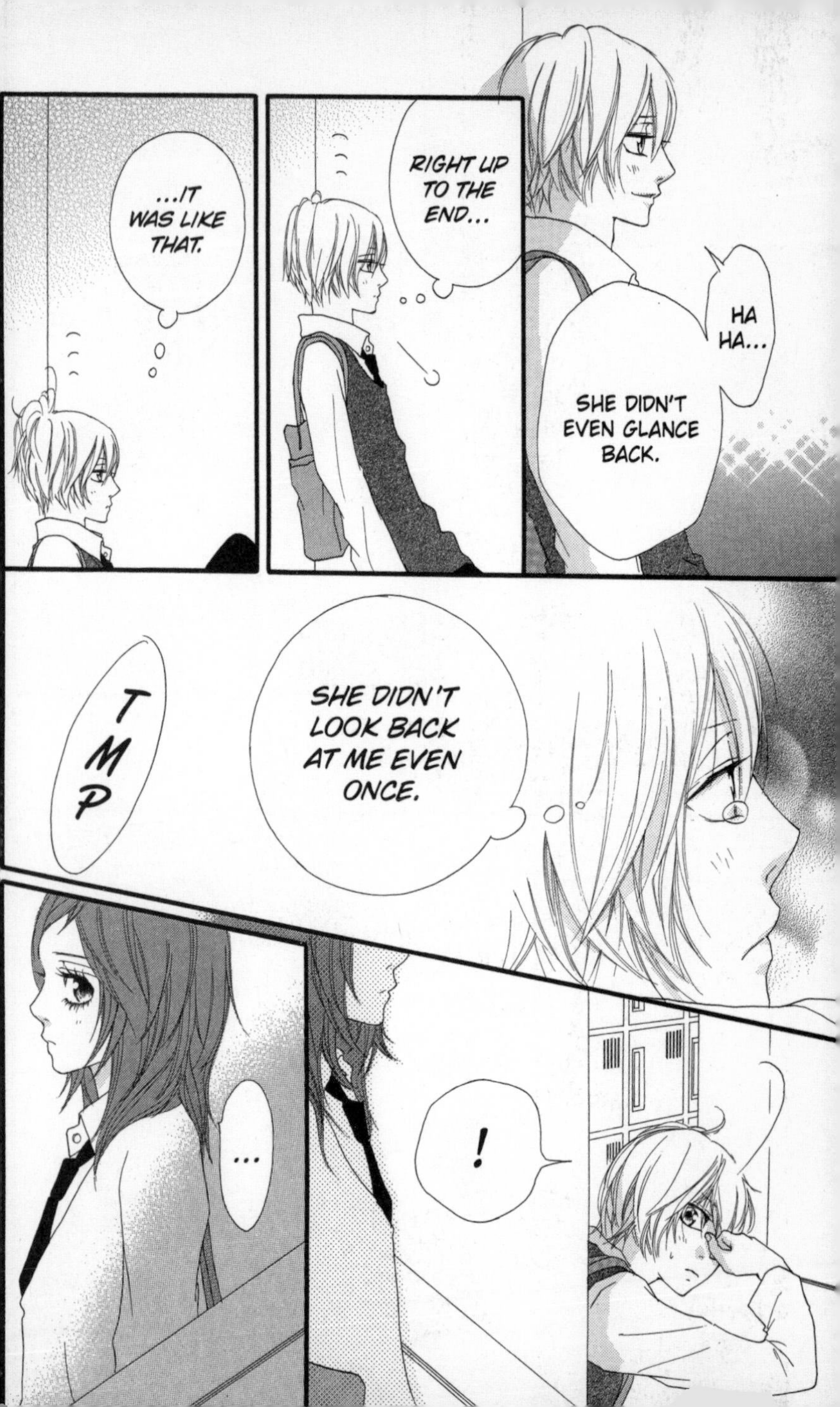
HA HA...
SHE DIDN'T EVEN GLANCE BACK.
RIGHT UP TO THE END...
...IT WAS LIKE THAT.
SHE DIDN'T LOOK BACK AT ME EVEN ONCE.
TMP
!
...

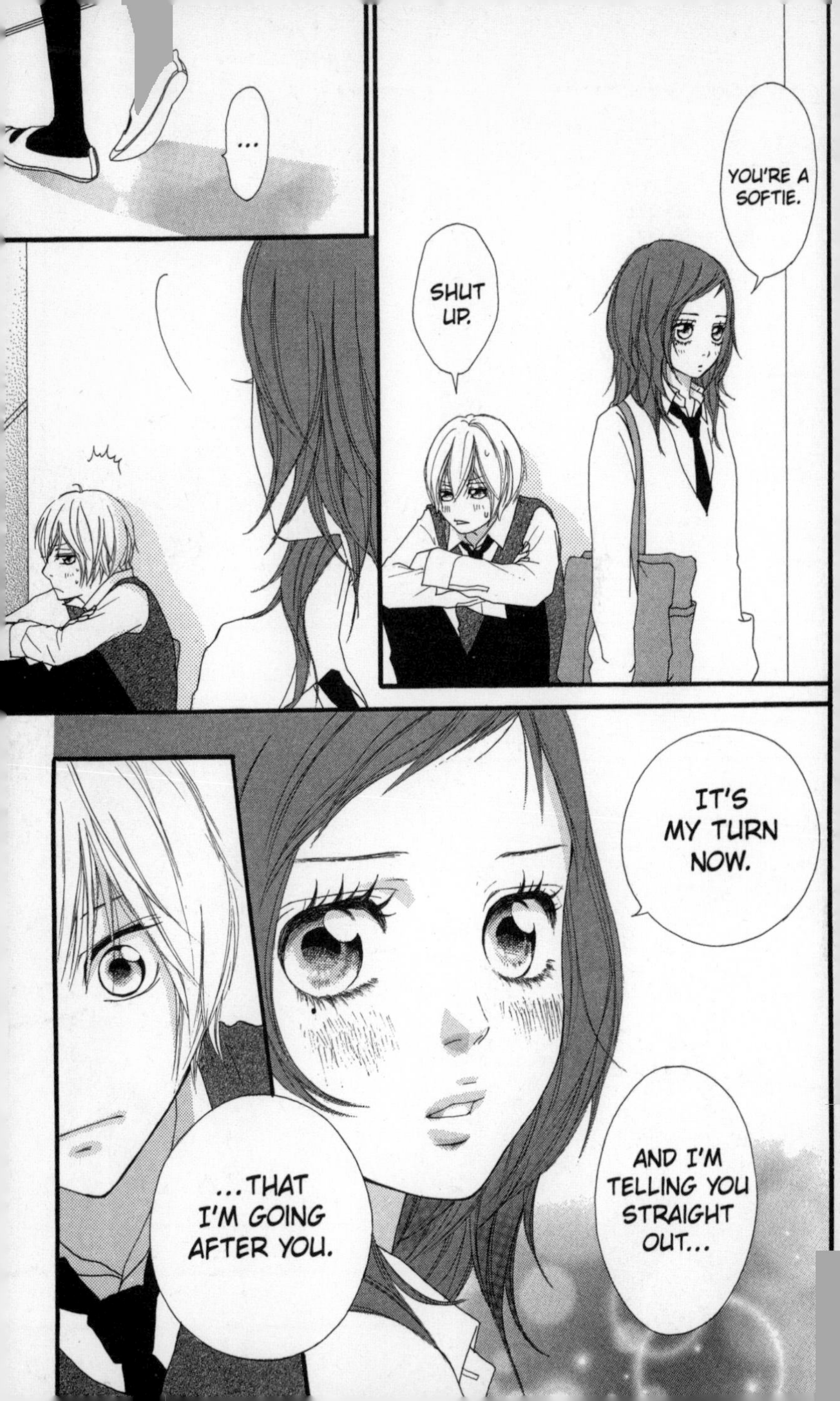
YOU'RE A SOFTIE.
SHUT UP.
...
IT'S MY TURN NOW.
AND I'M TELLING YOU STRAIGHT OUT...
...THAT I'M GOING AFTER YOU.

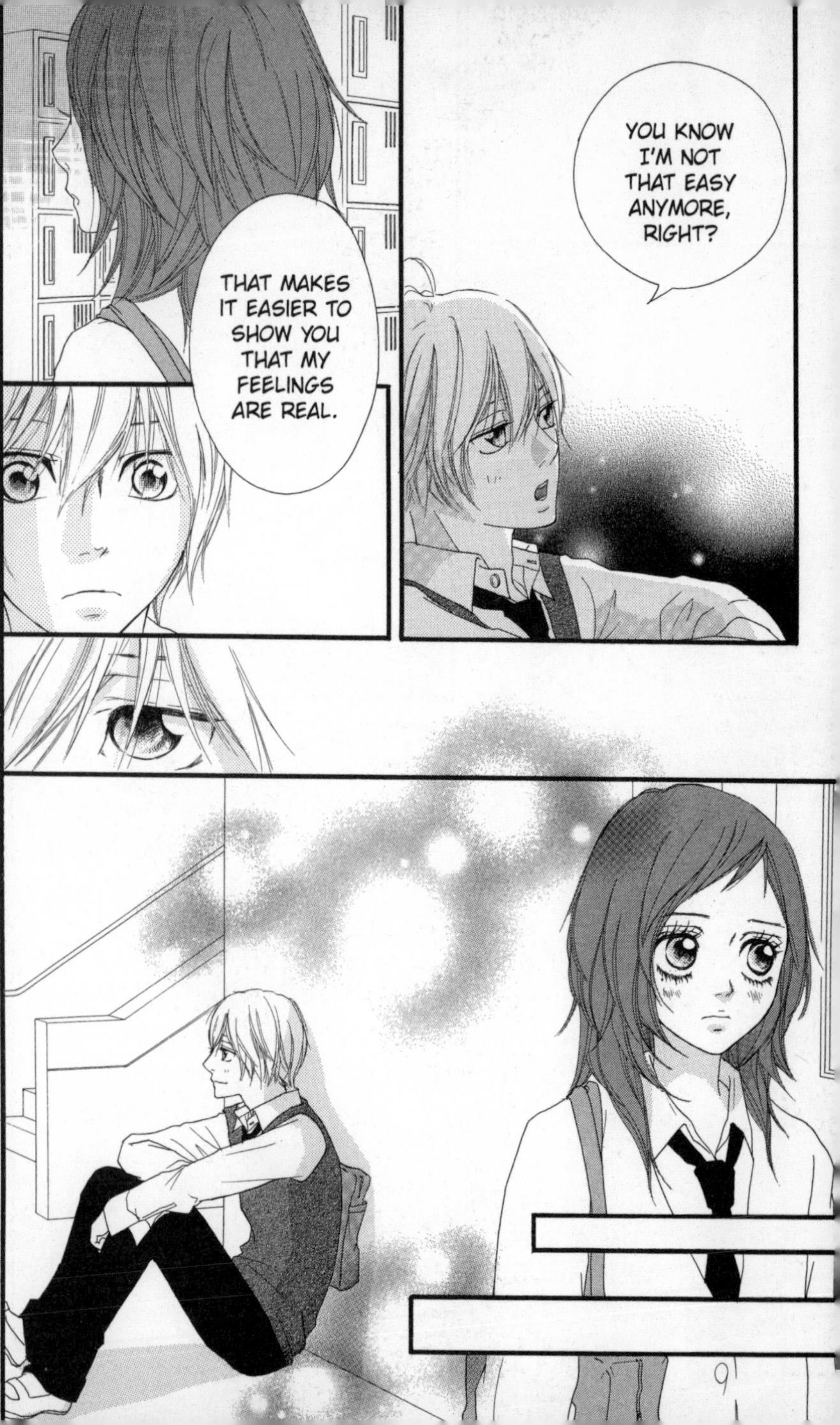
YOU KNOW I'M NOT THAT EASY ANYMORE, RIGHT?
THAT MAKES IT EASIER TO SHOW YOU THAT MY FEELINGS ARE REAL.

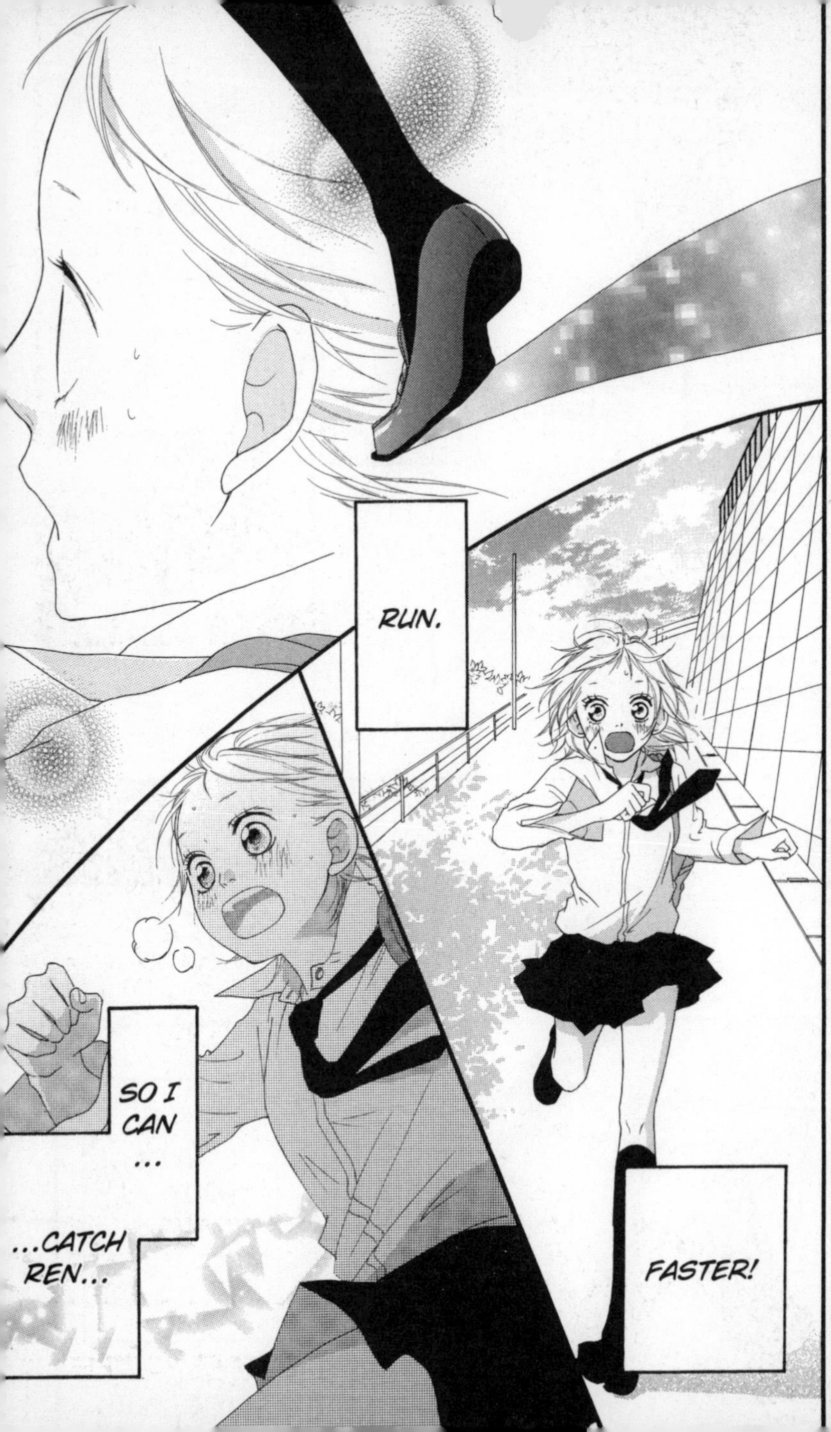
RUN.
FASTER!
SO I CAN ...
...CATCH REN...

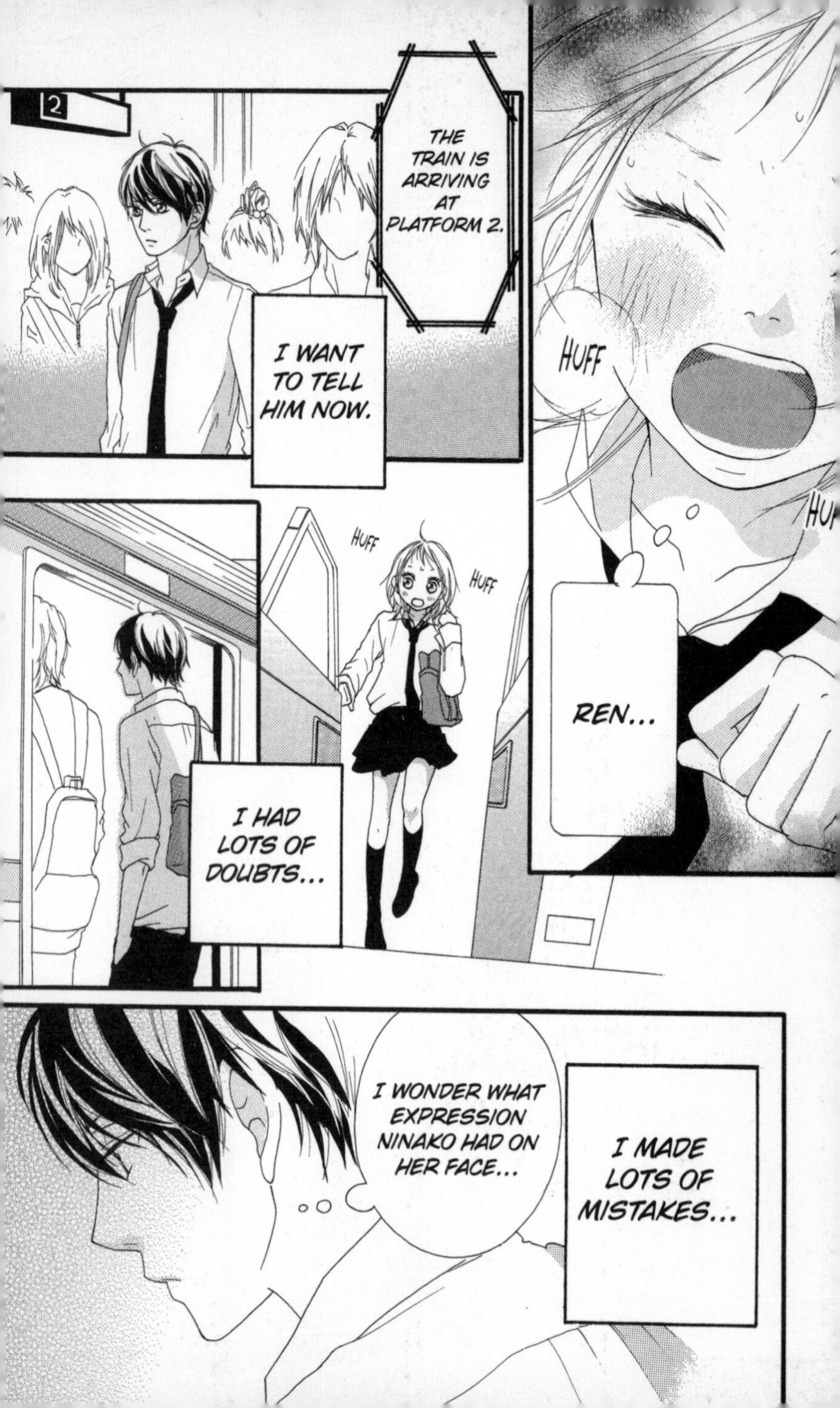
HUFF
REN...
2
THE TRAIN IS ARRIVING AT PLATFORM 2.
I WANT TO TELL HIM NOW.
HUFF
HUFF
I HAD LOTS OF DOUBTS...
I MADE LOTS OF MISTAKES...
I WONDER WHAT EXPRESSION NINAKO HAD ON HER FACE...

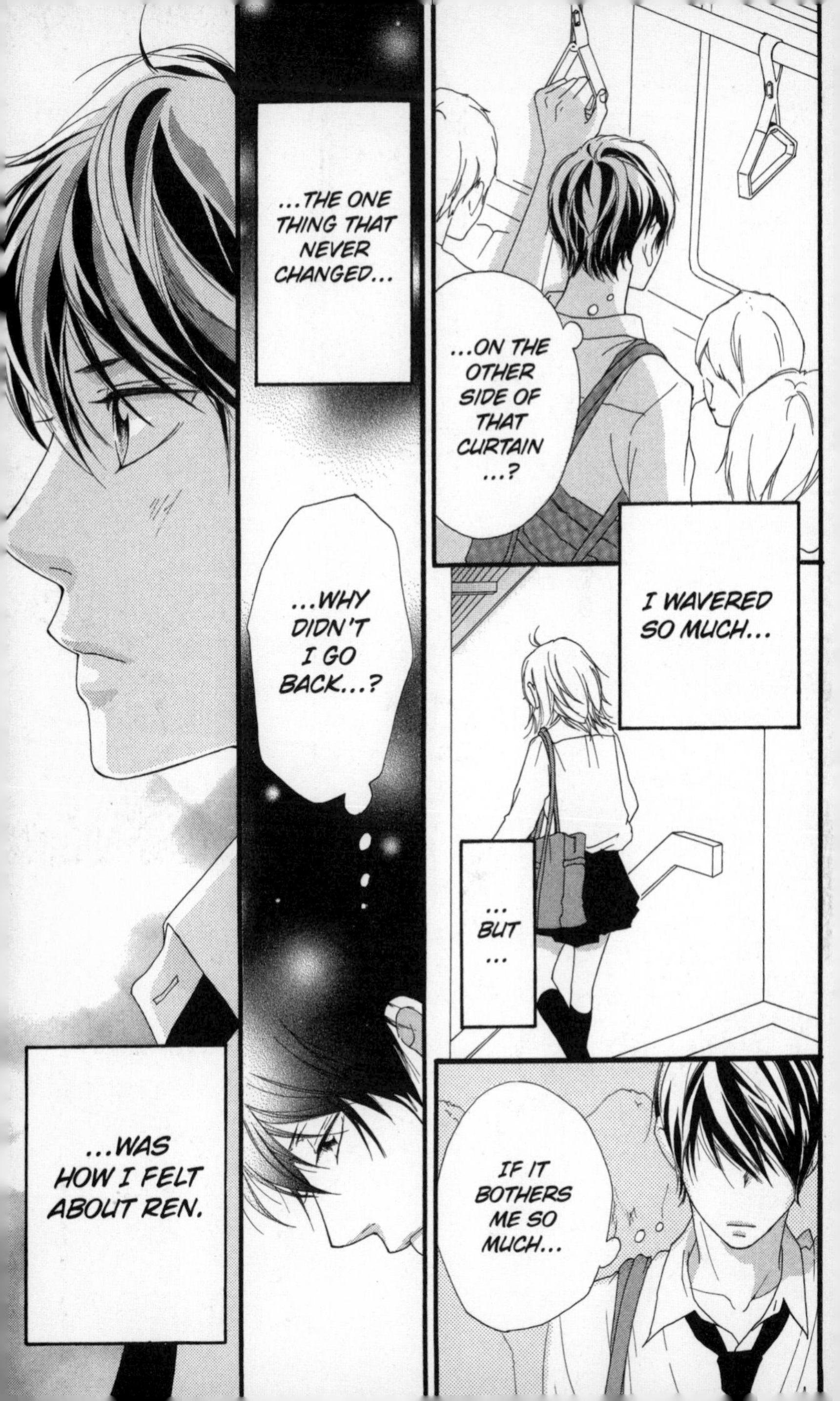

...ON THE OTHER SIDE OF THAT CURTAIN...?
I WAVERED SO MUCH...
...BUT...
IF IT BOTHERS ME SO MUCH...
...THE ONE THING THAT NEVER CHANGED...
...WHY DIDN'T I GO BACK...?
...WAS HOW I FELT ABOUT REN.

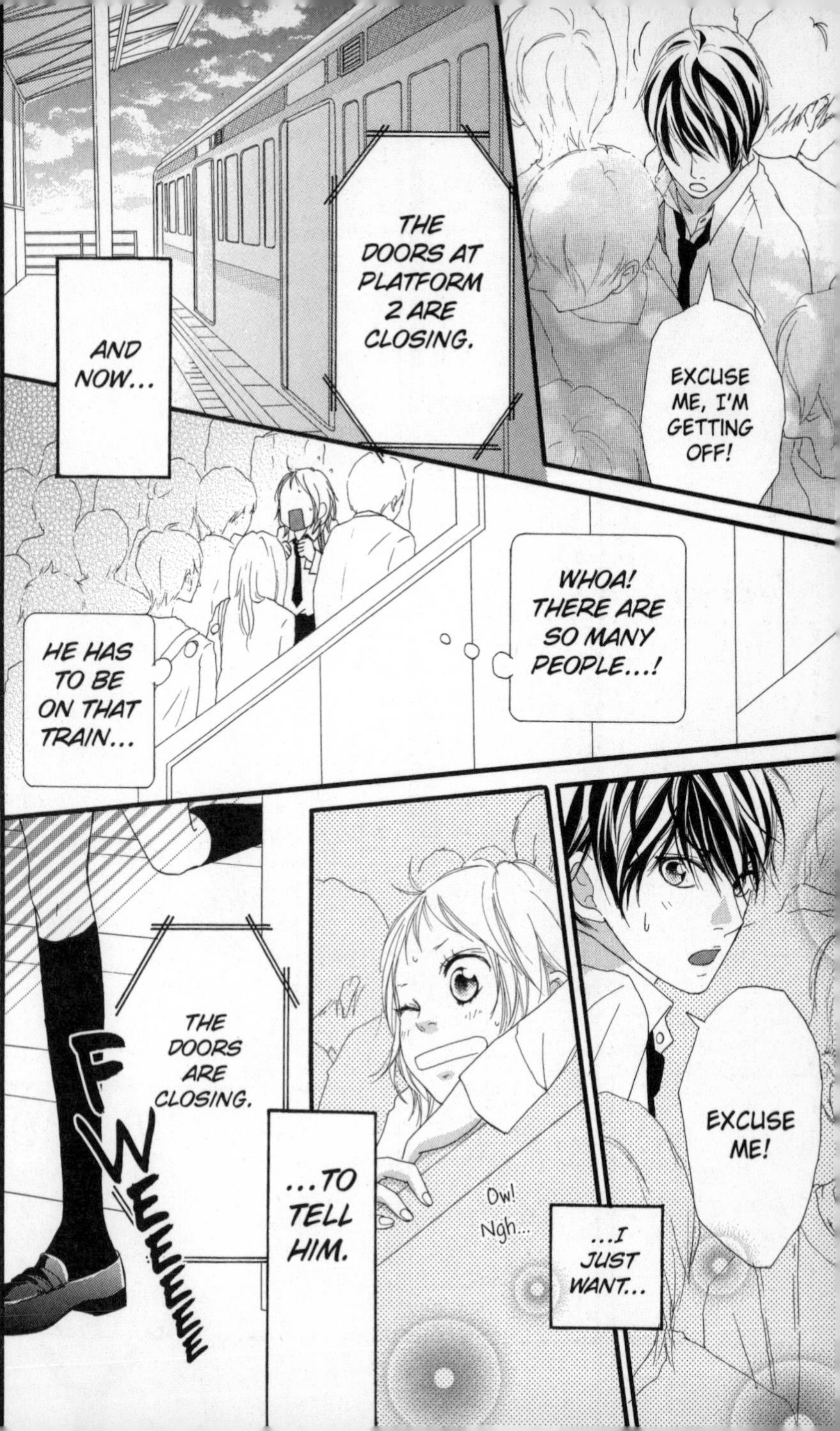
EXCUSE ME, I'M GETTING OFF!
THE DOORS AT PLATFORM 2 ARE CLOSING.
AND NOW...
WHOA! THERE ARE SO MANY PEOPLE...!
HE HAS TO BE ON THAT TRAIN...
EXCUSE ME!
...I JUST WANT...
Ow! Ngh...
...TO TELL HIM.
THE DOORS ARE CLOSING.
FWEEEEEEE

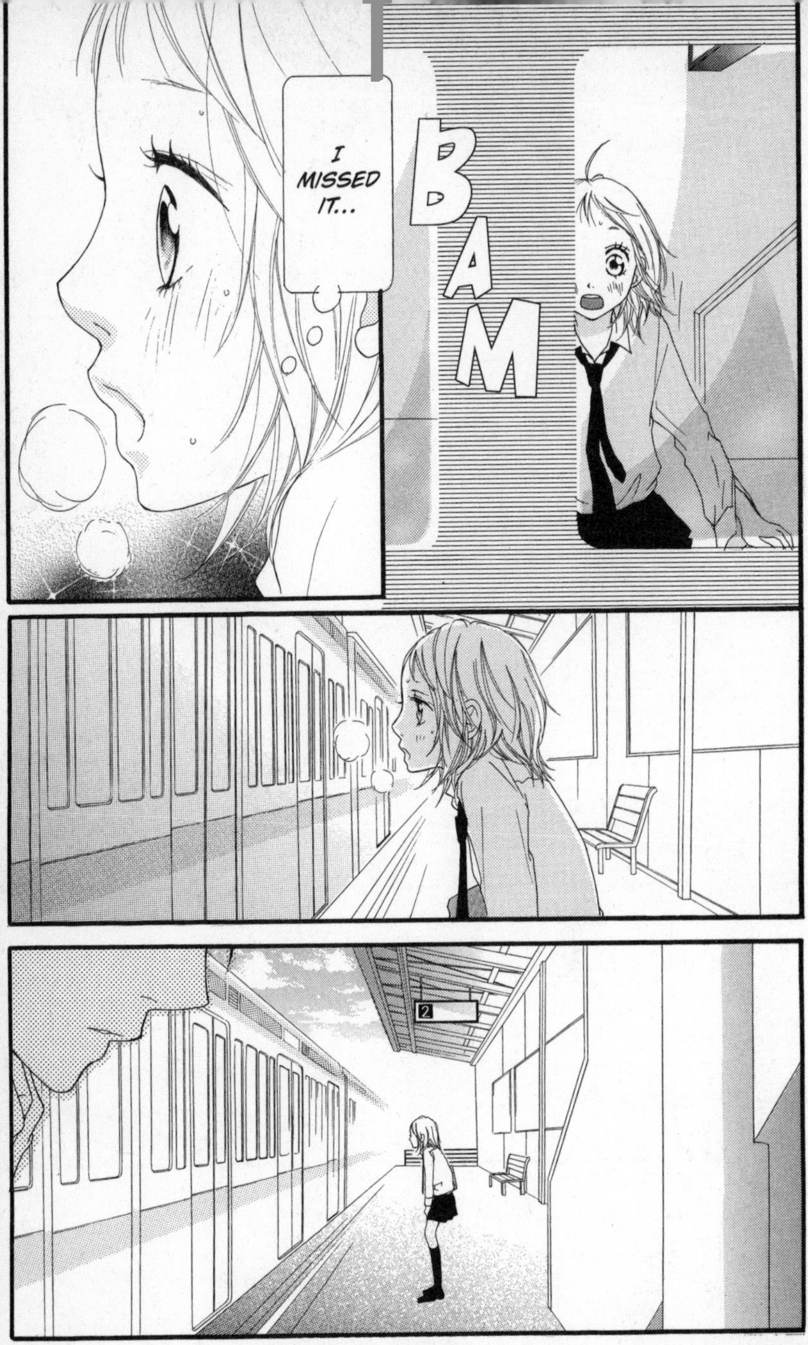
BAM
I MISSED IT...

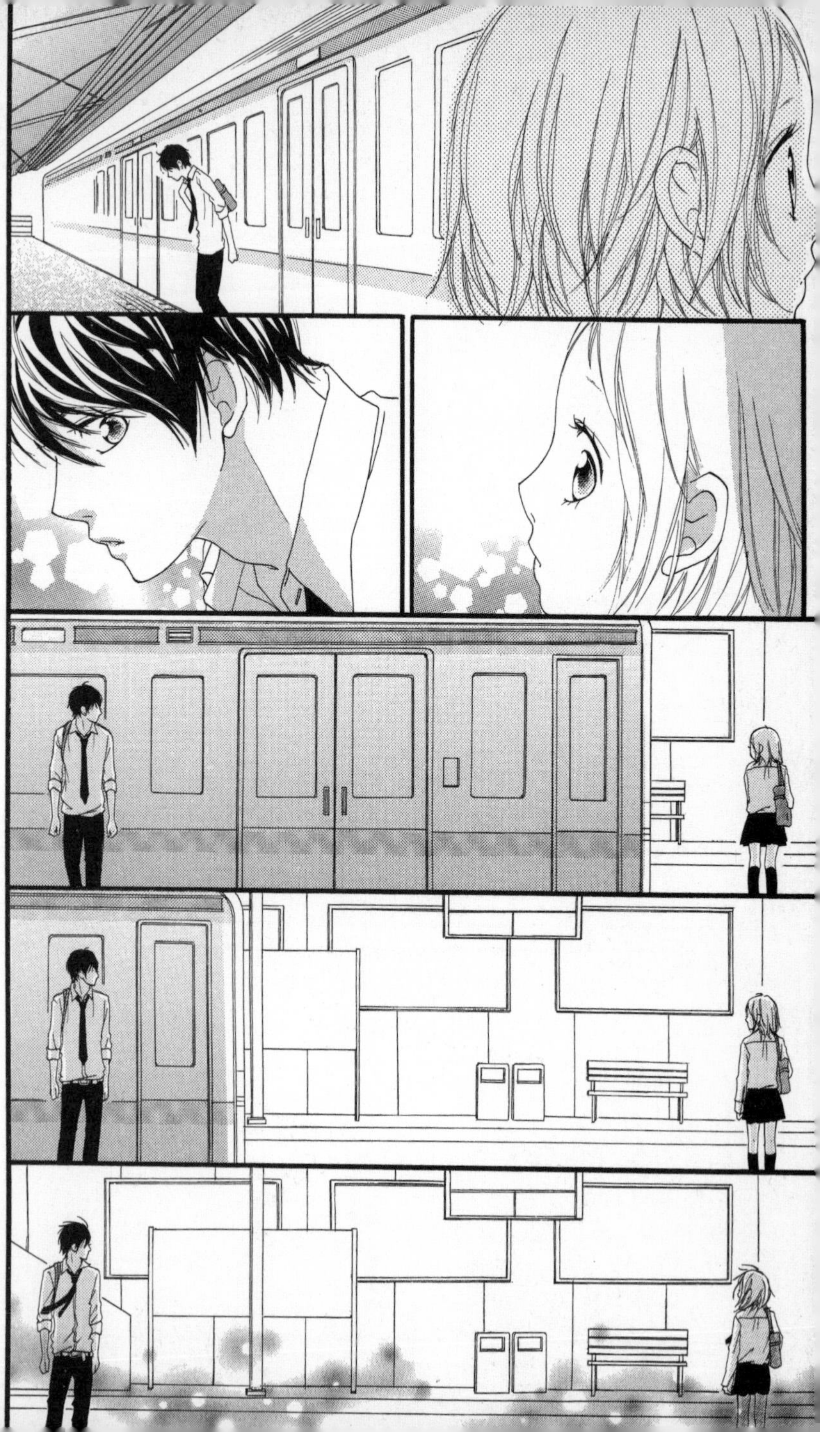

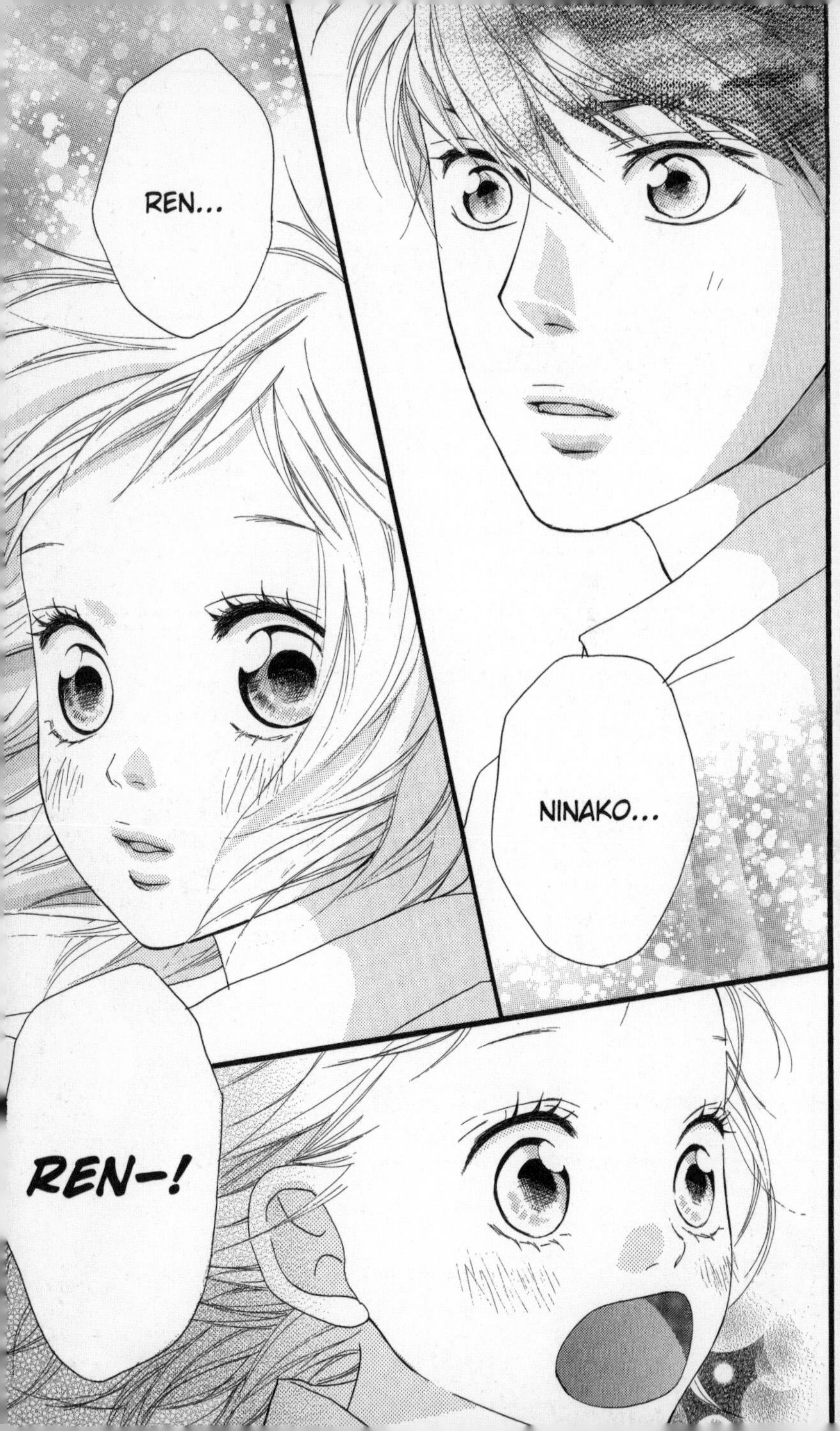
NINAKO...
REN...
REN-!

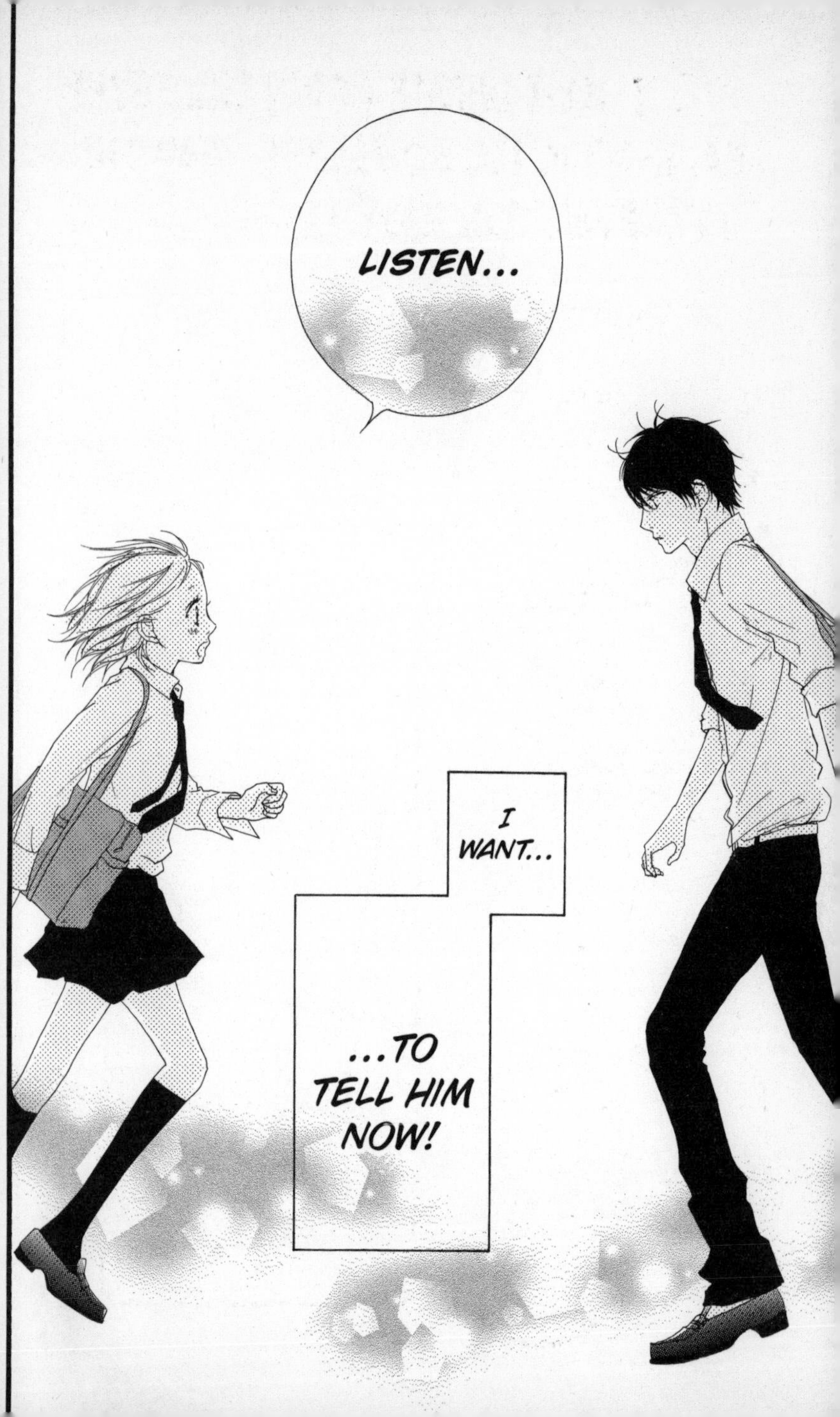
LISTEN...
I WANT...
...TO TELL HIM NOW!

THE "I JUST WROTE DOWN WHATEVER CAME TO MIND, SO PLEASE READ THIS WHENEVER YOU HAVE TIME!" CORNER

I'm still using the same desk chair. (See volumes 4-5!) It'll be good for quite a while yet!

I love my shampoo because it smells like lavender, so I was deeply hurt when someone told me it smells like a toilet. (Meaning a bathroom air freshener.) Well, no, that's an exaggeration. I was just a little ticked off.

My three chinchillas are very healthy.

When I was in elementary school, all we did in our secret hideout was eat dango! (That's sticky rice on sticks.)

Back when I was still in high school, I saw the celebrity Taro Yamada in front of a shop in Shimokitazawa. He asked, "Will you lend me your pen?" so I did. As a "thank-you," he gave me a chocolate ball. Just one. I ate it immediately.

After meeting with my editor, she gave me a gift. (Thank you for all your gifts, by the way!) When I opened the bag after I got home, there was a box of sweets and a small, mysterious bag. I looked inside and found a half-eaten croissant. It was my editor's snack. (She put it in by mistake.) Okay, try and imagine: it wasn't just a croissant, but a **partly nibbled** croissant. Is she a squirrel? I just loved it. She just took a nibble and put it away... Squirrel? Croissant + partly nibbled = awesome.

I tried to have a "remember when" conversation with Momoko Kouda, a Bessatsu Margaret author, but she didn't remember a thing. "Really? Is that how it went?" "Wait, wasn't it more like this?" She was wrong every time. Note to self: I can't chat with Momoko about memories.

★★★ I don't get out much so I don't know my town very well. I've lived here for about five years, but I really don't know where anything is. ★★★

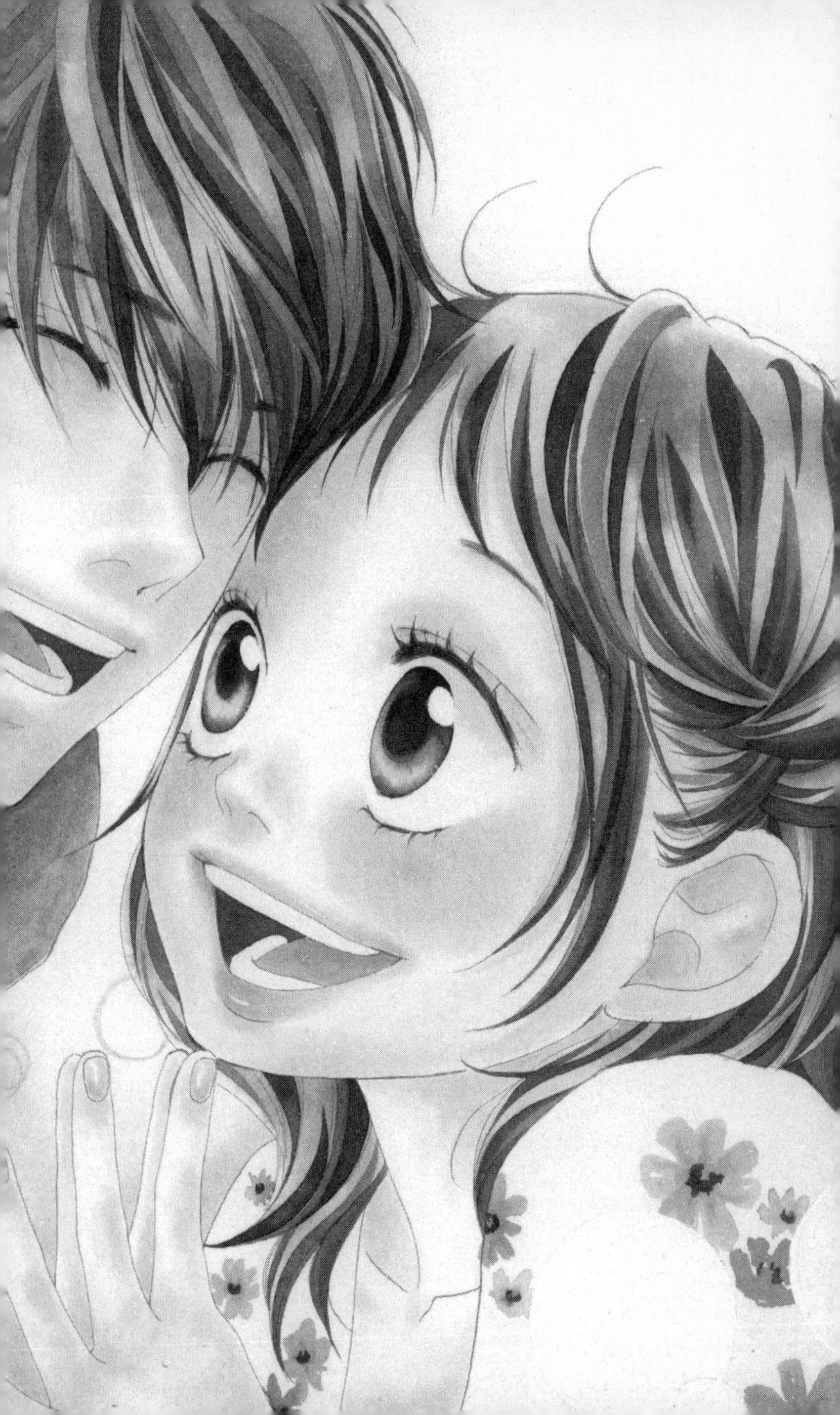

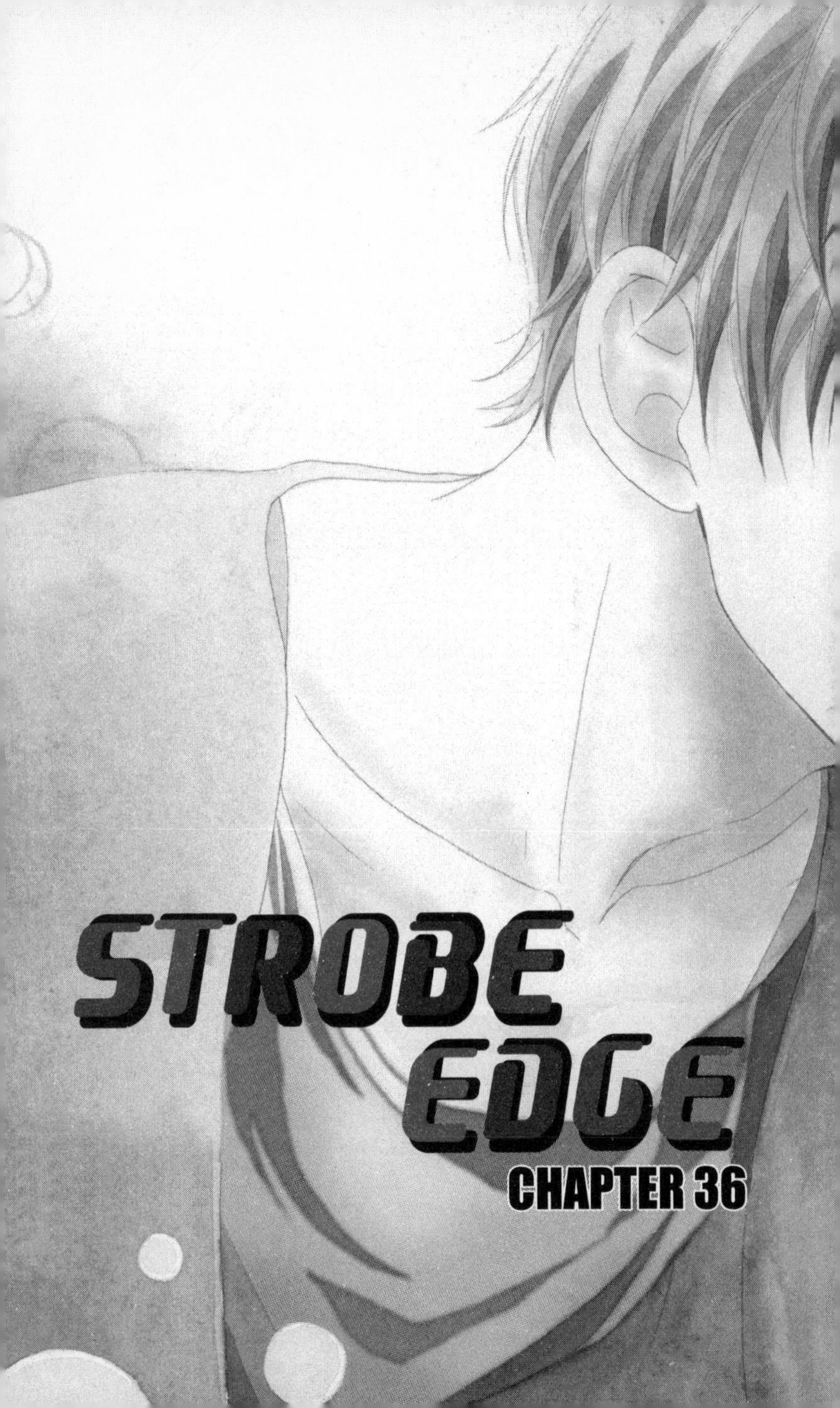
STROBE
EDGE
CHAPTER 36

STROBE EDGE trivia

I'LL TELL YOU BECAUSE WE'RE ALMOST DONE, BUT IT'S ALL USELESS Part 1

• We decided that one of Ninako's friends should have a larger role in the story, and therefore she should have a last name. That was Sayuri Uehara. When I was chatting about it on the phone with my editor, I happened to be listening to a CD by Maximum the Hormone, and I happen to be a huge fan of their bass player, Ue. Yes, that's right. Sayuri's name was taken from Ue of Maximum the Hormone. It took only about three seconds to decide— Sorry! His bass playing is awesome.

• I've told you before that the Chihuahua incident is pretty much exactly as it happened, but the incident where Ninako hears "Coke, no ice" as "cocoa ice" is true as well. In reality, a foreign customer ordered 7UP in a non-Japanese accent, and the confused staff brought out Saran Wrap. I wanted to use it as-is, but decided against it since it names specific products. I also thought it would be a little hard to understand, since manga is a visual medium. Oh, and in "Colorless Dreamer" (included in volume 6), under "Qualifications" on the resume, where it says ""Girl Scouts: Blue Ribbon," that's true too. Oh, but none of this happened to me. It all happened to other people.

• In my imagination, Ren had a much older brother who was very offbeat, unshaven, and shaggy with wanderlust... I got this far and I thought my editor looked sad, so I decided the idea probably wouldn't work and buried it. Ren's mythical brother...

Continued in part 2...

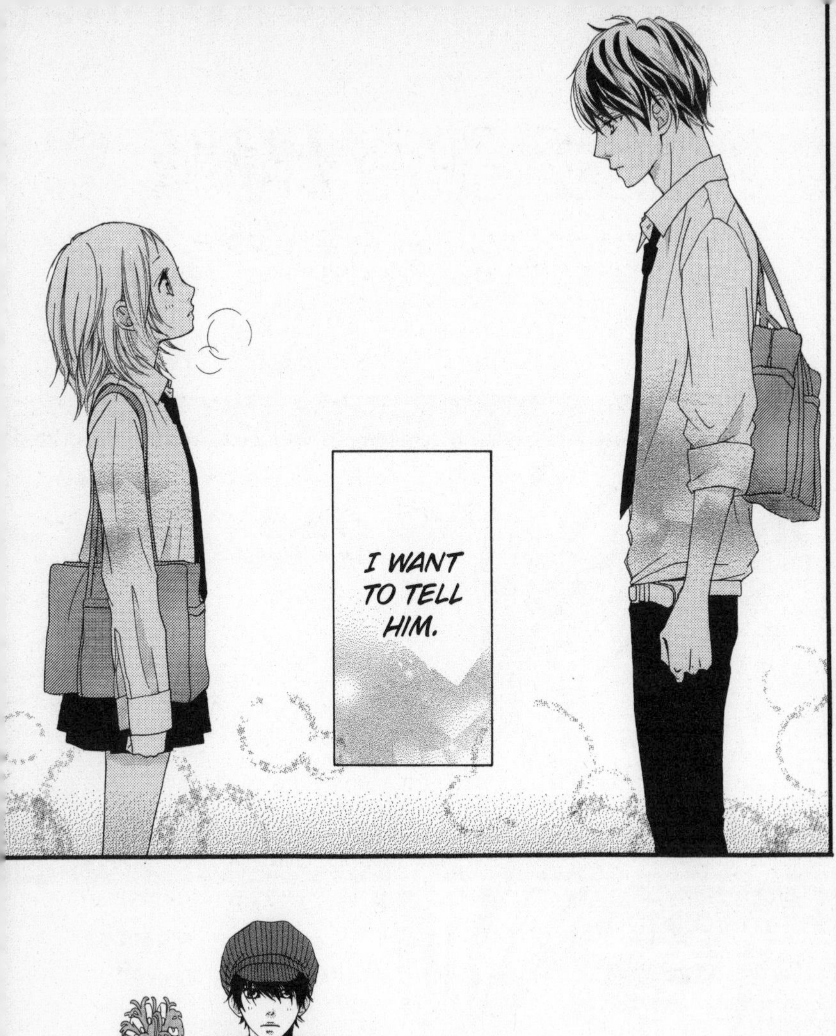
I WANT TO TELL HIM.

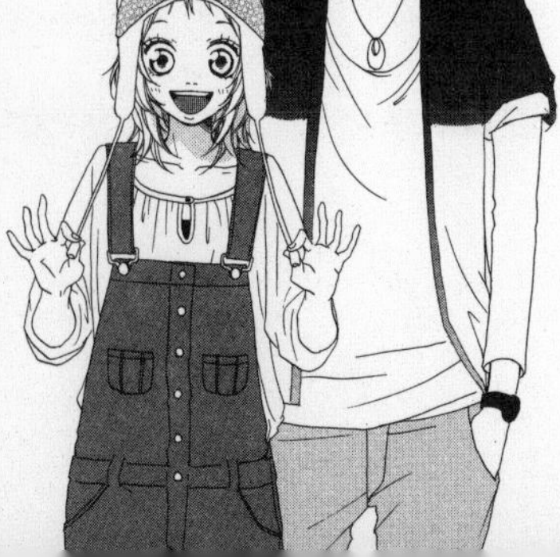

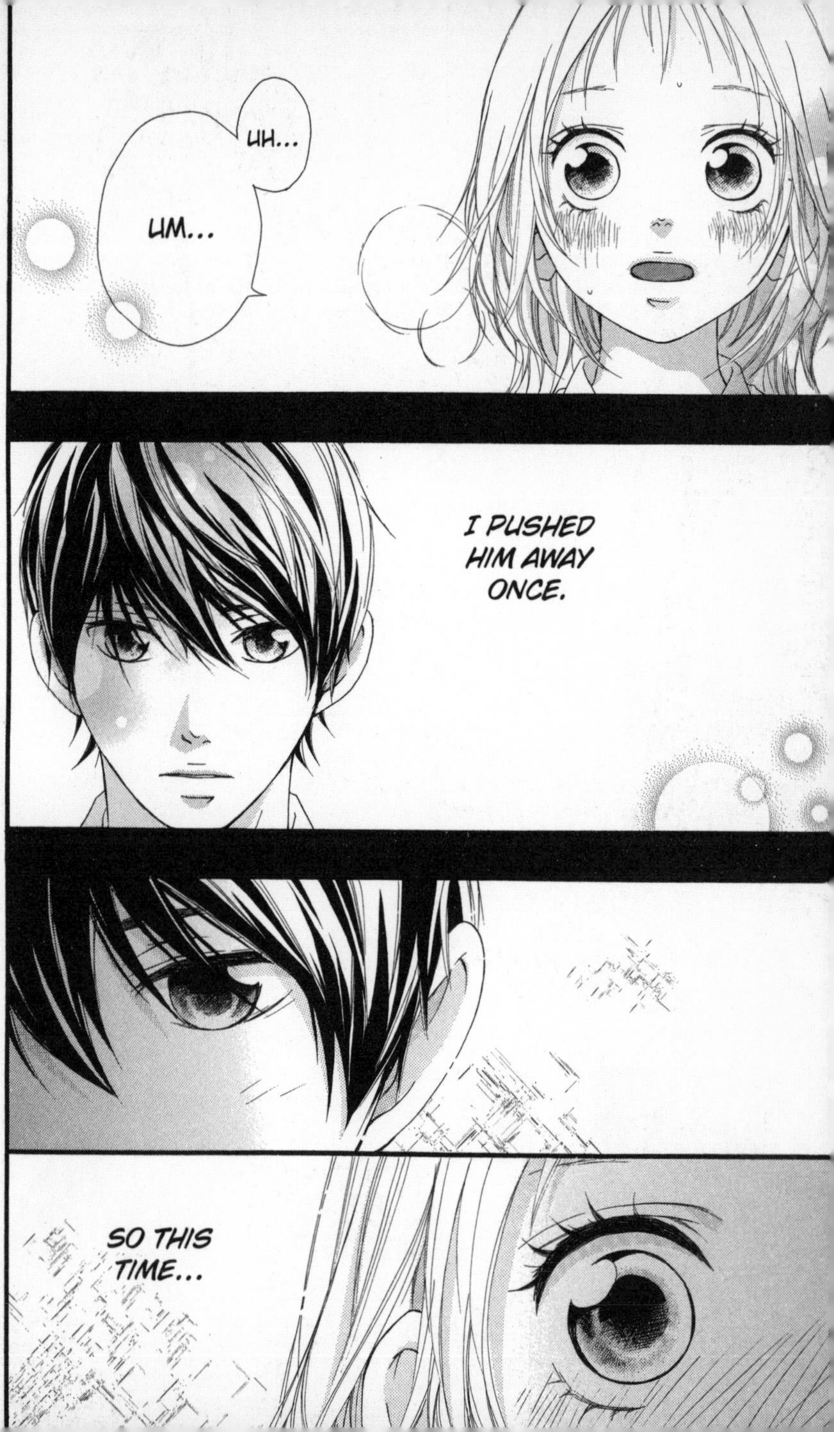
UH...
UM...
I PUSHED HIM AWAY ONCE.
SO THIS TIME...

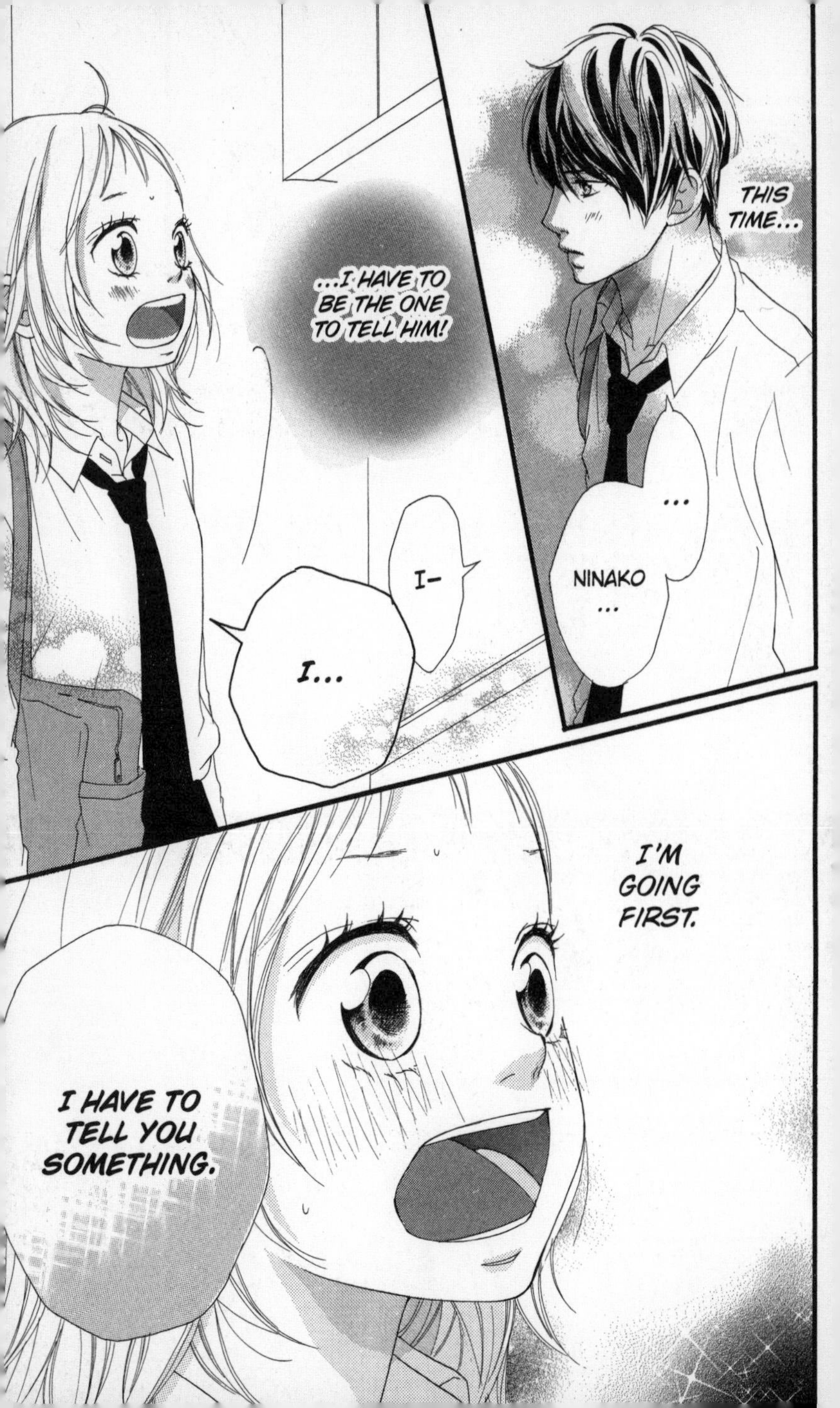
THIS TIME...
...
NINAKO ...
...I HAVE TO BE THE ONE TO TELL HIM!
I-
I...
I'M GOING FIRST.
I HAVE TO TELL YOU SOMETHING.

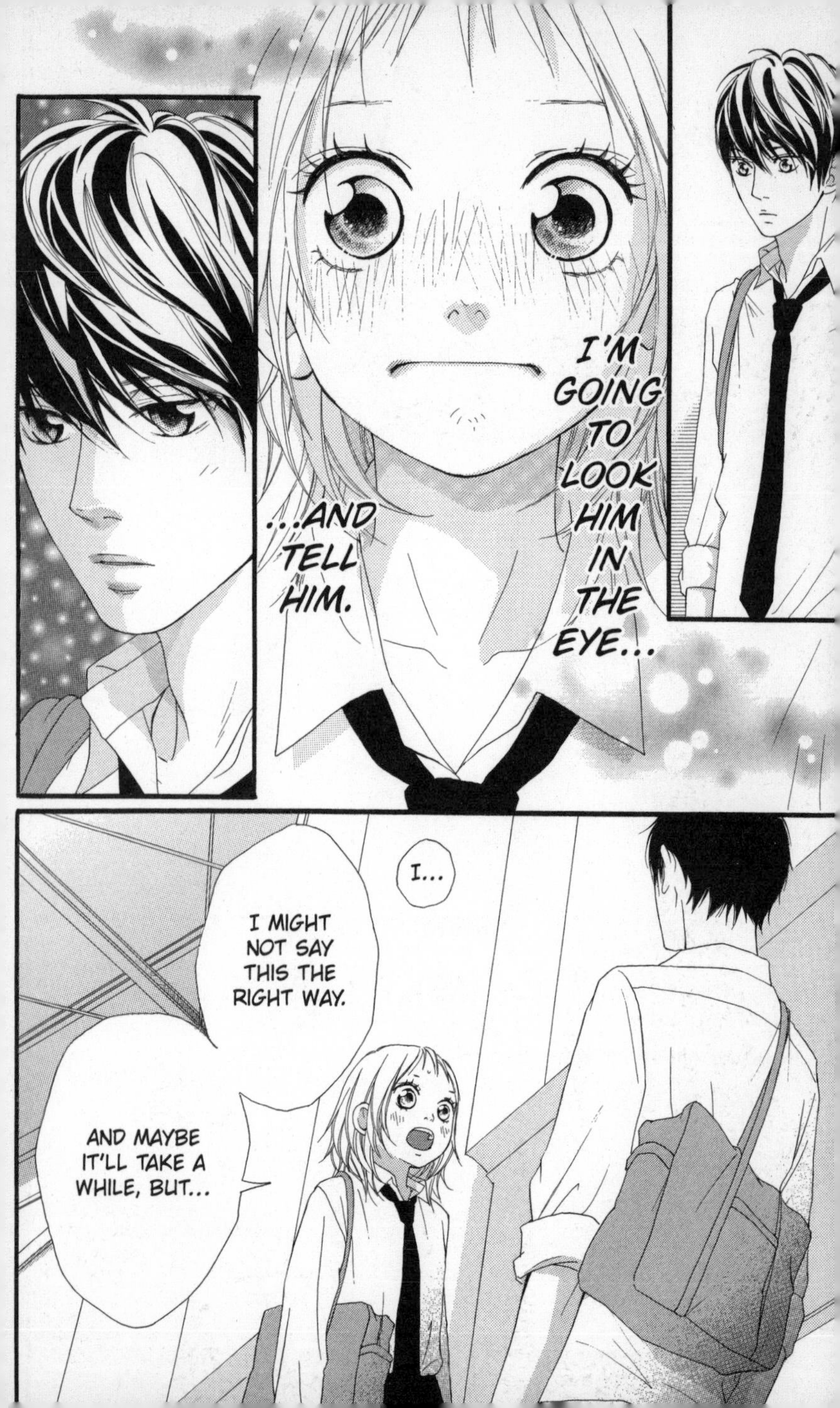
I'M GOING TO LOOK HIM IN THE EYE...
...AND TELL HIM.
I...
I MIGHT NOT SAY THIS THE RIGHT WAY.
AND MAYBE IT'LL TAKE A WHILE, BUT...

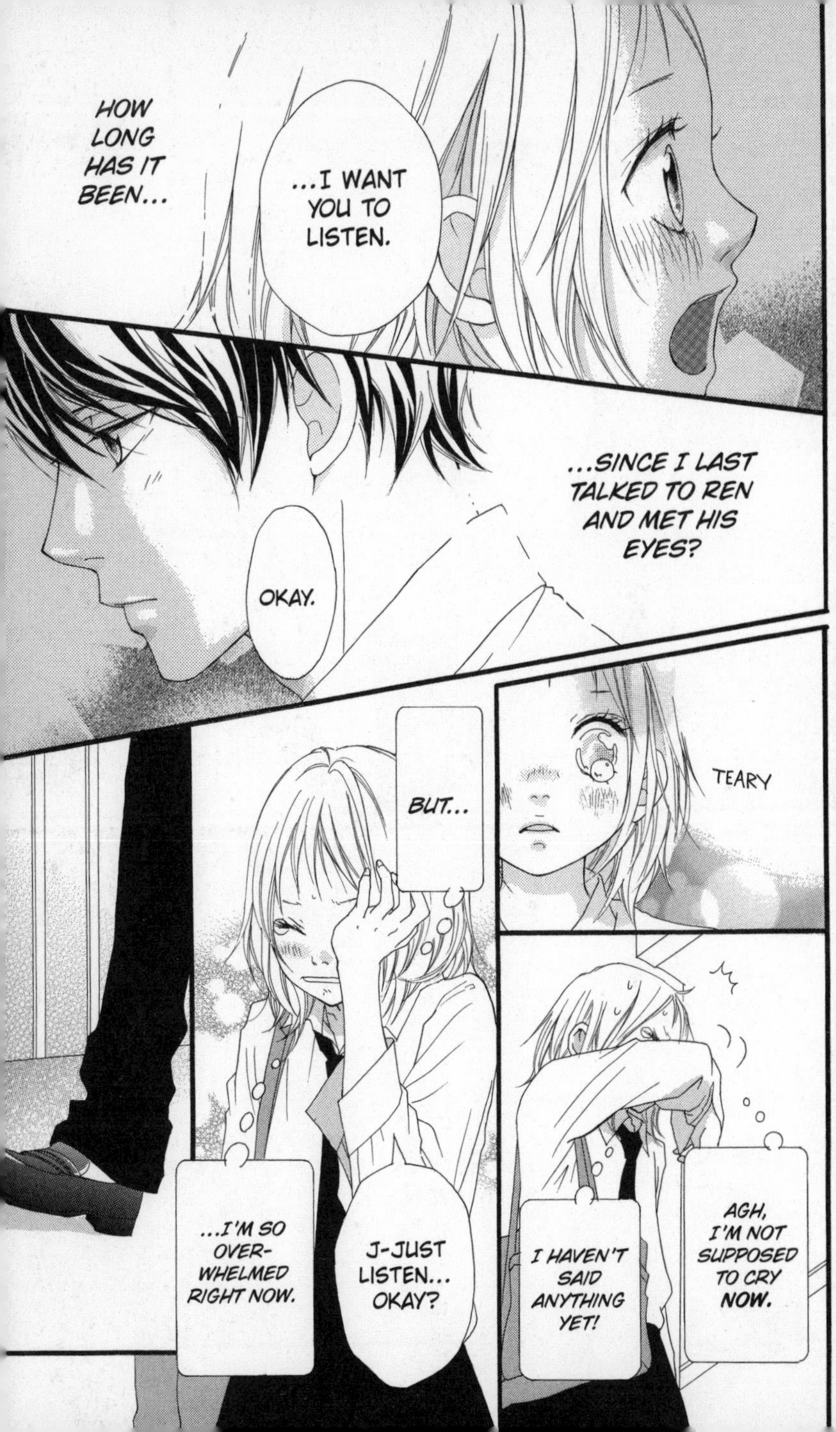
...I WANT YOU TO LISTEN.
HOW LONG HAS IT BEEN...
...SINCE I LAST TALKED TO REN AND MET HIS EYES?
OKAY.
TEARY
AGH, I'M NOT SUPPOSED TO CRY NOW.
I HAVEN'T SAID ANYTHING YET!
BUT...
J-JUST LISTEN... OKAY?
...I'M SO OVER-WHELMED RIGHT NOW.

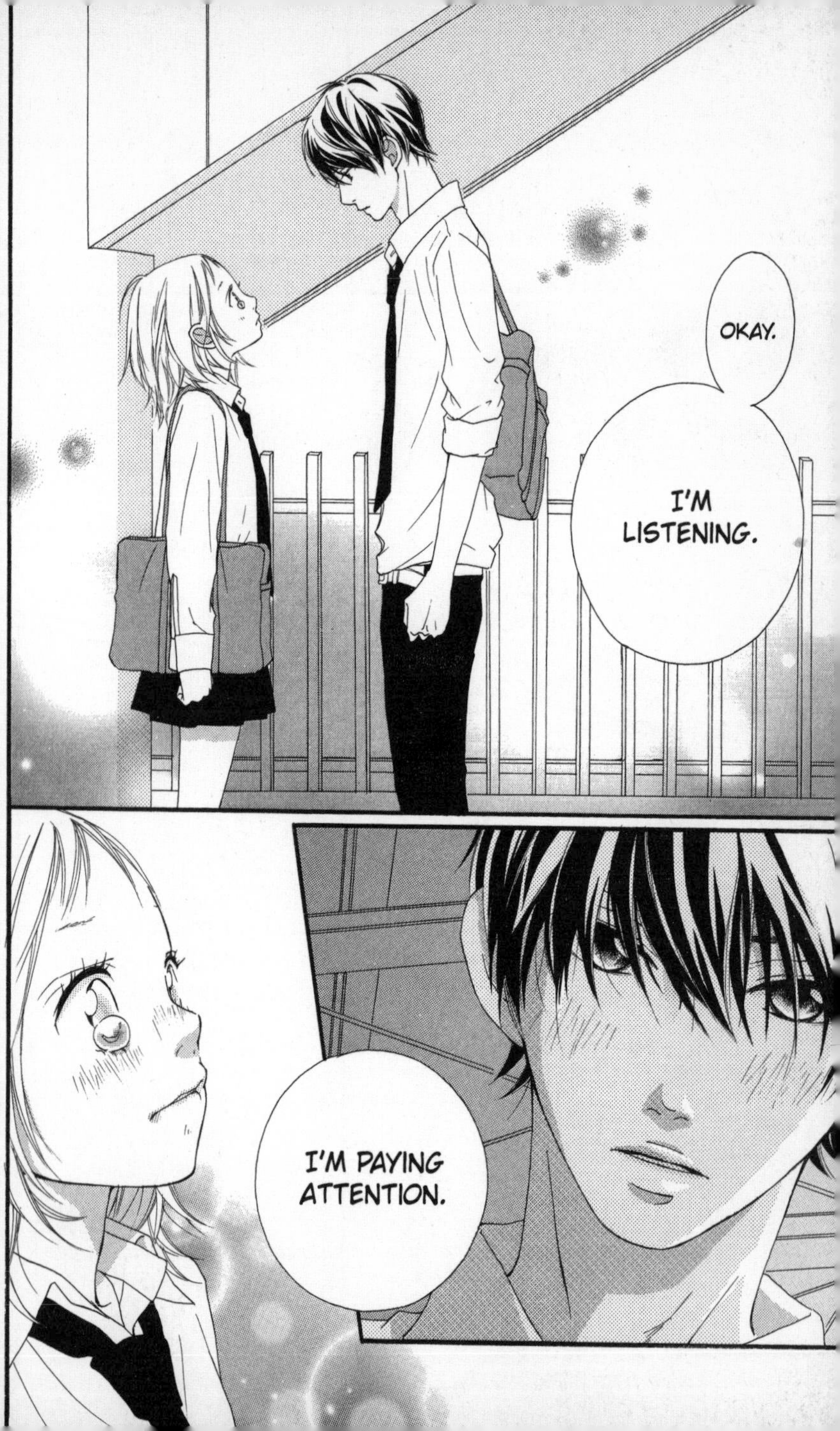
OKAY.
I'M LISTENING.
I'M PAYING ATTENTION.

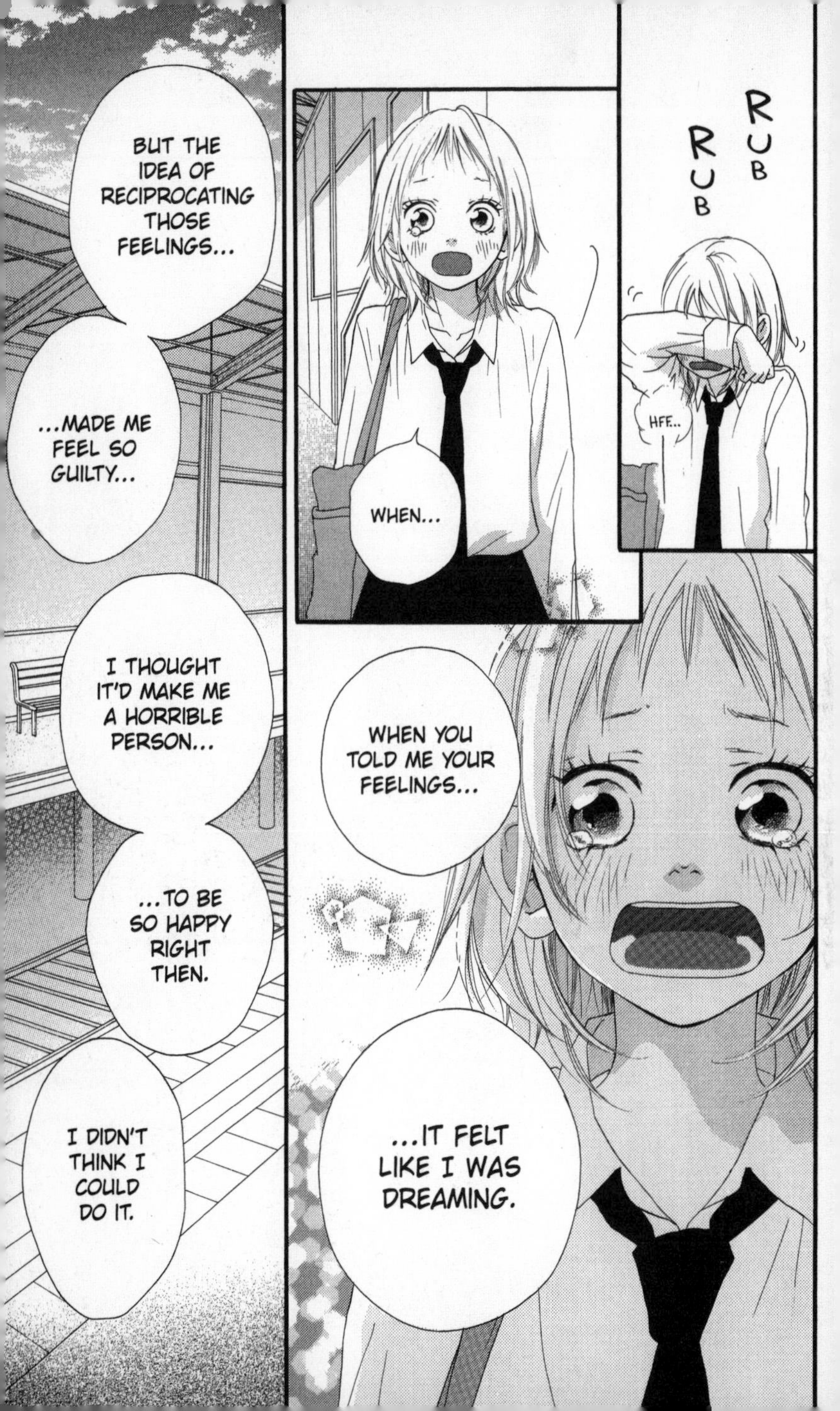
RUB RUB
HFF...
WHEN...
WHEN YOU TOLD ME YOUR FEELINGS...
...IT FELT LIKE I WAS DREAMING.
BUT THE IDEA OF RECIPROCATING THOSE FEELINGS...
...MADE ME FEEL SO GUILTY...
I THOUGHT IT'D MAKE ME A HORRIBLE PERSON...
...TO BE SO HAPPY RIGHT THEN.
I DIDN'T THINK I COULD DO IT.

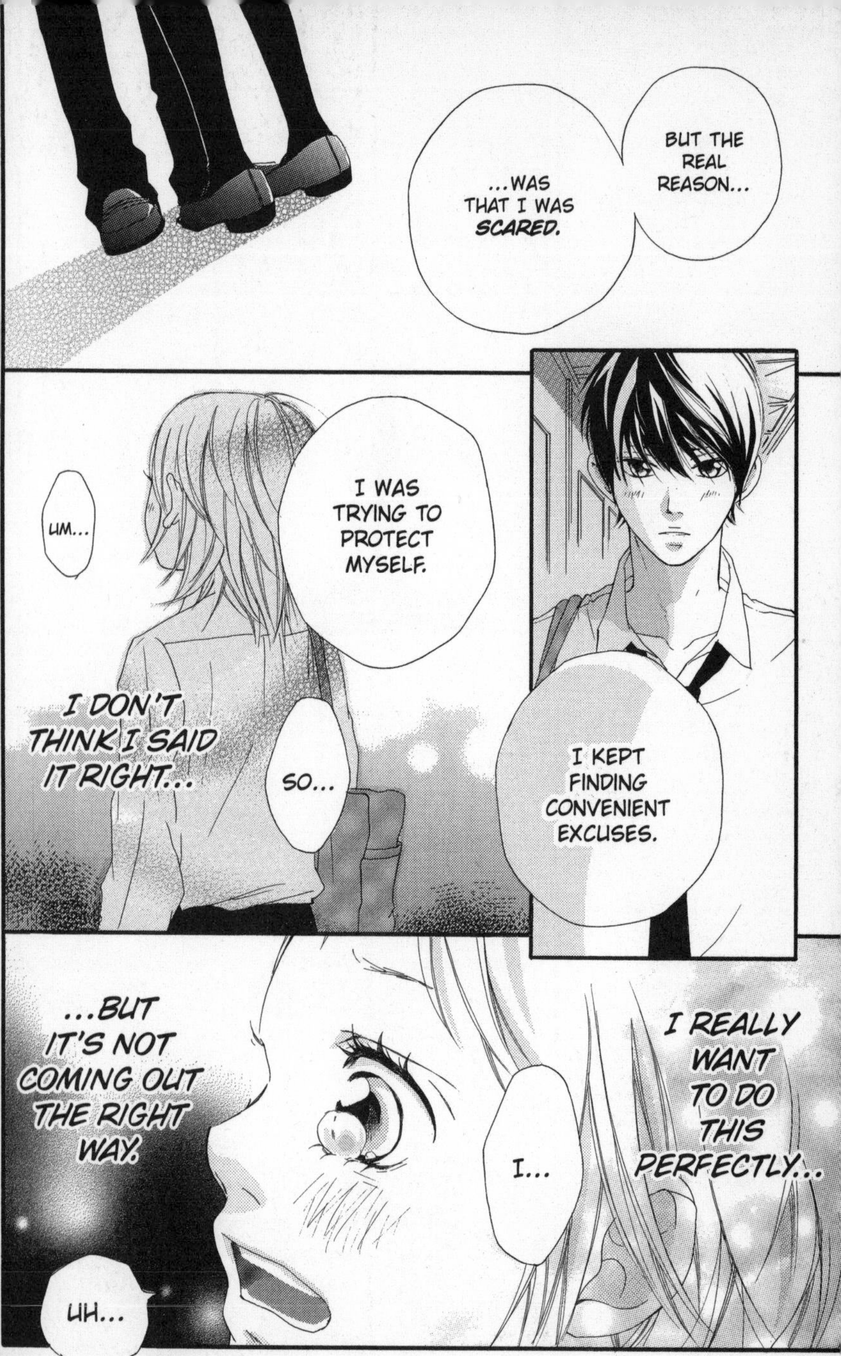
BUT THE REAL REASON...
...WAS THAT I WAS *SCARED.*
I KEPT FINDING CONVENIENT EXCUSES.
I WAS TRYING TO PROTECT MYSELF.
UM...
SO...
I DON'T THINK I SAID IT RIGHT...
I REALLY WANT TO DO THIS PERFECTLY...
I...
...BUT IT'S NOT COMING OUT THE RIGHT WAY.
UH...

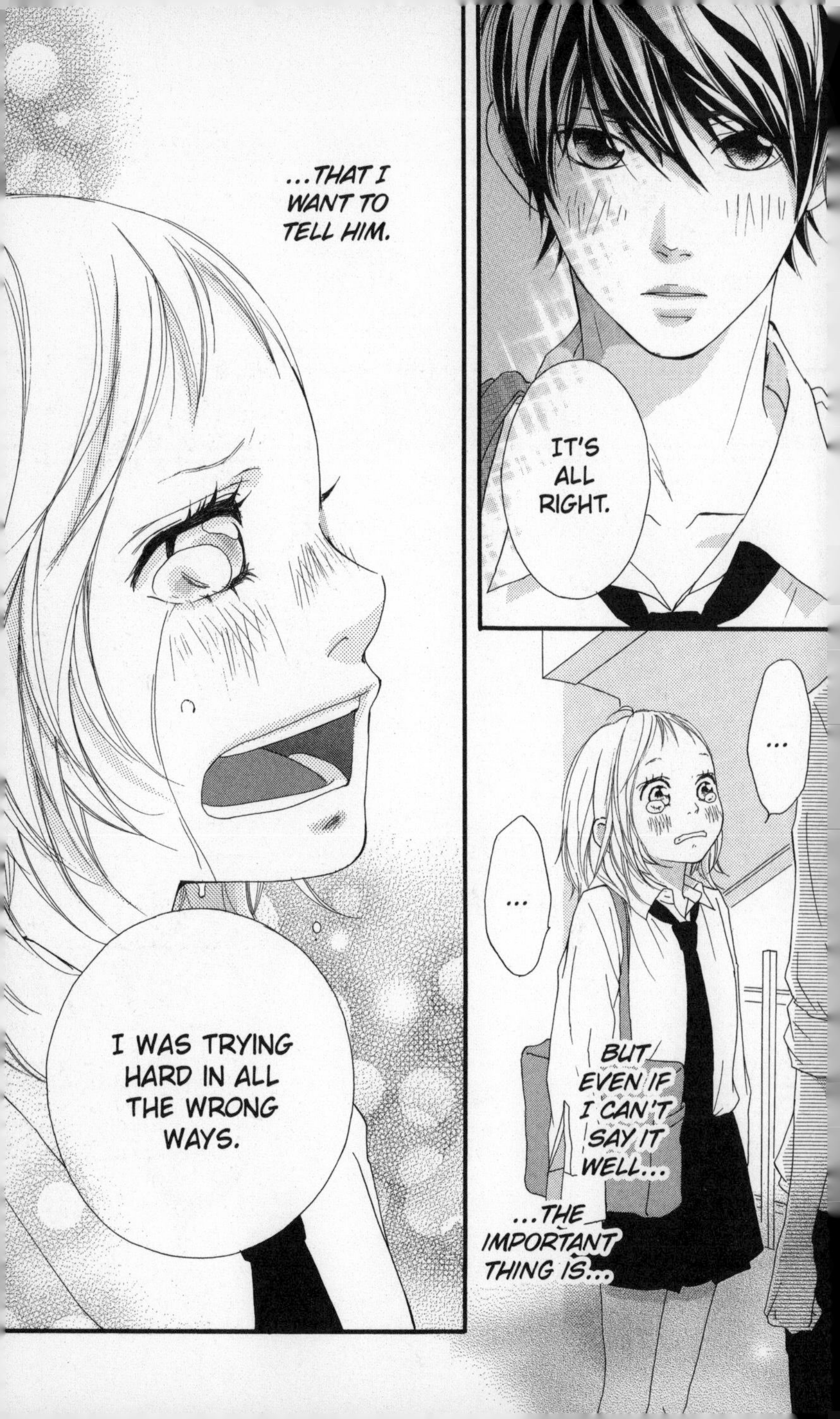
IT'S ALL RIGHT.
...
...
BUT EVEN IF I CAN'T SAY IT WELL...
...THE IMPORTANT THING IS...
...THAT I WANT TO TELL HIM.
I WAS TRYING HARD IN ALL THE WRONG WAYS.

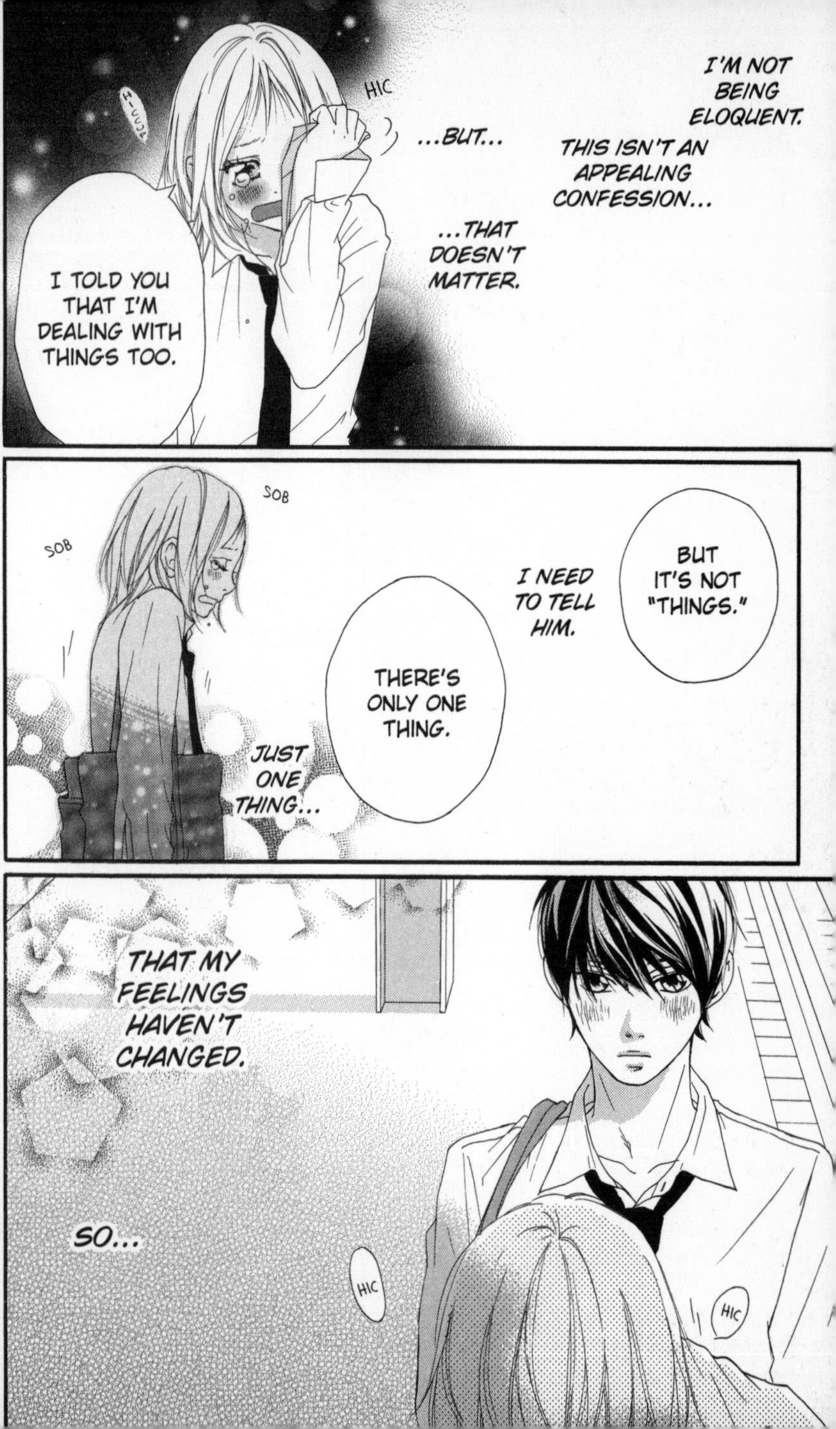
I'M NOT BEING ELOQUENT.
THIS ISN'T AN APPEALING CONFESSION...
...BUT...
HIC
...THAT DOESN'T MATTER.
HICCUP
I TOLD YOU THAT I'M DEALING WITH THINGS TOO.
BUT IT'S NOT "THINGS."
I NEED TO TELL HIM.
THERE'S ONLY ONE THING.
SOB
JUST ONE THING...
SOB
HIC
THAT MY FEELINGS HAVEN'T CHANGED.
HIC
SO...

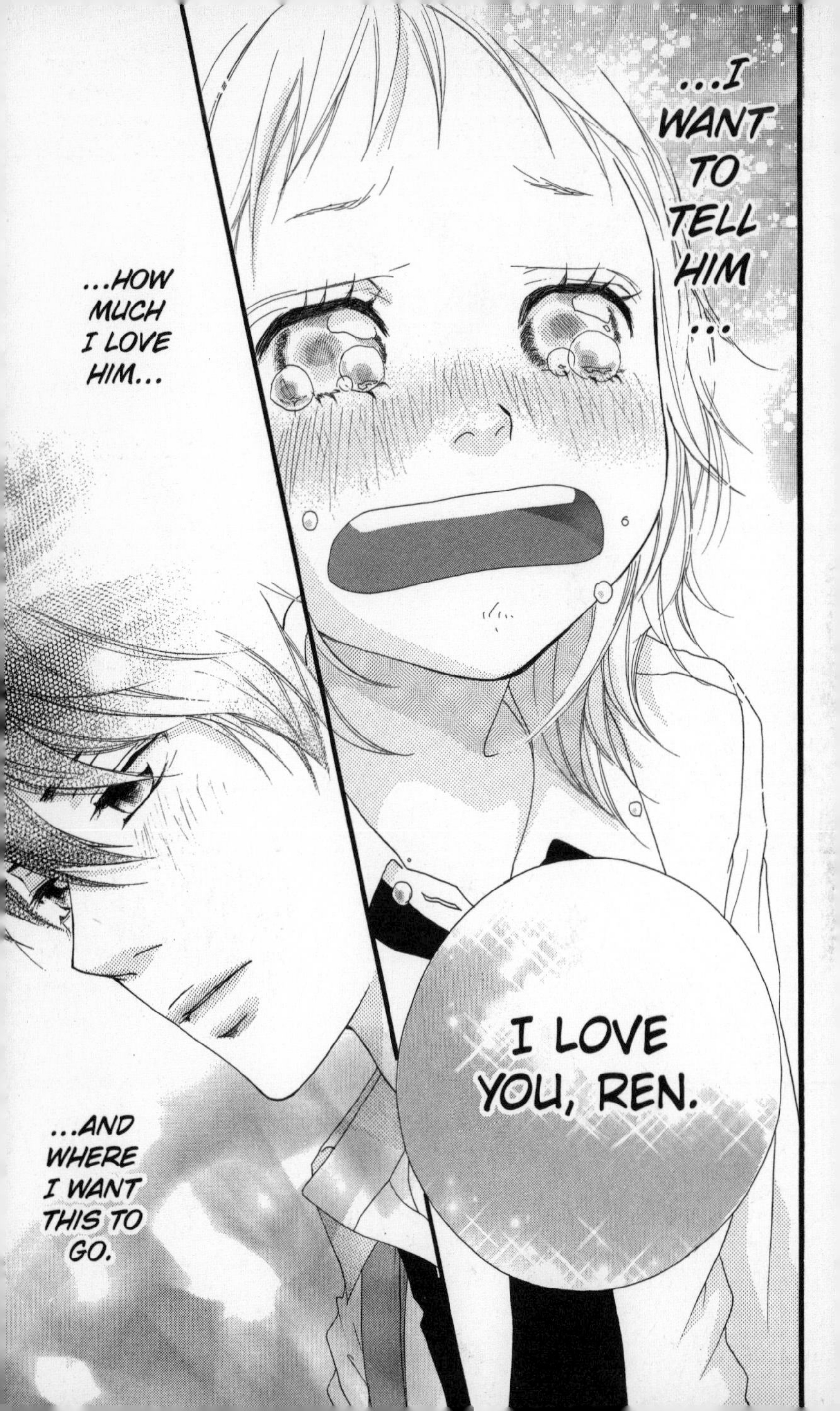
...I WANT TO TELL HIM...
...HOW MUCH I LOVE HIM...
I LOVE YOU, REN.
...AND WHERE I WANT THIS TO GO.

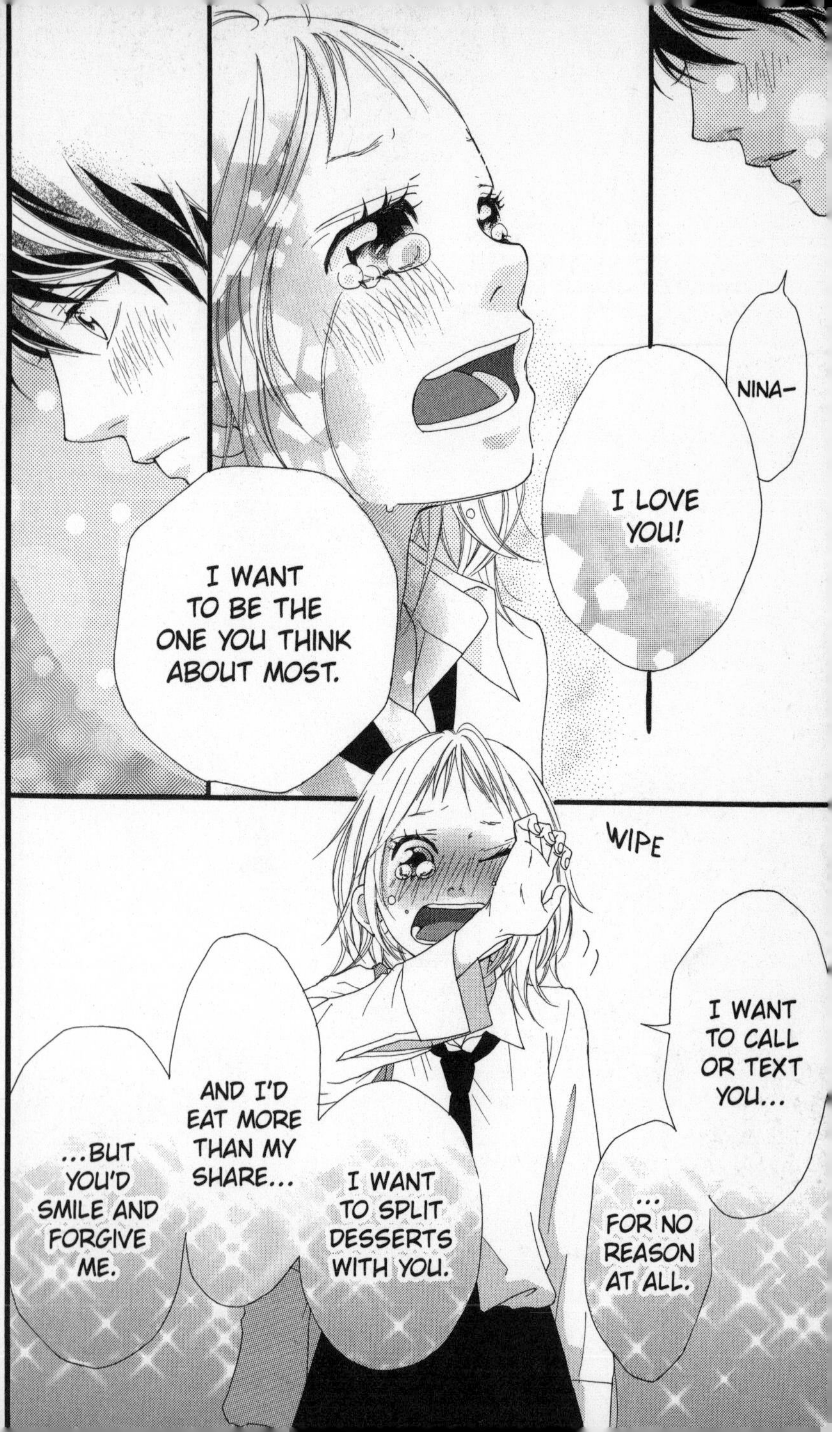
NINA-
I LOVE YOU!
I WANT TO BE THE ONE YOU THINK ABOUT MOST.
WIPE
I WANT TO CALL OR TEXT YOU...
...FOR NO REASON AT ALL.
I WANT TO SPLIT DESSERTS WITH YOU.
AND I'D EAT MORE THAN MY SHARE...
...BUT YOU'D SMILE AND FORGIVE ME.

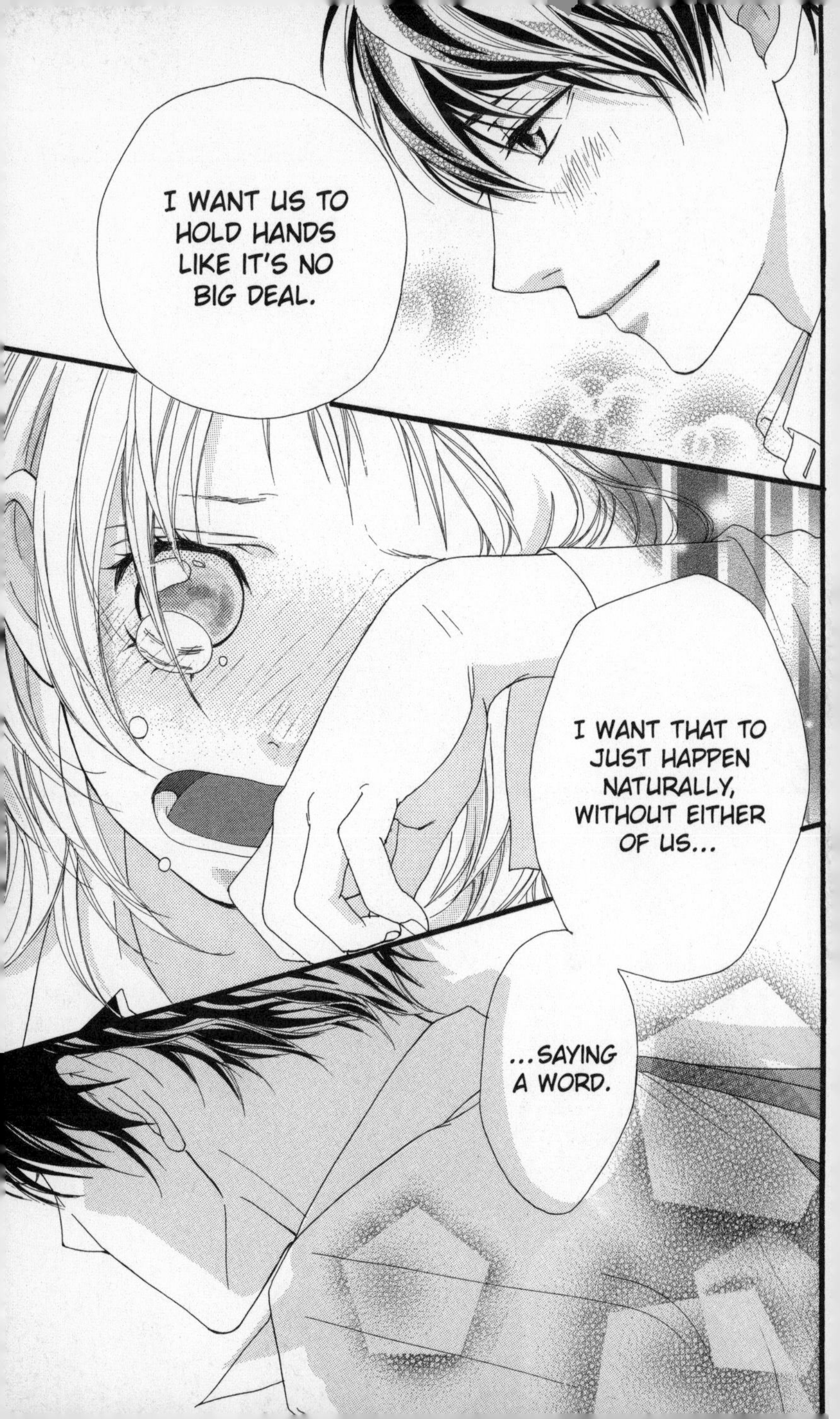
I WANT US TO HOLD HANDS LIKE IT'S NO BIG DEAL.
I WANT THAT TO JUST HAPPEN NATURALLY, WITHOUT EITHER OF US...
...SAYING A WORD.

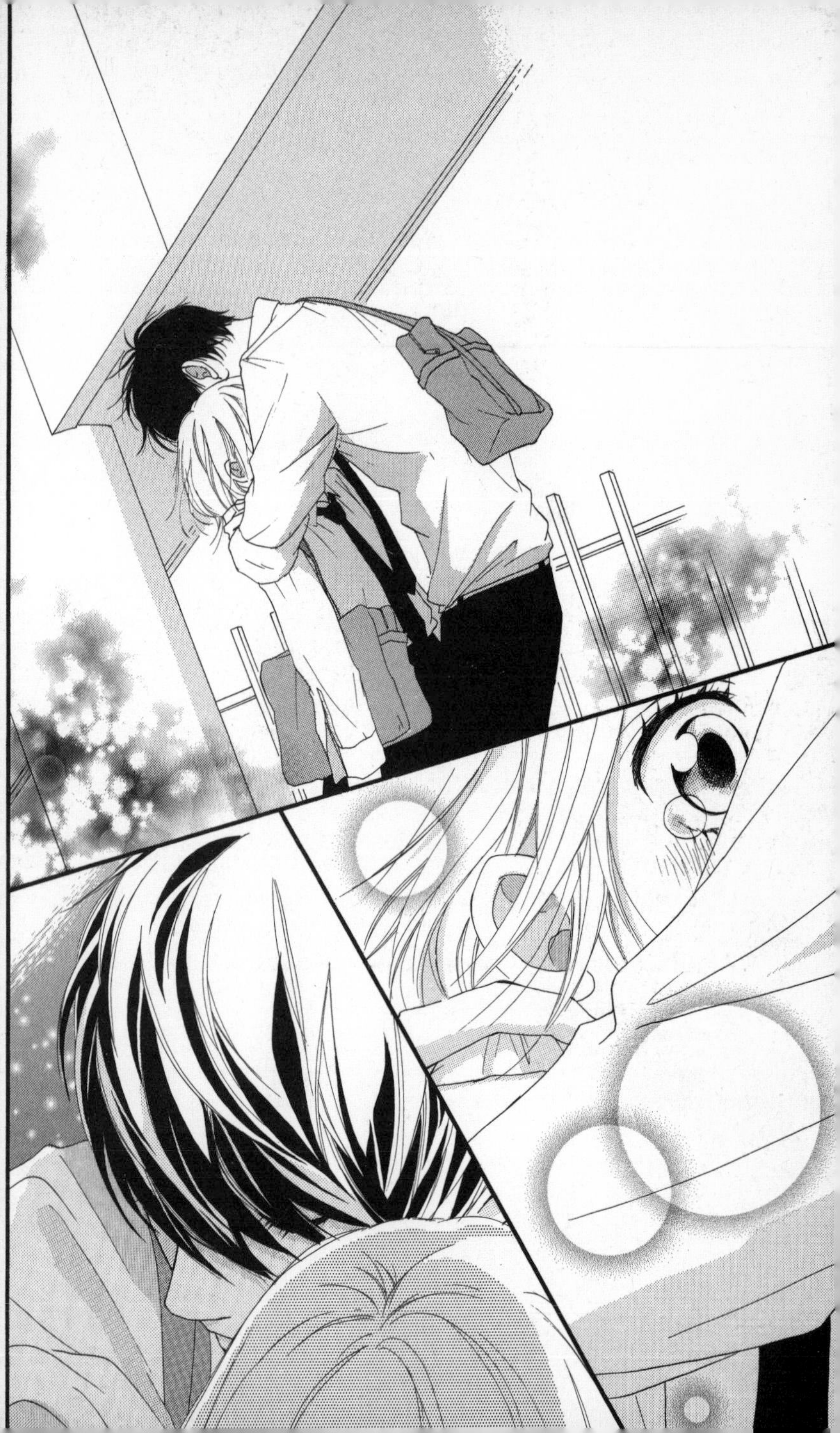

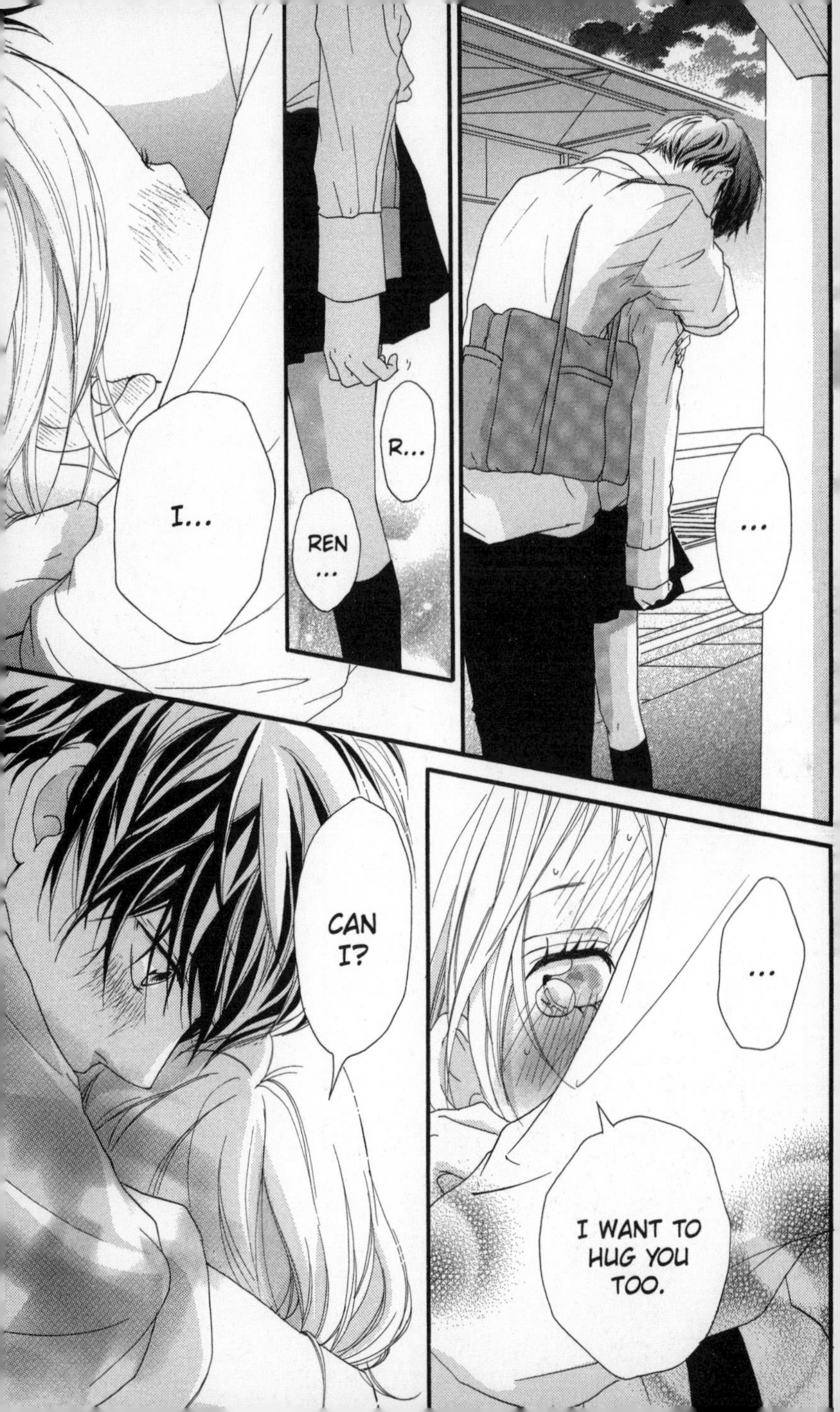
...
R...
REN ...
I...
...
I WANT TO HUG YOU TOO.
CAN I?

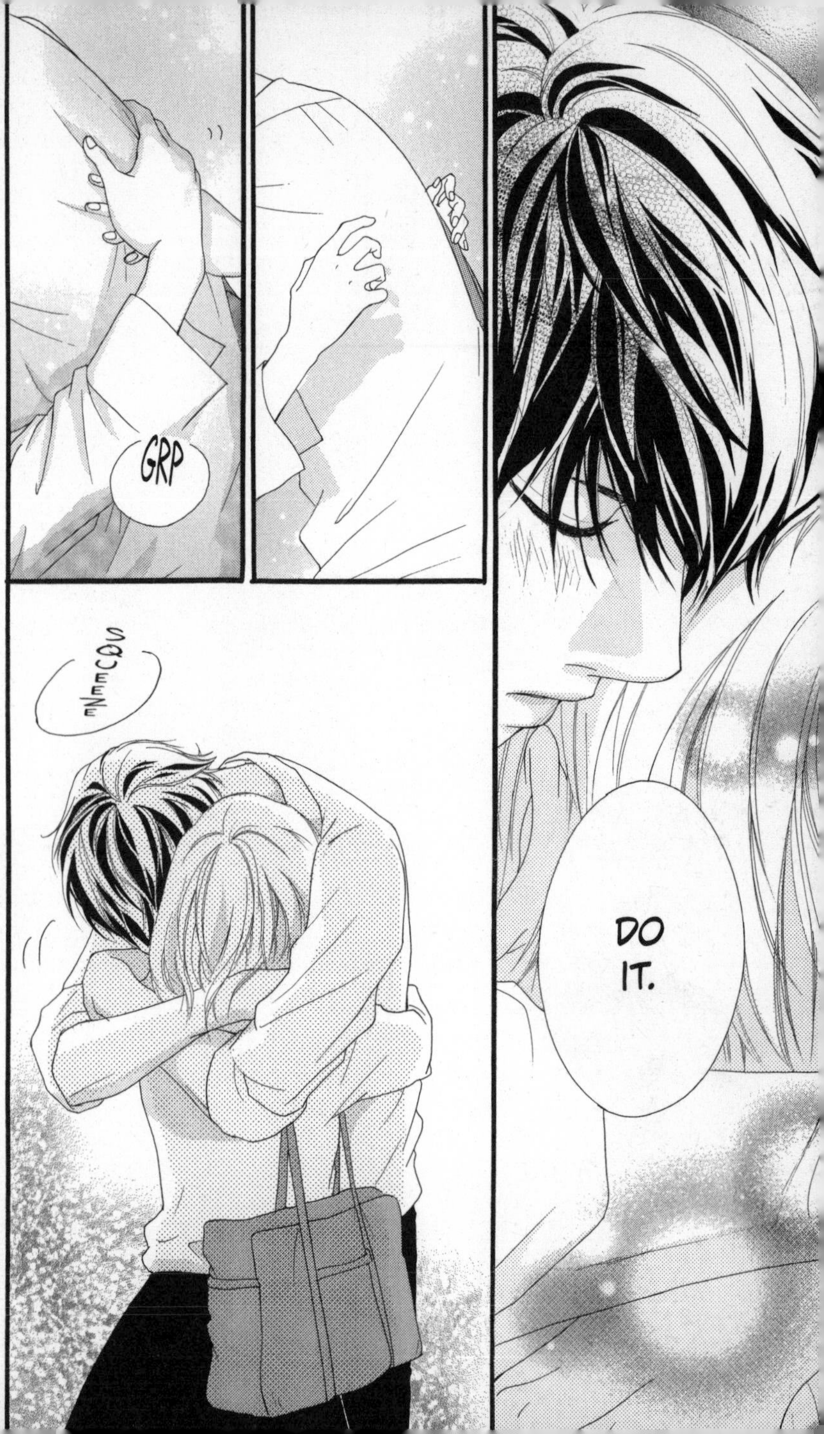
DO IT.
GRP
SQUEEZE

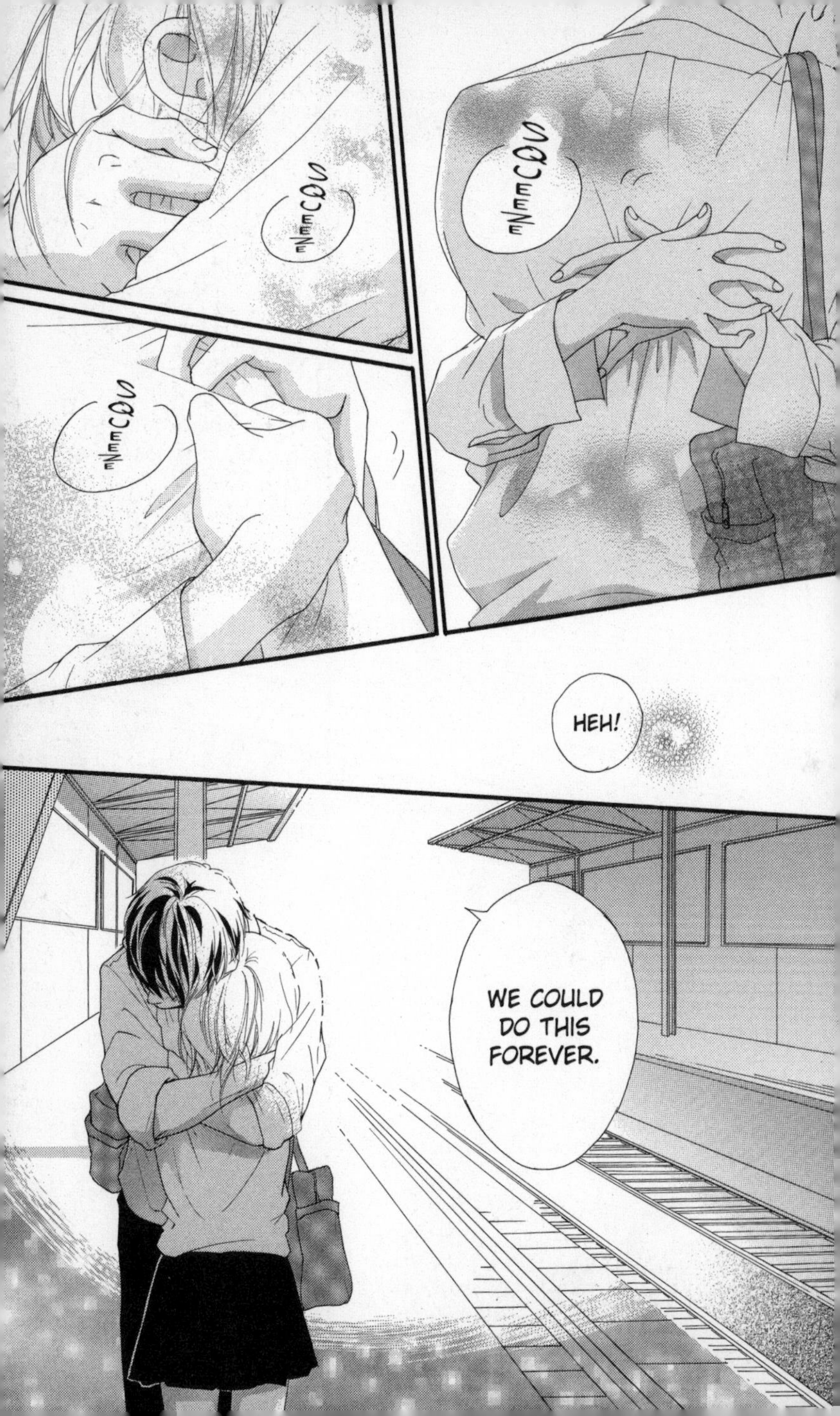
SQUEEEZE
SQUEEEZE
SQUEEEZE
HEH!
WE COULD DO THIS FOREVER.

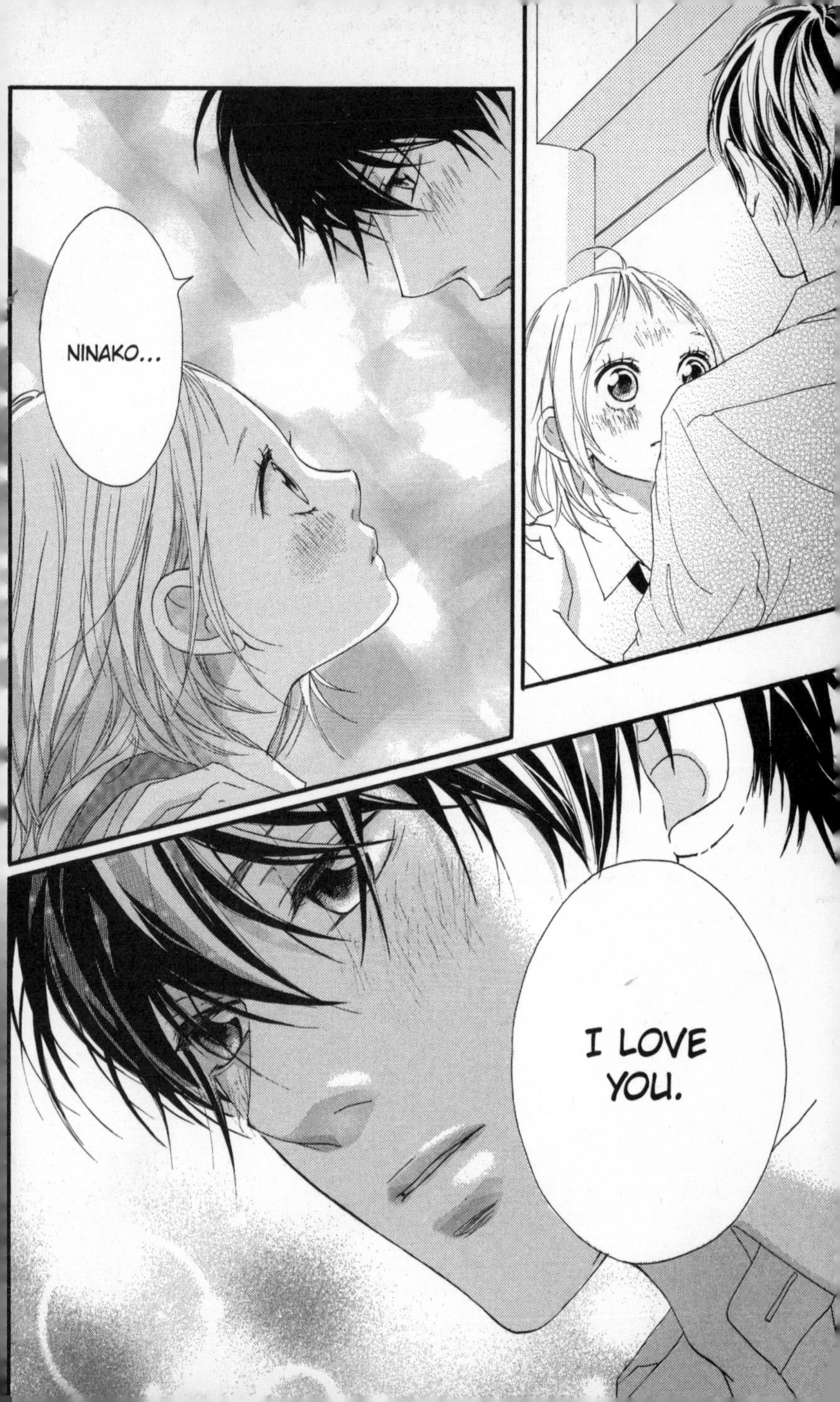
NINAKO...
I LOVE YOU.

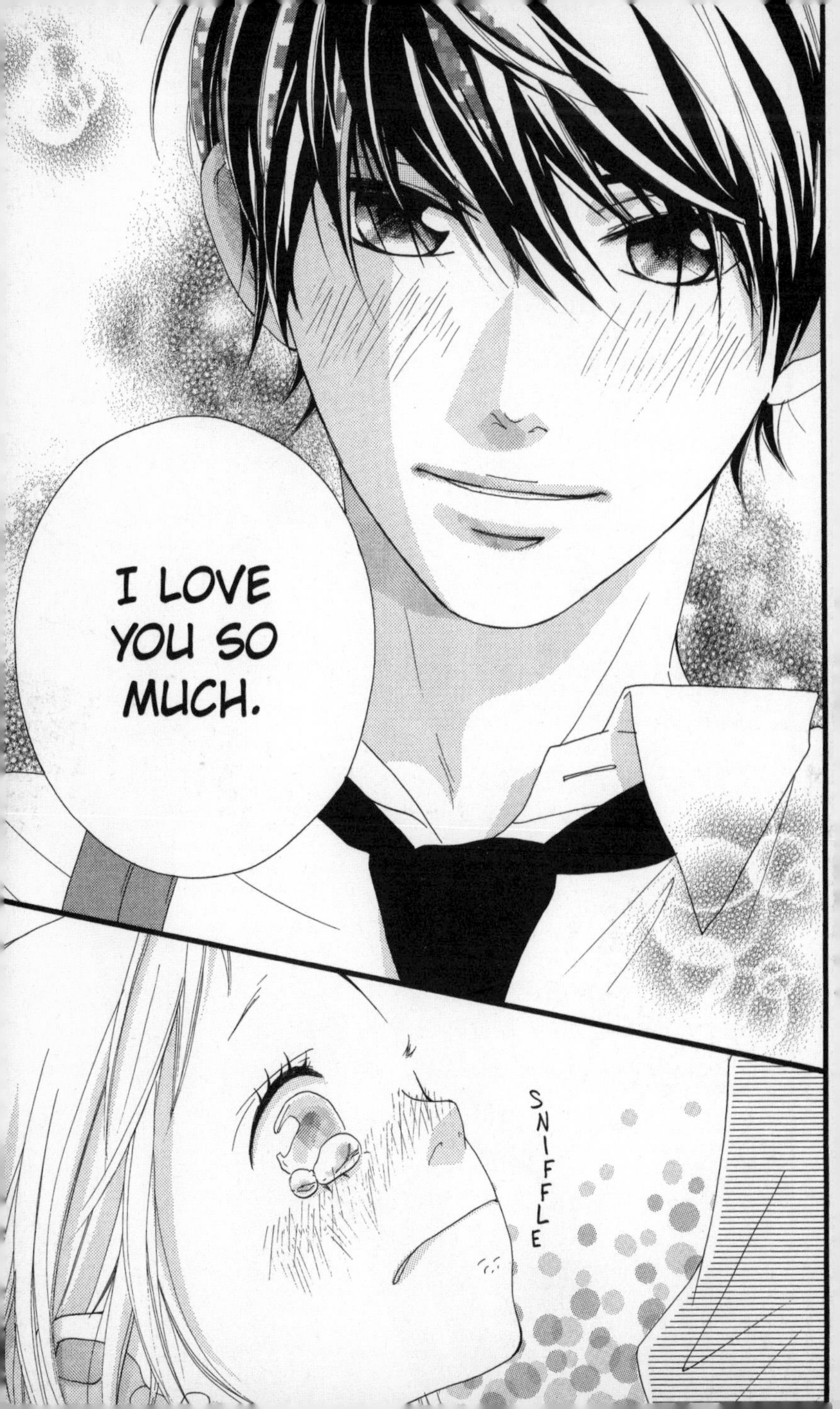
I LOVE YOU SO MUCH.
SNIFFLE

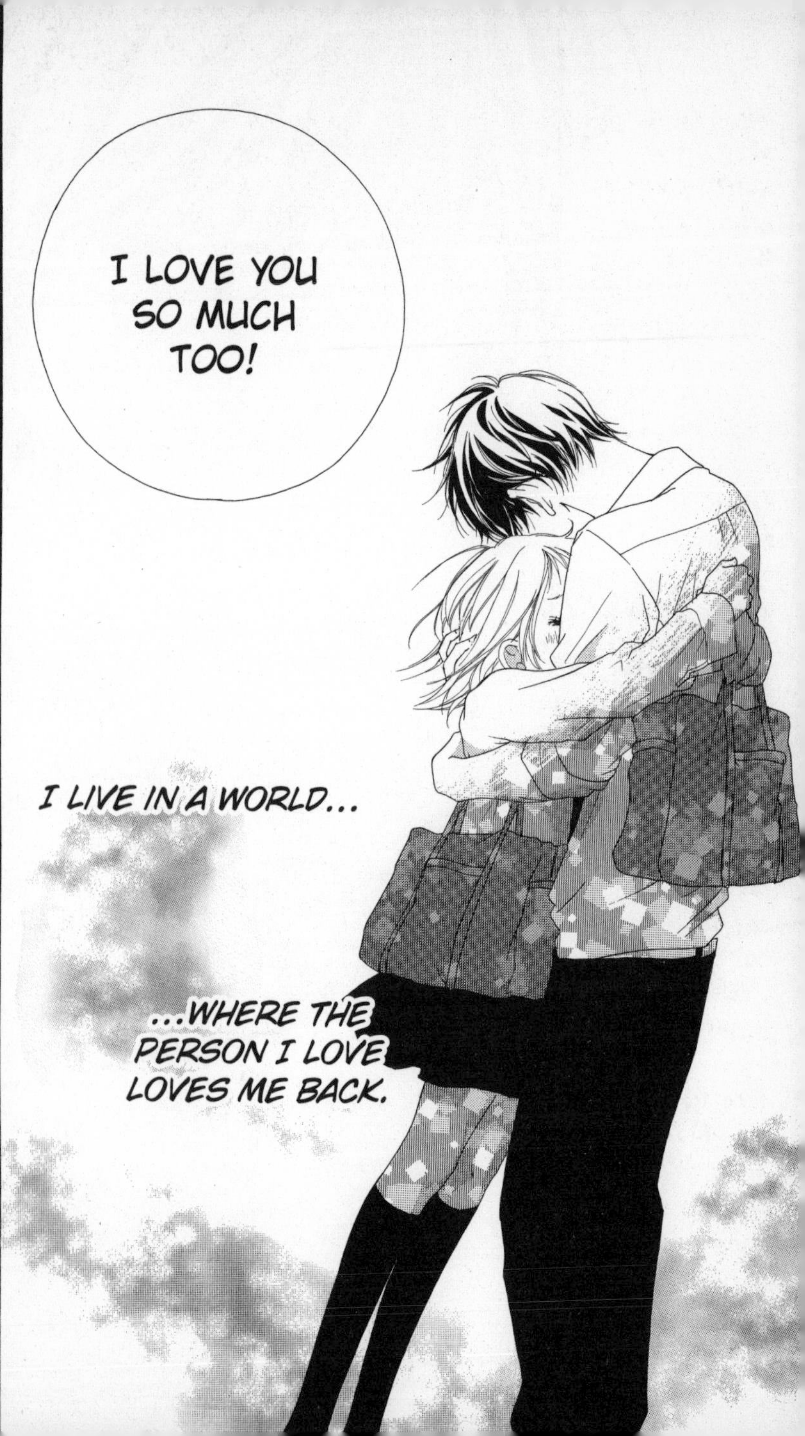
I LOVE YOU SO MUCH TOO!
I LIVE IN A WORLD...
...WHERE THE PERSON I LOVE LOVES ME BACK.

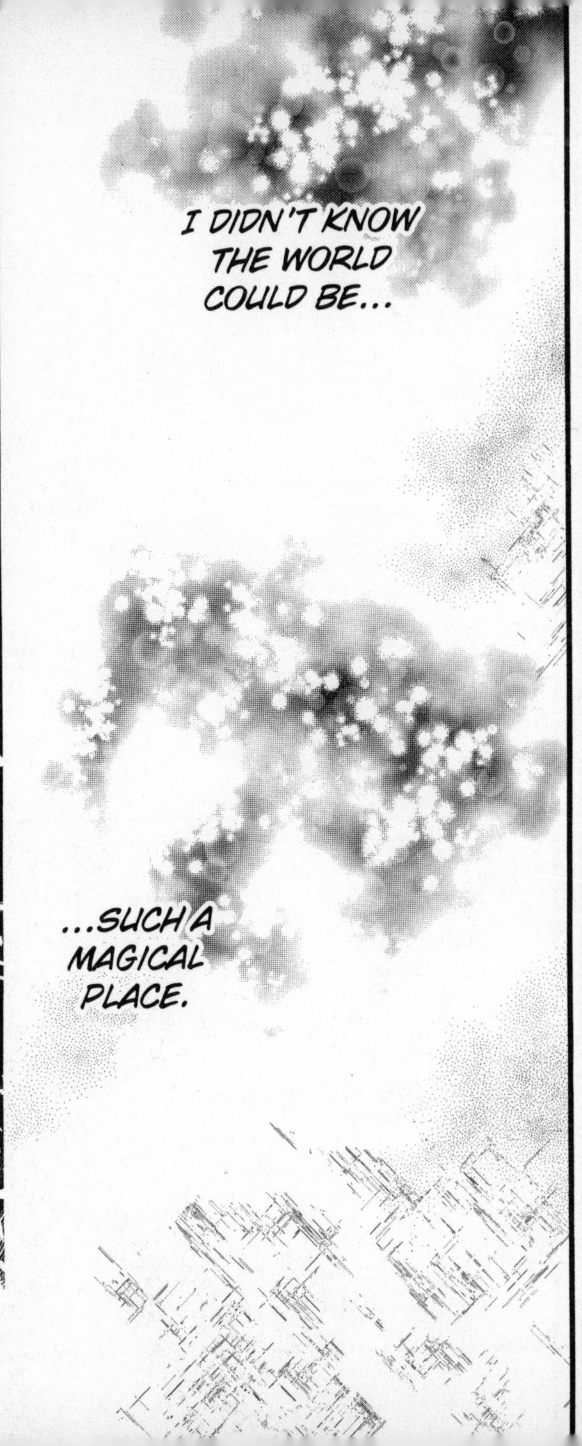
I DIDN'T KNOW THE WORLD COULD BE...
...SUCH A MAGICAL PLACE.

When I was in high school, I really wanted square nails. While trying to get them, I always cut my nails too short. That really hurt! And cutting them short doesn't mean that they'll grow square, but I thought putting nail polish on those nails would look so cute, especially if it were red... I think that's why my nails aren't in great shape now. They aren't tapered or square. They're just really nondescript. Even now, when I see a woman with manicured square nails (especially with a matte polish), I get jealous. It's so cute!

Completely off topic, but I want to get a new cell phone. I'm still using a 901. Isn't that impressive?

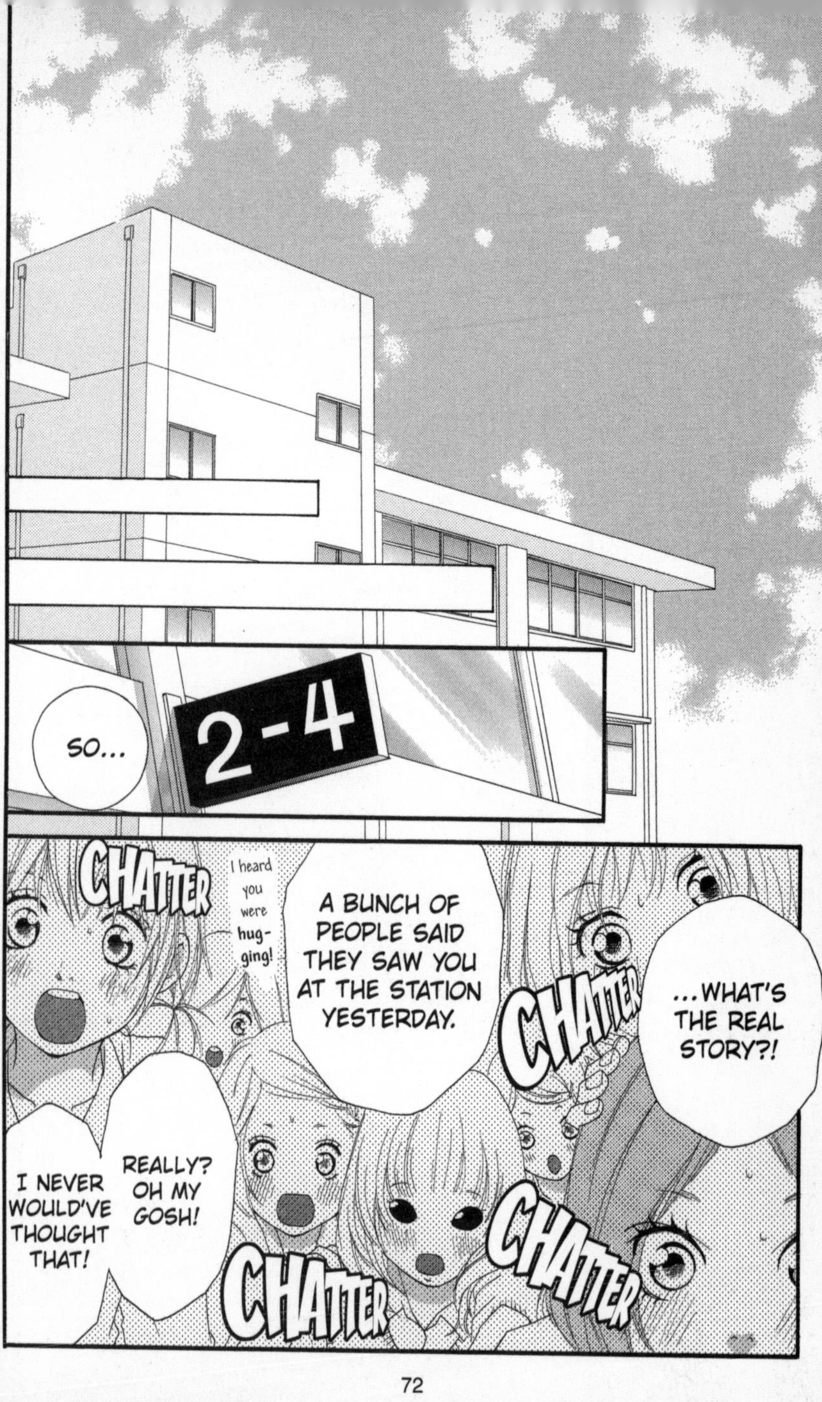
2-4
SO...
...WHAT'S THE REAL STORY?!
CHATTER
A BUNCH OF PEOPLE SAID THEY SAW YOU AT THE STATION YESTERDAY.
I heard you were hug-ging!
CHATTER
CHATTER
REALLY? OH MY GOSH!
I NEVER WOULD'VE THOUGHT THAT!
CHATTER

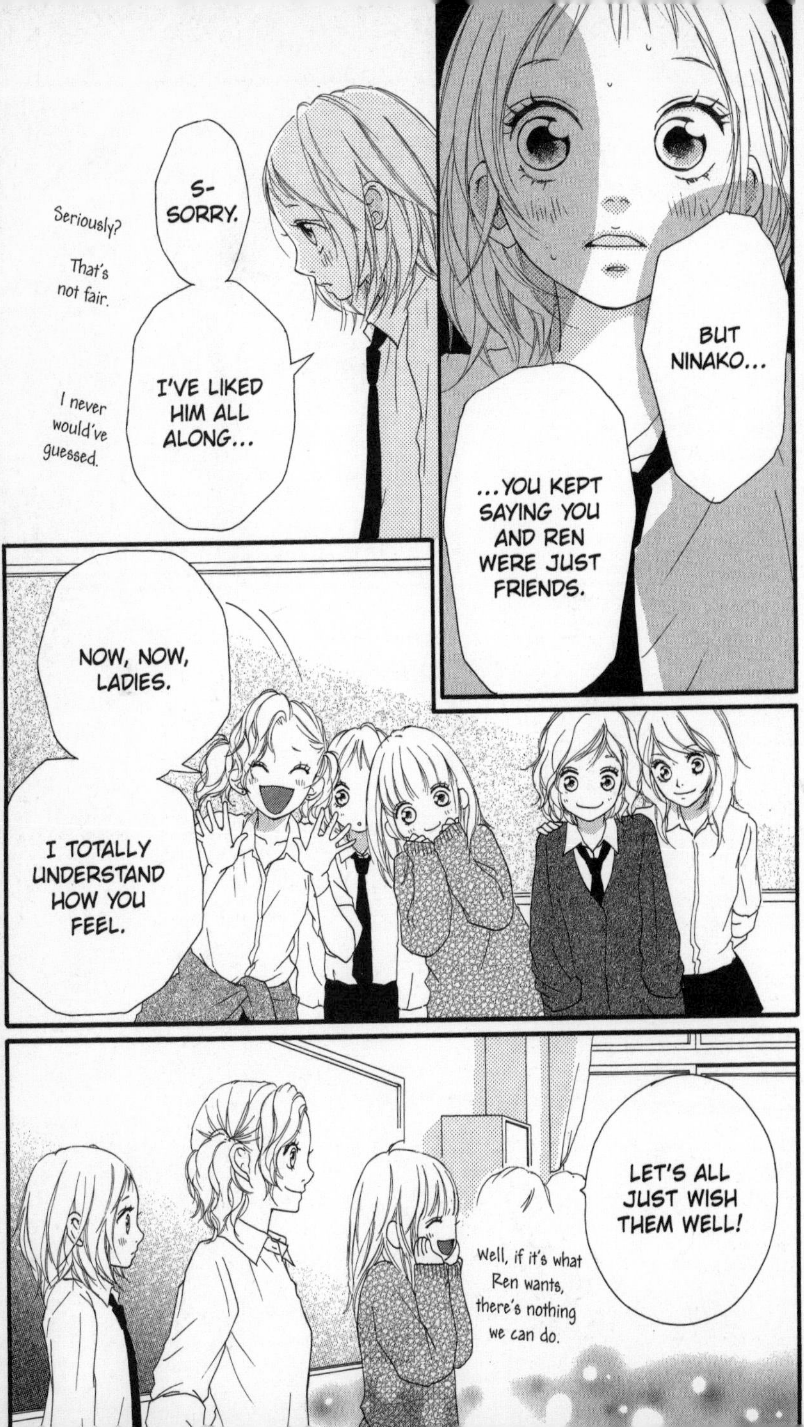
BUT NINAKO...
...YOU KEPT SAYING YOU AND REN WERE JUST FRIENDS.
S-SORRY.
I'VE LIKED HIM ALL ALONG...
Seriously?
That's not fair.
I never would've guessed.
NOW, NOW, LADIES.
I TOTALLY UNDERSTAND HOW YOU FEEL.
LET'S ALL JUST WISH THEM WELL!
Well, if it's what Ren wants, there's nothing we can do.

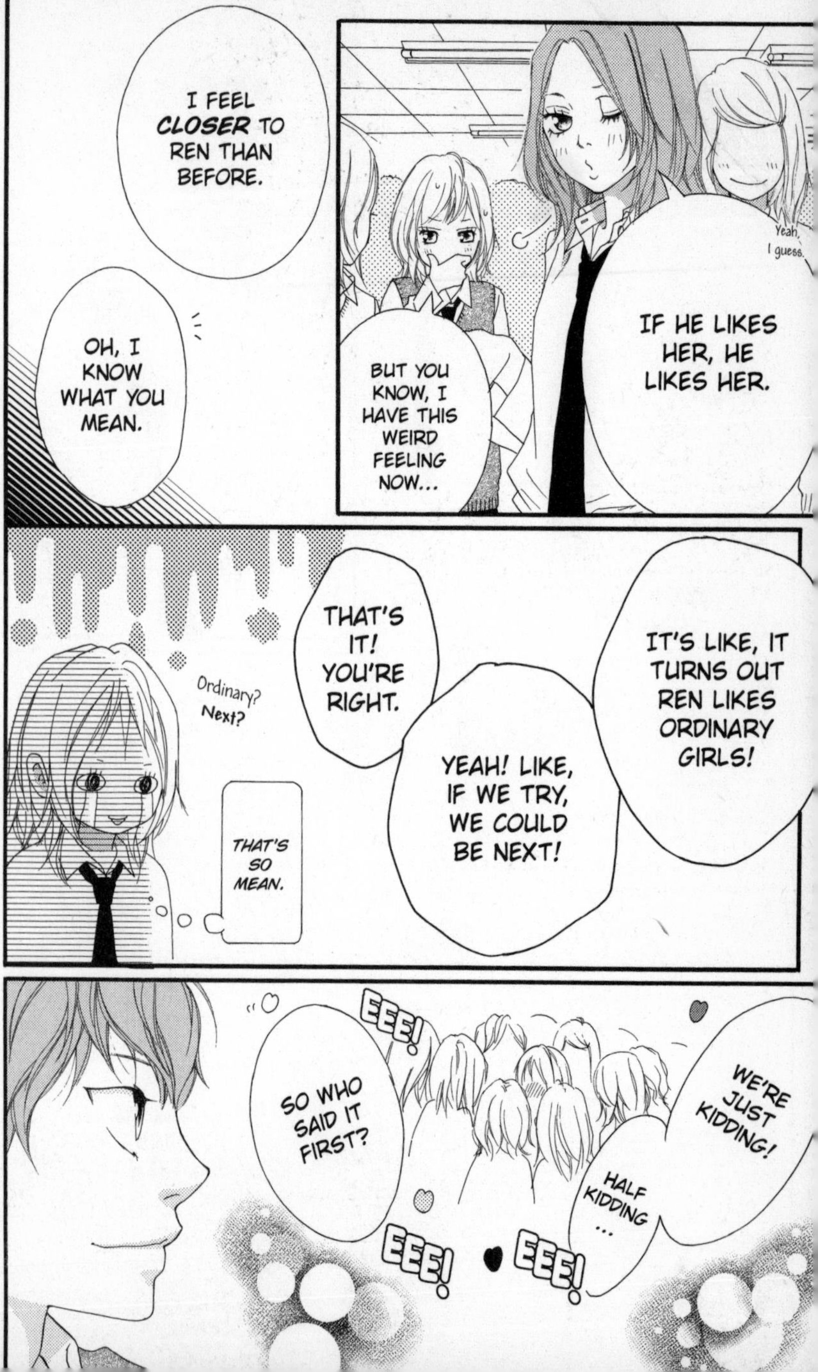

Yeah, I guess.
IF HE LIKES HER, HE LIKES HER.
BUT YOU KNOW, I HAVE THIS WEIRD FEELING NOW...
I FEEL CLOSER TO REN THAN BEFORE.
OH, I KNOW WHAT YOU MEAN.
IT'S LIKE, IT TURNS OUT REN LIKES ORDINARY GIRLS!
THAT'S IT! YOU'RE RIGHT.
YEAH! LIKE, IF WE TRY, WE COULD BE NEXT!
Ordinary? Next?
THAT'S SO MEAN.
WE'RE JUST KIDDING!
HALF KIDDING...
EEE!
SO WHO SAID IT FIRST?
EEE!
EEE!

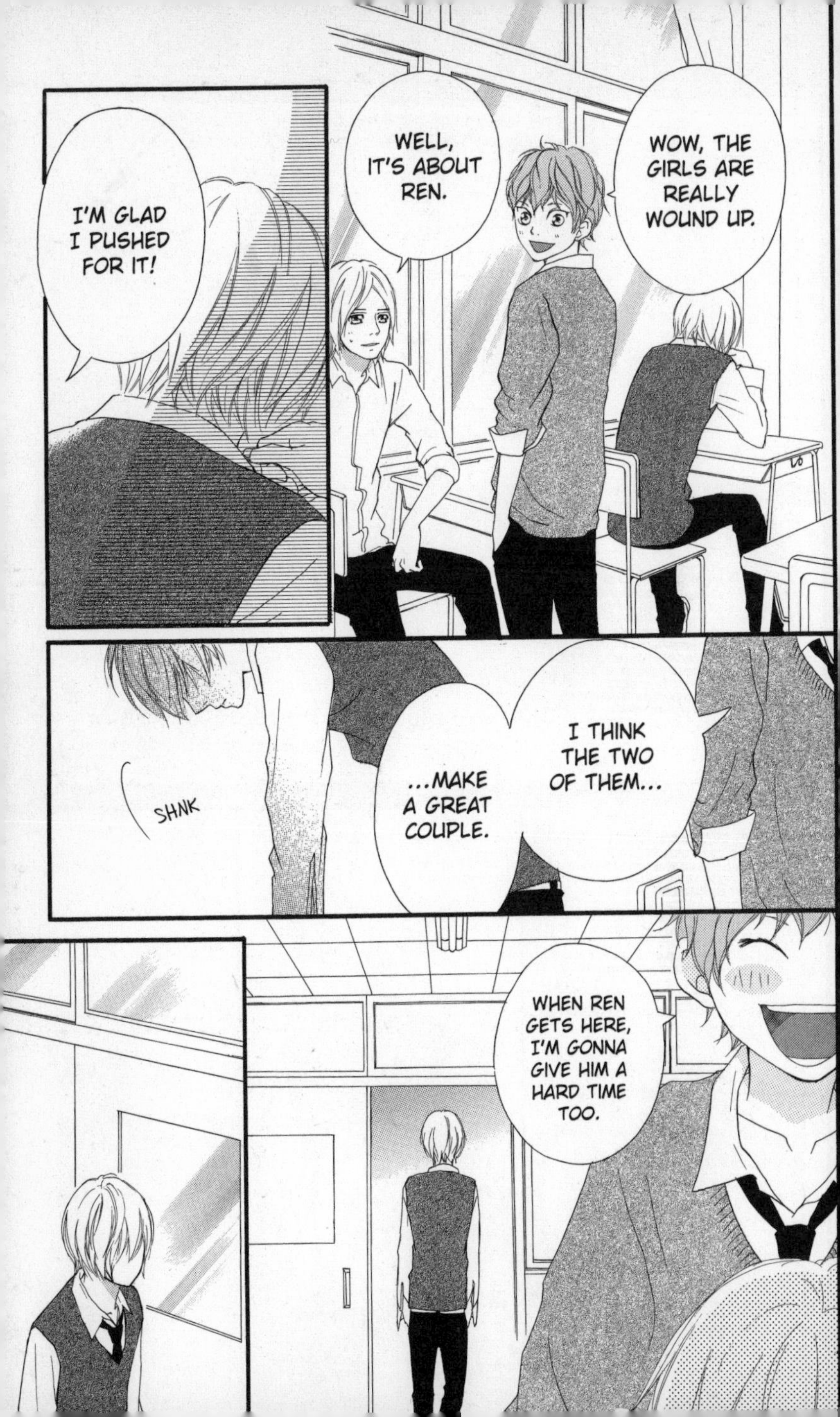
WOW, THE GIRLS ARE REALLY WOUND UP.
WELL, IT'S ABOUT REN.
I'M GLAD I PUSHED FOR IT!
I THINK THE TWO OF THEM...
...MAKE A GREAT COUPLE.
SHNK
WHEN REN GETS HERE, I'M GONNA GIVE HIM A HARD TIME TOO.

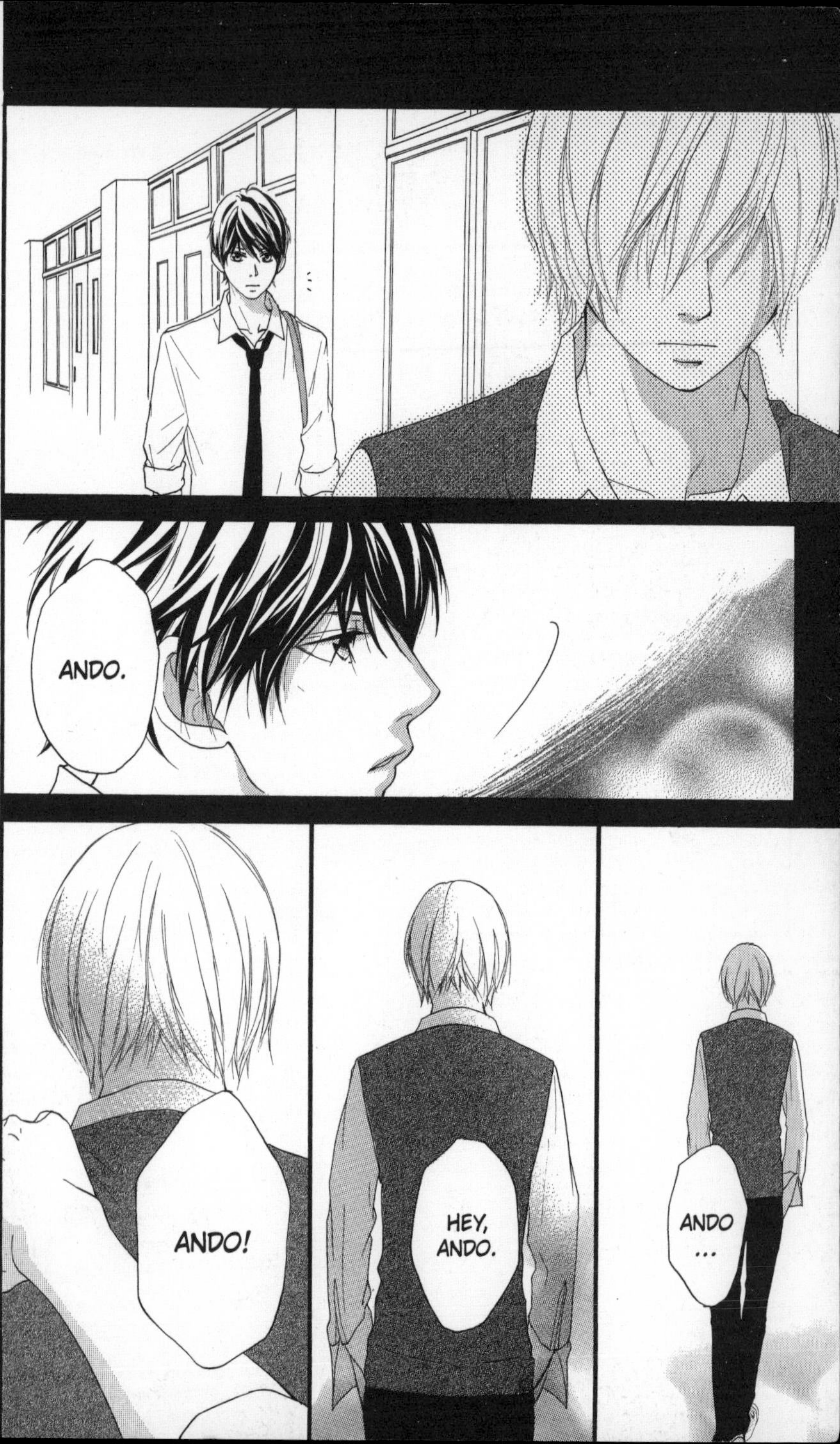
ANDO.
ANDO ...
HEY, ANDO.
ANDO!

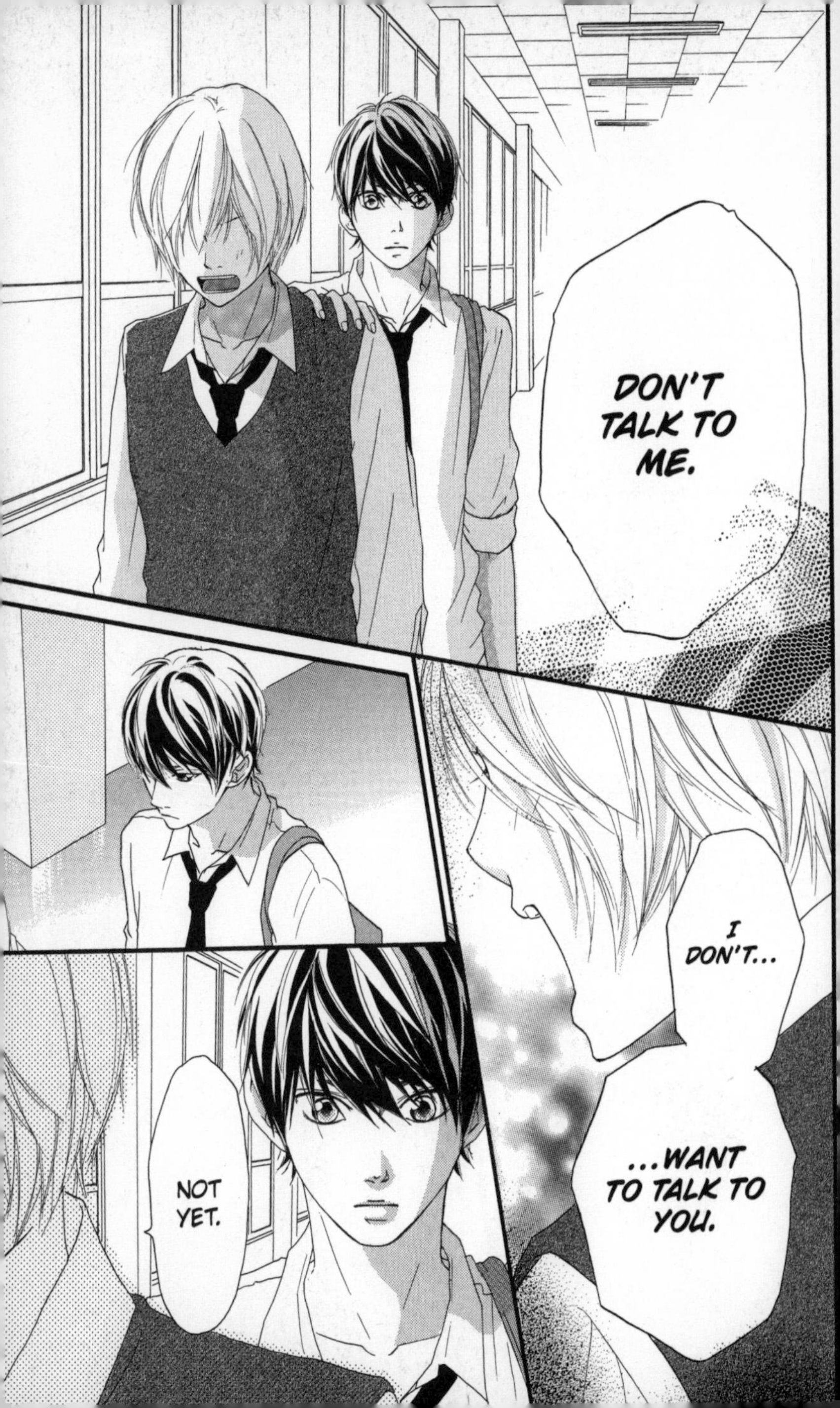
DON'T TALK TO ME.
I DON'T...
...WANT TO TALK TO YOU.
NOT YET.

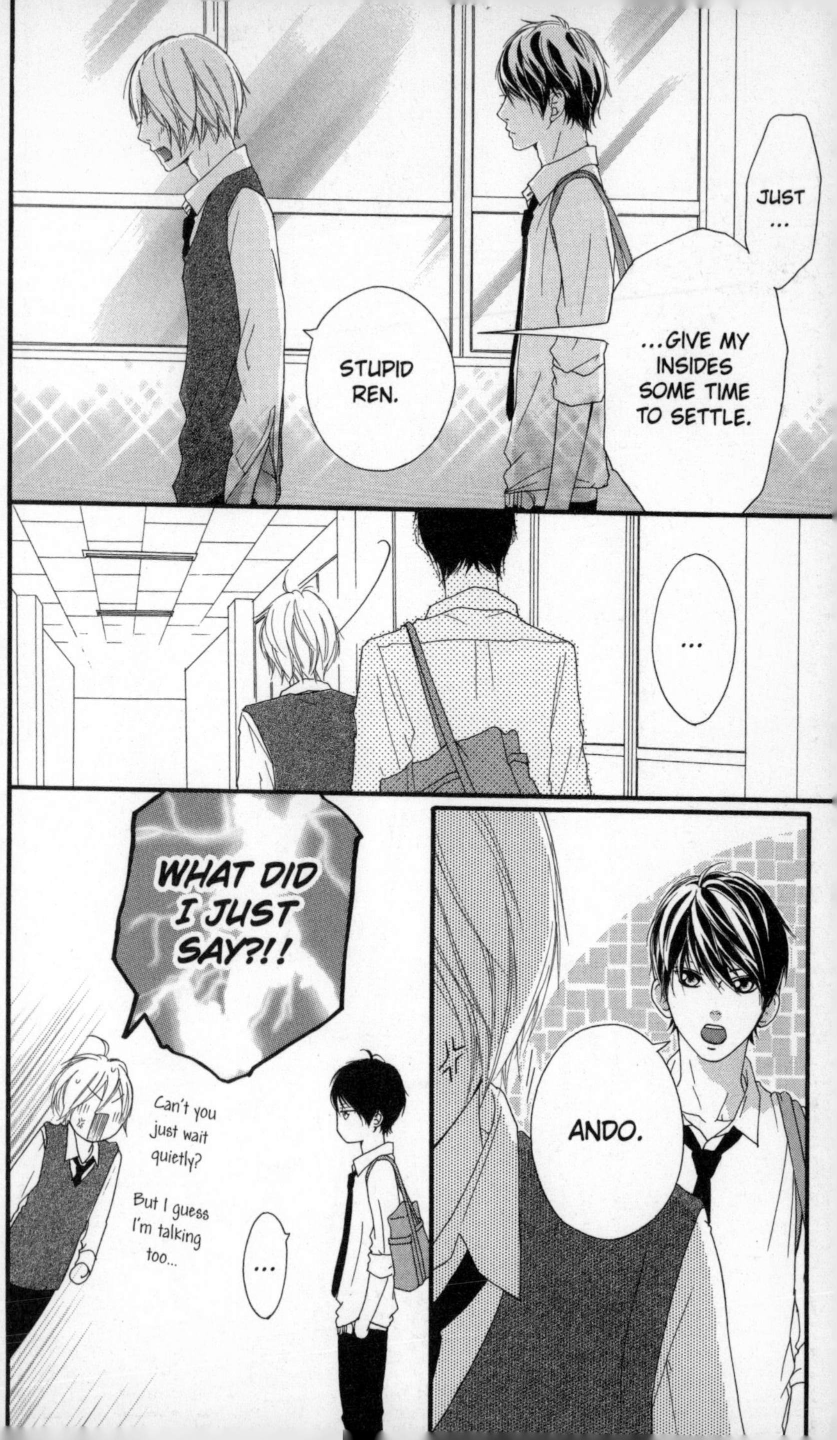
JUST ...
...GIVE MY INSIDES SOME TIME TO SETTLE.
STUPID REN.
...
ANDO.
WHAT DID I JUST SAY?!!
Can't you just wait quietly?
But I guess I'm talking too...
...

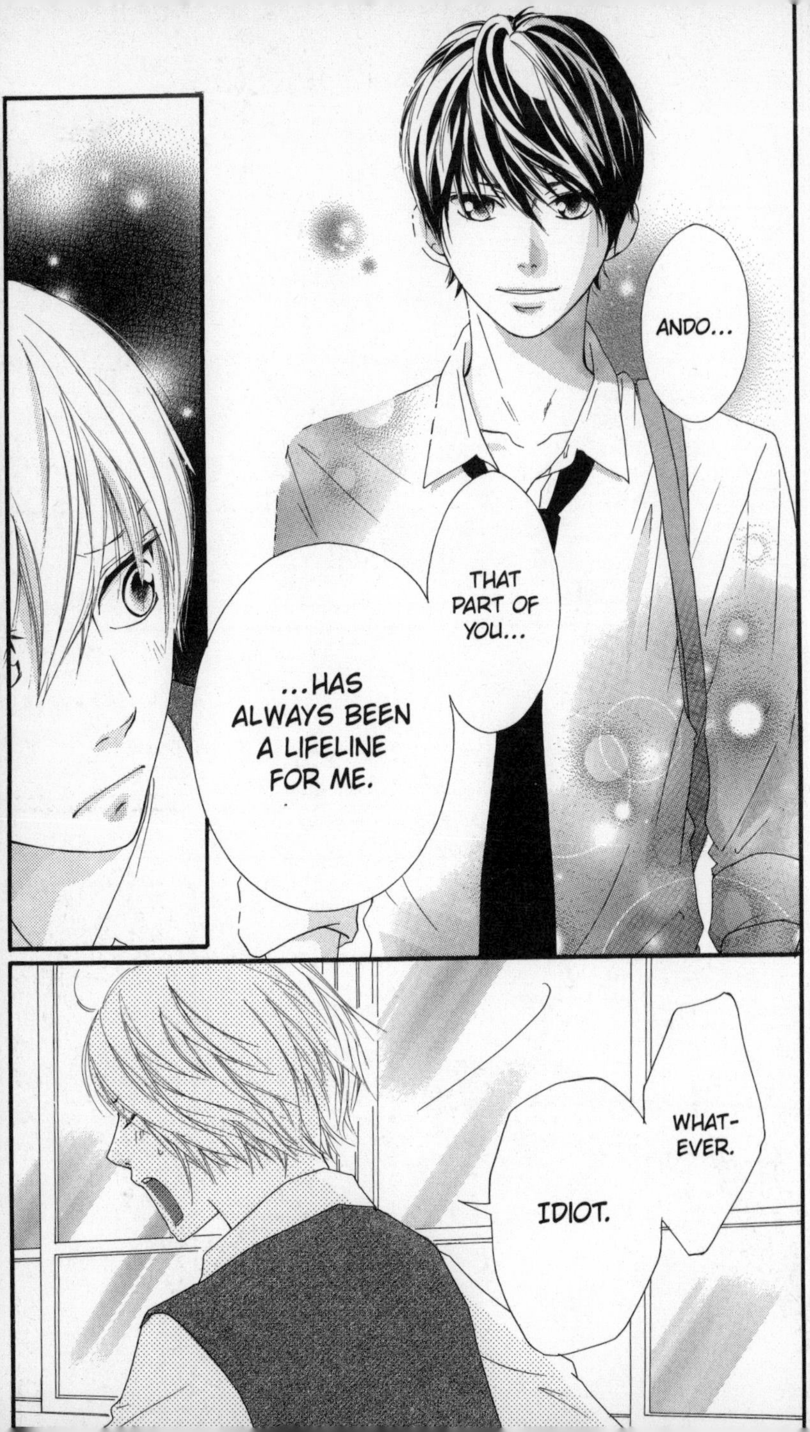
ANDO...
THAT PART OF YOU...
...HAS ALWAYS BEEN A LIFELINE FOR ME.
WHAT-EVER.
IDIOT.

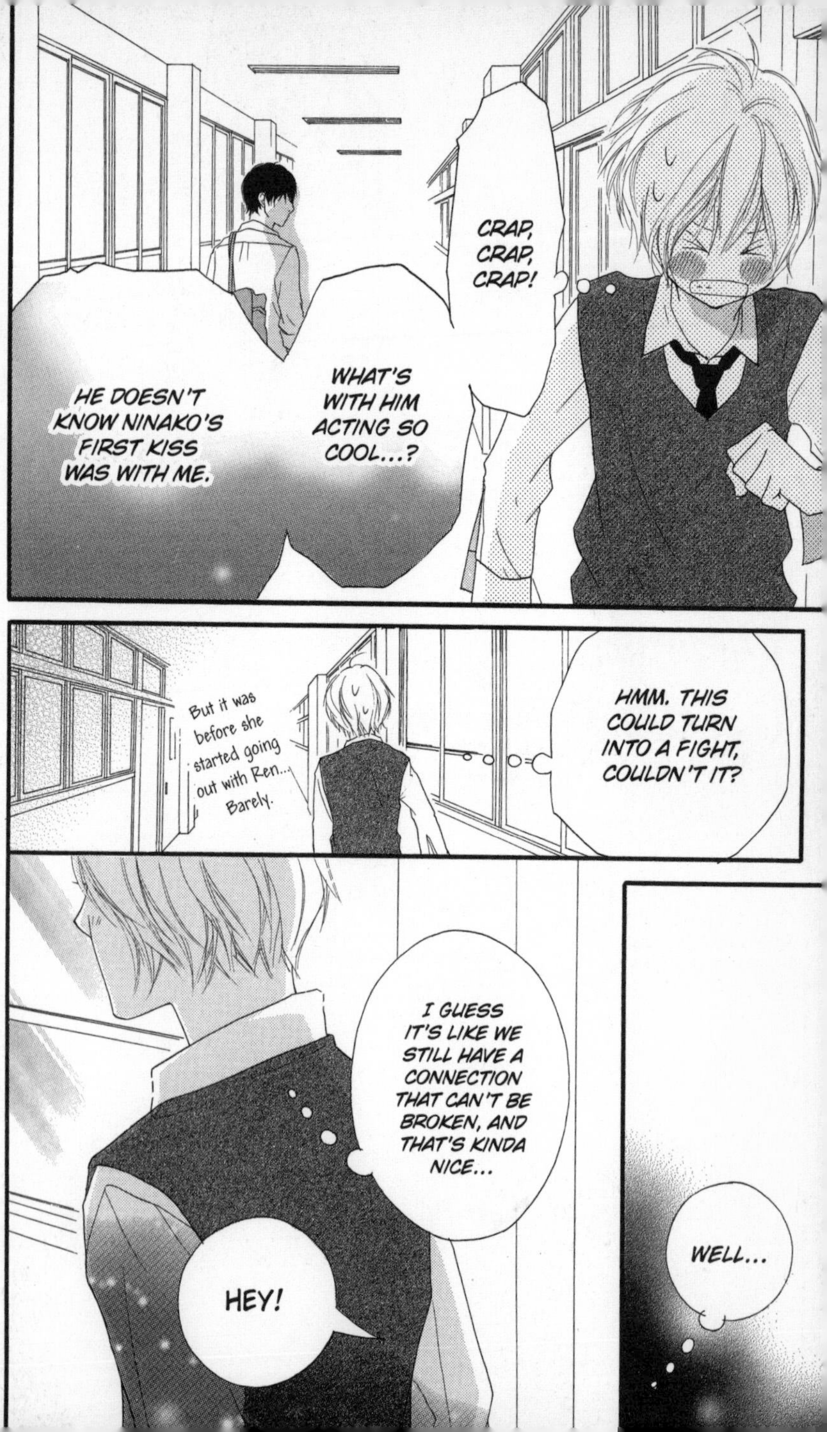
CRAP, CRAP, CRAP!
WHAT'S WITH HIM ACTING SO COOL...?
HE DOESN'T KNOW NINAKO'S FIRST KISS WAS WITH ME.
HMM. THIS COULD TURN INTO A FIGHT, COULDN'T IT?
But it was before she started going out with Ren... Barely.
WELL...
I GUESS IT'S LIKE WE STILL HAVE A CONNECTION THAT CAN'T BE BROKEN, AND THAT'S KINDA NICE...
HEY!

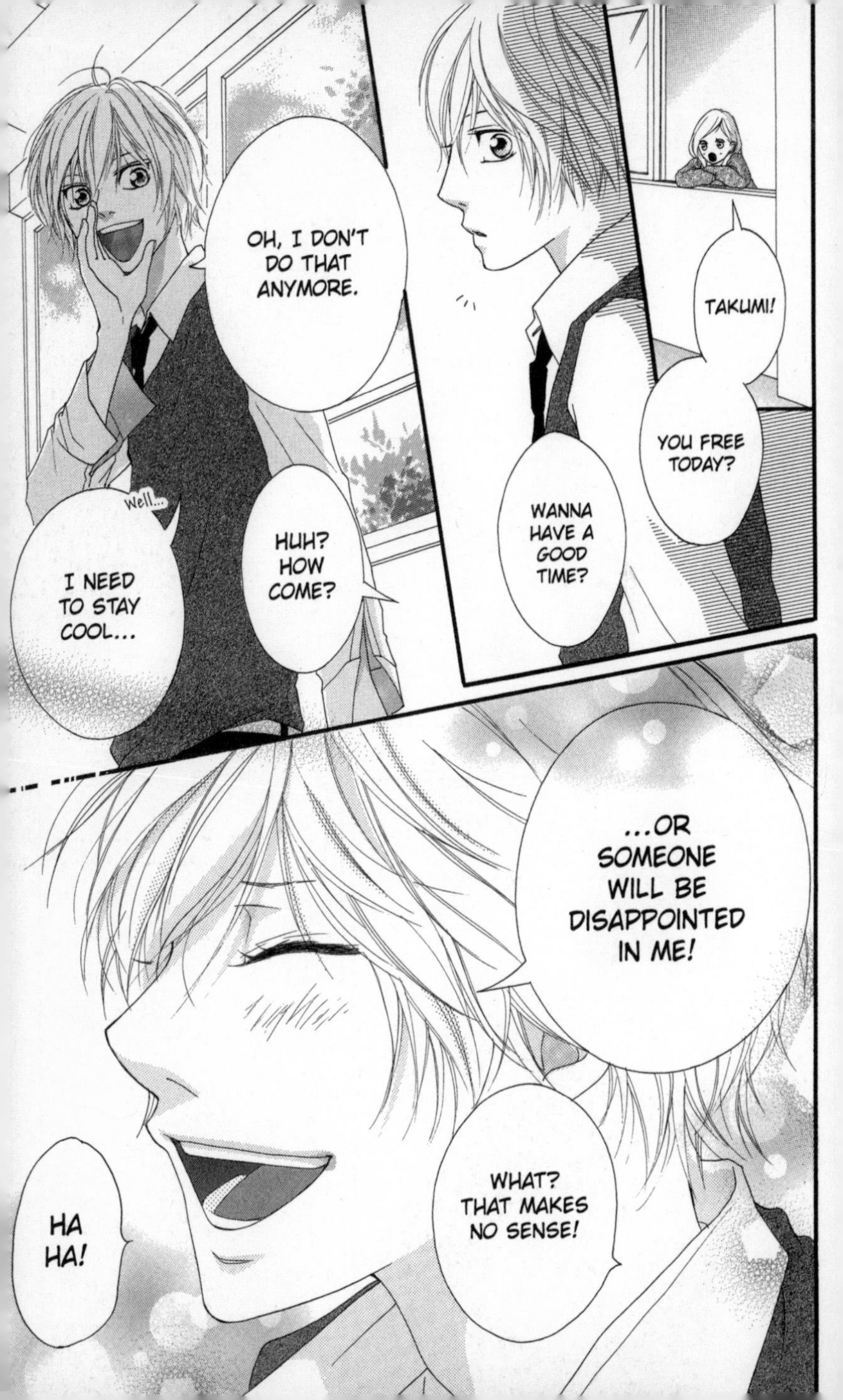
TAKUMI!
YOU FREE TODAY?
WANNA HAVE A GOOD TIME?
OH, I DON'T DO THAT ANYMORE.
HUH? HOW COME?
Well...
I NEED TO STAY COOL...
...OR SOMEONE WILL BE DISAPPOINTED IN ME!
WHAT? THAT MAKES NO SENSE!
HA HA!

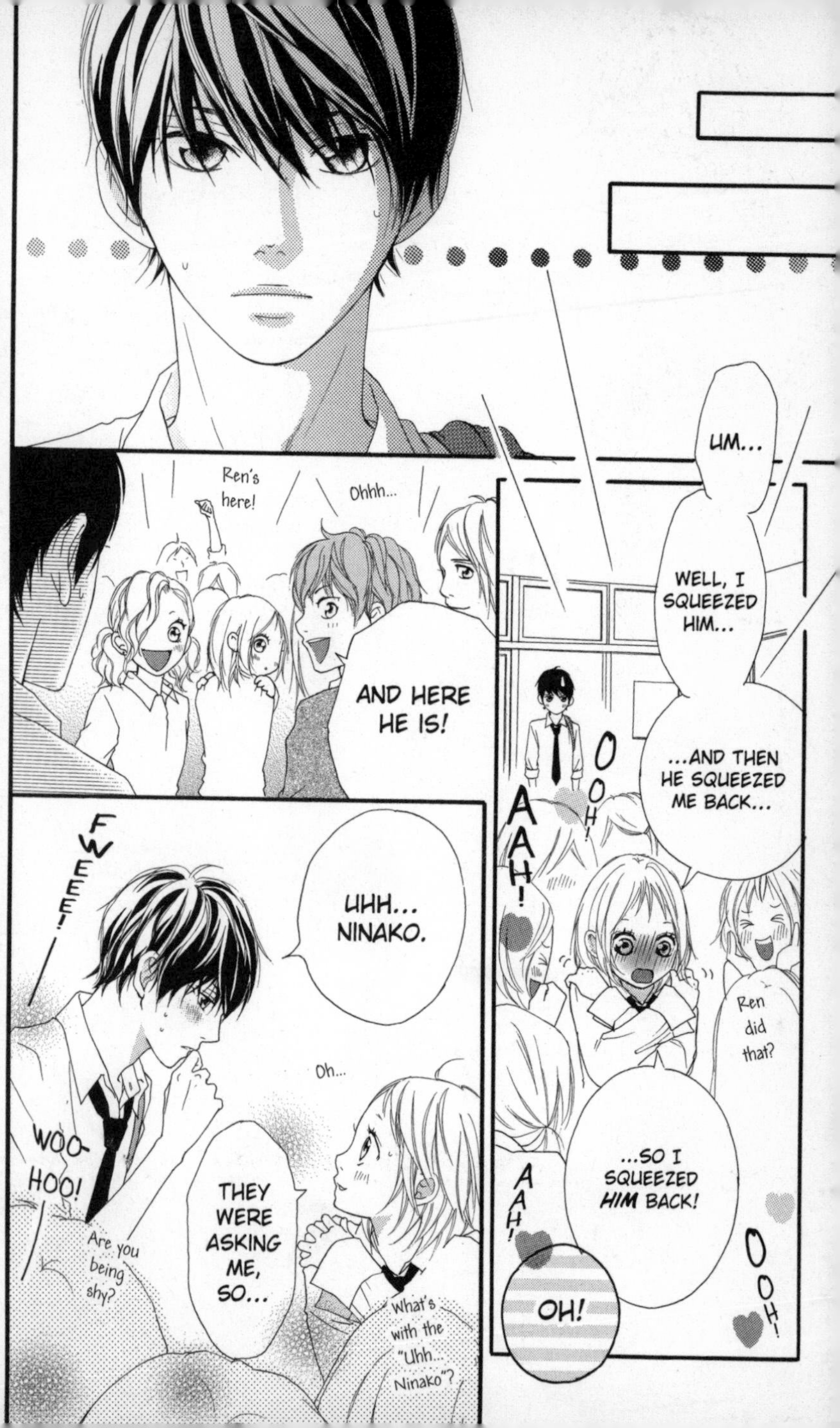
UM...
WELL, I SQUEEZED HIM...
...AND THEN HE SQUEEZED ME BACK...
OOH!
AAH!
Ren did that?
...SO I SQUEEZED *HIM* BACK!
OOH!
AAH!
OH!
Ohhh...
Ren's here!
AND HERE HE IS!
UHH... NINAKO.
FWEEE!
Oh...
THEY WERE ASKING ME, SO...
What's with the "Uhh... Ninako"?
WOO-HOO!
Are you being shy?

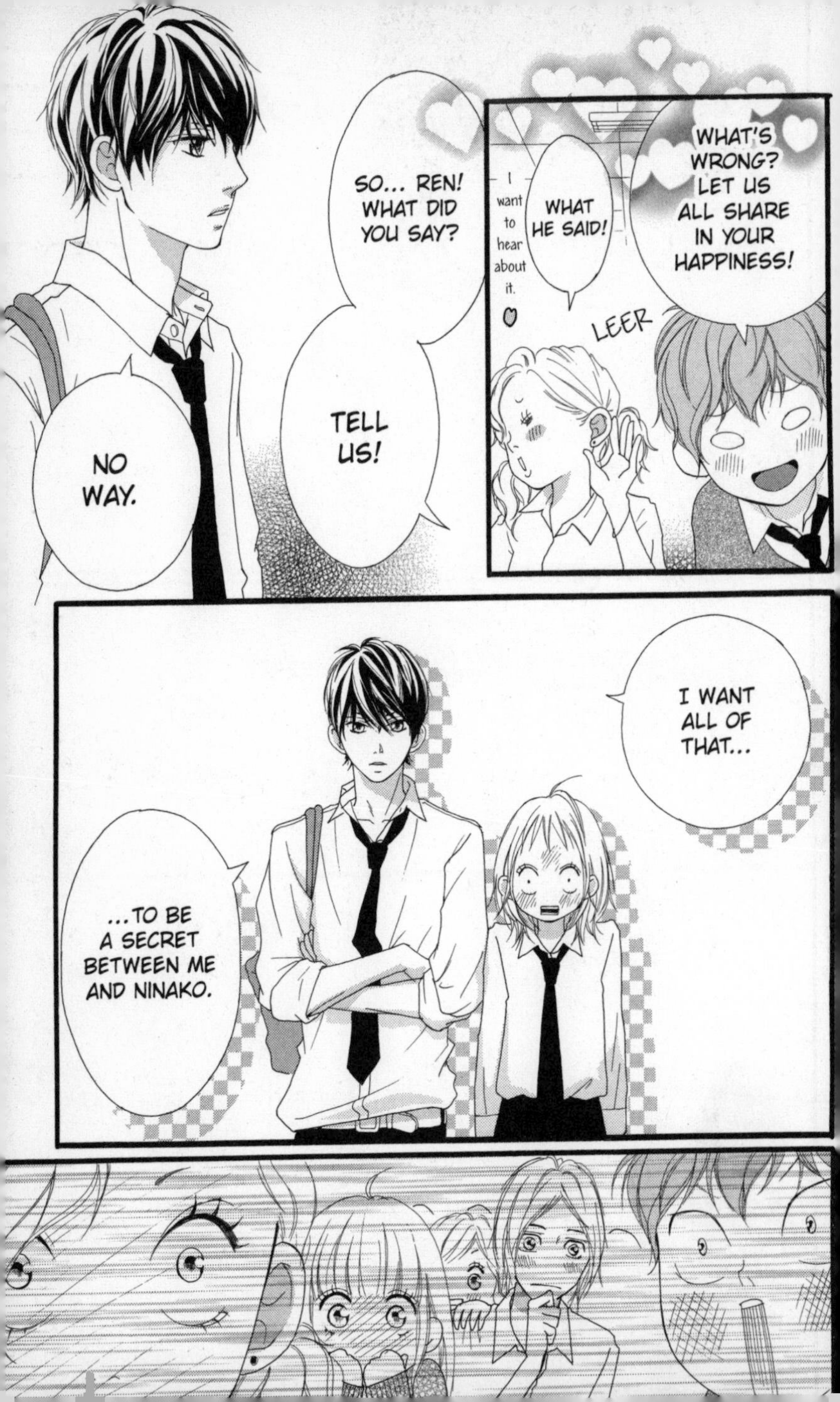
WHAT'S WRONG? LET US ALL SHARE IN YOUR HAPPINESS!
WHAT HE SAID!
I want to hear about it.
LEER
SO... REN! WHAT DID YOU SAY?
TELL US!
NO WAY.
I WANT ALL OF THAT...
...TO BE A SECRET BETWEEN ME AND NINAKO.

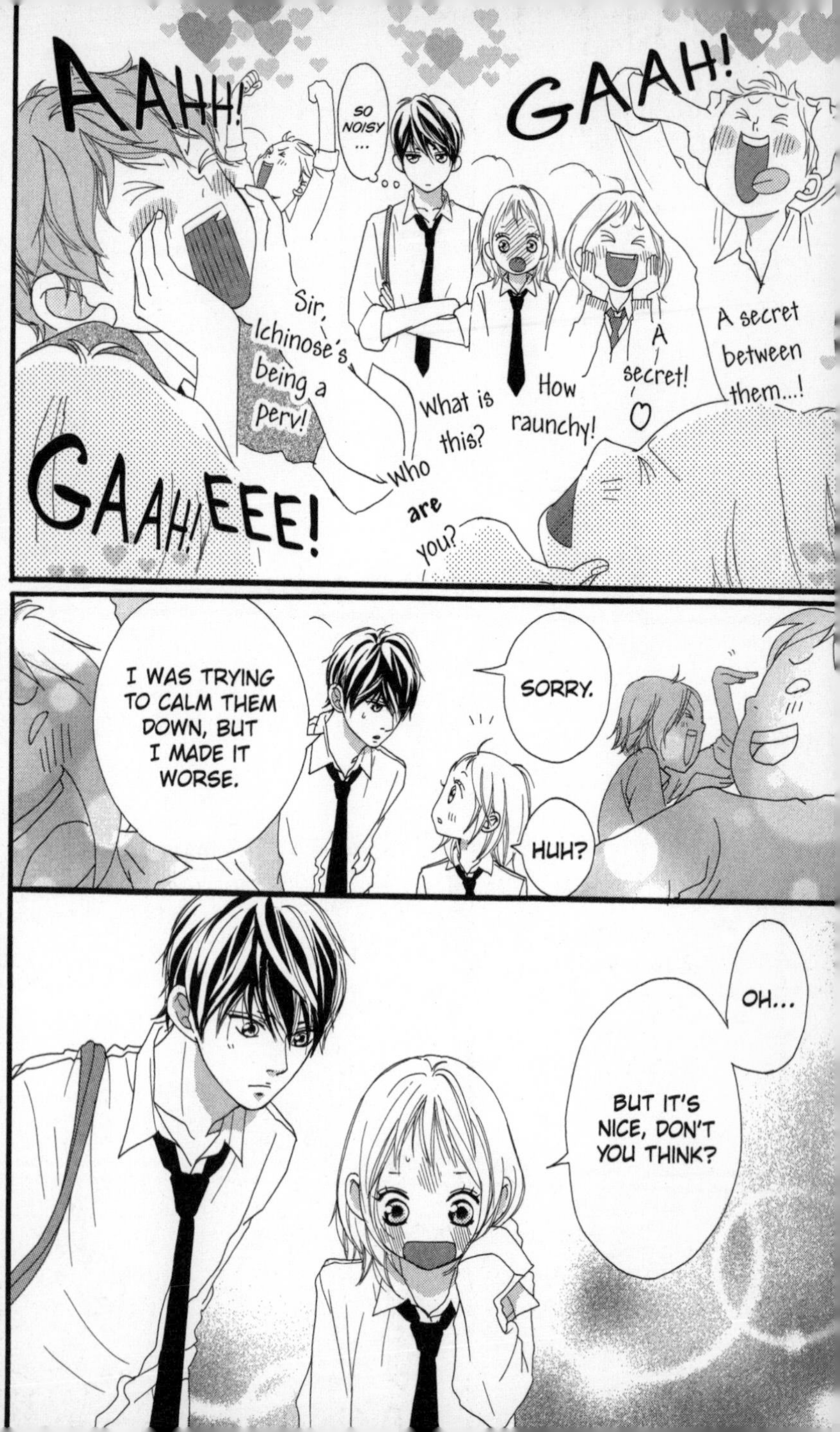
GAAH!
A secret between them...!
A secret! ♡
SO NOISY ...
How raunchy!
What is this?
AAHH!
Sir, Ichinose's being a perv!
Who are you?
GAAH! EEE!
SORRY.
HUH?
I WAS TRYING TO CALM THEM DOWN, BUT I MADE IT WORSE.
OH...
BUT IT'S NICE, DON'T YOU THINK?

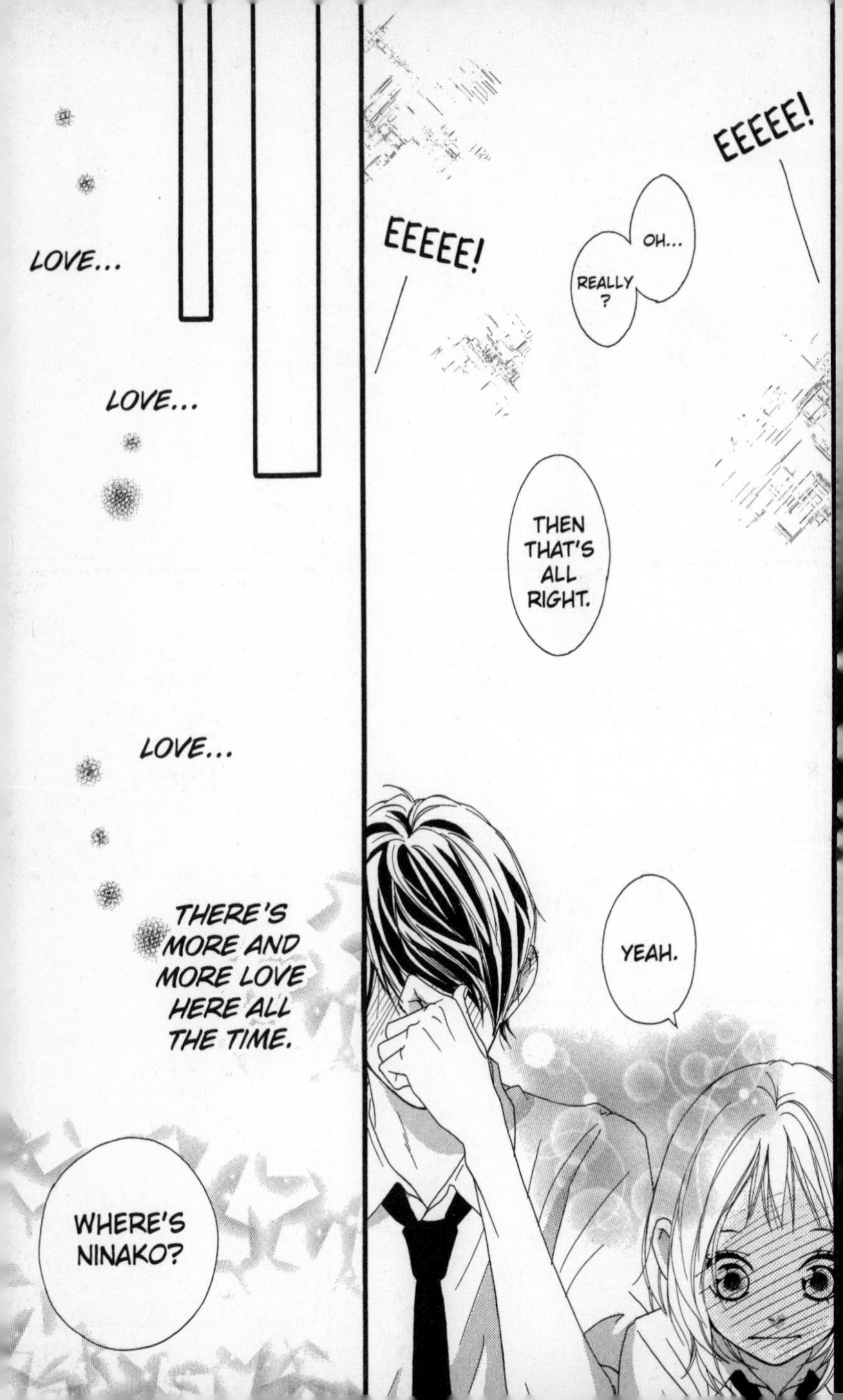
EEEEE!
OH... REALLY?
EEEEE!
THEN THAT'S ALL RIGHT.
YEAH.
LOVE...
LOVE...
LOVE...
THERE'S MORE AND MORE LOVE HERE ALL THE TIME.
WHERE'S NINAKO?

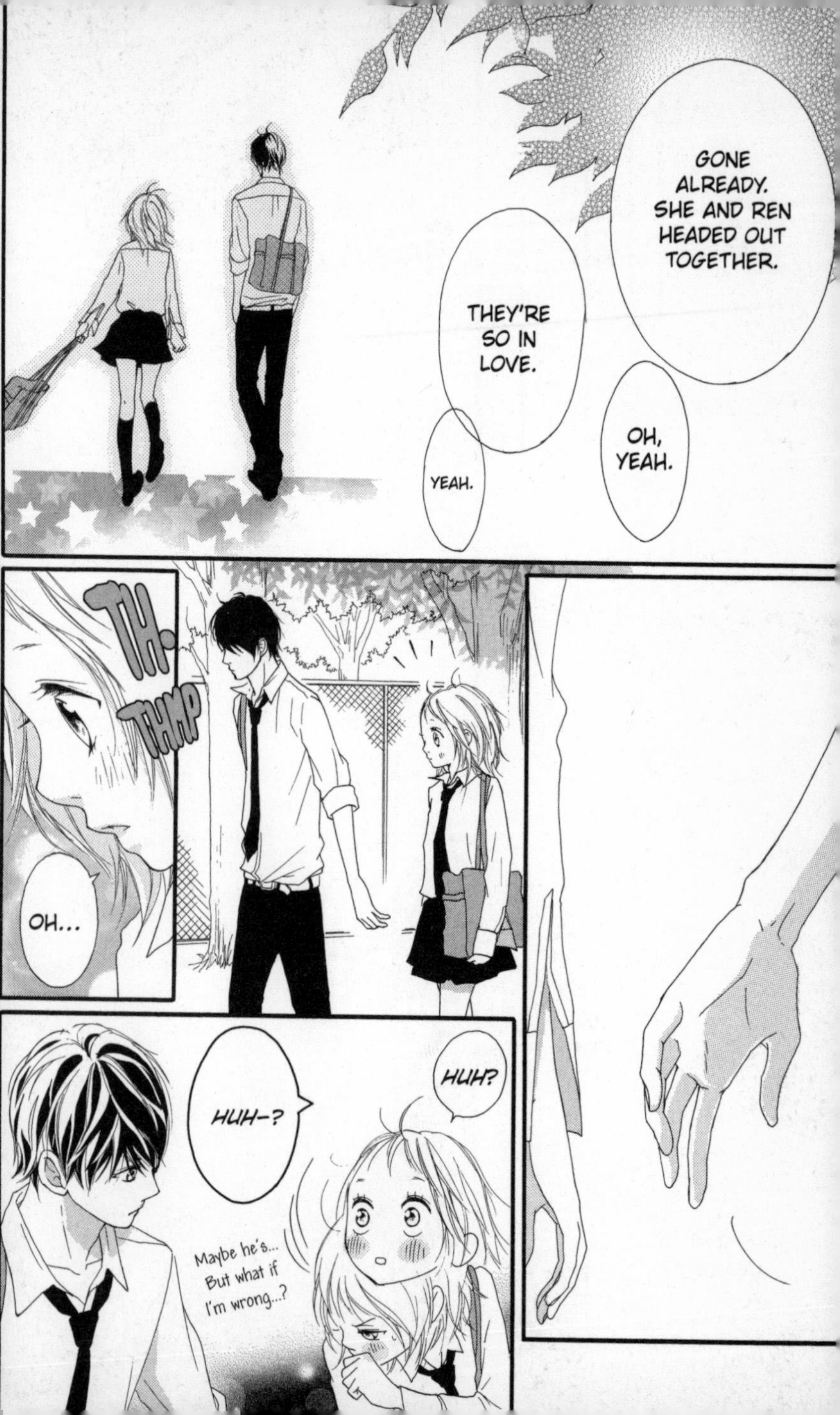
GONE ALREADY. SHE AND REN HEADED OUT TOGETHER.
OH, YEAH.
THEY'RE SO IN LOVE.
YEAH.
TH-THMP
OH...
HUH?
HUH-?
Maybe he's... But what if I'm wrong...?

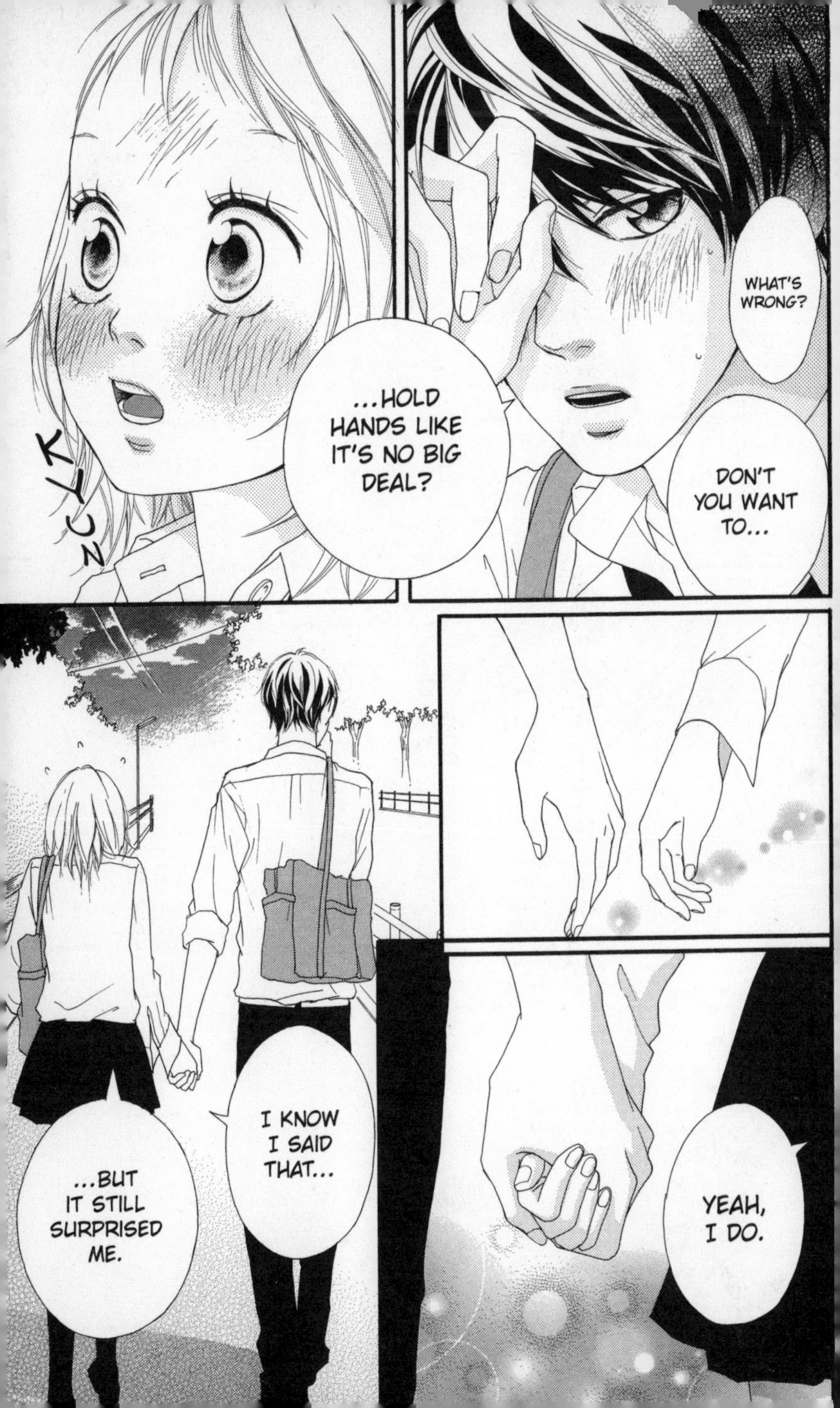
WHAT'S WRONG?
DON'T YOU WANT TO...
...HOLD HANDS LIKE IT'S NO BIG DEAL?
KYUN
YEAH, I DO.
I KNOW I SAID THAT...
...BUT IT STILL SURPRISED ME.

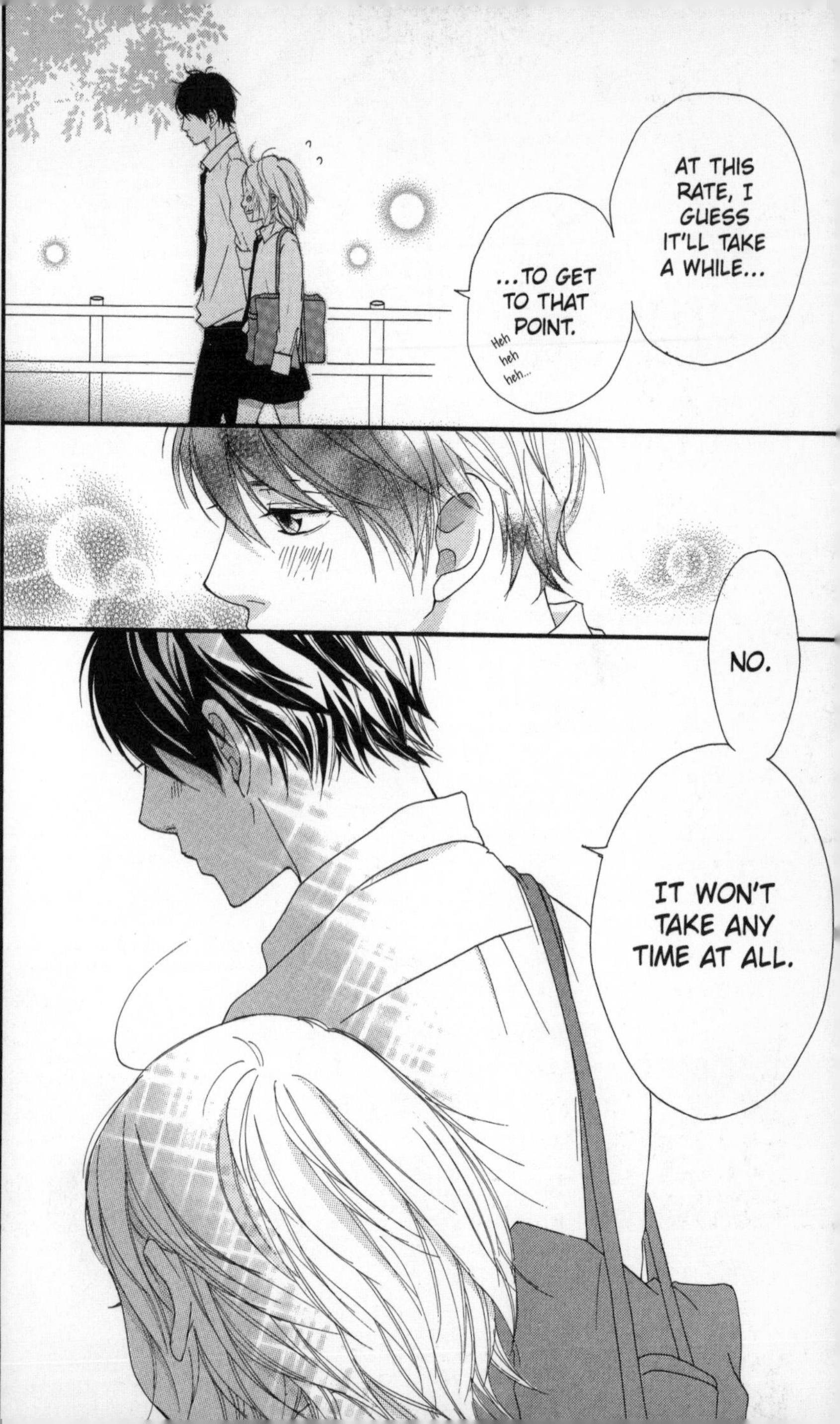
AT THIS RATE, I GUESS IT'LL TAKE A WHILE...
...TO GET TO THAT POINT.
Heh heh heh...
NO.
IT WON'T TAKE ANY TIME AT ALL.

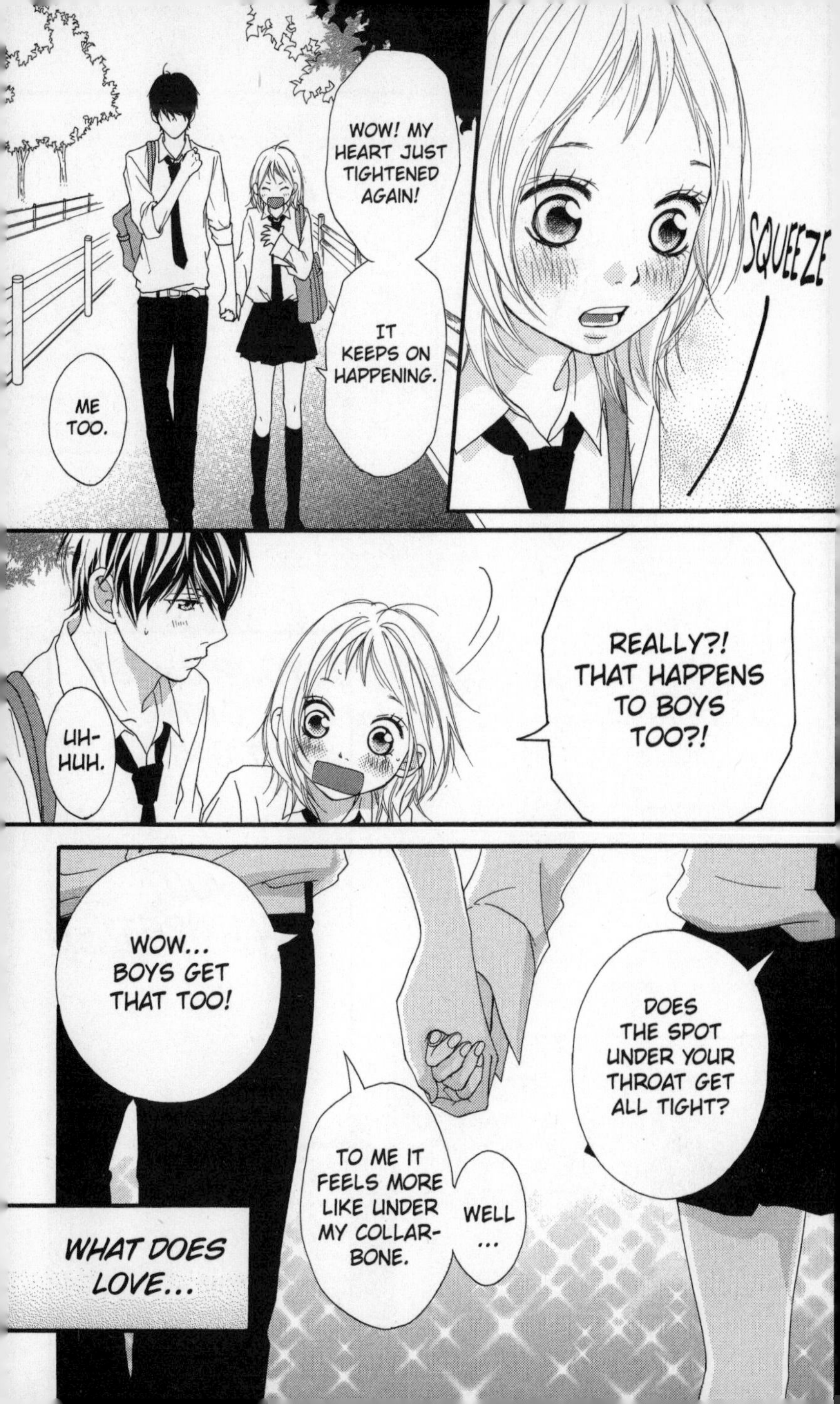
SQUEEZE
WOW! MY HEART JUST TIGHTENED AGAIN!
IT KEEPS ON HAPPENING.
ME TOO.
REALLY?! THAT HAPPENS TO BOYS TOO?!
UH-HUH.
WOW... BOYS GET THAT TOO!
DOES THE SPOT UNDER YOUR THROAT GET ALL TIGHT?
WELL...
TO ME IT FEELS MORE LIKE UNDER MY COLLAR-BONE.
WHAT DOES LOVE...

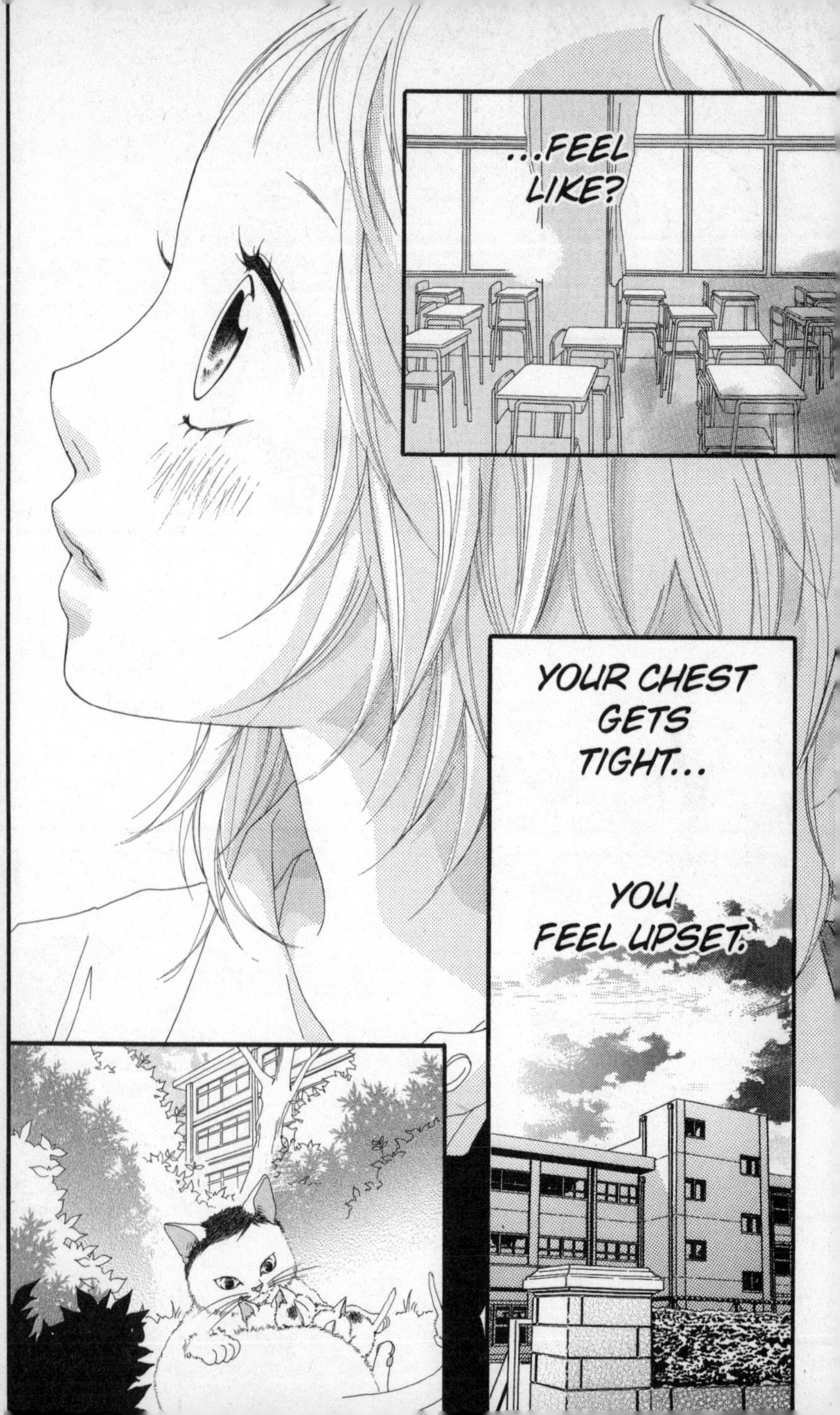
...FEEL LIKE?
YOUR CHEST GETS TIGHT...
YOU FEEL UPSET.

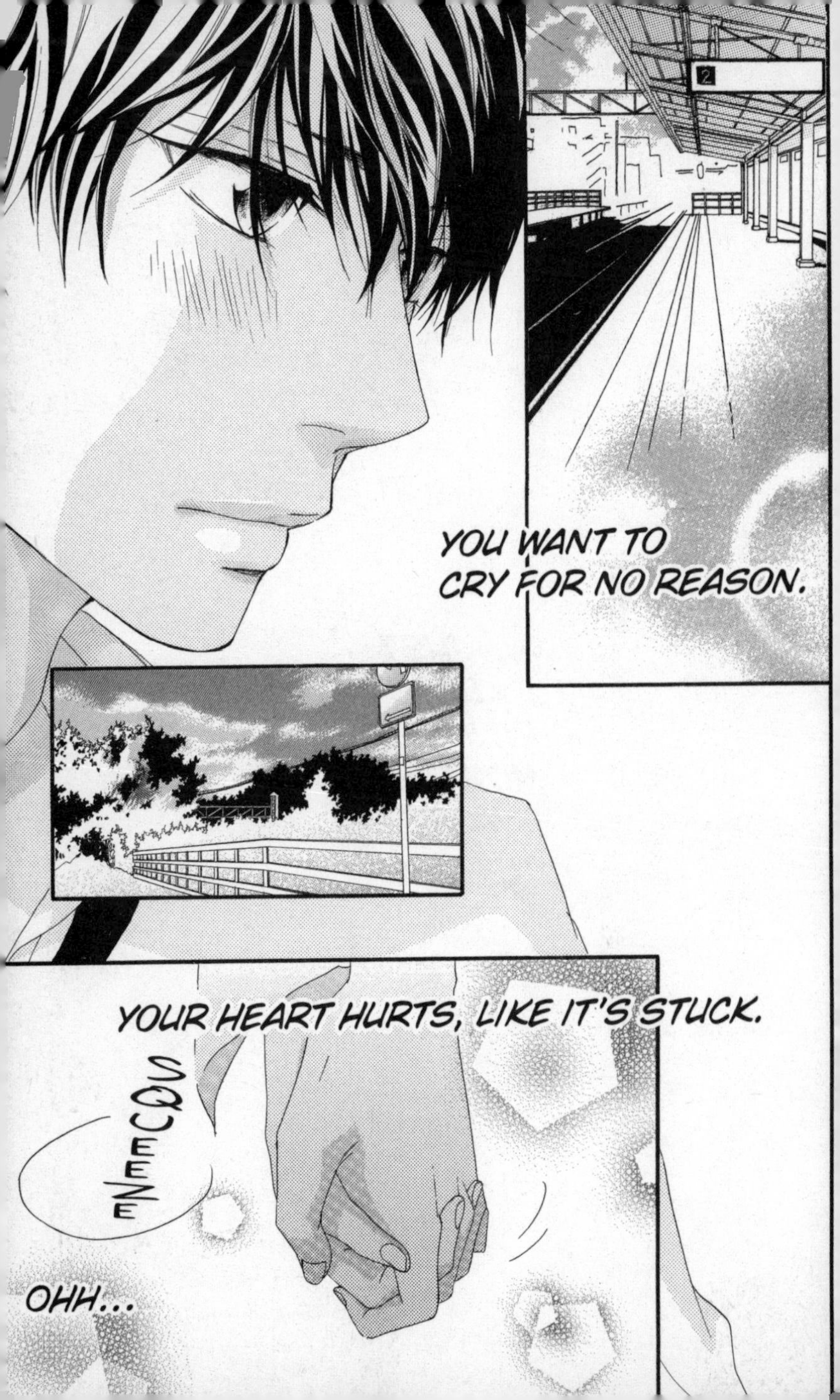
YOU WANT TO CRY FOR NO REASON.
YOUR HEART HURTS, LIKE IT'S STUCK.
SQUEEEZE
OHH...

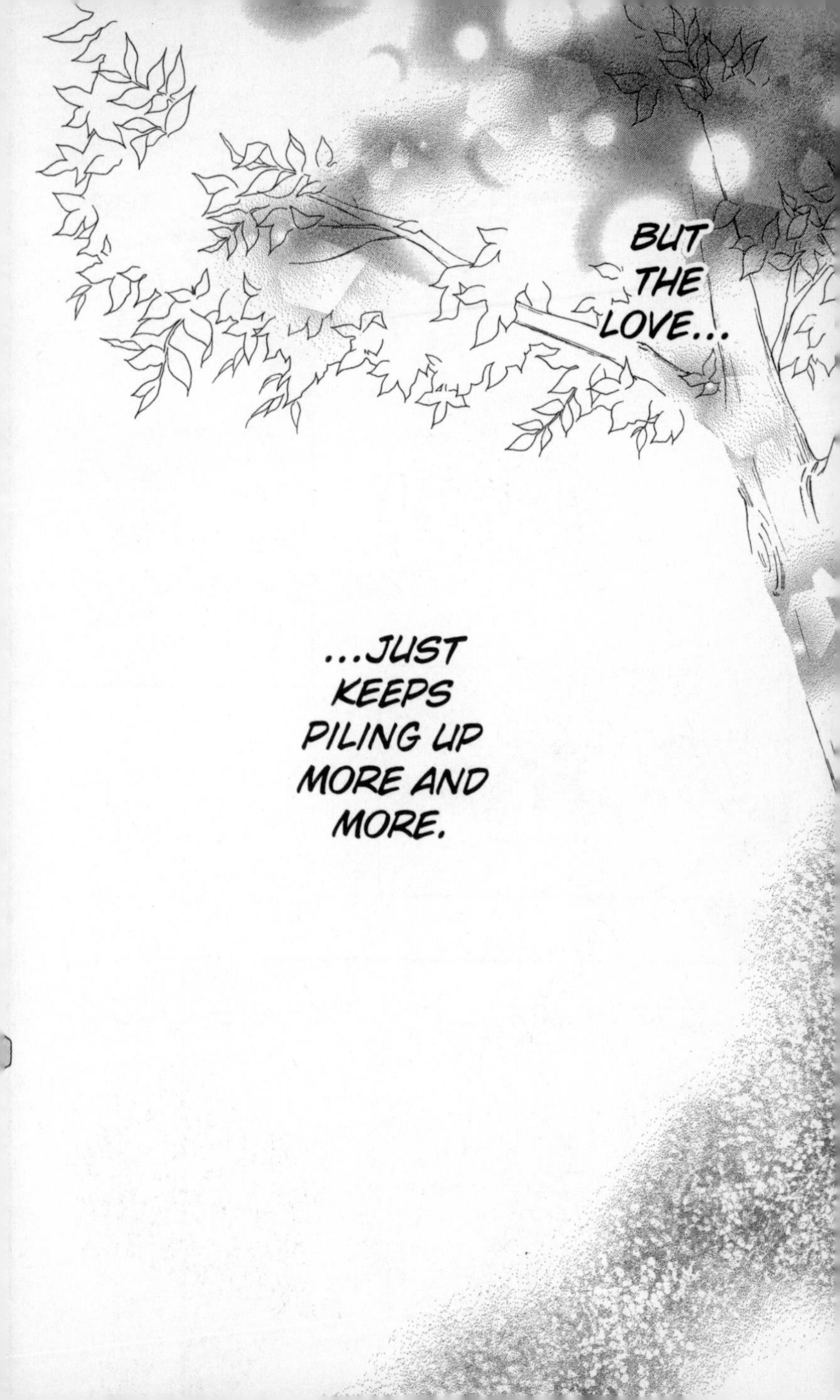
BUT THE LOVE...
...JUST KEEPS PILING UP MORE AND MORE.

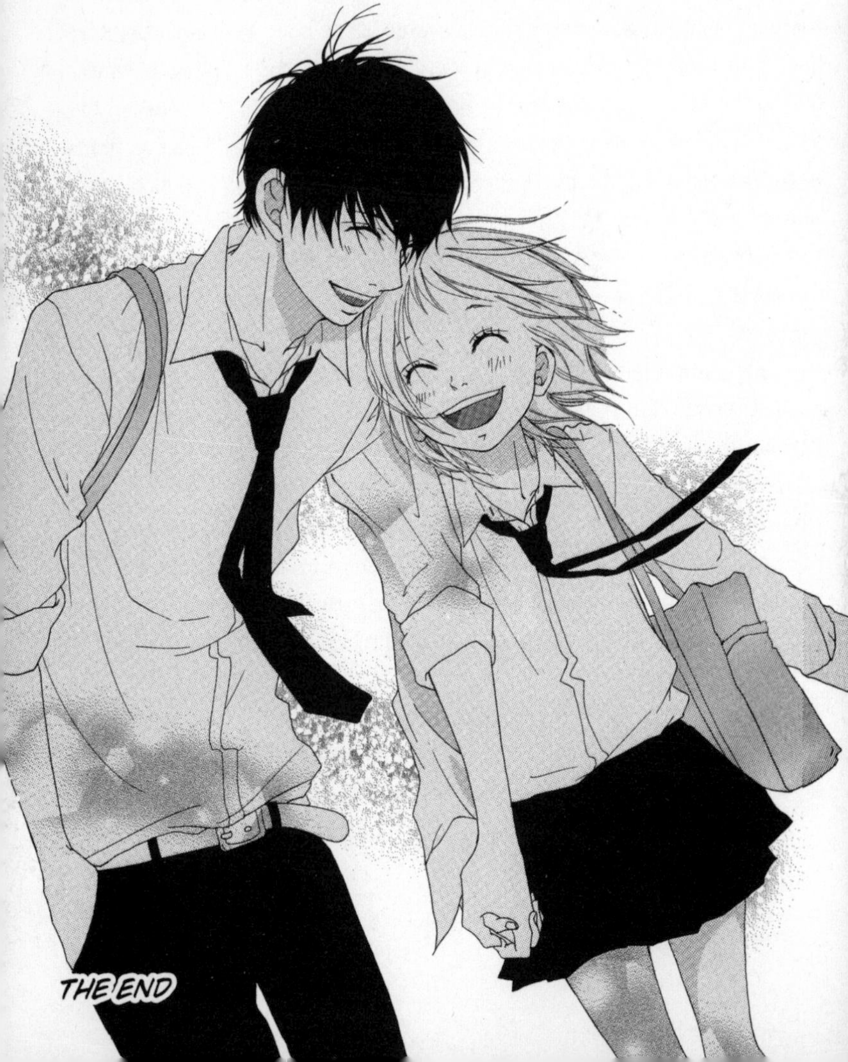
THE END

STROBE EDGE TRIVIA

I'LL TELL YOU BECAUSE WE'RE ALMOST DONE, BUT IT'S ALL USELESS Part 2

• When Ren feels a "love squeeze," it makes his collarbone feel tight. (Actually, that happens to me too. Is it unusual to have your collarbone feel tight?) To show that, I drew Ren pressing his collarbone a couple of times during the series, very subtly. The first time was when Ninako brushed the cherry blossom off him. When you read that scene, you can think, oh, that's when he was feeling the love squeeze. And this one is hard to notice, but you can see it in the overhead view during the field trip when the two of them are sitting on the bench. And then the one with the headphones, or the nurse's office... Wait a minute, Ren! That's too many love squeezes!

• I really wanted to write a side story for the cheer squad leader. There was a small window, but it just didn't happen. That's why he has a full name: Keisuke Toda. It didn't come up at all in the series. He really is loud!

• Ninako is based on a girl (not a model) I saw in a hair magazine whom I thought was gorgeous. So I imagined what she'd be like and thought, "I'd like to be friends with her!" I created her that way. She was really very cute. But I wasn't able to make Ninako look very much like her, just the hair.

• In Mayuka's side story in volume 2, there's a drawing of Ren looking like he had wings growing out of his back. I didn't really know how feathers worked, so I used my feather duster as a model.

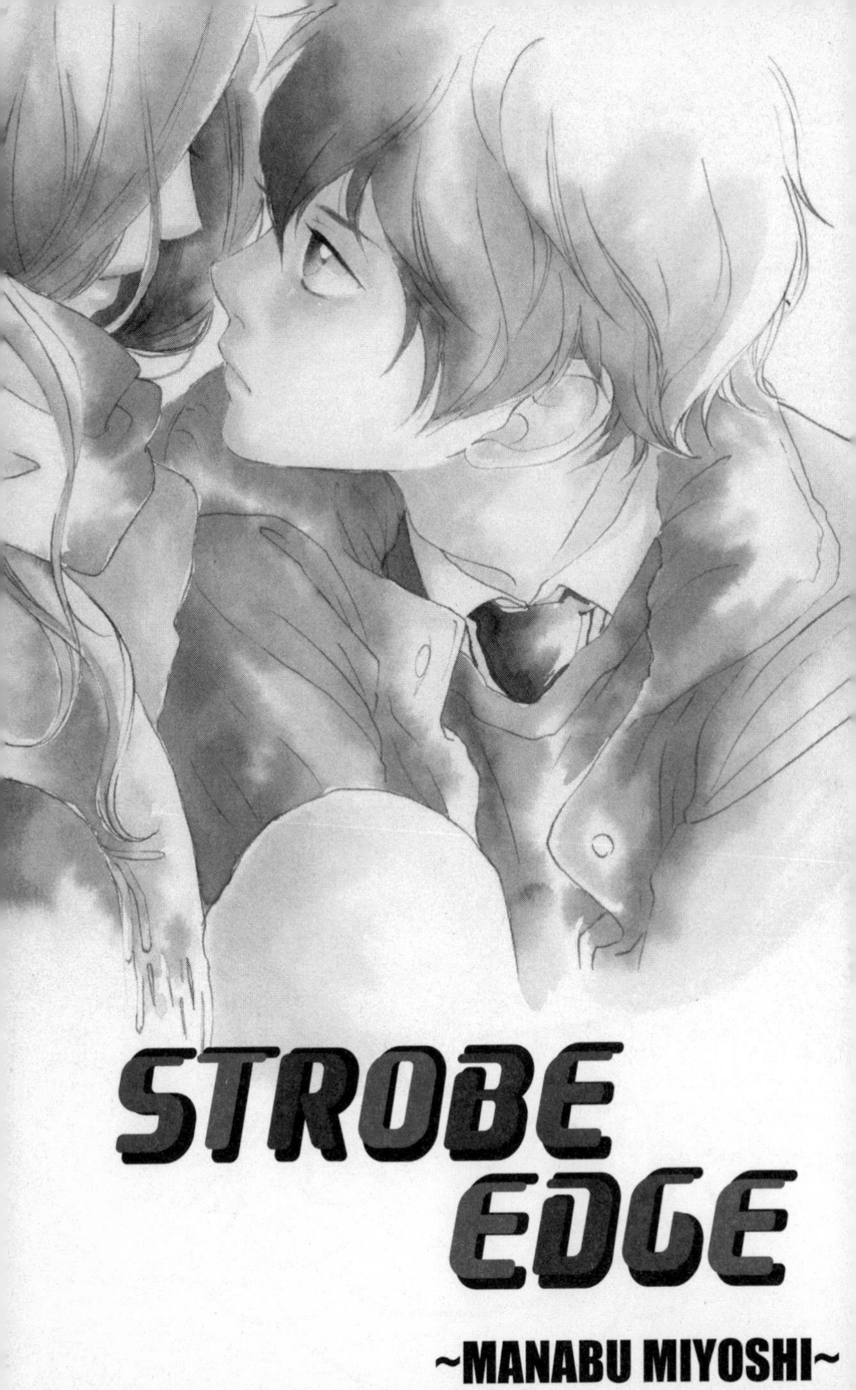

STROBE EDGE

~MANABU MIYOSHI~

ABOUT THE STROBE EDGE

~MANABU MIYOSHI~ SIDE STORY

Manabu looks very energetic and cute, and he has a really enthusiastic personality. He likes strong girls, and once he falls in love, he goes for it. That's the fundamental thing about Manabu.

Within *Strobe Edge*, he's definitely not one of the hot guys. So how can he be so enthusiastic? Who does he think he is? (I know it's cruel of me to say that, since I created him and all.)

Thoughts like that are how I decided to write this side story. While I was working on it, I really loved Manabu. Even though I was the one drawing it, I was rooting for him and telling him to go for it!

I'm sure it's because of this side of his personality that Manabu gets so impatient with Ren's initial super-cautious approach.

It would make me so happy if you read this little story and love Manabu too!

So now, without further delay, here's the last *Strobe Edge* side story!

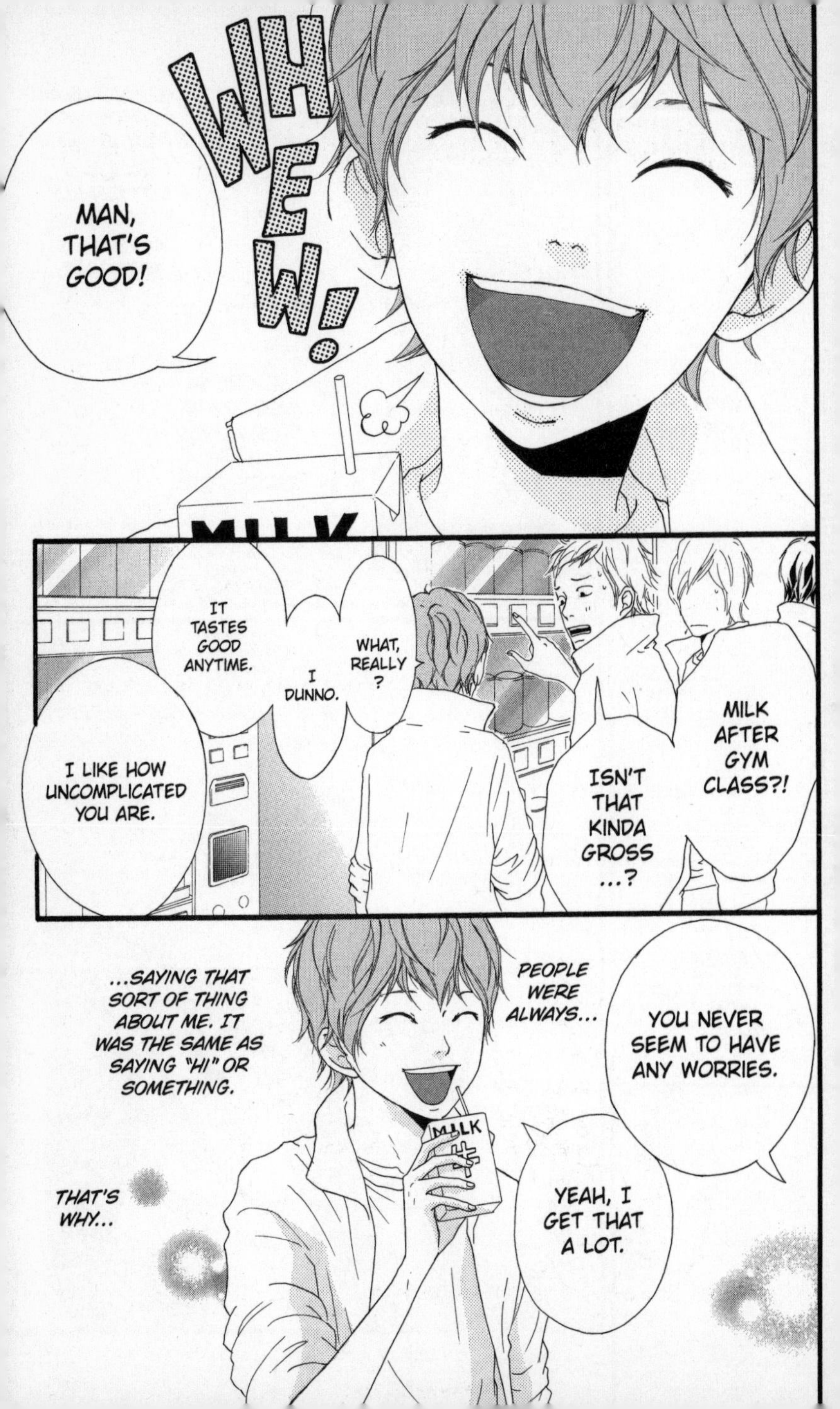
WHEW!
MAN, THAT'S GOOD!
MILK AFTER GYM CLASS?!
ISN'T THAT KINDA GROSS ...?
WHAT, REALLY ?
I DUNNO.
IT TASTES GOOD ANYTIME.
I LIKE HOW UNCOMPLICATED YOU ARE.
YOU NEVER SEEM TO HAVE ANY WORRIES.
PEOPLE WERE ALWAYS...
...SAYING THAT SORT OF THING ABOUT ME. IT WAS THE SAME AS SAYING "HI" OR SOMETHING.
MILK
YEAH, I GET THAT A LOT.
THAT'S WHY...

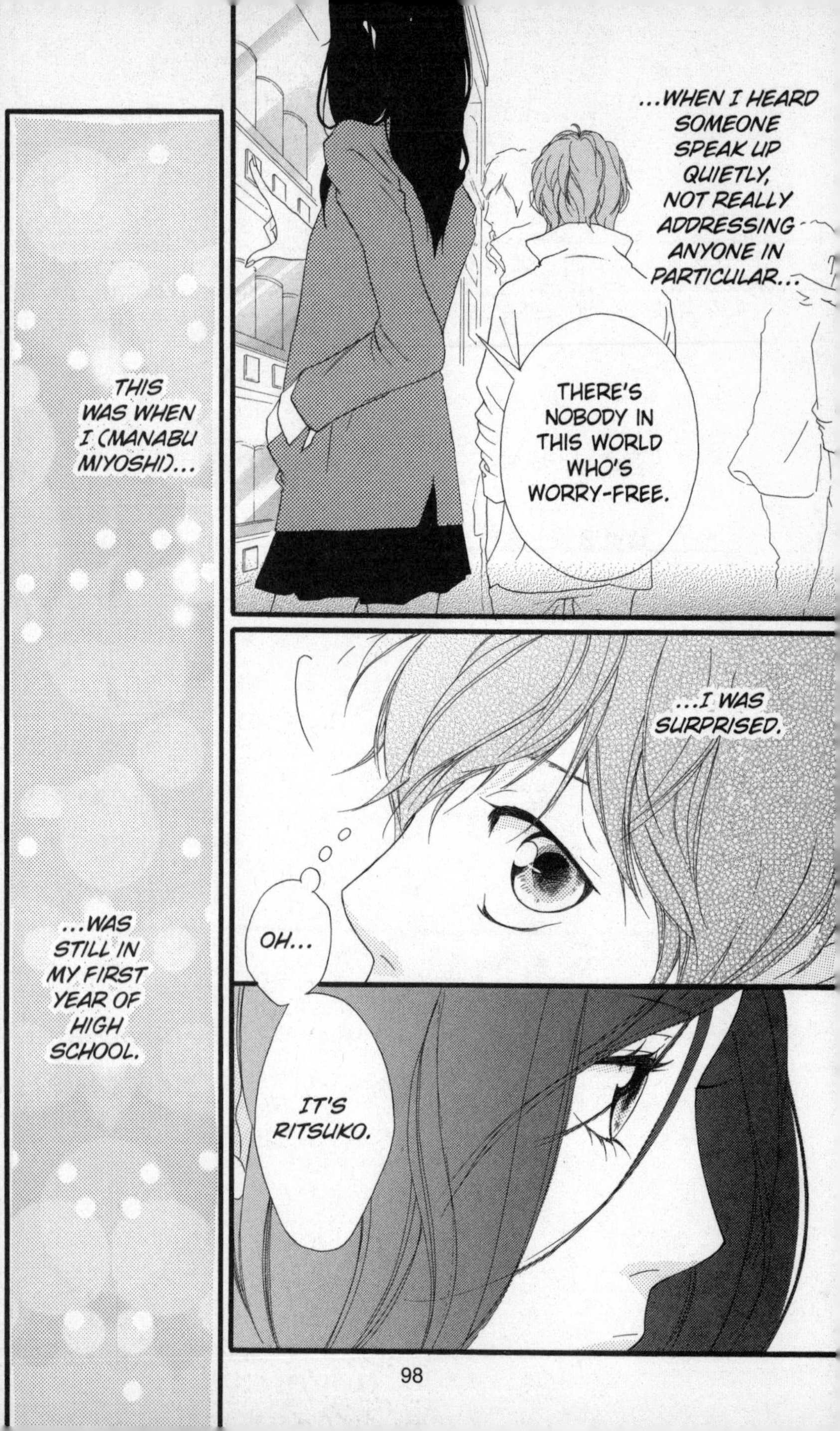
...WHEN I HEARD SOMEONE SPEAK UP QUIETLY, NOT REALLY ADDRESSING ANYONE IN PARTICULAR...
THERE'S NOBODY IN THIS WORLD WHO'S WORRY-FREE.
...I WAS SURPRISED.
OH...
IT'S RITSUKO.
THIS WAS WHEN I (MANABU MIYOSHI)...
...WAS STILL IN MY FIRST YEAR OF HIGH SCHOOL.

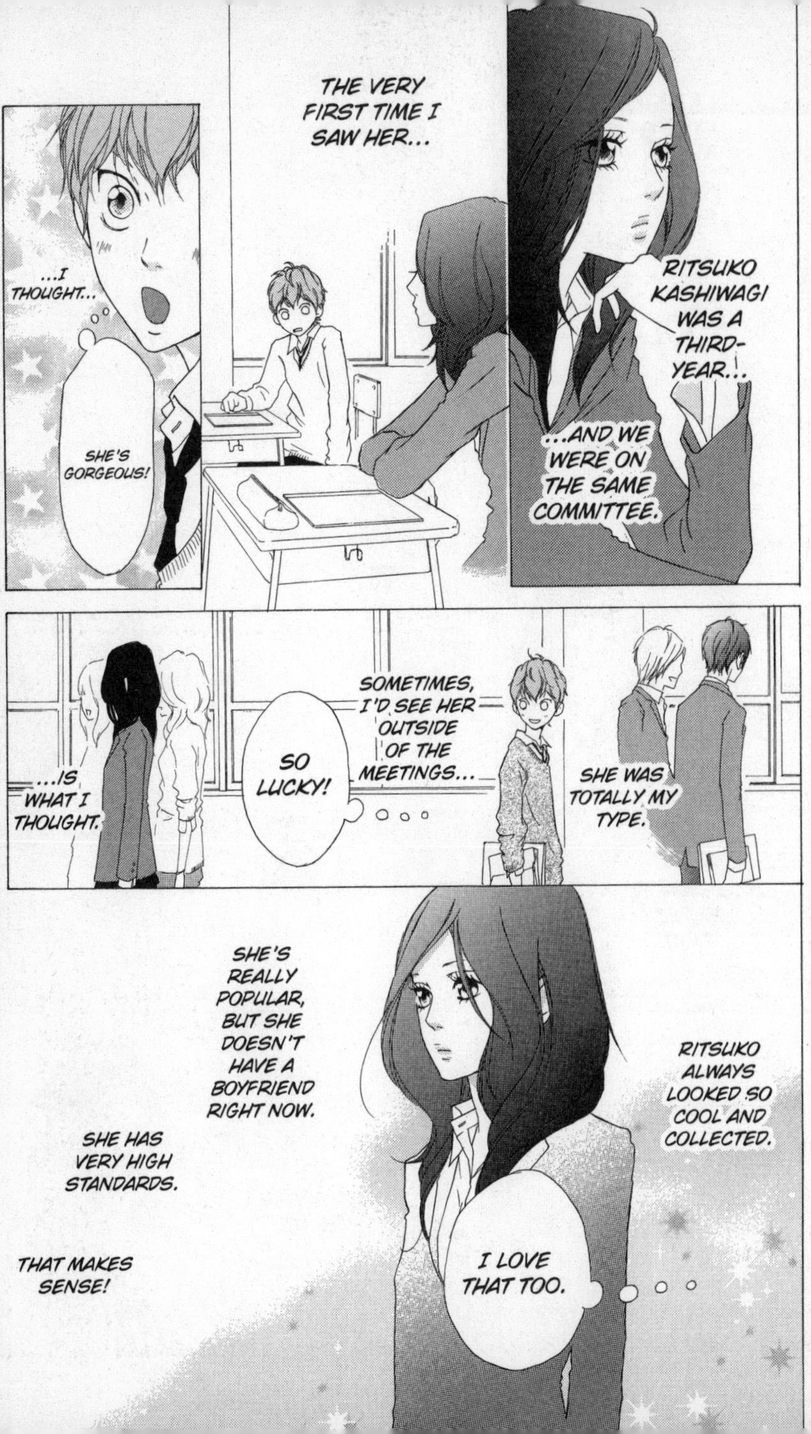
RITSUKO KASHIWAGI WAS A THIRD-YEAR...
...AND WE WERE ON THE SAME COMMITTEE.
THE VERY FIRST TIME I SAW HER...
...I THOUGHT...
SHE'S GORGEOUS!
SHE WAS TOTALLY MY TYPE.
SOMETIMES, I'D SEE HER OUTSIDE OF THE MEETINGS...
SO LUCKY!
...IS WHAT I THOUGHT.
RITSUKO ALWAYS LOOKED SO COOL AND COLLECTED.
I LOVE THAT TOO.
SHE'S REALLY POPULAR, BUT SHE DOESN'T HAVE A BOYFRIEND RIGHT NOW.
SHE HAS VERY HIGH STANDARDS.
THAT MAKES SENSE!

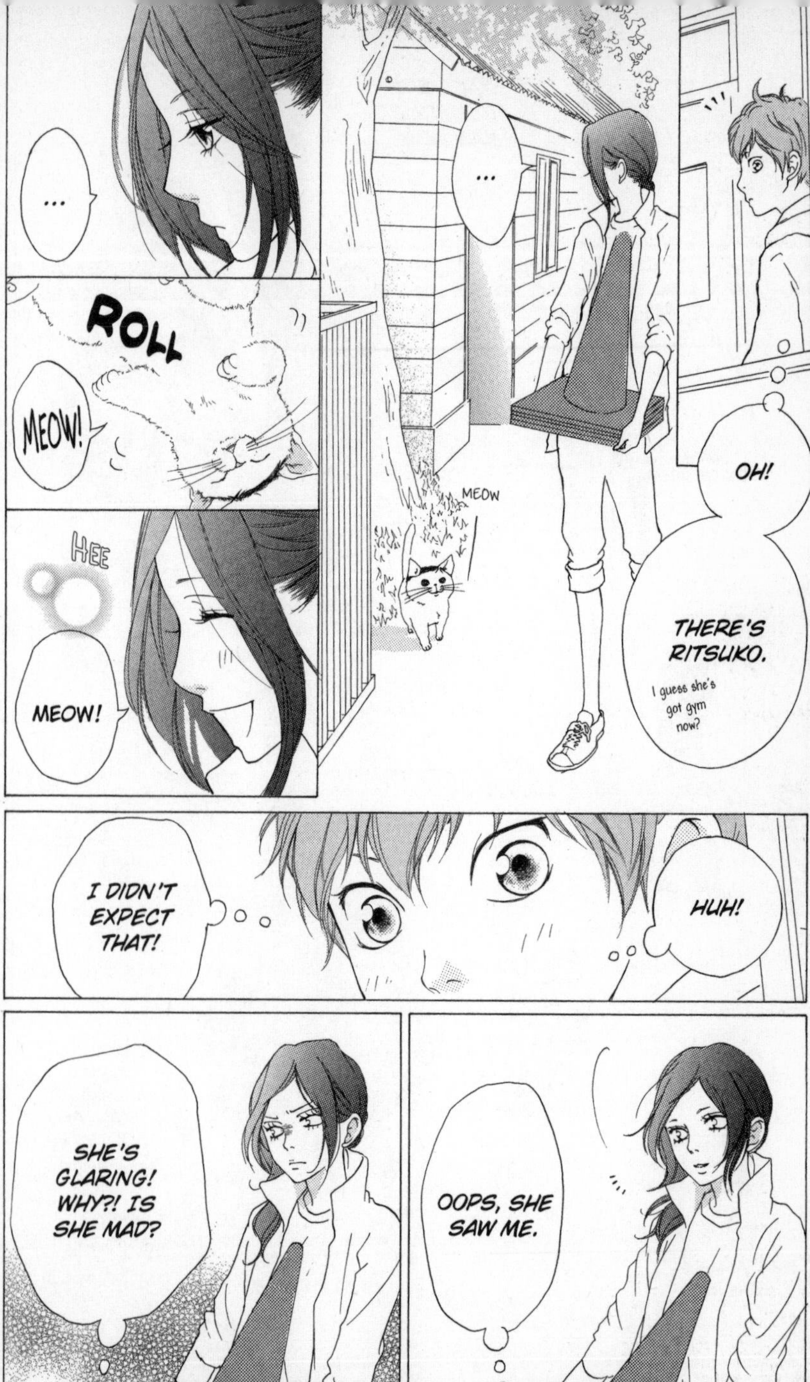
OH!
THERE'S RITSUKO.
I guess she's got gym now?
...
MEOW
...
ROLL
MEOW!
HEE
MEOW!
HUH!
I DIDN'T EXPECT THAT!
OOPS, SHE SAW ME.
SHE'S GLARING! WHY?! IS SHE MAD?

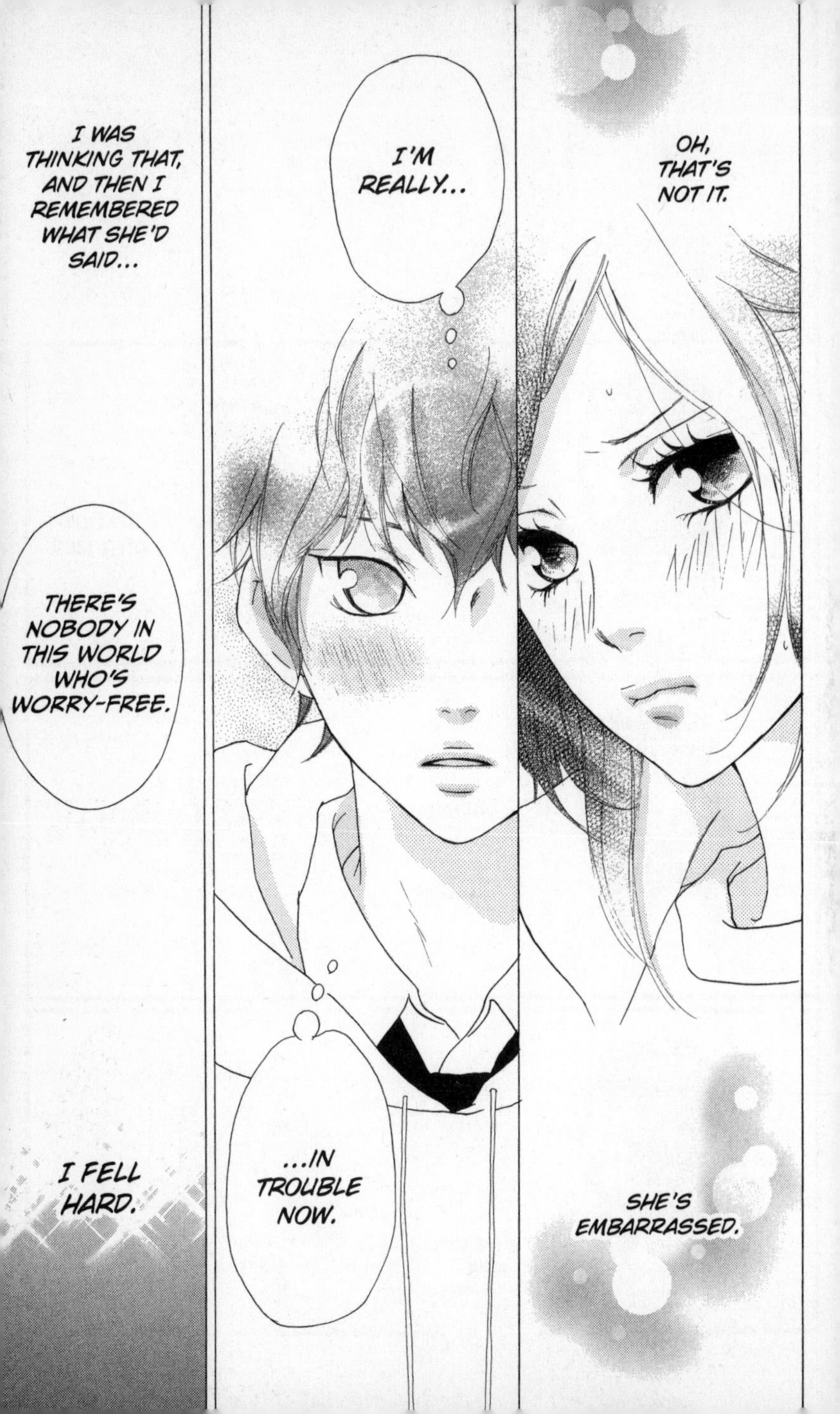
OH, THAT'S NOT IT.
SHE'S EMBARRASSED.
I'M REALLY...
...IN TROUBLE NOW.
I WAS THINKING THAT, AND THEN I REMEMBERED WHAT SHE'D SAID...
THERE'S NOBODY IN THIS WORLD WHO'S WORRY-FREE.
I FELL HARD.

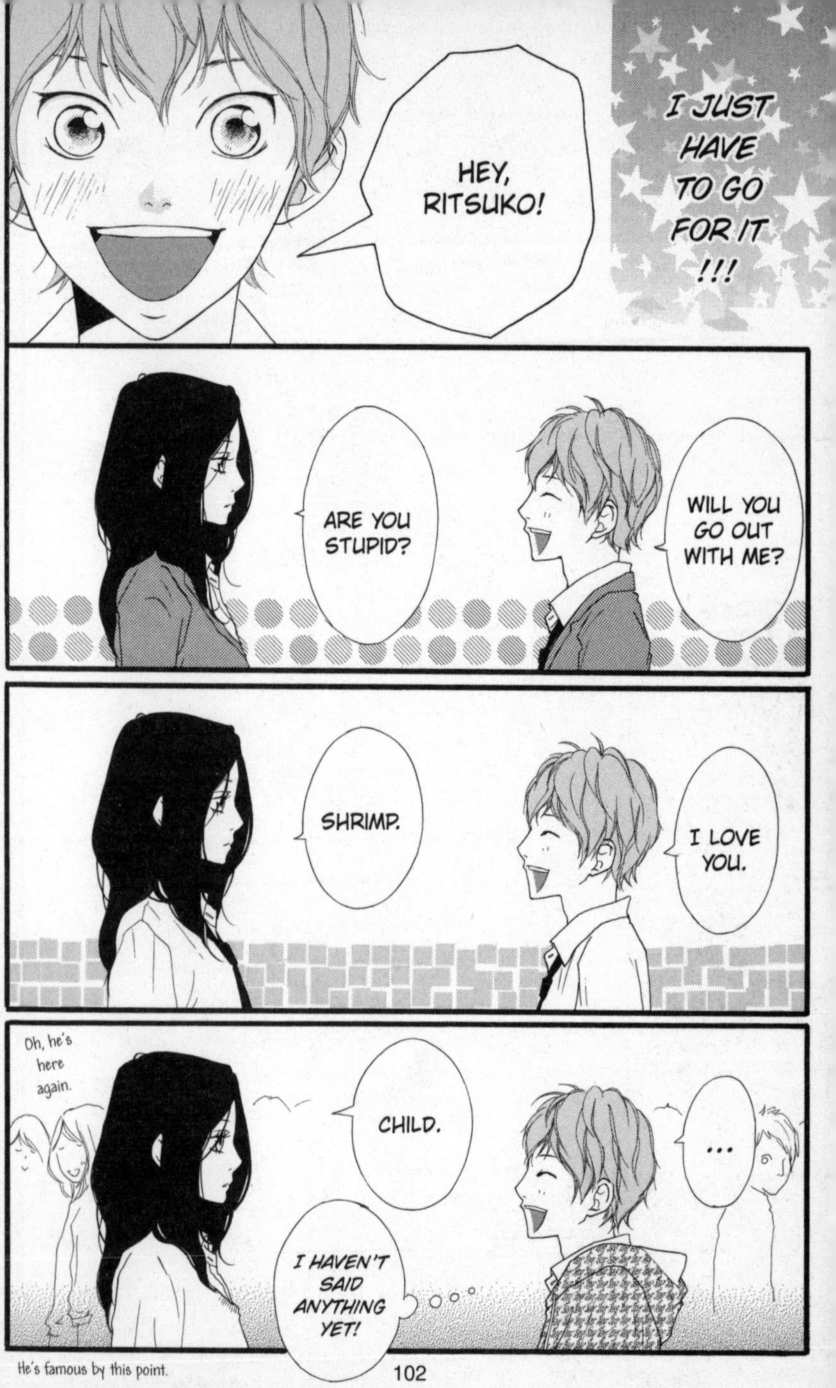
I JUST HAVE TO GO FOR IT !!!
HEY, RITSUKO!
WILL YOU GO OUT WITH ME?
ARE YOU STUPID?
I LOVE YOU.
SHRIMP.
...
Oh, he's here again.
CHILD.
I HAVEN'T SAID ANYTHING YET!

He's famous by this point.

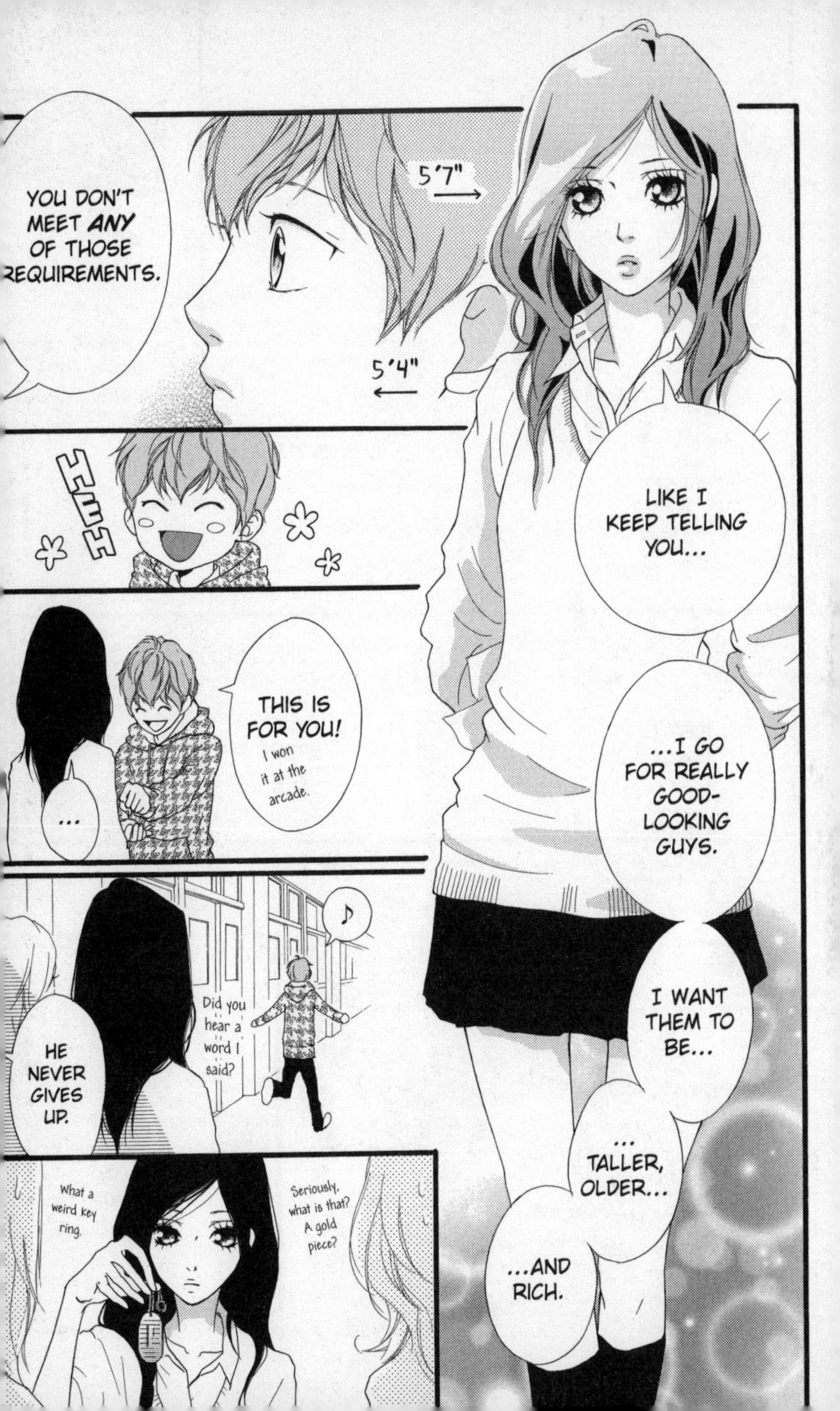
LIKE I KEEP TELLING YOU...
...I GO FOR REALLY GOOD-LOOKING GUYS.
I WANT THEM TO BE...
...TALLER, OLDER...
...AND RICH.
5'7"
5'4"
YOU DON'T MEET ANY OF THOSE REQUIREMENTS.
HEH
THIS IS FOR YOU! I won it at the arcade.
...
♪
Did you hear a word I said?
HE NEVER GIVES UP.
Seriously, what is that? A gold piece?
What a weird key ring.

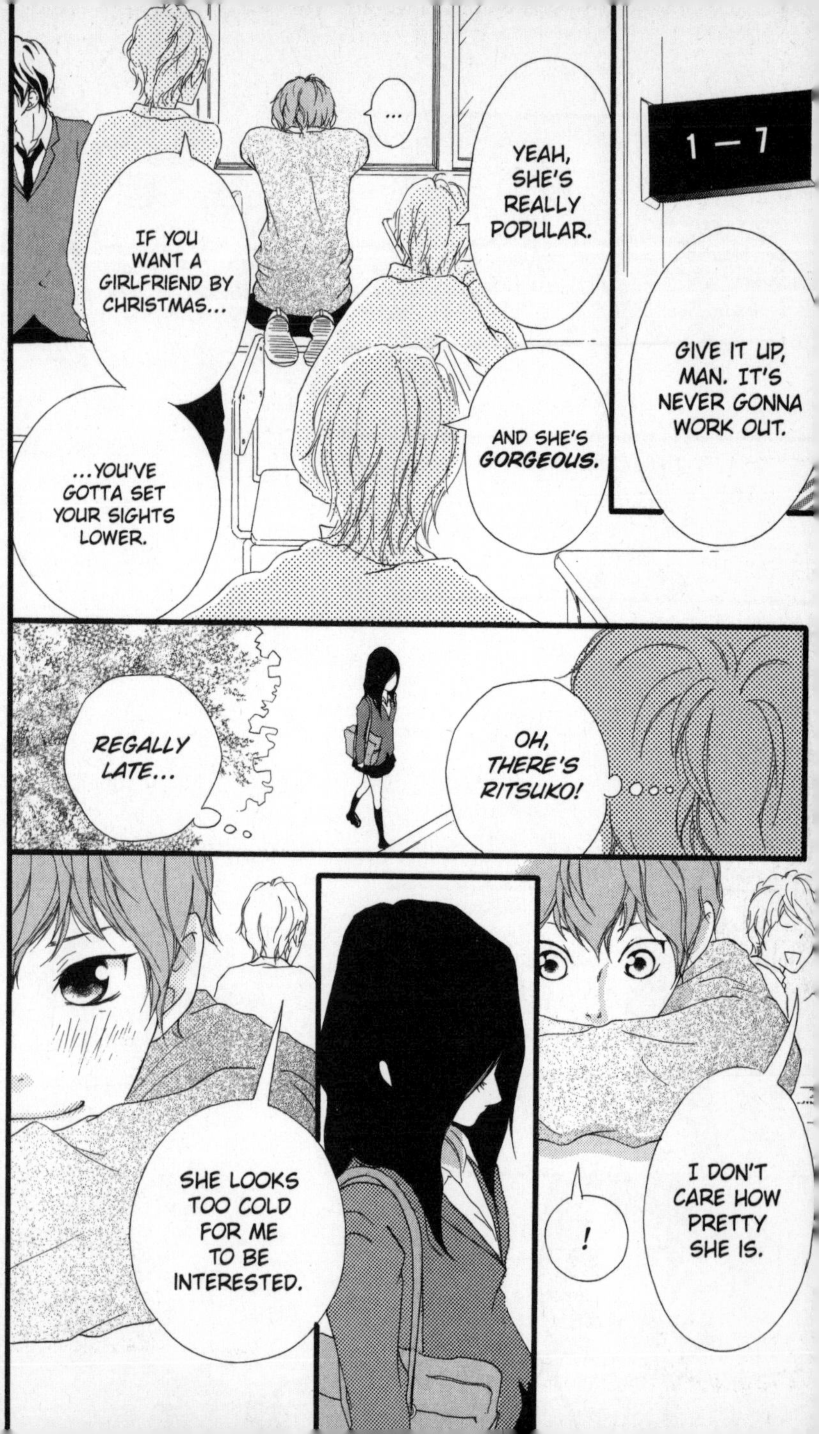
1 — 7
GIVE IT UP, MAN. IT'S NEVER GONNA WORK OUT.
YEAH, SHE'S REALLY POPULAR.
AND SHE'S *GORGEOUS*.
...
IF YOU WANT A GIRLFRIEND BY CHRISTMAS...
...YOU'VE GOTTA SET YOUR SIGHTS LOWER.
OH, THERE'S RITSUKO!
REGALLY LATE...
I DON'T CARE HOW PRETTY SHE IS.
!
SHE LOOKS TOO COLD FOR ME TO BE INTERESTED.

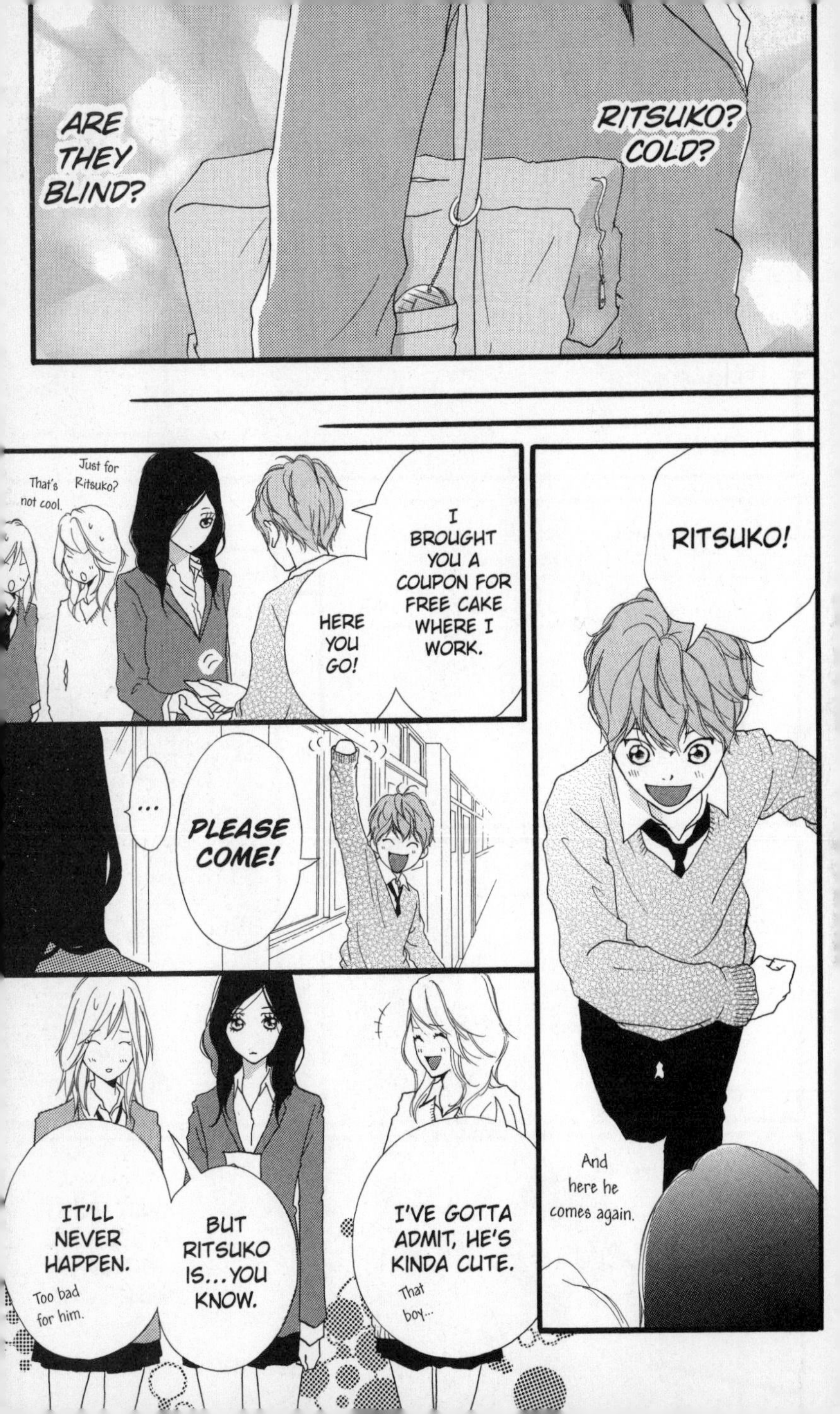
RITSUKO? COLD?
ARE THEY BLIND?
RITSUKO!
And here he comes again.
I BROUGHT YOU A COUPON FOR FREE CAKE WHERE I WORK.
HERE YOU GO!
Just for Ritsuko?
That's not cool.
PLEASE COME!
...
I'VE GOTTA ADMIT, HE'S KINDA CUTE.
That boy...
BUT RITSUKO IS...YOU KNOW.
IT'LL NEVER HAPPEN.
Too bad for him.

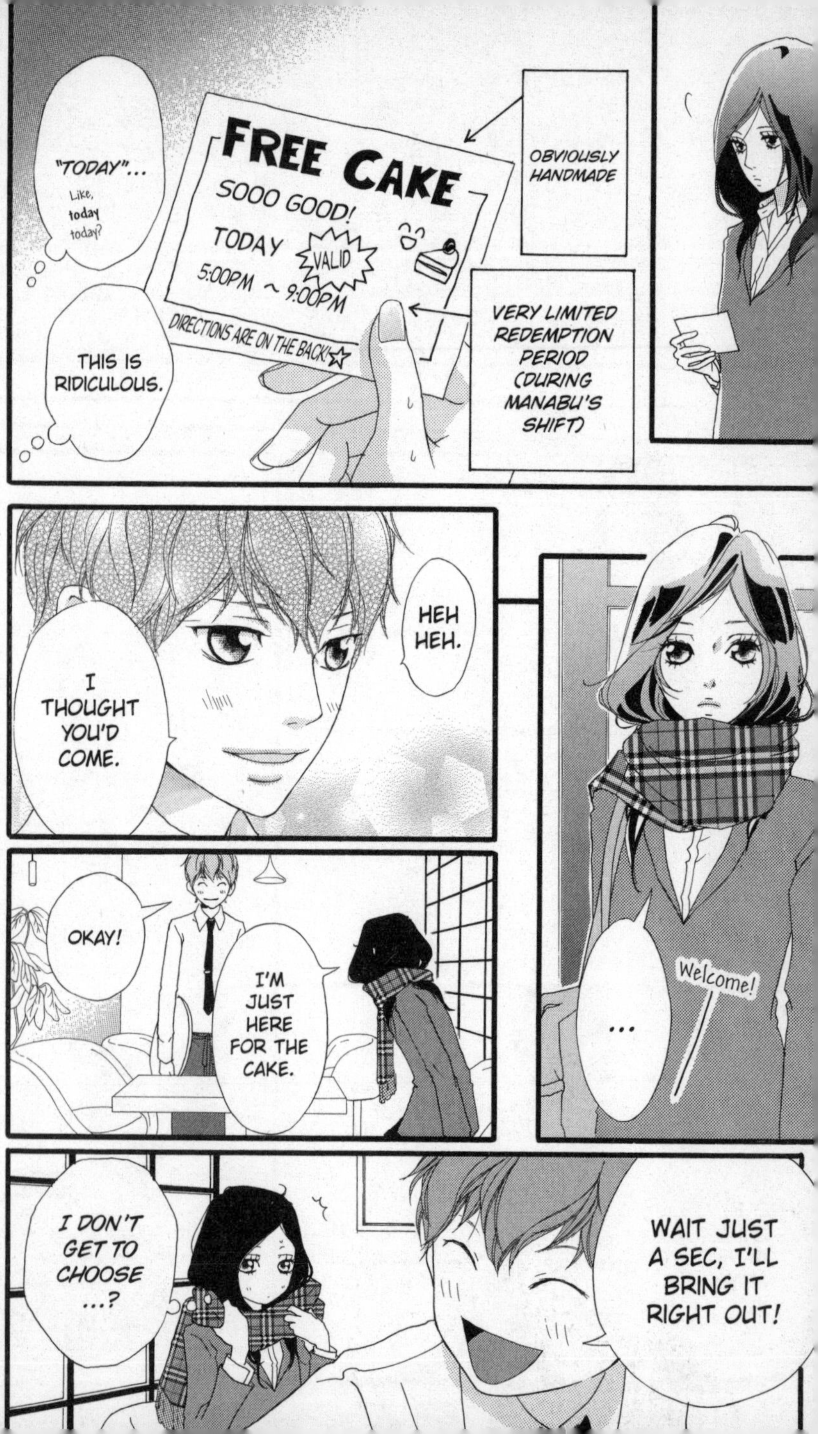
OBVIOUSLY HANDMADE
FREE CAKE
SOOO GOOD!
TODAY VALID
5:00PM ~ 9:00PM
DIRECTIONS ARE ON THE BACK!☆
VERY LIMITED REDEMPTION PERIOD (DURING MANABU'S SHIFT)
"TODAY"... Like, today today?
THIS IS RIDICULOUS.
Welcome!
...
HEH HEH.
I THOUGHT YOU'D COME.
I'M JUST HERE FOR THE CAKE.
OKAY!
WAIT JUST A SEC, I'LL BRING IT RIGHT OUT!
I DON'T GET TO CHOOSE ...?

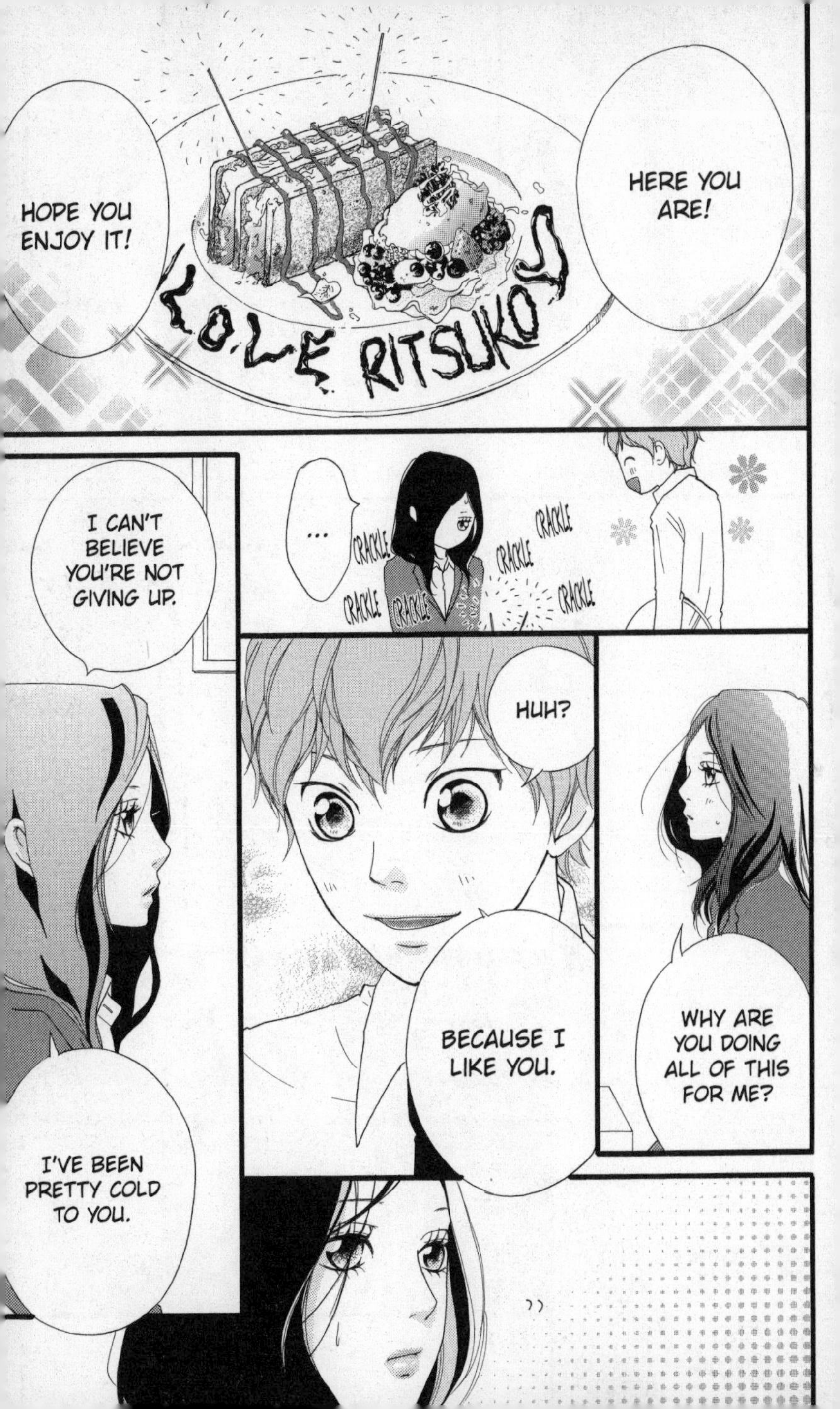
HERE YOU ARE!
HOPE YOU ENJOY IT!
L.O.V.E RITSUKO
...
CRACKLE
CRACKLE
CRACKLE
CRACKLE
CRACKLE
CRACKLE
WHY ARE YOU DOING ALL OF THIS FOR ME?
HUH?
BECAUSE I LIKE YOU.
I CAN'T BELIEVE YOU'RE NOT GIVING UP.
I'VE BEEN PRETTY COLD TO YOU.

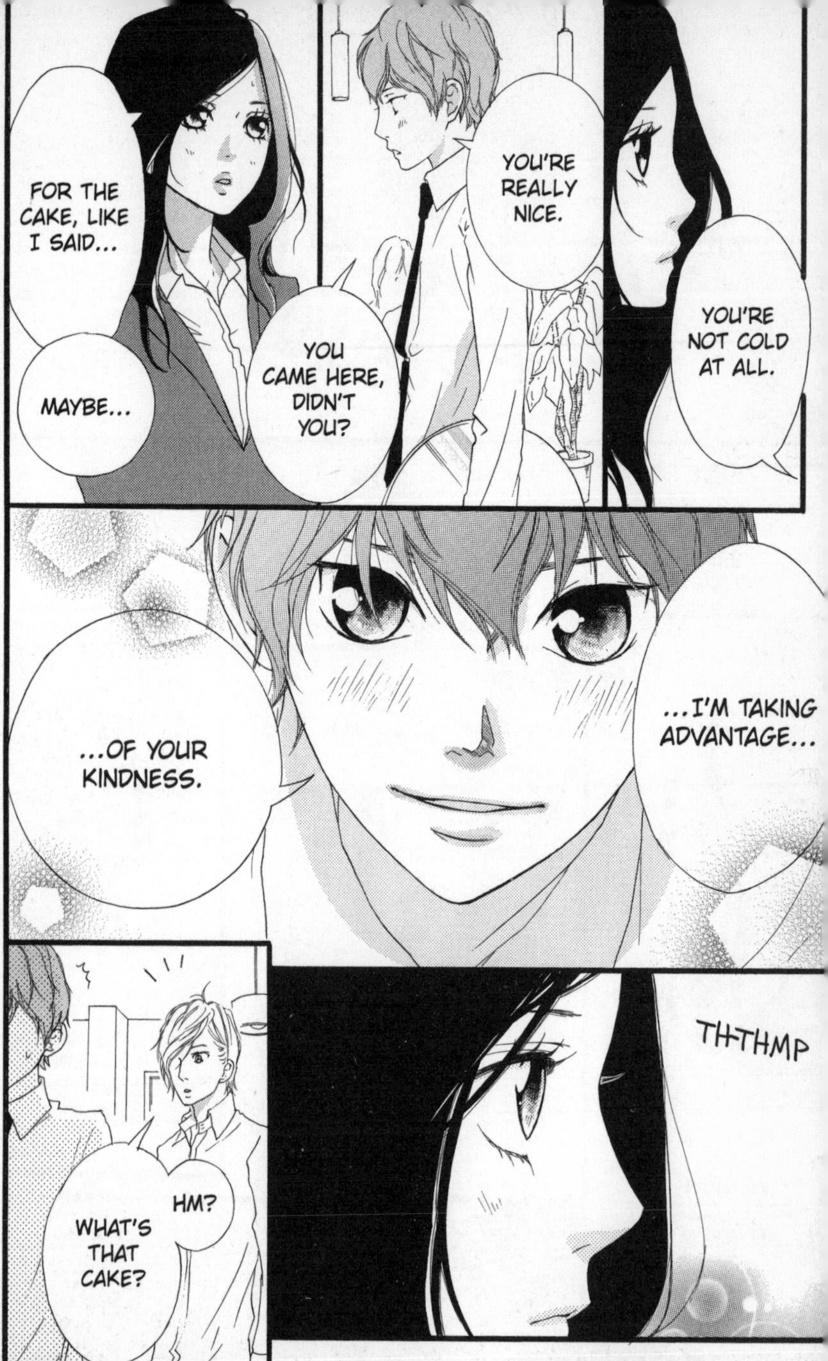
YOU'RE NOT COLD AT ALL.
YOU'RE REALLY NICE.
YOU CAME HERE, DIDN'T YOU?
FOR THE CAKE, LIKE I SAID...
MAYBE...
...I'M TAKING ADVANTAGE...
...OF YOUR KINDNESS.
TH-THMP
HM?
WHAT'S THAT CAKE?

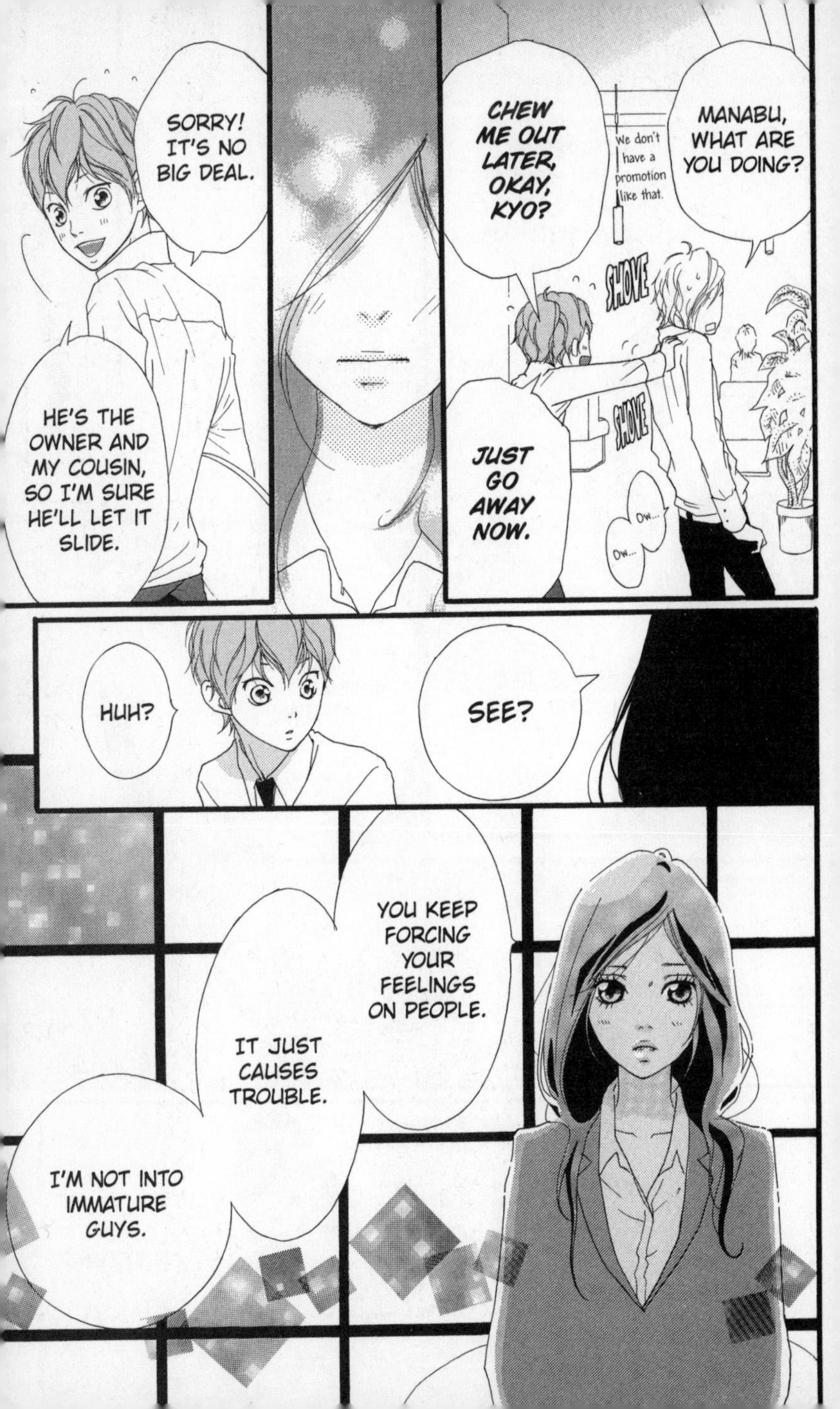
MANABU, WHAT ARE YOU DOING?
We don't have a promotion like that.
CHEW ME OUT LATER, OKAY, KYO?
SHOVE
SHOVE
JUST GO AWAY NOW.
Ow...
Ow...
SORRY! IT'S NO BIG DEAL.
HE'S THE OWNER AND MY COUSIN, SO I'M SURE HE'LL LET IT SLIDE.
SEE?
HUH?
YOU KEEP FORCING YOUR FEELINGS ON PEOPLE.
IT JUST CAUSES TROUBLE.
I'M NOT INTO IMMATURE GUYS.

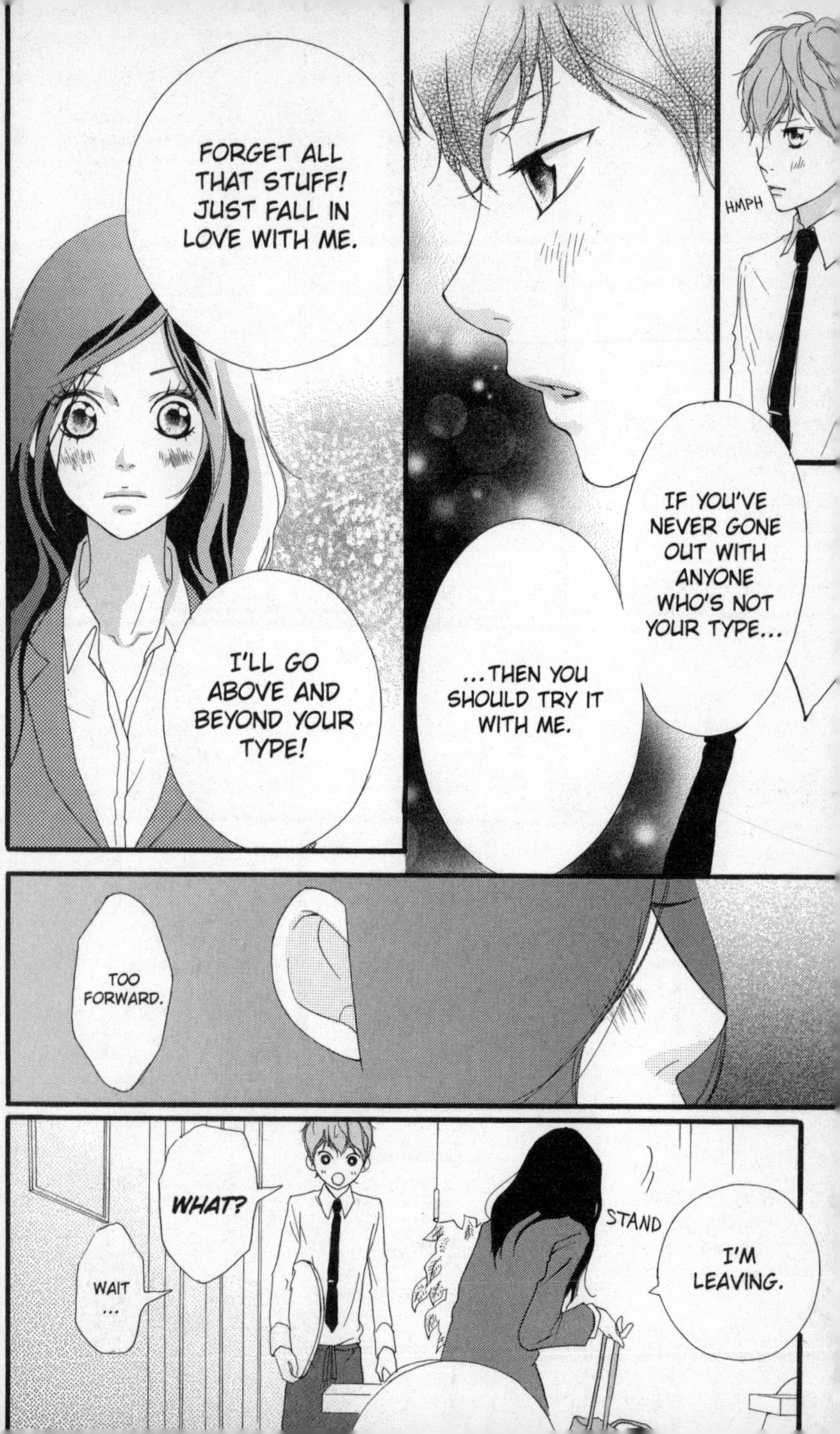
HMPH
IF YOU'VE NEVER GONE OUT WITH ANYONE WHO'S NOT YOUR TYPE...
...THEN YOU SHOULD TRY IT WITH ME.
FORGET ALL THAT STUFF! JUST FALL IN LOVE WITH ME.
I'LL GO ABOVE AND BEYOND YOUR TYPE!
TOO FORWARD.
I'M LEAVING.
STAND
WHAT?
WAIT ...

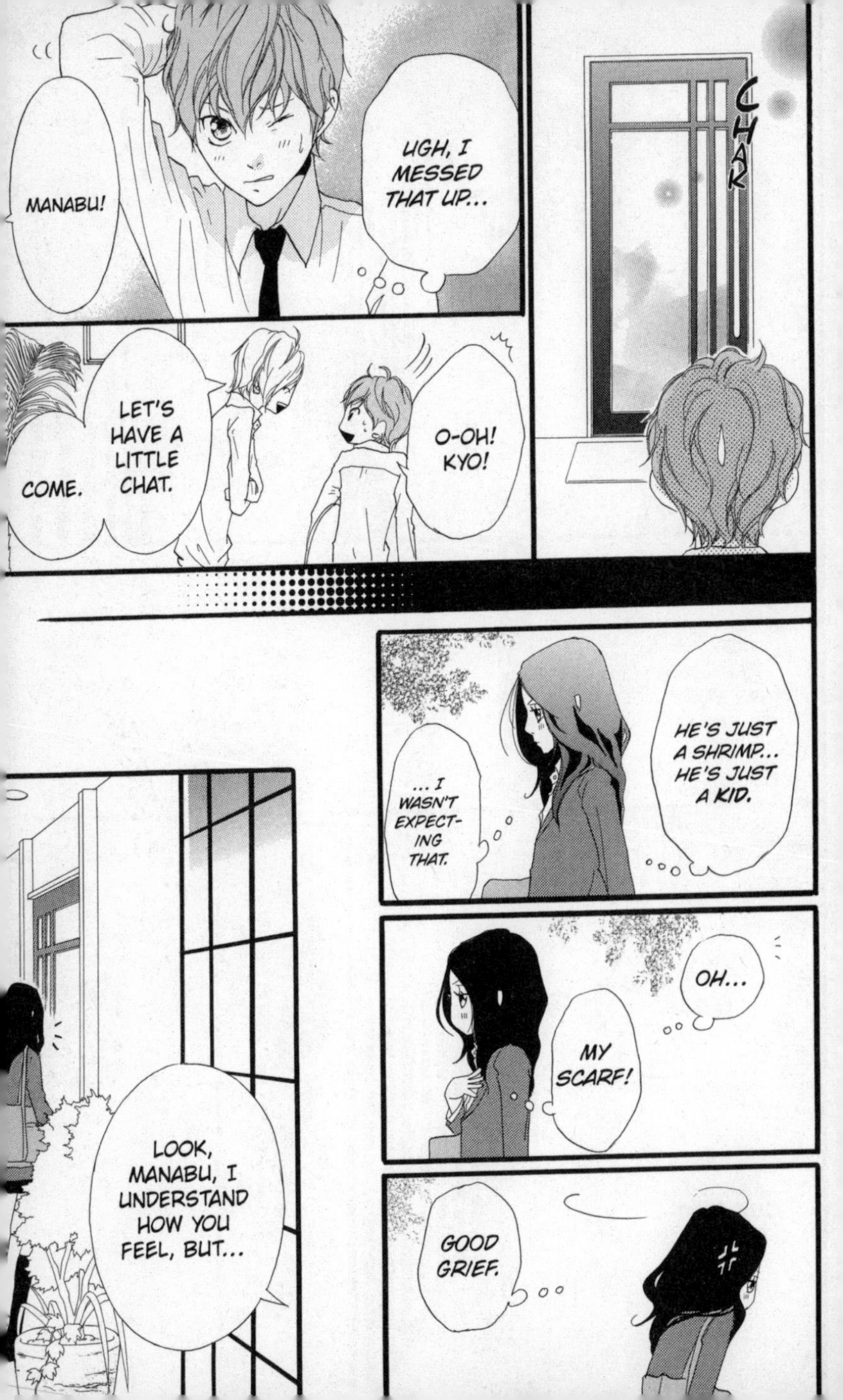
CHAK
UGH, I MESSED THAT UP...
MANABU!
O-OH! KYO!
LET'S HAVE A LITTLE CHAT.
COME.
HE'S JUST A SHRIMP... HE'S JUST A KID.
... I WASN'T EXPECTING THAT.
OH...
MY SCARF!
GOOD GRIEF.
LOOK, MANABU, I UNDERSTAND HOW YOU FEEL, BUT...

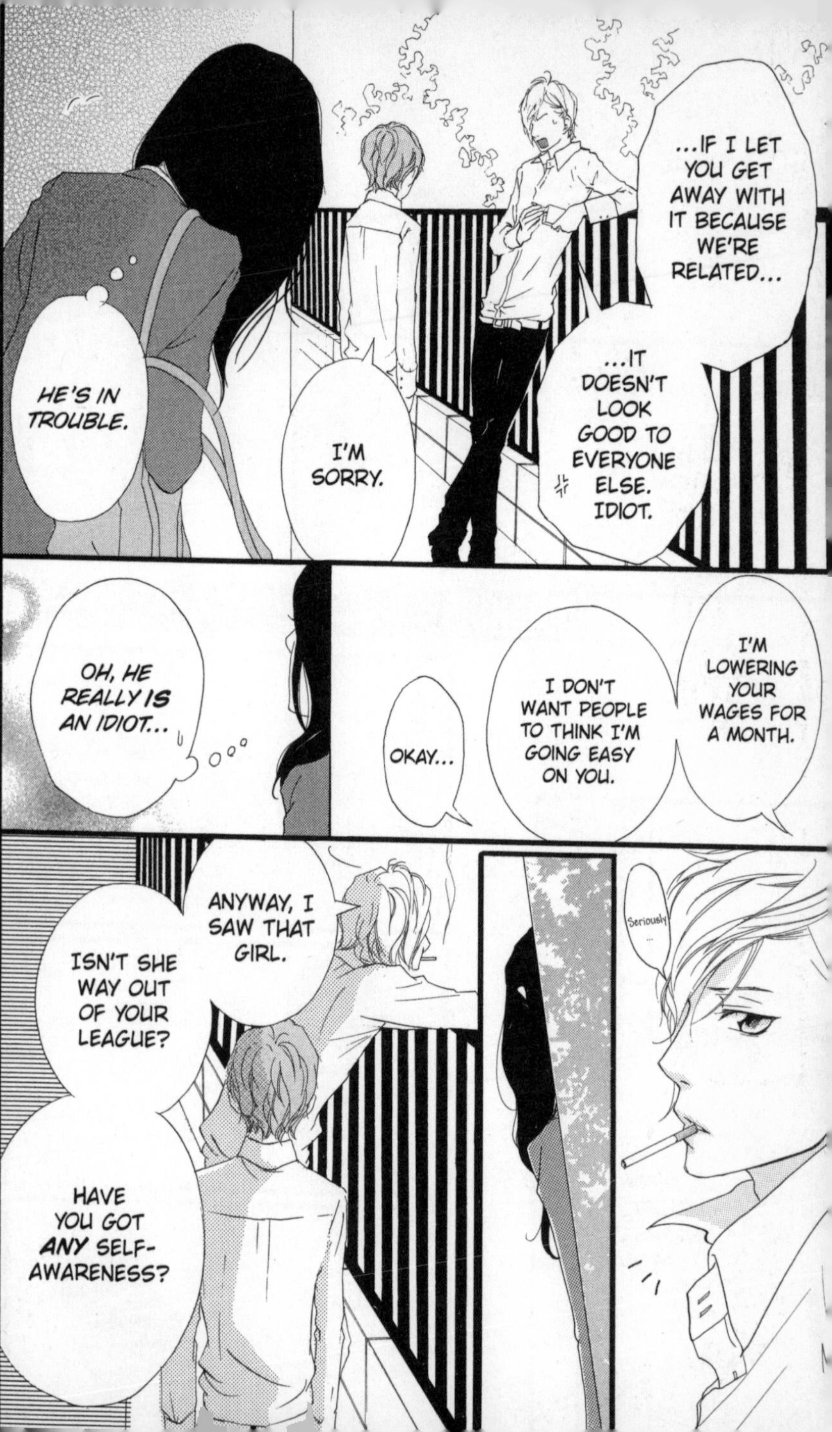
...IF I LET YOU GET AWAY WITH IT BECAUSE WE'RE RELATED...
...IT DOESN'T LOOK GOOD TO EVERYONE ELSE. IDIOT.
I'M SORRY.
HE'S IN TROUBLE.
I'M LOWERING YOUR WAGES FOR A MONTH.
I DON'T WANT PEOPLE TO THINK I'M GOING EASY ON YOU.
OKAY...
OH, HE REALLY *IS* AN IDIOT...
Seriously...
ANYWAY, I SAW THAT GIRL.
ISN'T SHE WAY OUT OF YOUR LEAGUE?
HAVE YOU GOT *ANY* SELF-AWARENESS?

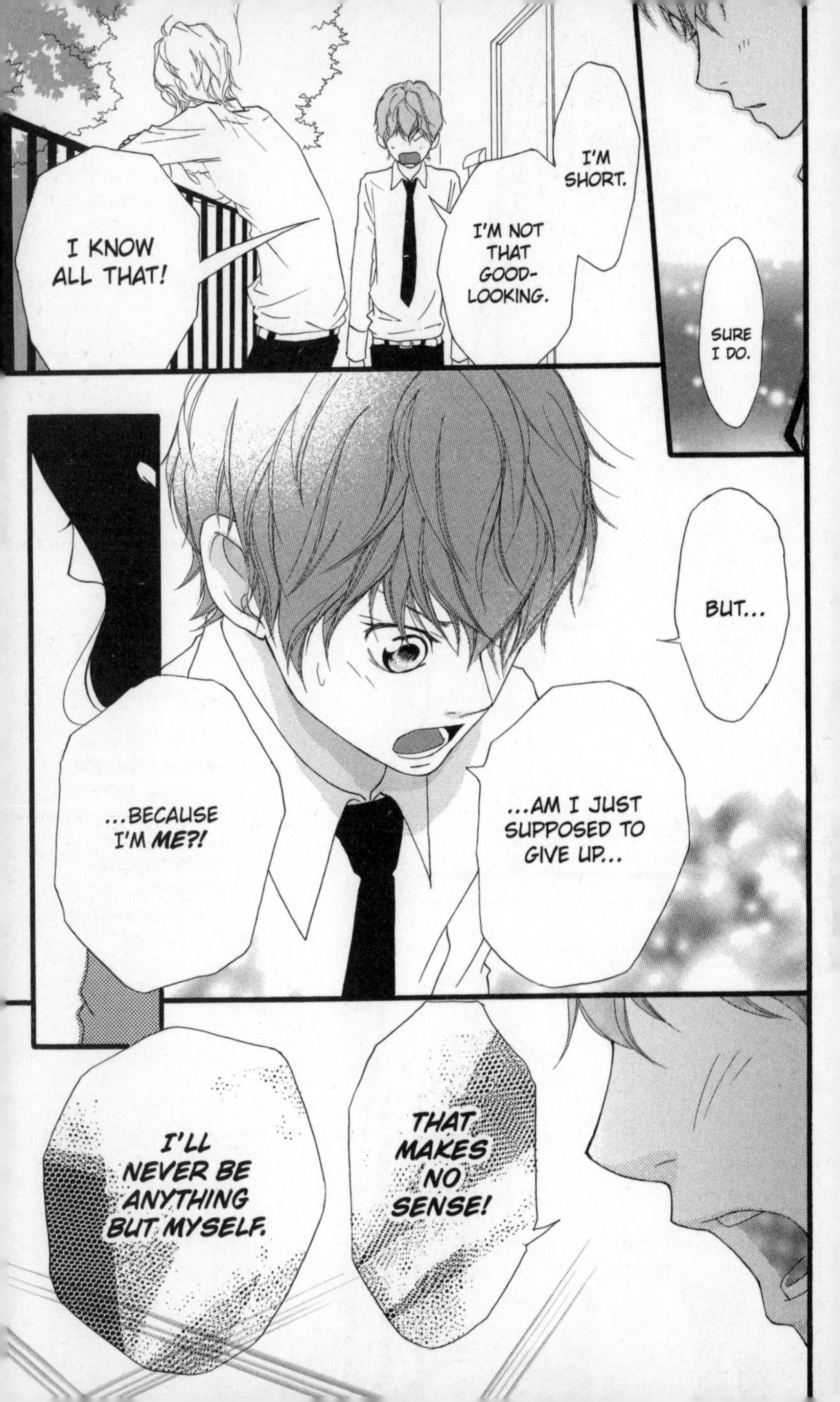
SURE I DO.
I'M SHORT.
I'M NOT THAT GOOD-LOOKING.
I KNOW ALL THAT!
BUT...
...AM I JUST SUPPOSED TO GIVE UP...
...BECAUSE I'M *ME?!*
THAT MAKES NO SENSE!
I'LL NEVER BE ANYTHING BUT MYSELF.

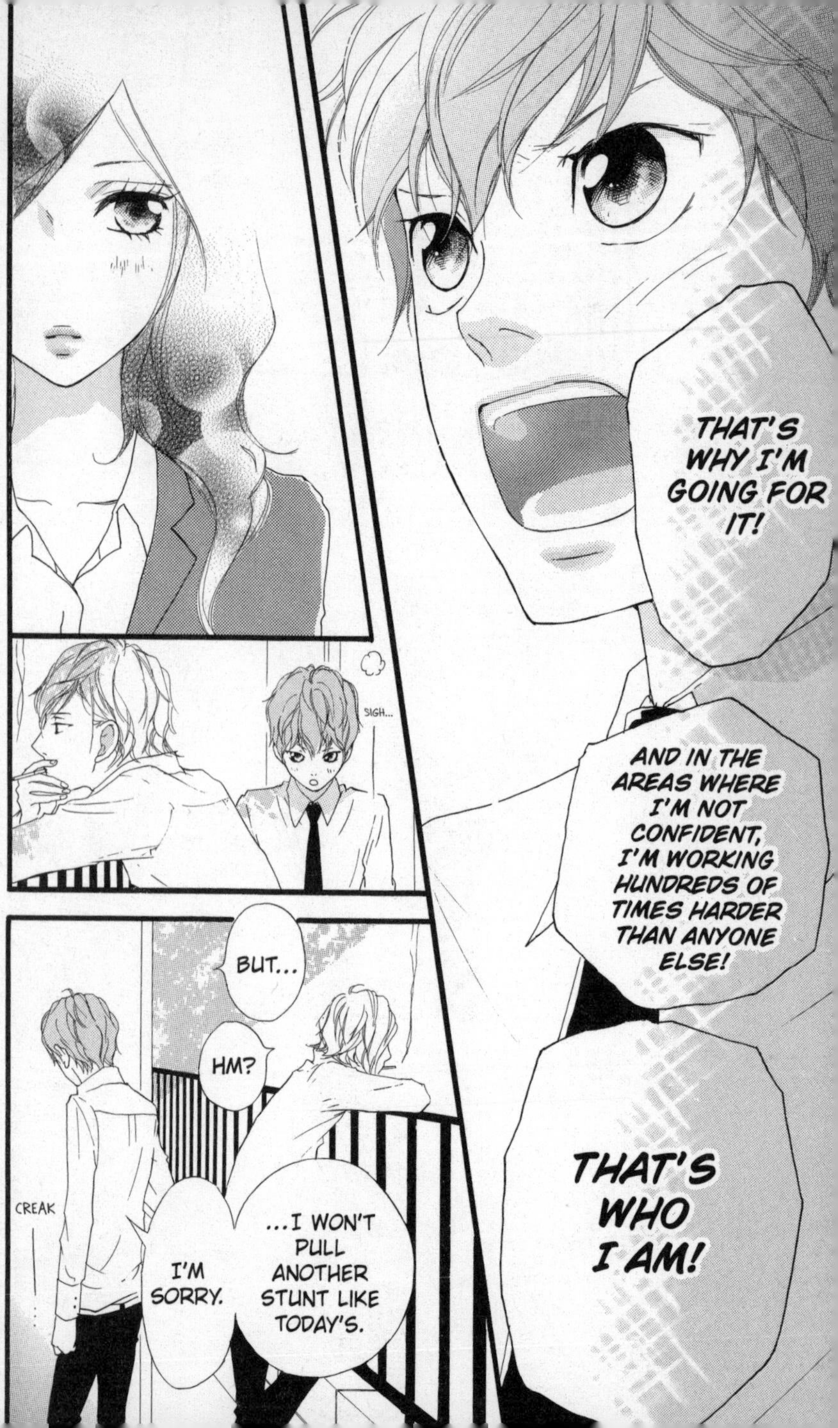
THAT'S WHY I'M GOING FOR IT!
AND IN THE AREAS WHERE I'M NOT CONFIDENT, I'M WORKING HUNDREDS OF TIMES HARDER THAN ANYONE ELSE!
THAT'S WHO I AM!
SIGH...
BUT...
HM?
...I WON'T PULL ANOTHER STUNT LIKE TODAY'S.
I'M SORRY.
CREAK

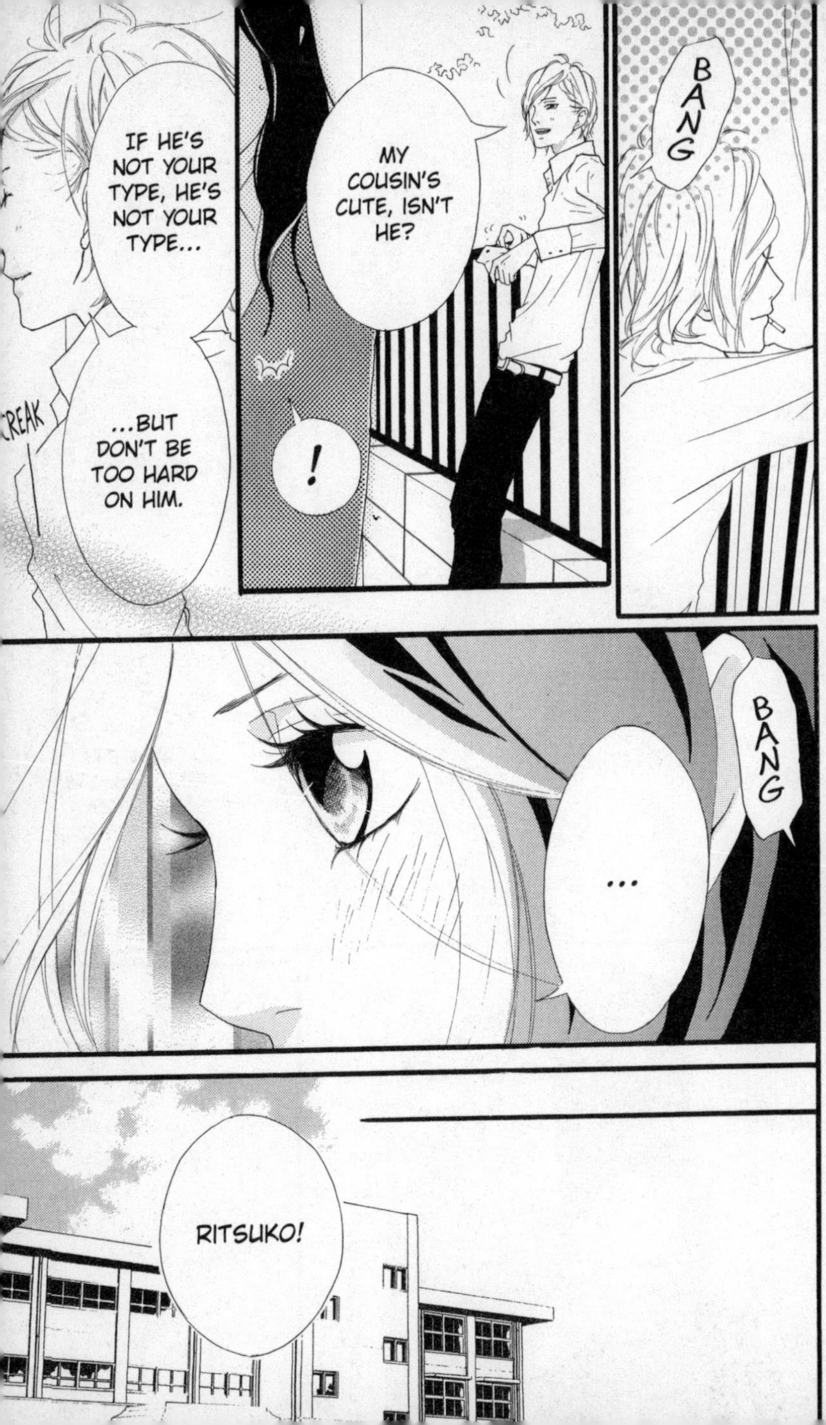
BANG
MY COUSIN'S CUTE, ISN'T HE?
!
IF HE'S NOT YOUR TYPE, HE'S NOT YOUR TYPE...
...BUT DON'T BE TOO HARD ON HIM.
CREAK
BANG
...
RITSUKO!

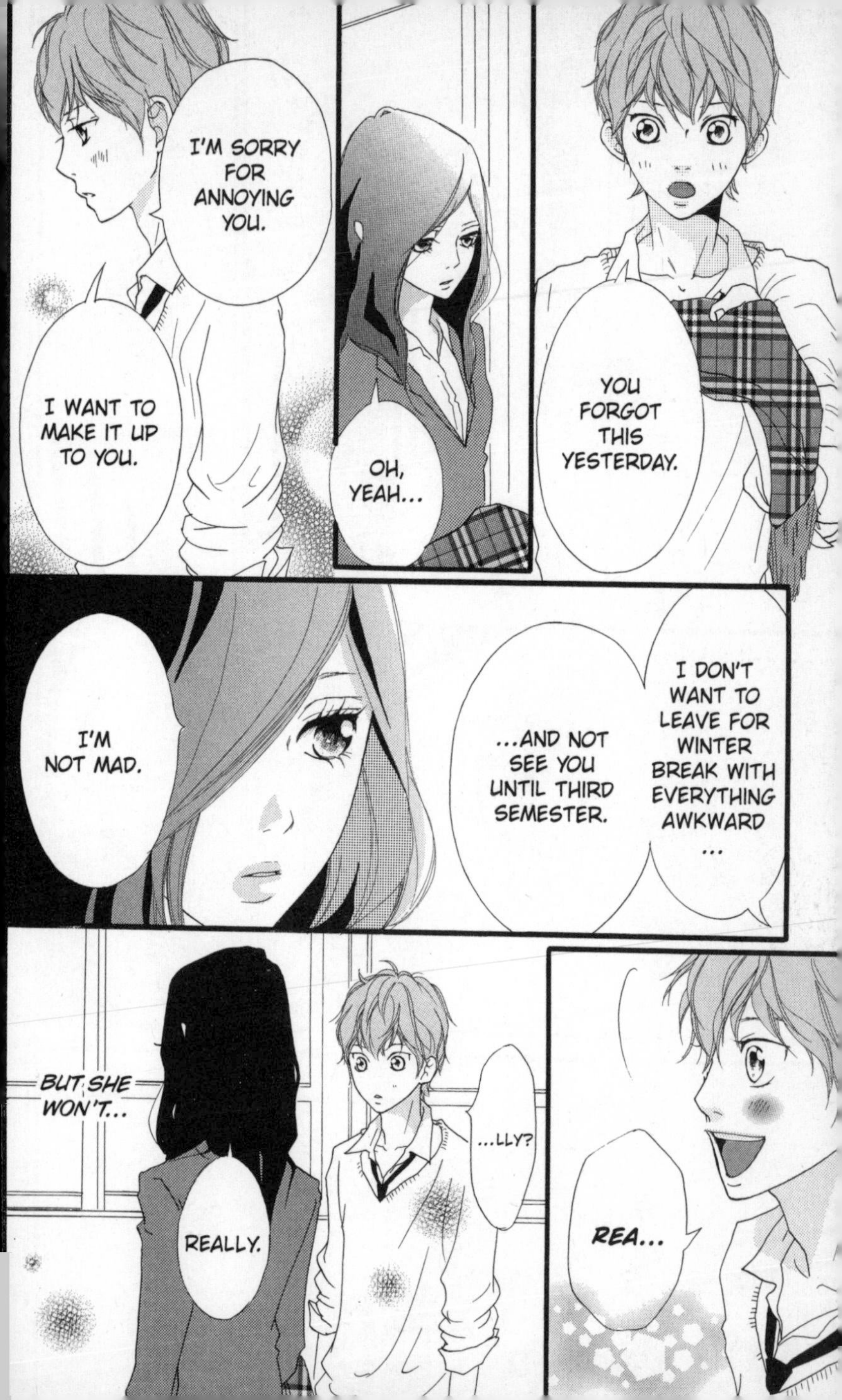
YOU FORGOT THIS YESTERDAY.
OH, YEAH...
I'M SORRY FOR ANNOYING YOU.
I WANT TO MAKE IT UP TO YOU.
I DON'T WANT TO LEAVE FOR WINTER BREAK WITH EVERYTHING AWKWARD ...
...AND NOT SEE YOU UNTIL THIRD SEMESTER.
I'M NOT MAD.
REA...
...LLY?
BUT SHE WON'T...
REALLY.

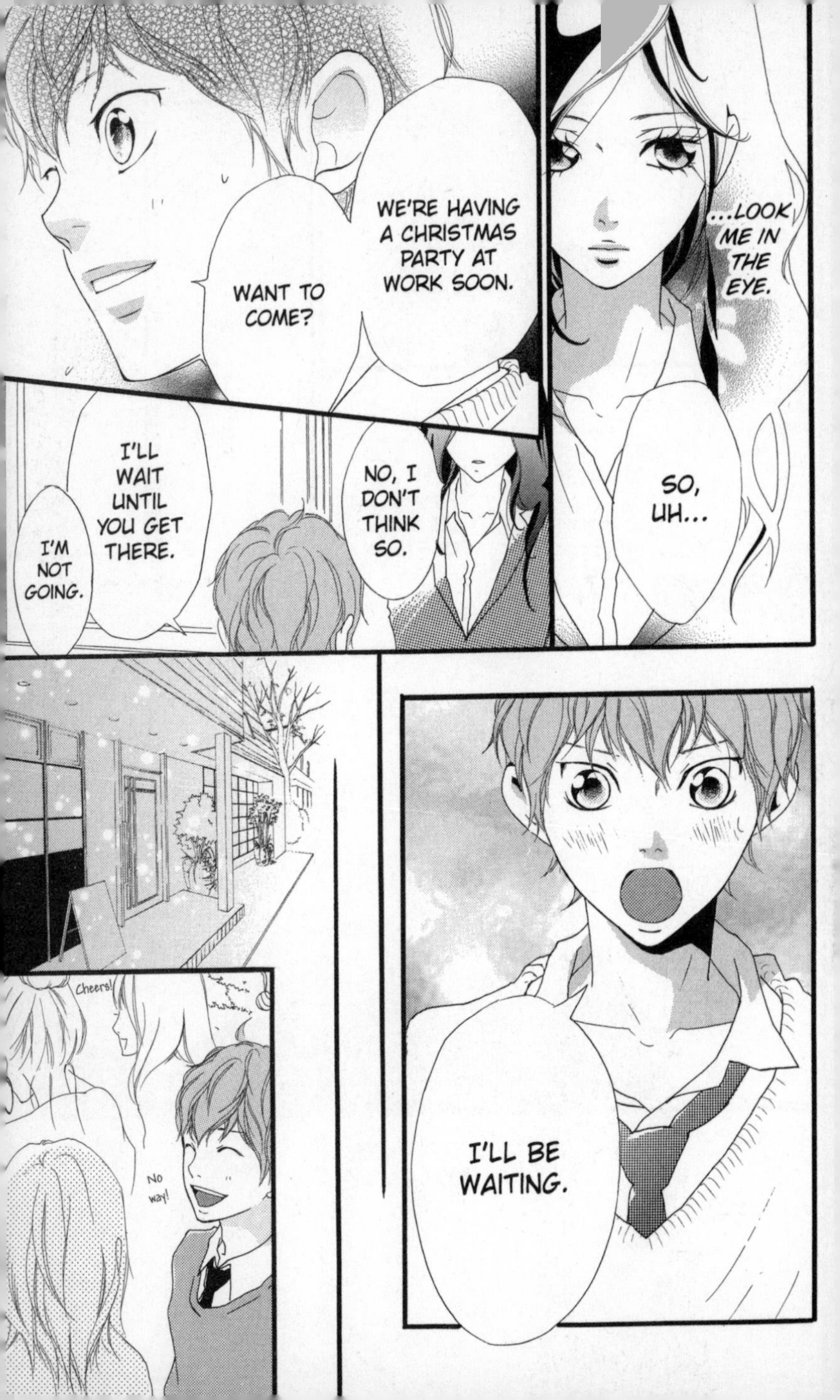
...LOOK ME IN THE EYE.
SO, UH...
WE'RE HAVING A CHRISTMAS PARTY AT WORK SOON.
WANT TO COME?
NO, I DON'T THINK SO.
I'LL WAIT UNTIL YOU GET THERE.
I'M NOT GOING.
I'LL BE WAITING.
Cheers!
No way!

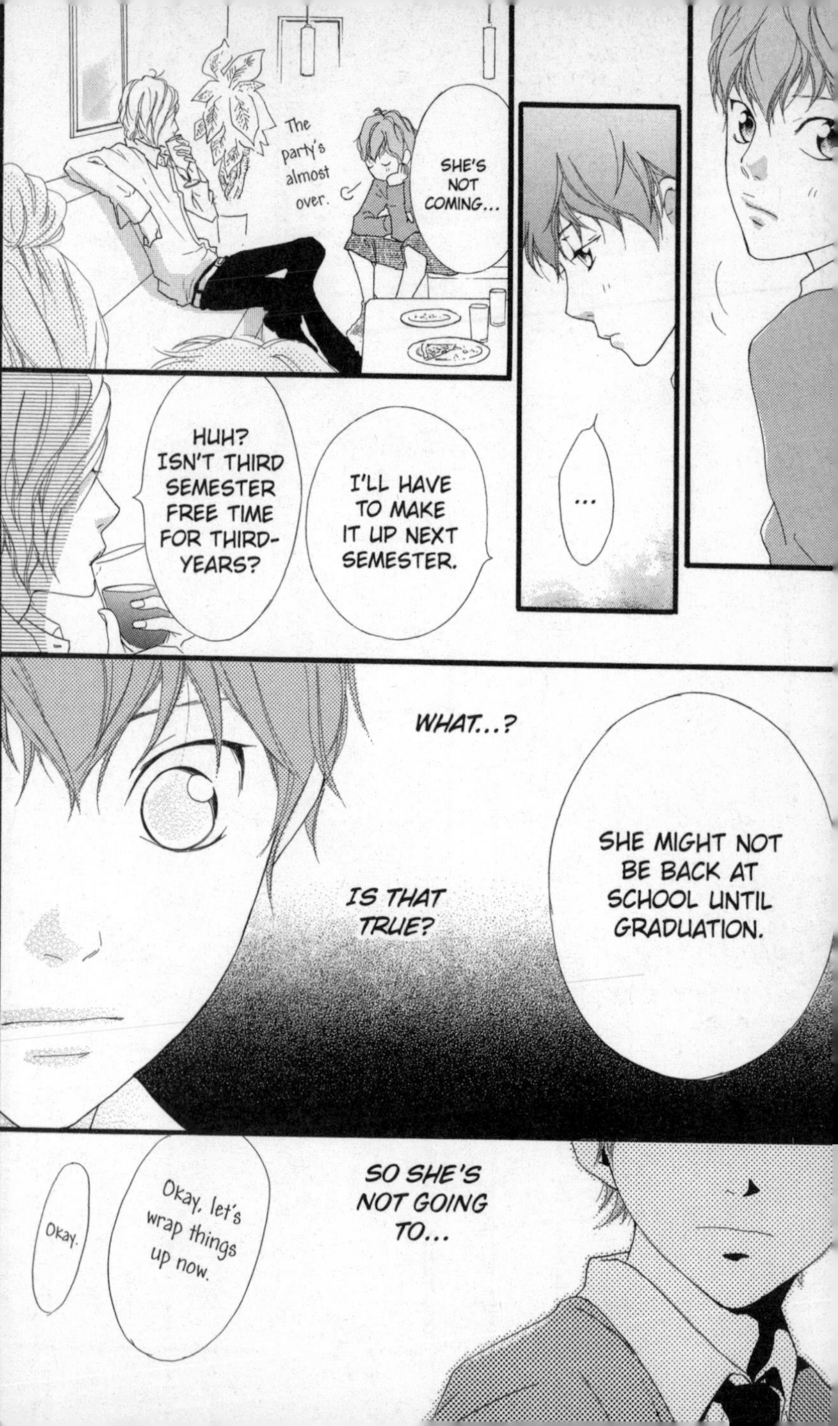
SHE'S NOT COMING...
The party's almost over.
I'LL HAVE TO MAKE IT UP NEXT SEMESTER.
HUH? ISN'T THIRD SEMESTER FREE TIME FOR THIRD-YEARS?
...
SHE MIGHT NOT BE BACK AT SCHOOL UNTIL GRADUATION.
WHAT...?
IS THAT TRUE?
SO SHE'S NOT GOING TO...
Okay, let's wrap things up now.
Okay.

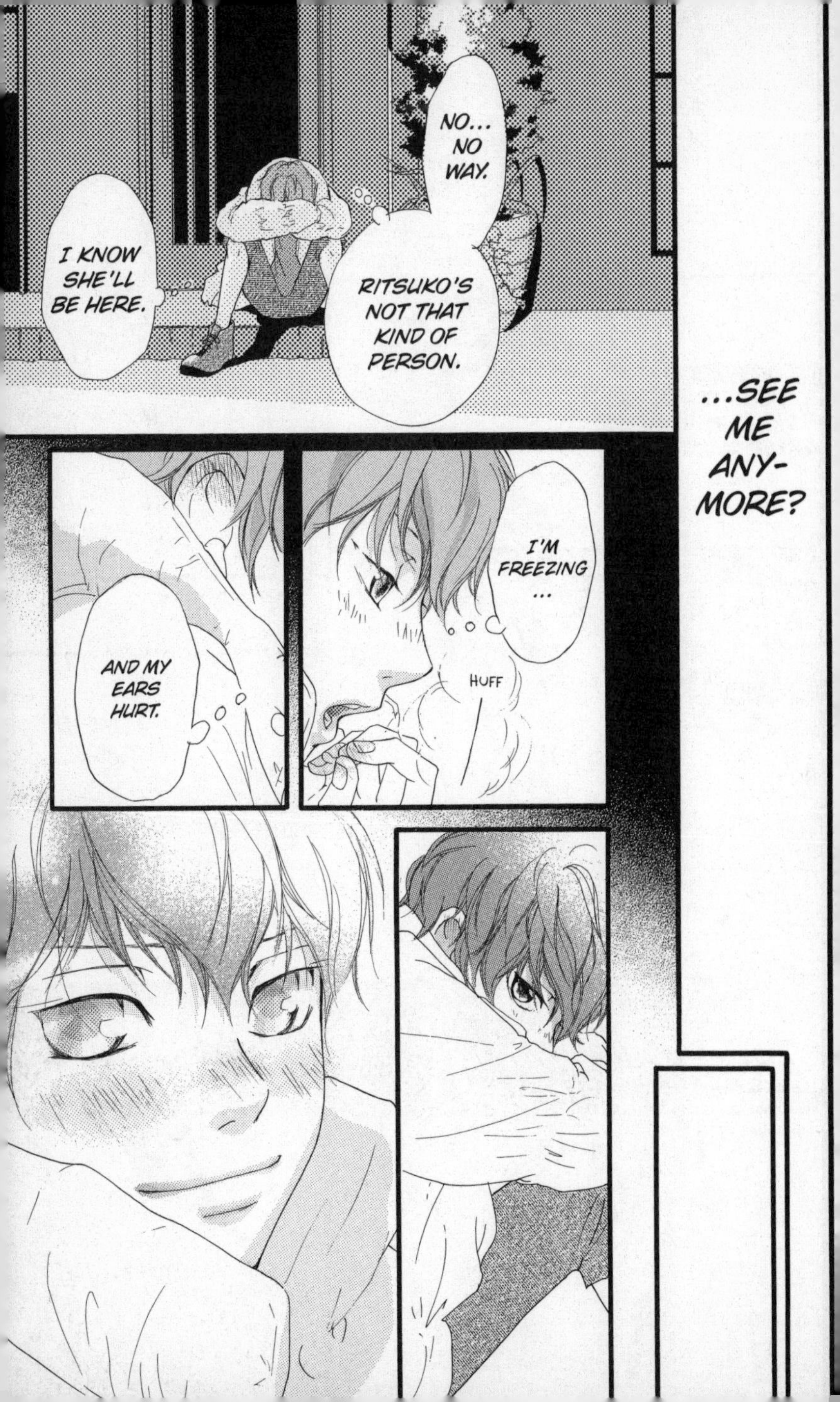
...SEE ME ANY-MORE?
NO... NO WAY.
RITSUKO'S NOT THAT KIND OF PERSON.
I KNOW SHE'LL BE HERE.
I'M FREEZING ...
HUFF
AND MY EARS HURT.

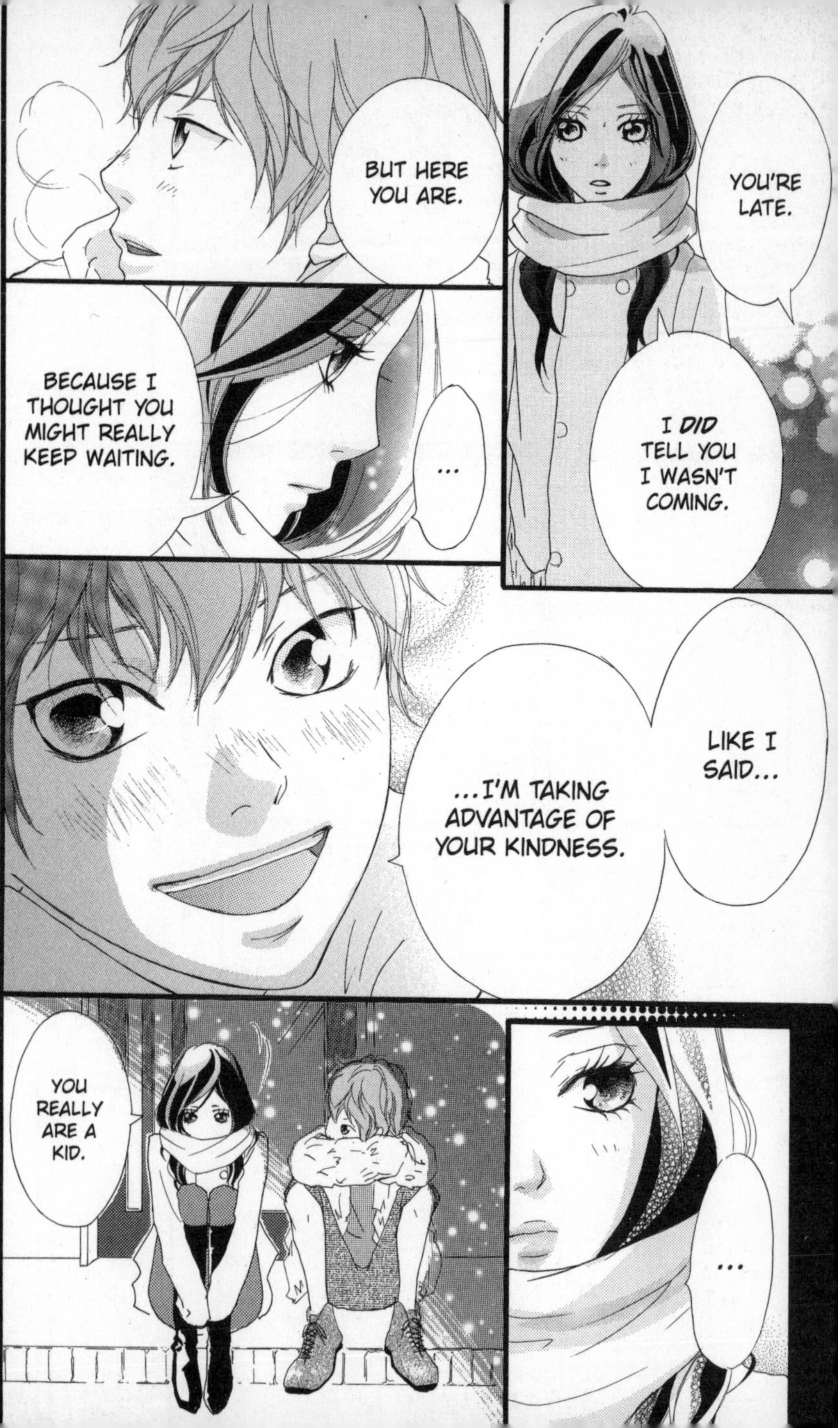
YOU'RE LATE.
I *DID* TELL YOU I WASN'T COMING.
BUT HERE YOU ARE.
...
BECAUSE I THOUGHT YOU MIGHT REALLY KEEP WAITING.
LIKE I SAID...
...I'M TAKING ADVANTAGE OF YOUR KINDNESS.
...
YOU REALLY ARE A KID.

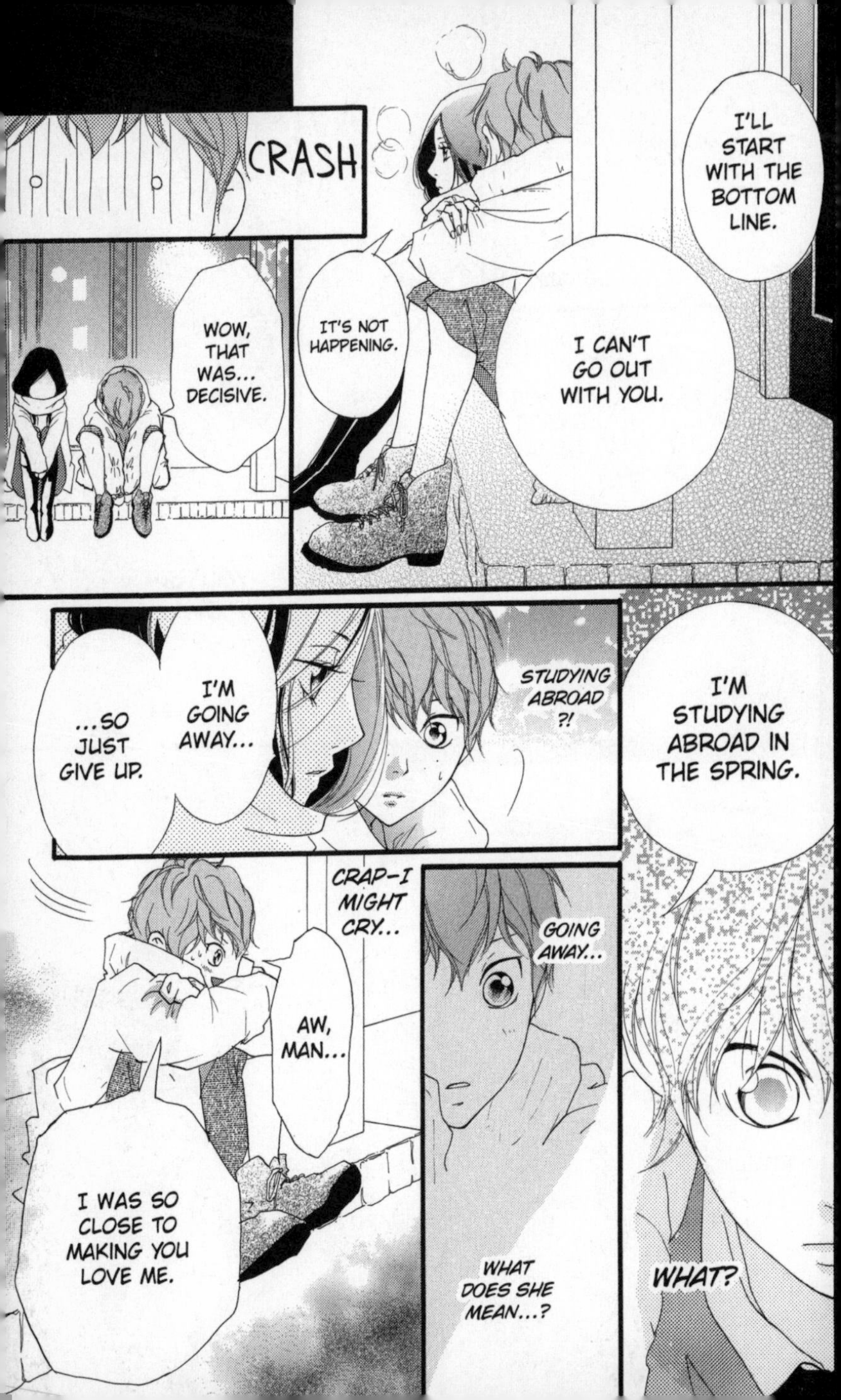
I'LL START WITH THE BOTTOM LINE.
I CAN'T GO OUT WITH YOU.
IT'S NOT HAPPENING.
CRASH
WOW, THAT WAS... DECISIVE.
I'M STUDYING ABROAD IN THE SPRING.
WHAT?
STUDYING ABROAD ?!
I'M GOING AWAY...
...SO JUST GIVE UP.
GOING AWAY...
WHAT DOES SHE MEAN...?
CRAP—I MIGHT CRY...
AW, MAN...
I WAS SO CLOSE TO MAKING YOU LOVE ME.

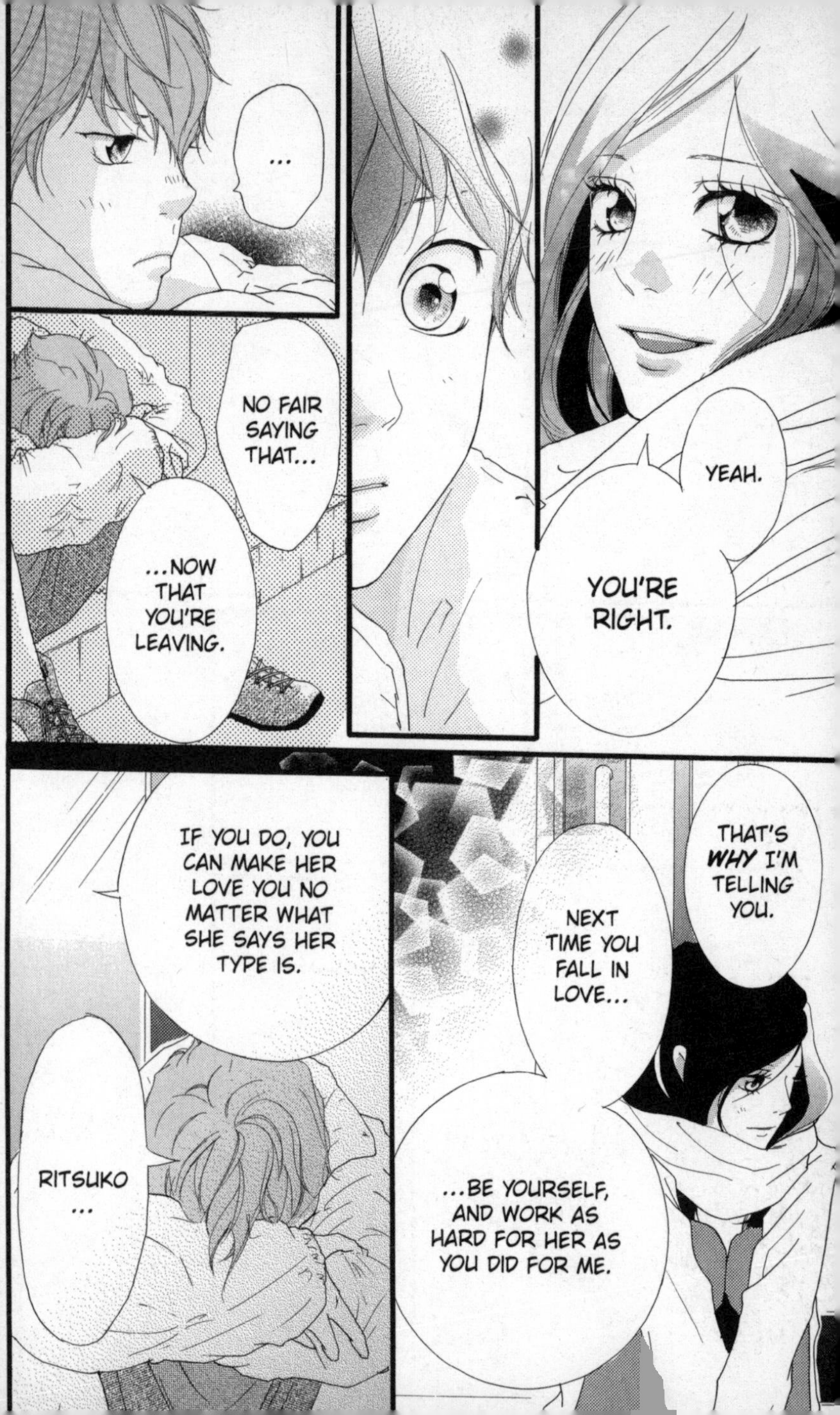
YEAH.
YOU'RE RIGHT.
...
NO FAIR SAYING THAT...
...NOW THAT YOU'RE LEAVING.
THAT'S *WHY* I'M TELLING YOU.
NEXT TIME YOU FALL IN LOVE...
...BE YOURSELF, AND WORK AS HARD FOR HER AS YOU DID FOR ME.
IF YOU DO, YOU CAN MAKE HER LOVE YOU NO MATTER WHAT SHE SAYS HER TYPE IS.
RITSUKO...

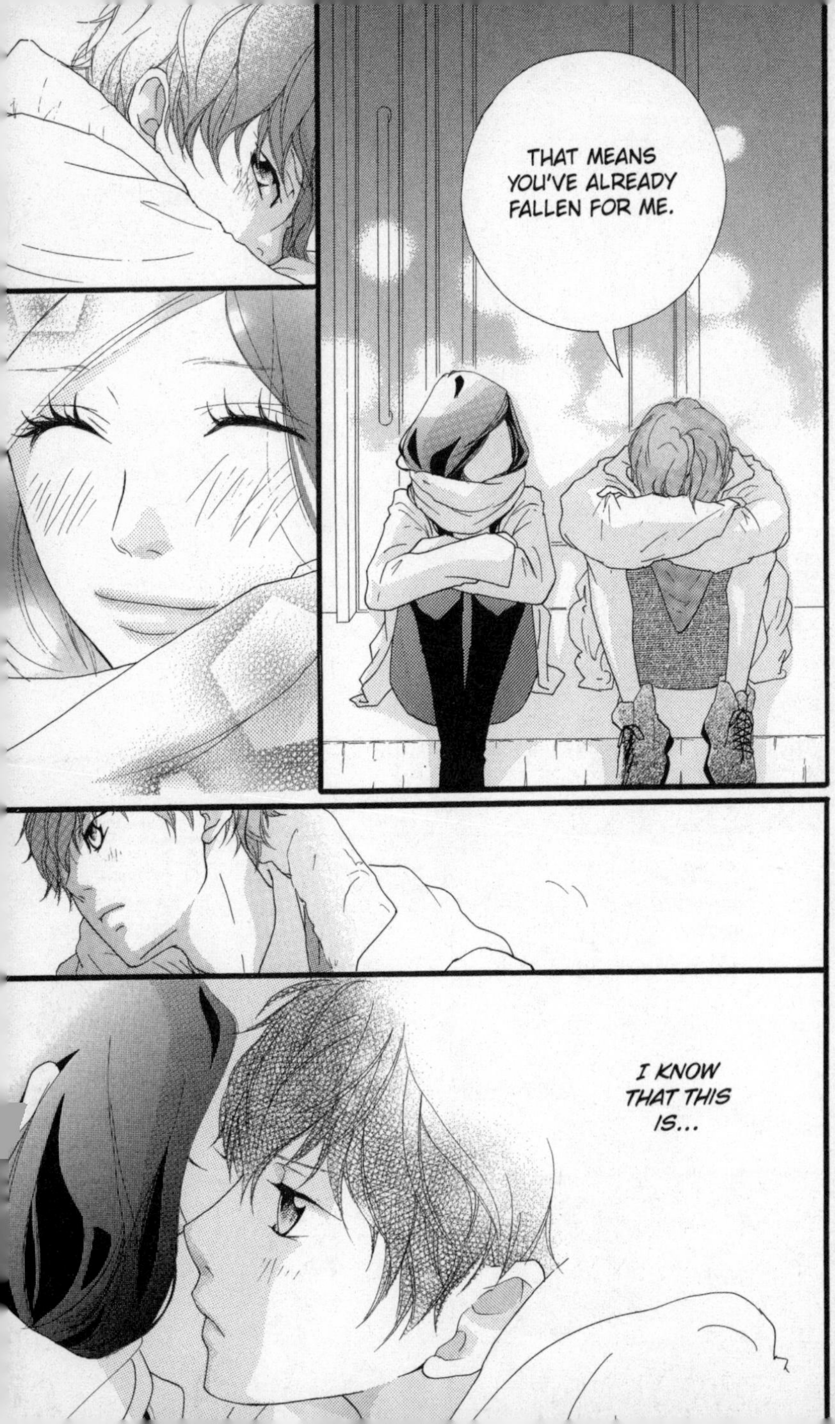
THAT MEANS YOU'VE ALREADY FALLEN FOR ME.
I KNOW THAT THIS IS...

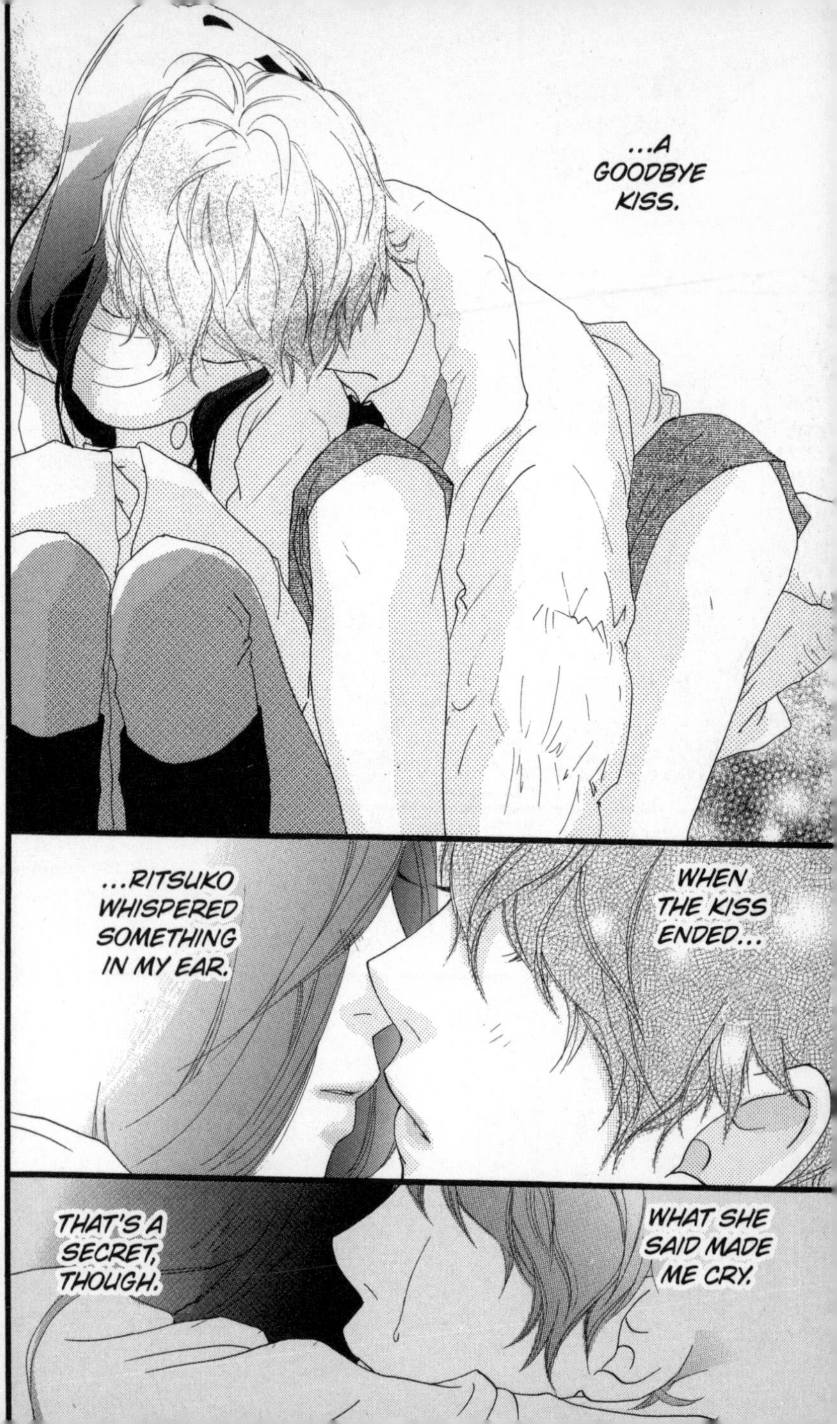
...A GOODBYE KISS.
WHEN THE KISS ENDED...
...RITSUKO WHISPERED SOMETHING IN MY EAR.
WHAT SHE SAID MADE ME CRY.
THAT'S A SECRET, THOUGH.

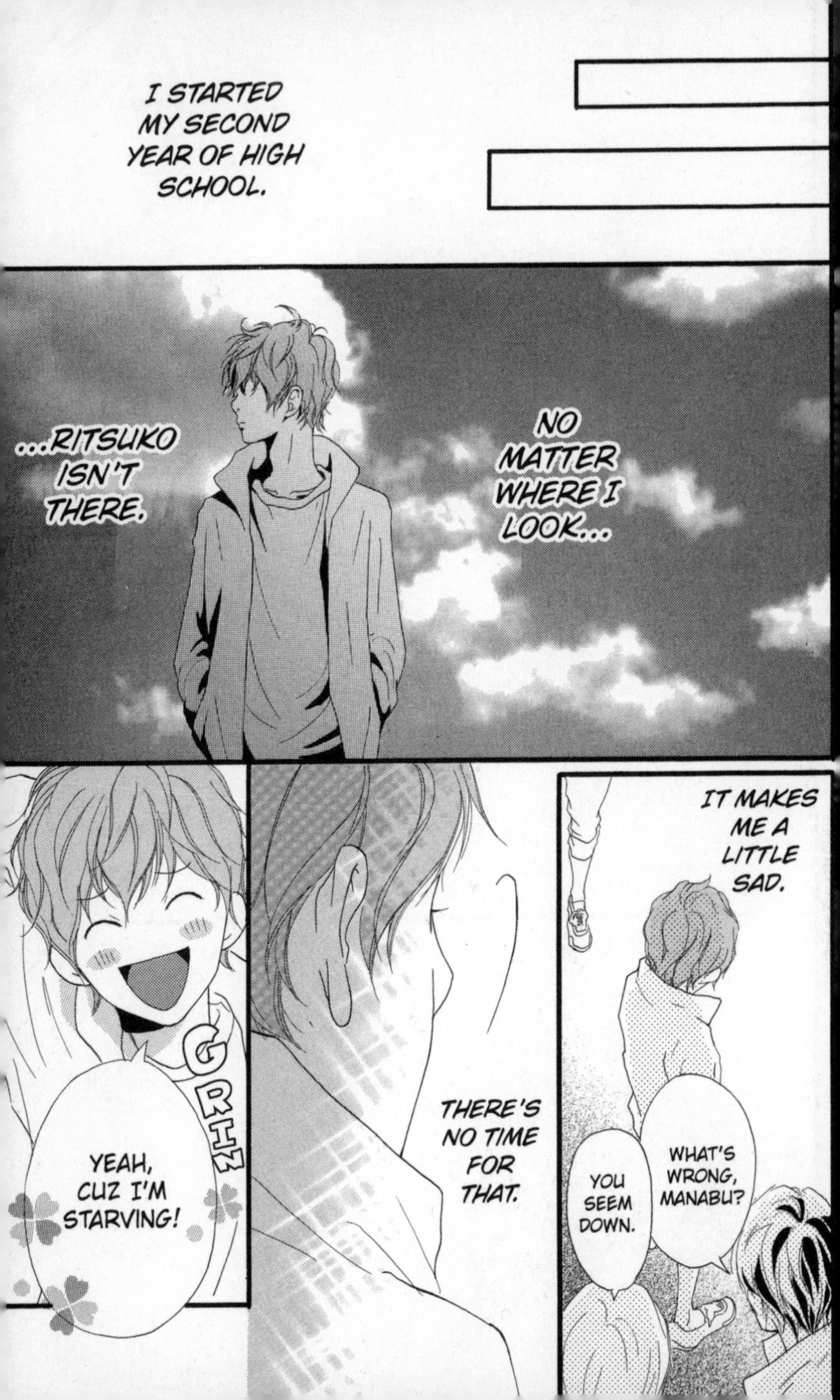
I STARTED MY SECOND YEAR OF HIGH SCHOOL.
NO MATTER WHERE I LOOK...
...RITSUKO ISN'T THERE.
IT MAKES ME A LITTLE SAD.
WHAT'S WRONG, MANABU?
YOU SEEM DOWN.
THERE'S NO TIME FOR THAT.
GRIN
YEAH, CUZ I'M STARVING!

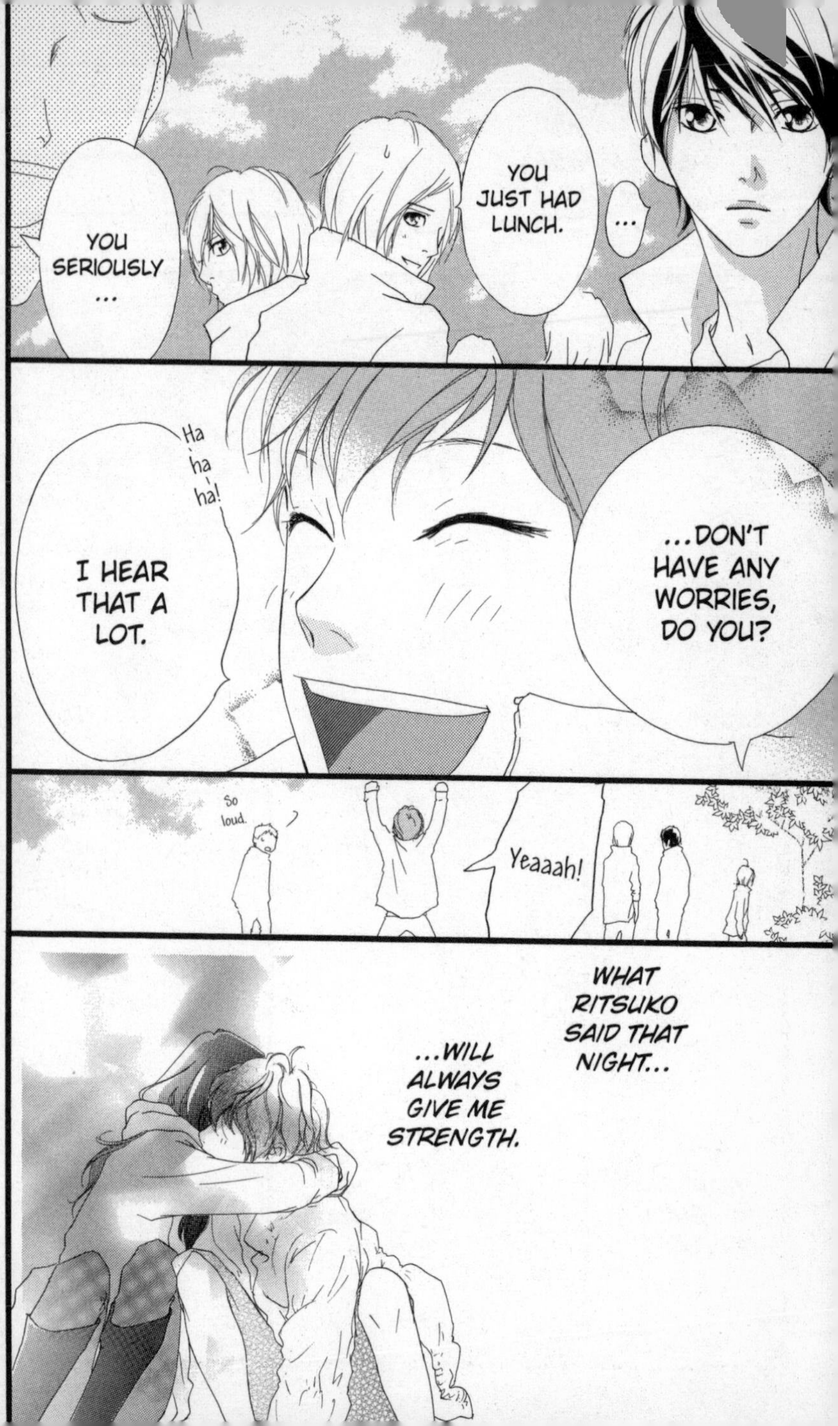
...
YOU JUST HAD LUNCH.
YOU SERIOUSLY ...
...DON'T HAVE ANY WORRIES, DO YOU?
Ha ha ha!
I HEAR THAT A LOT.
Yeaaah!
So loud.
WHAT RITSUKO SAID THAT NIGHT...
...WILL ALWAYS GIVE ME STRENGTH.

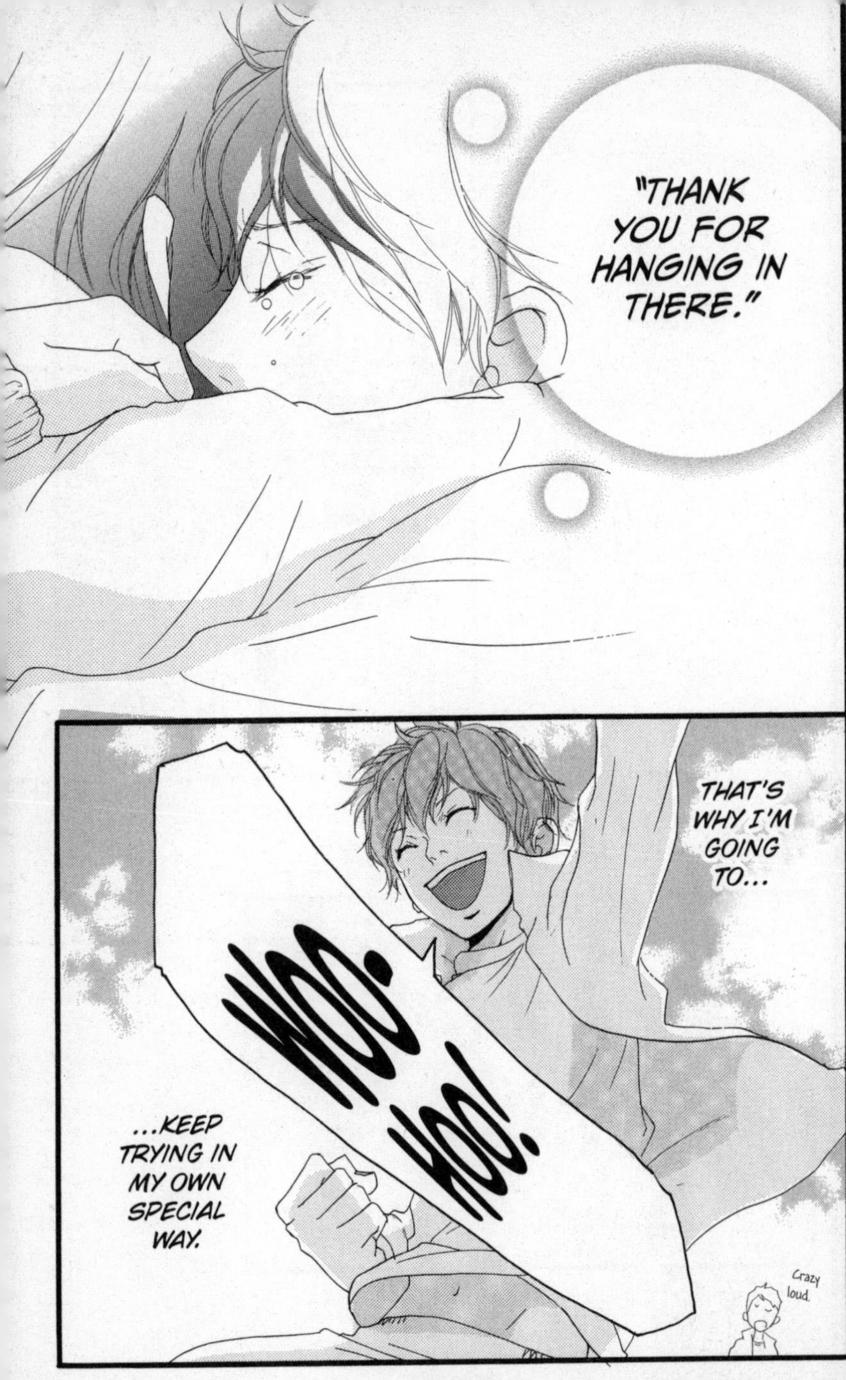
"THANK YOU FOR HANGING IN THERE."
THAT'S WHY I'M GOING TO...
WOO! HOO!
...KEEP TRYING IN MY OWN SPECIAL WAY.
Crazy loud.

THE END

I hope the two of them can be happy together someday.

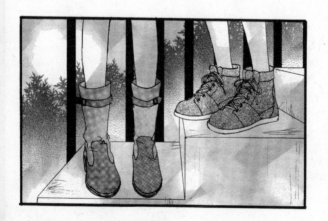

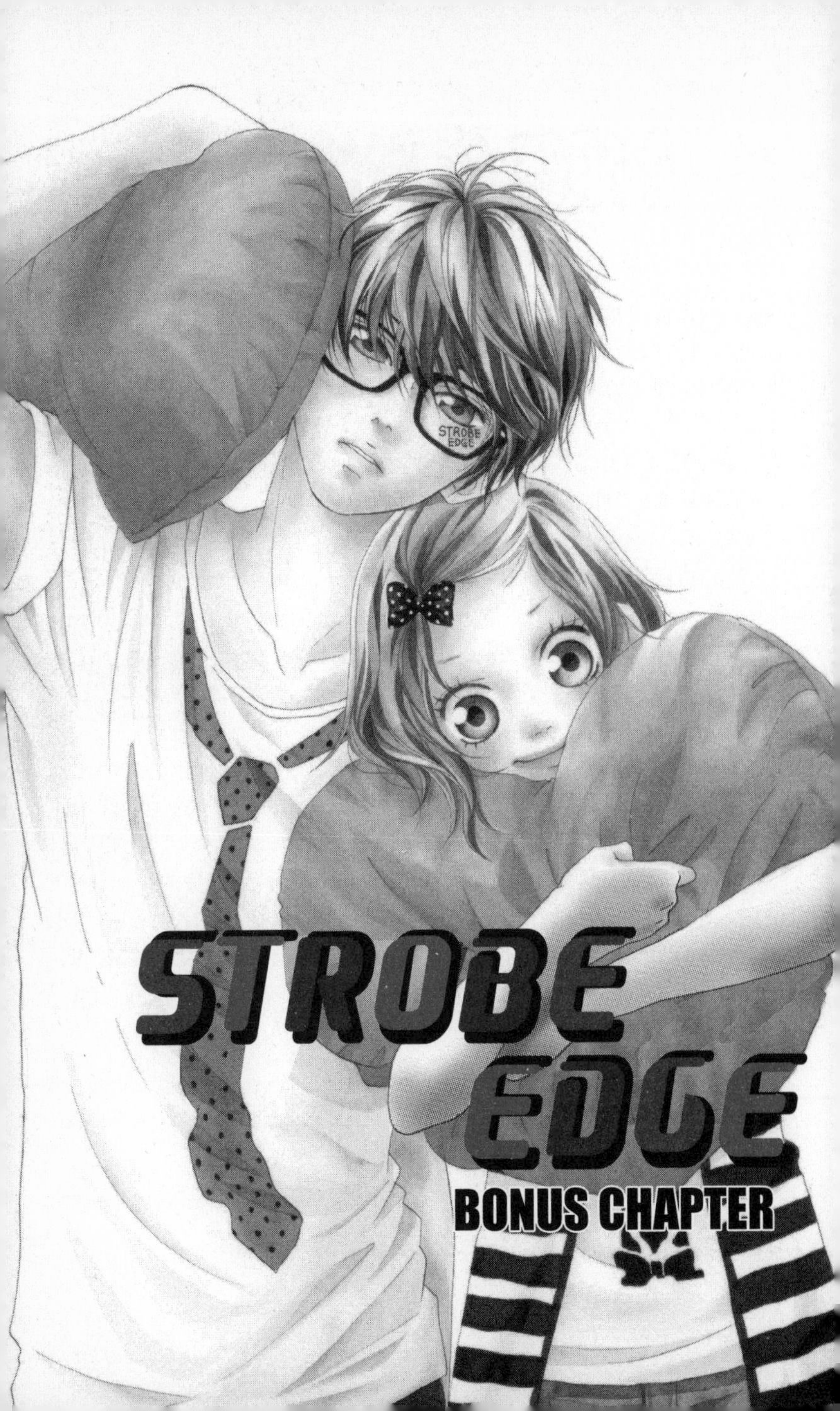
STROBE EDGE
STROBE EDGE
BONUS CHAPTER

A PAGE OF APOLOGY

I'M SORRY.

I need to apologize to everyone about something! I'm sure some of you out there have already noticed, but Ando's profile in *Strobe Edge* volume 8 says his first love was when he was ten years old. But, um...

ANDO'S FIRST LOVE WAS ACTUALLY IN HIS SECOND YEAR OF JUNIOR HIGH!!!

I'm sorry, I'm sorry, I'm sorry! I am really sorry!!! A reader wrote and asked, "Which is it? ☺," and that's the first time I noticed. In that instant, you could hear all the blood leaving my body! Whoosh...! What have I done?

I even wrote a bonus story for Ando, and yet I blithely wrote "ten years old"! I am truly sorry! It was a huge mistake. I'd like you all to get a red pen right now, and write in "Junior High Year 2" or "13" in his profile. (Is 13 the right age if it's before your birthday?) I am so disappointed in myself for this sloppy work. I'm sure mistakes like this will pop up if you look for them, so please don't look. (Run away!) If you do notice, then just smirk and say, "Oh, here's another one." I'll be super careful going forward! Sorry!

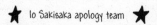 ★ Io Sakisaka apology team ★

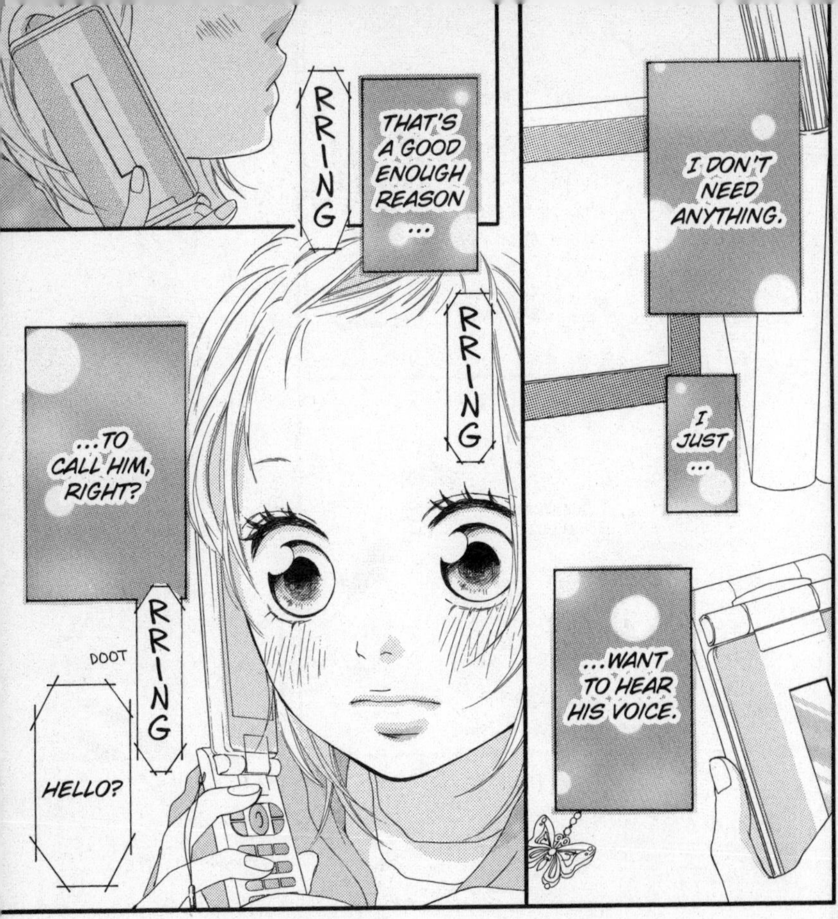
I DON'T NEED ANYTHING.
I JUST ...
...WANT TO HEAR HIS VOICE.
THAT'S A GOOD ENOUGH REASON ...
RRING
...TO CALL HIM, RIGHT?
RRING
RRING
DOOT
HELLO?

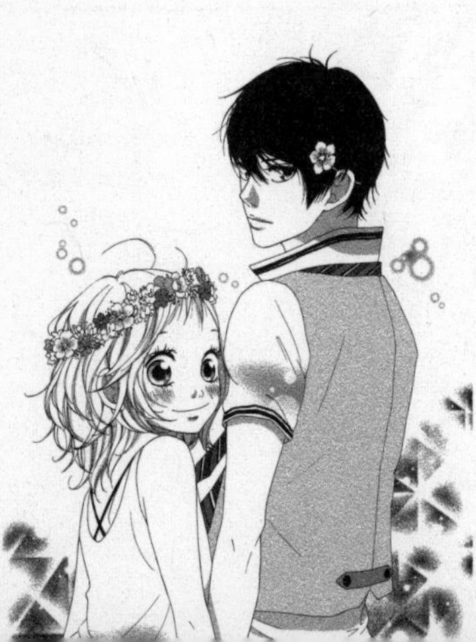

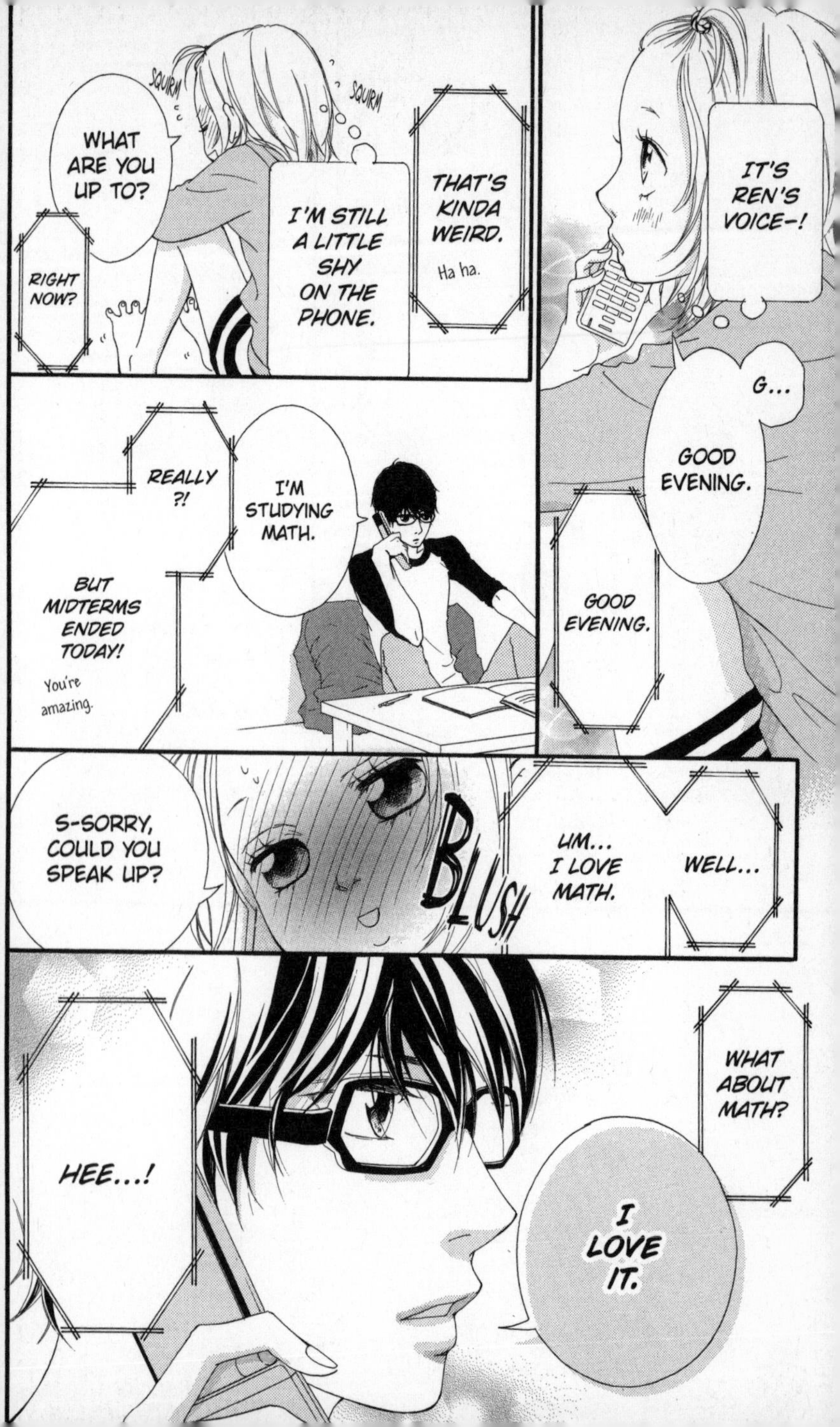
IT'S REN'S VOICE-!
G...
GOOD EVENING.
GOOD EVENING.
THAT'S KINDA WEIRD.
Ha ha.
I'M STILL A LITTLE SHY ON THE PHONE.
SQUIRM
SQUIRM
WHAT ARE YOU UP TO?
RIGHT NOW?
I'M STUDYING MATH.
REALLY?!
BUT MIDTERMS ENDED TODAY!
You're amazing.
WELL...
UM... I LOVE MATH.
BLUSH
S-SORRY, COULD YOU SPEAK UP?
WHAT ABOUT MATH?
I LOVE IT.
HEE...!

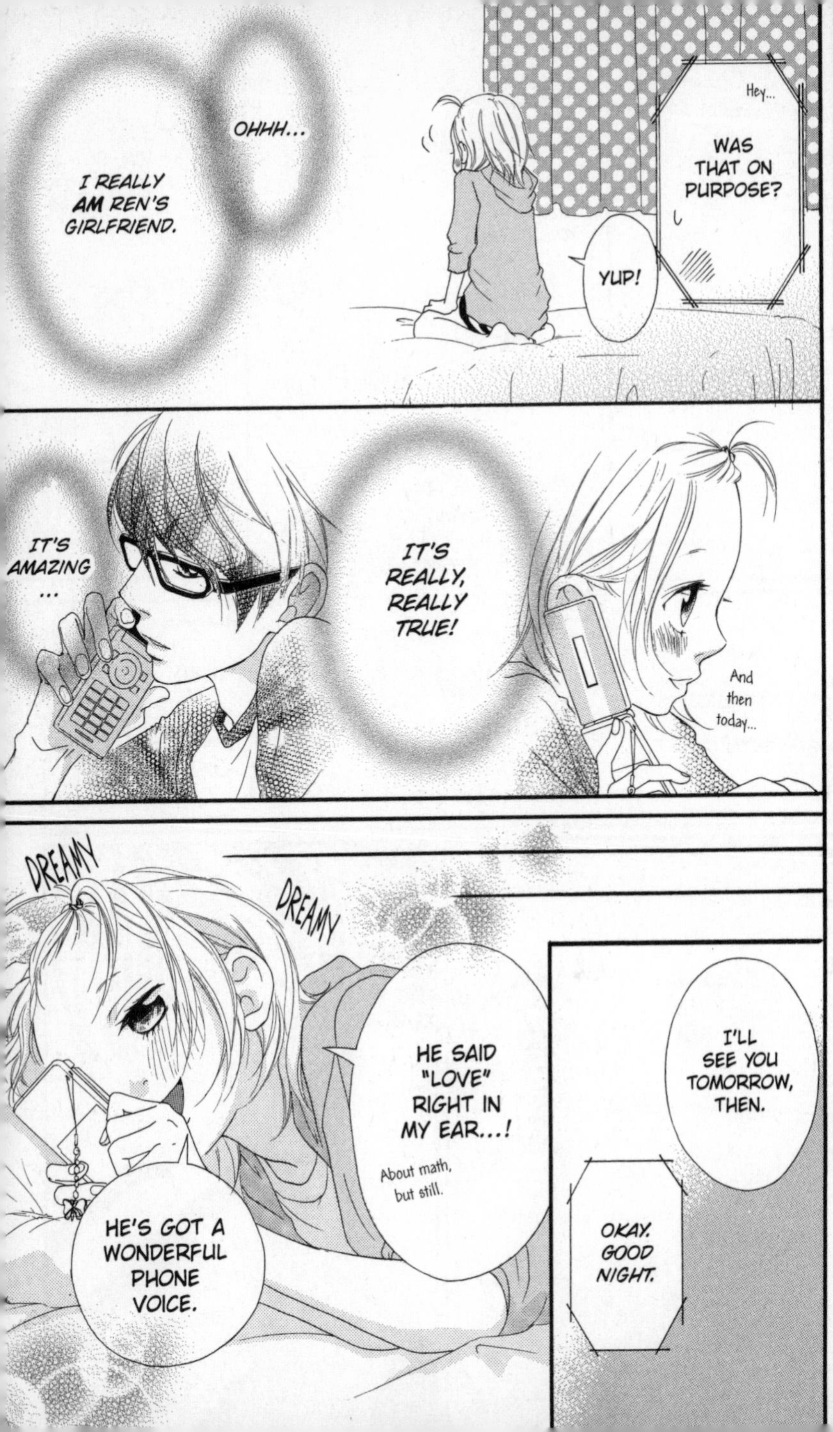
Hey... WAS THAT ON PURPOSE?
YUP!
OHHH...
I REALLY AM REN'S GIRLFRIEND.
And then today...
IT'S REALLY, REALLY TRUE!
IT'S AMAZING ...
I'LL SEE YOU TOMORROW, THEN.
OKAY. GOOD NIGHT.
DREAMY
DREAMY
HE SAID "LOVE" RIGHT IN MY EAR...!
About math, but still.
HE'S GOT A WONDERFUL PHONE VOICE.

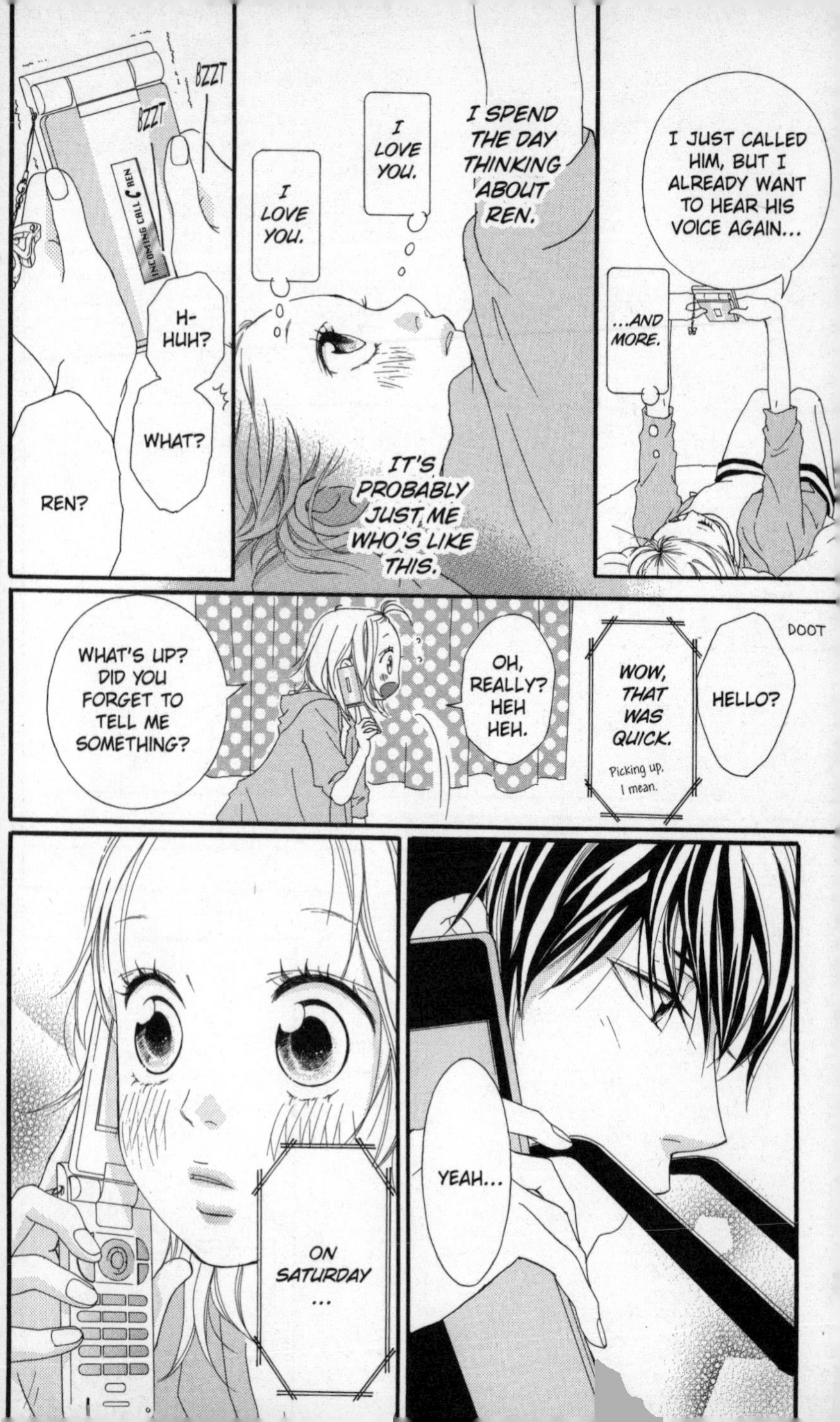
I JUST CALLED HIM, BUT I ALREADY WANT TO HEAR HIS VOICE AGAIN...
...AND MORE.
I SPEND THE DAY THINKING ABOUT REN.
I LOVE YOU.
I LOVE YOU.
IT'S PROBABLY JUST ME WHO'S LIKE THIS.
BZZT
BZZT
INCOMING CALL REN
H-HUH?
WHAT?
REN?
DOOT
HELLO?
WOW, THAT WAS QUICK.
Picking up, I mean.
OH, REALLY? HEH HEH.
WHAT'S UP? DID YOU FORGET TO TELL ME SOMETHING?
YEAH...
ON SATURDAY ...

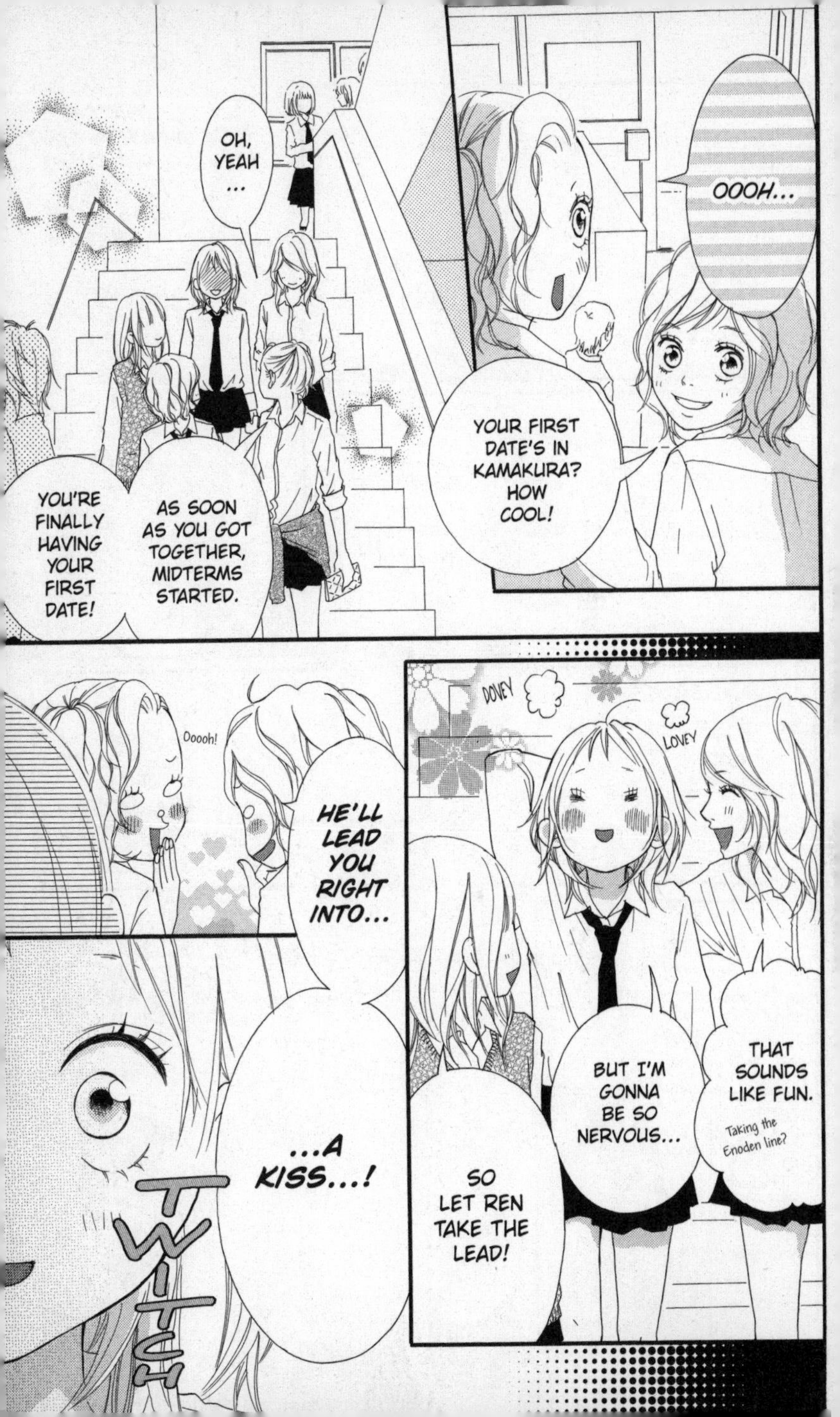
OOOH...
YOUR FIRST DATE'S IN KAMAKURA? HOW COOL!
OH, YEAH...
AS SOON AS YOU GOT TOGETHER, MIDTERMS STARTED.
YOU'RE FINALLY HAVING YOUR FIRST DATE!
DOVEY
LOVEY
THAT SOUNDS LIKE FUN.
Taking the Enoden line?
BUT I'M GONNA BE SO NERVOUS...
SO LET REN TAKE THE LEAD!
Ooooh!
HE'LL LEAD YOU RIGHT INTO...
...A KISS...!
TWITCH

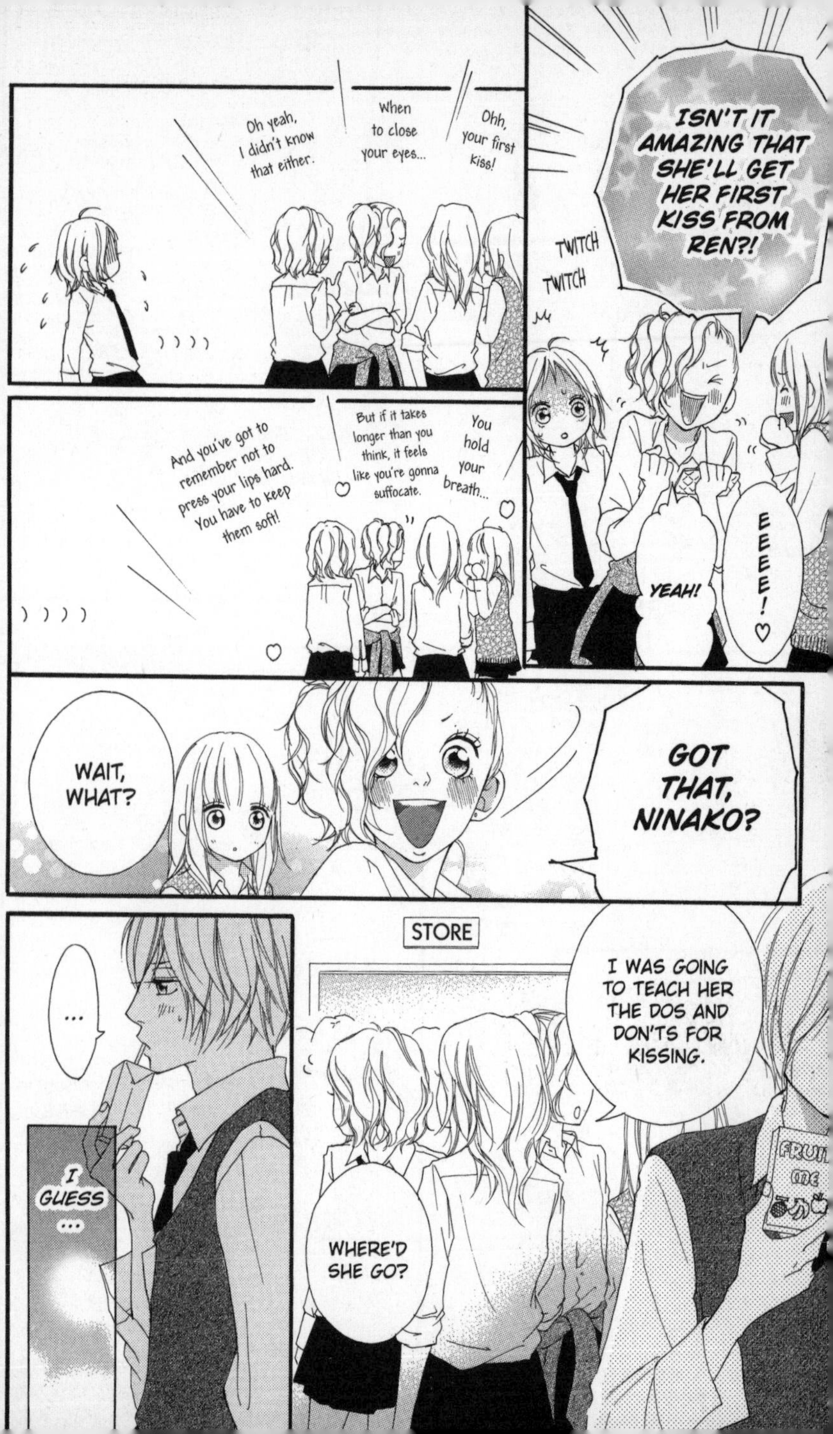

ISN'T IT AMAZING THAT SHE'LL GET HER FIRST KISS FROM REN?!
TWITCH
TWITCH
YEAH!
EEEE! ♡
Ohh, your first kiss!
When to close your eyes...
Oh yeah, I didn't know that either.
You hold your breath...
But if it takes longer than you think, it feels like you're gonna suffocate.
And you've got to remember not to press your lips hard. You have to keep them soft!
GOT THAT, NINAKO?
WAIT, WHAT?
STORE
I WAS GOING TO TEACH HER THE DOS AND DON'TS FOR KISSING.
WHERE'D SHE GO?
FRUIT ONE
...
I GUESS...

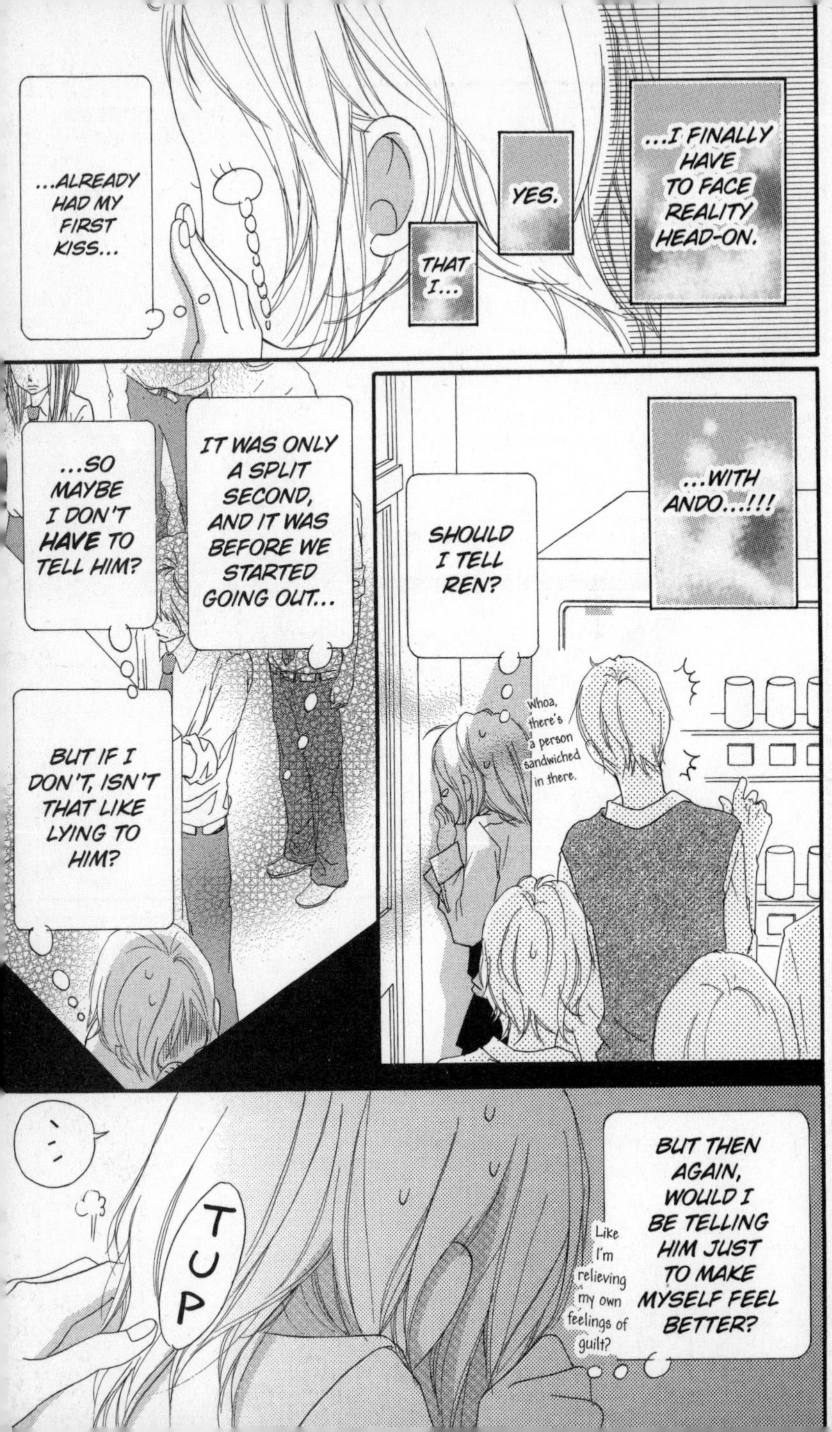
...I FINALLY HAVE TO FACE REALITY HEAD-ON.
YES.
THAT I...
...ALREADY HAD MY FIRST KISS...
...WITH ANDO...!!!
SHOULD I TELL REN?
Whoa, there's a person sandwiched in there.
IT WAS ONLY A SPLIT SECOND, AND IT WAS BEFORE WE STARTED GOING OUT...
...SO MAYBE I DON'T HAVE TO TELL HIM?
BUT IF I DON'T, ISN'T THAT LIKE LYING TO HIM?
BUT THEN AGAIN, WOULD I BE TELLING HIM JUST TO MAKE MYSELF FEEL BETTER?
Like I'm relieving my own feelings of guilt?
TUP
...

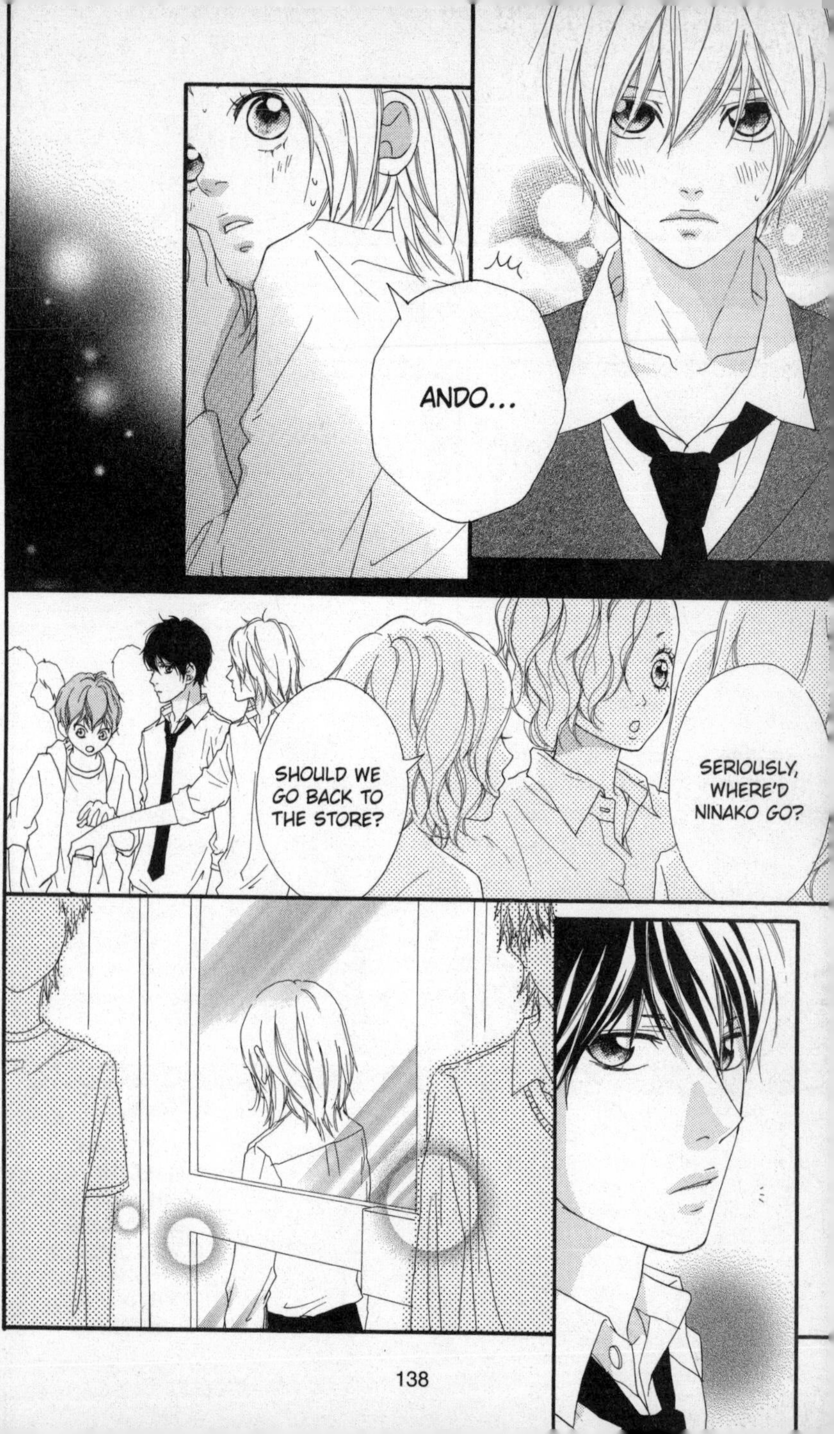
ANDO...
SERIOUSLY, WHERE'D NINAKO GO?
SHOULD WE GO BACK TO THE STORE?

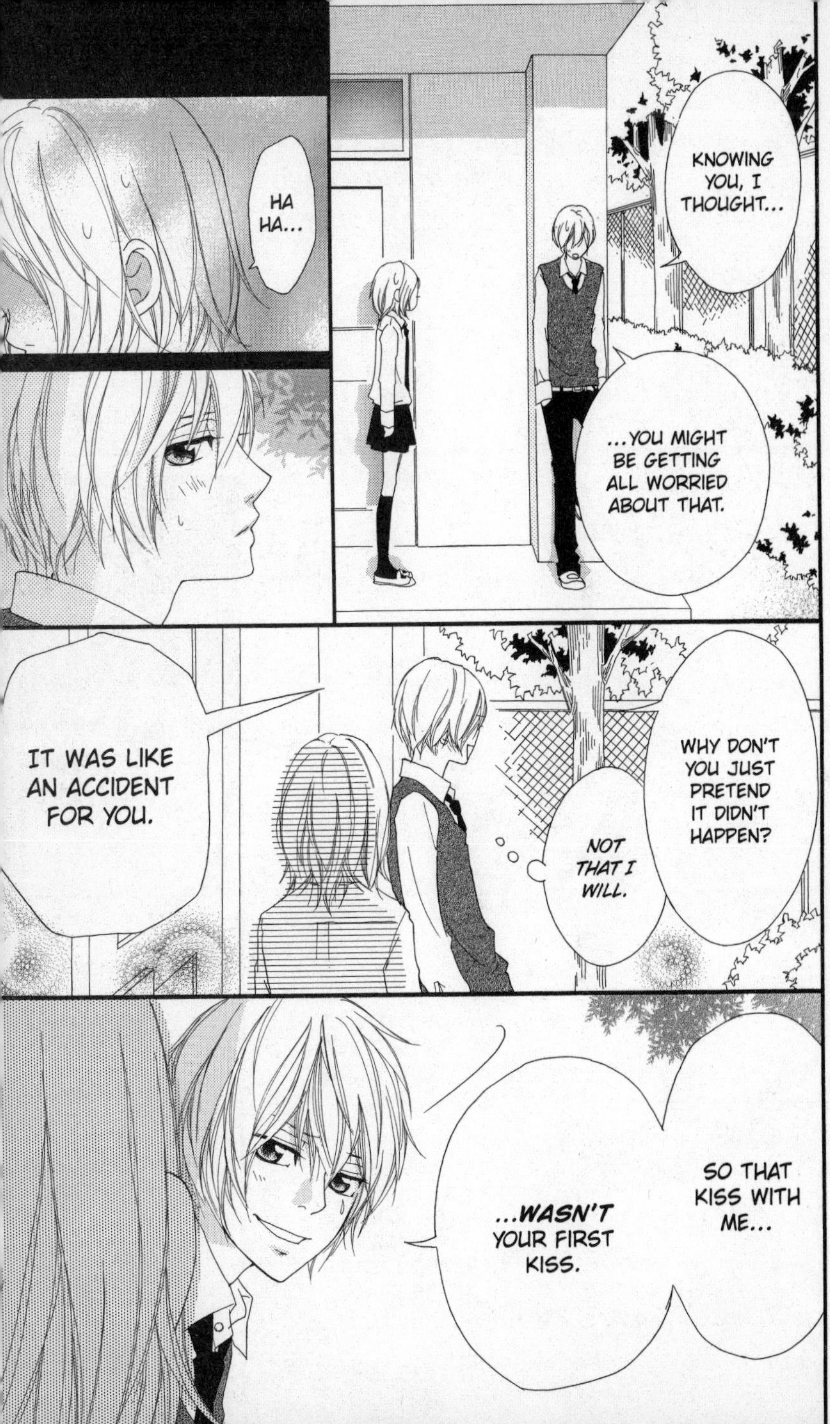
KNOWING YOU, I THOUGHT...
...YOU MIGHT BE GETTING ALL WORRIED ABOUT THAT.
HA HA...
WHY DON'T YOU JUST PRETEND IT DIDN'T HAPPEN?
NOT THAT I WILL.
IT WAS LIKE AN ACCIDENT FOR YOU.
SO THAT KISS WITH ME...
...***WASN'T*** YOUR FIRST KISS.

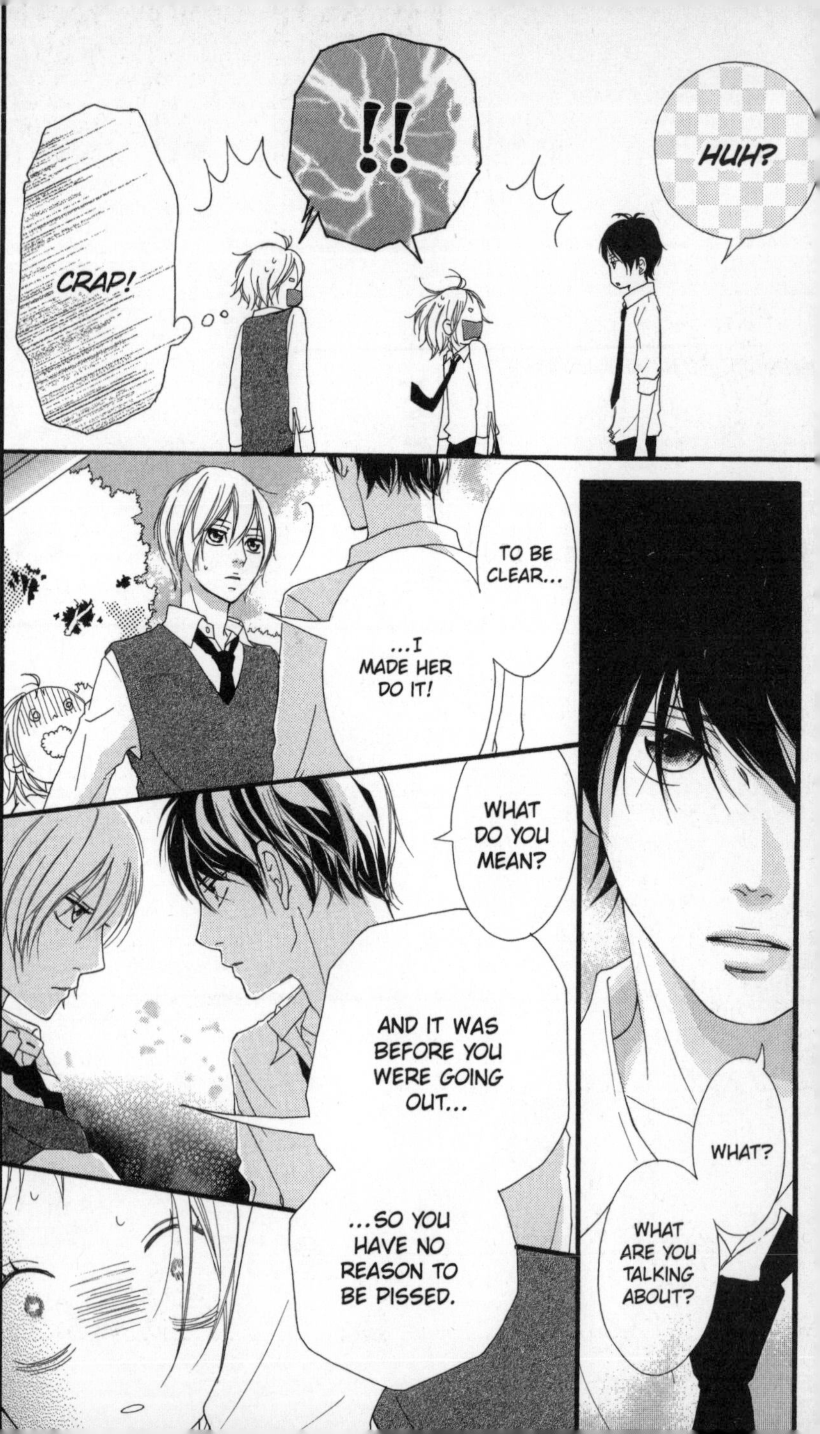
HUH?
!!
CRAP!
WHAT?
WHAT ARE YOU TALKING ABOUT?
TO BE CLEAR...
...I MADE HER DO IT!
WHAT DO YOU MEAN?
AND IT WAS BEFORE YOU WERE GOING OUT...
...SO YOU HAVE NO REASON TO BE PISSED.

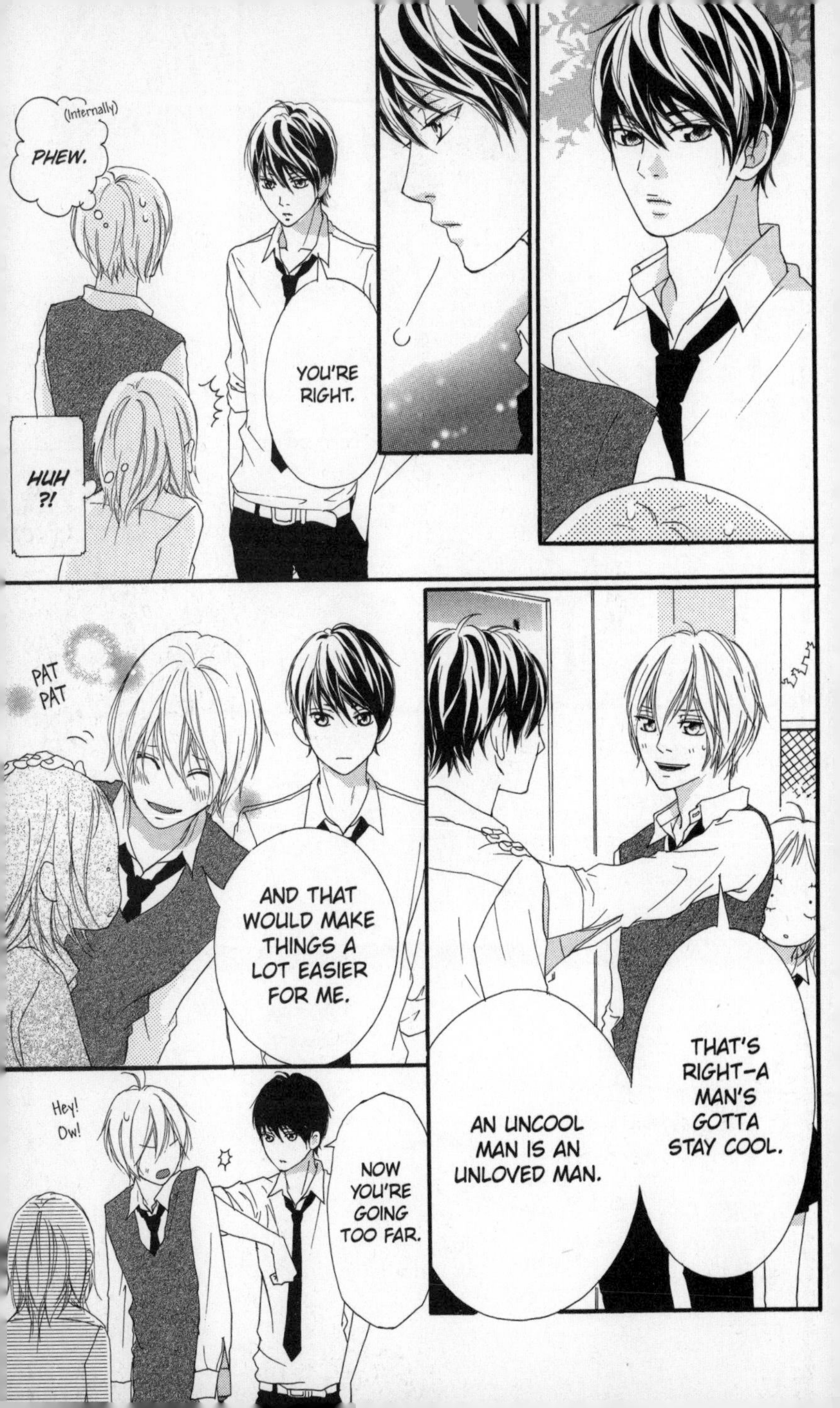
(Internally)
PHEW.
YOU'RE RIGHT.
HUH?!
THAT'S RIGHT—A MAN'S GOTTA STAY COOL.
AN UNCOOL MAN IS AN UNLOVED MAN.
PAT PAT
AND THAT WOULD MAKE THINGS A LOT EASIER FOR ME.
NOW YOU'RE GOING TOO FAR.
Hey! Ow!

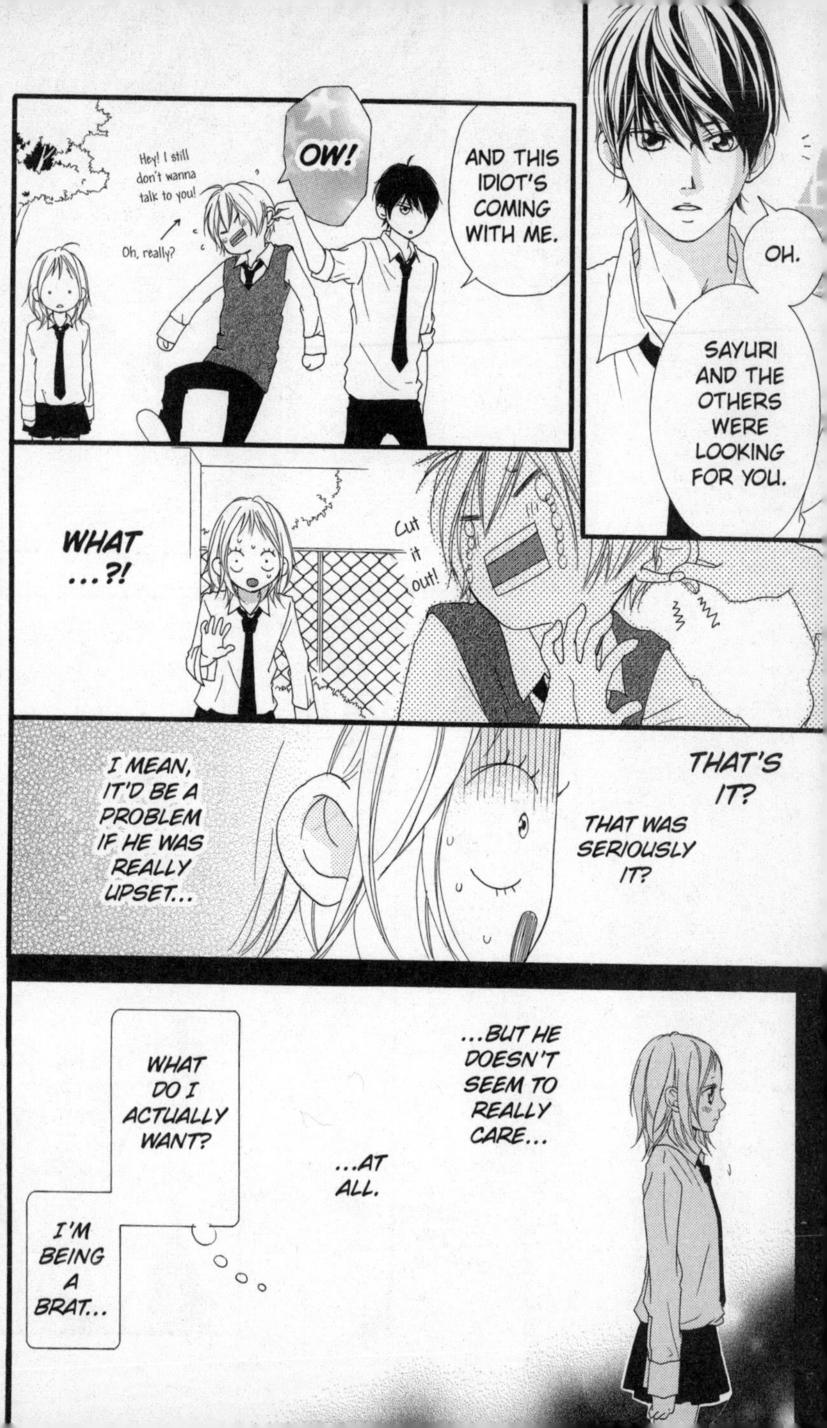
OH.
SAYURI AND THE OTHERS WERE LOOKING FOR YOU.
AND THIS IDIOT'S COMING WITH ME.
OW!
Hey! I still don't wanna talk to you!
Oh, really?
Cut it out!
WHAT ...?!
THAT'S IT?
THAT WAS SERIOUSLY IT?
I MEAN, IT'D BE A PROBLEM IF HE WAS REALLY UPSET...
...BUT HE DOESN'T SEEM TO REALLY CARE...
...AT ALL.
WHAT DO I ACTUALLY WANT?
I'M BEING A BRAT...

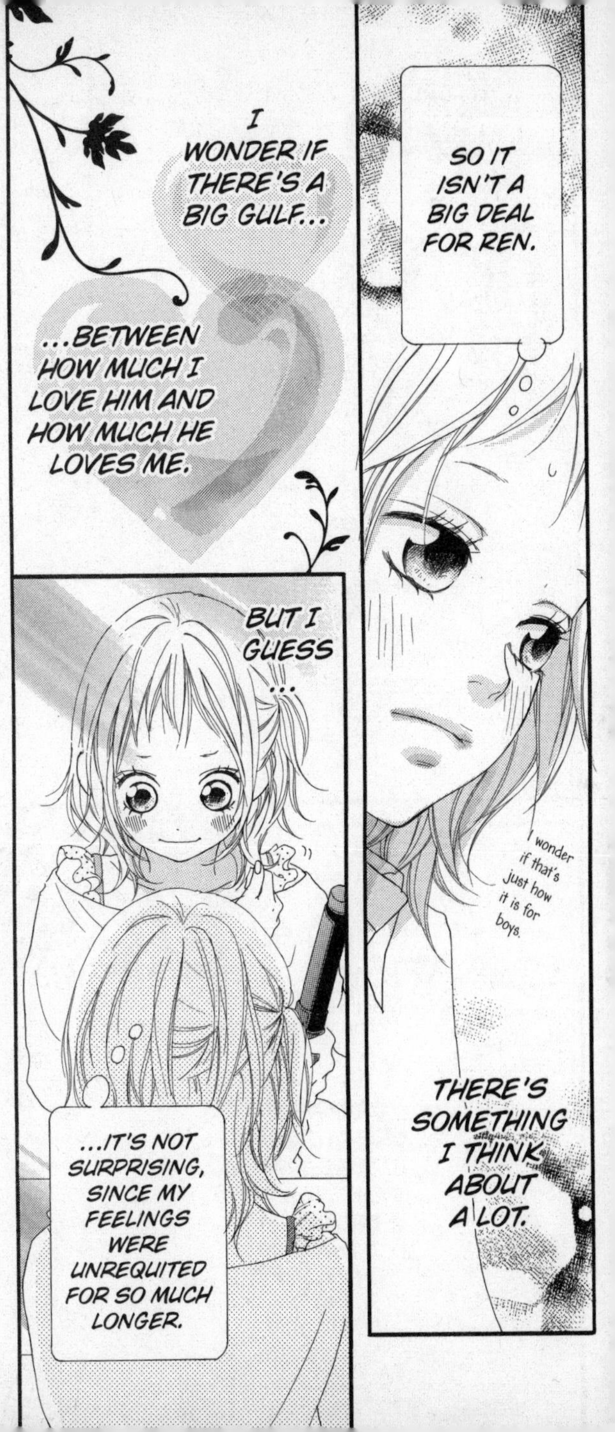
SO IT ISN'T A BIG DEAL FOR REN.
I wonder if that's just how it is for boys.
THERE'S SOMETHING I THINK ABOUT A LOT.
I WONDER IF THERE'S A BIG GULF...
...BETWEEN HOW MUCH I LOVE HIM AND HOW MUCH HE LOVES ME.
BUT I GUESS...
...IT'S NOT SURPRISING, SINCE MY FEELINGS WERE UNREQUITED FOR SO MUCH LONGER.

The people who helped me with the manuscript this time! ♡

Hanemi Ayase
Runchi Koyama
Emi Fujino
Natsumi Kaizaki
Chidan Mizuguchi

Thank you very, very much! I had a great time working on the copy with you. I hope we'll be able to work together again soon, and I thank you for all your hard work!!!

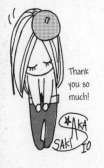

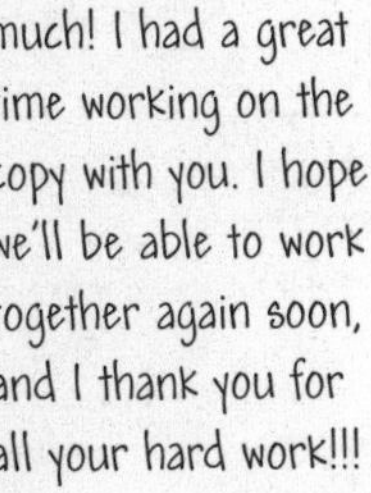
Thank you so much!
SAKISAKA IO

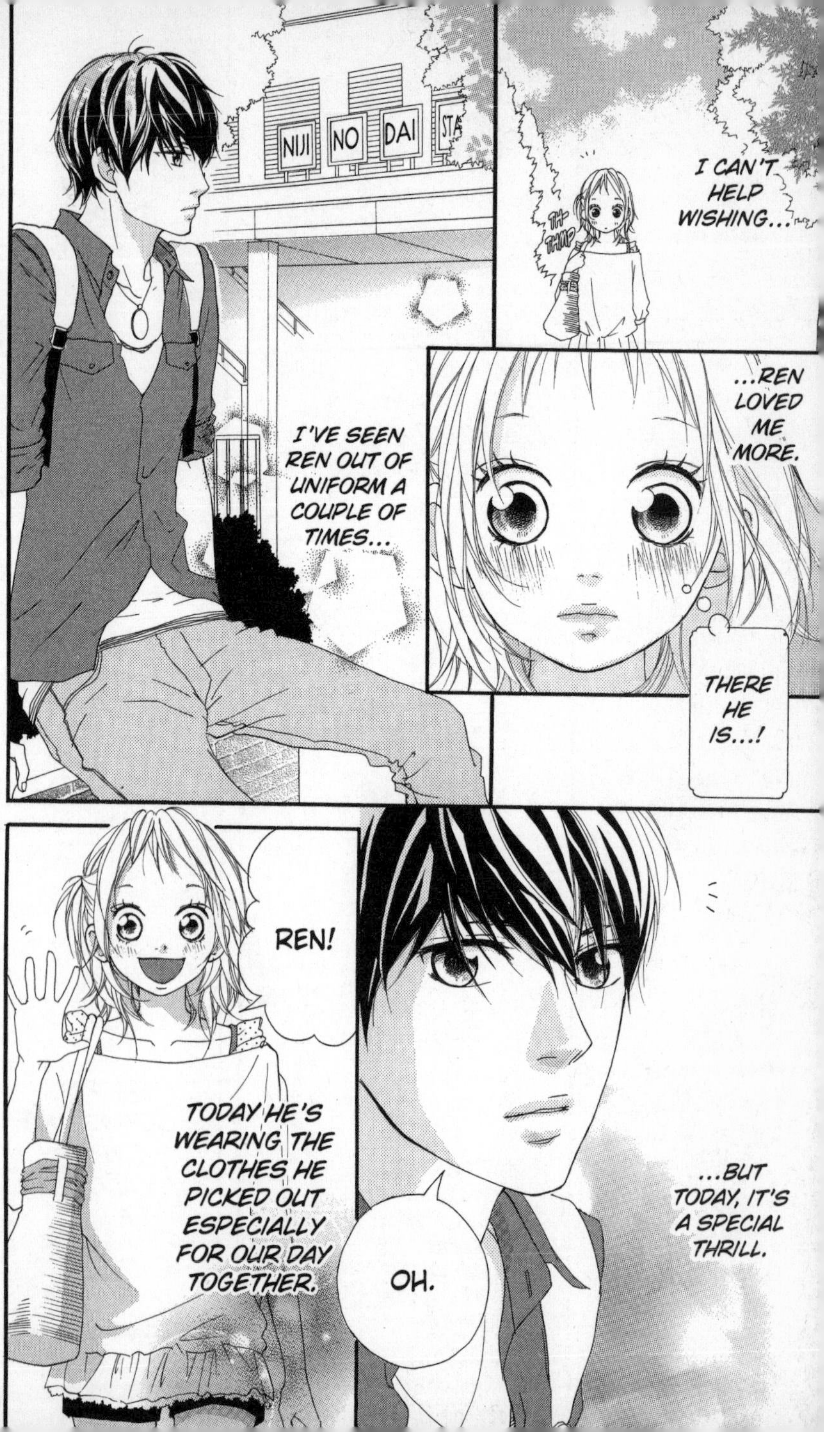
TH-THMP
I CAN'T HELP WISHING...
...REN LOVED ME MORE.
THERE HE IS...!
NIJI NO DAI STA
I'VE SEEN REN OUT OF UNIFORM A COUPLE OF TIMES...
...BUT TODAY, IT'S A SPECIAL THRILL.
OH.
REN!
TODAY HE'S WEARING THE CLOTHES HE PICKED OUT ESPECIALLY FOR OUR DAY TOGETHER.

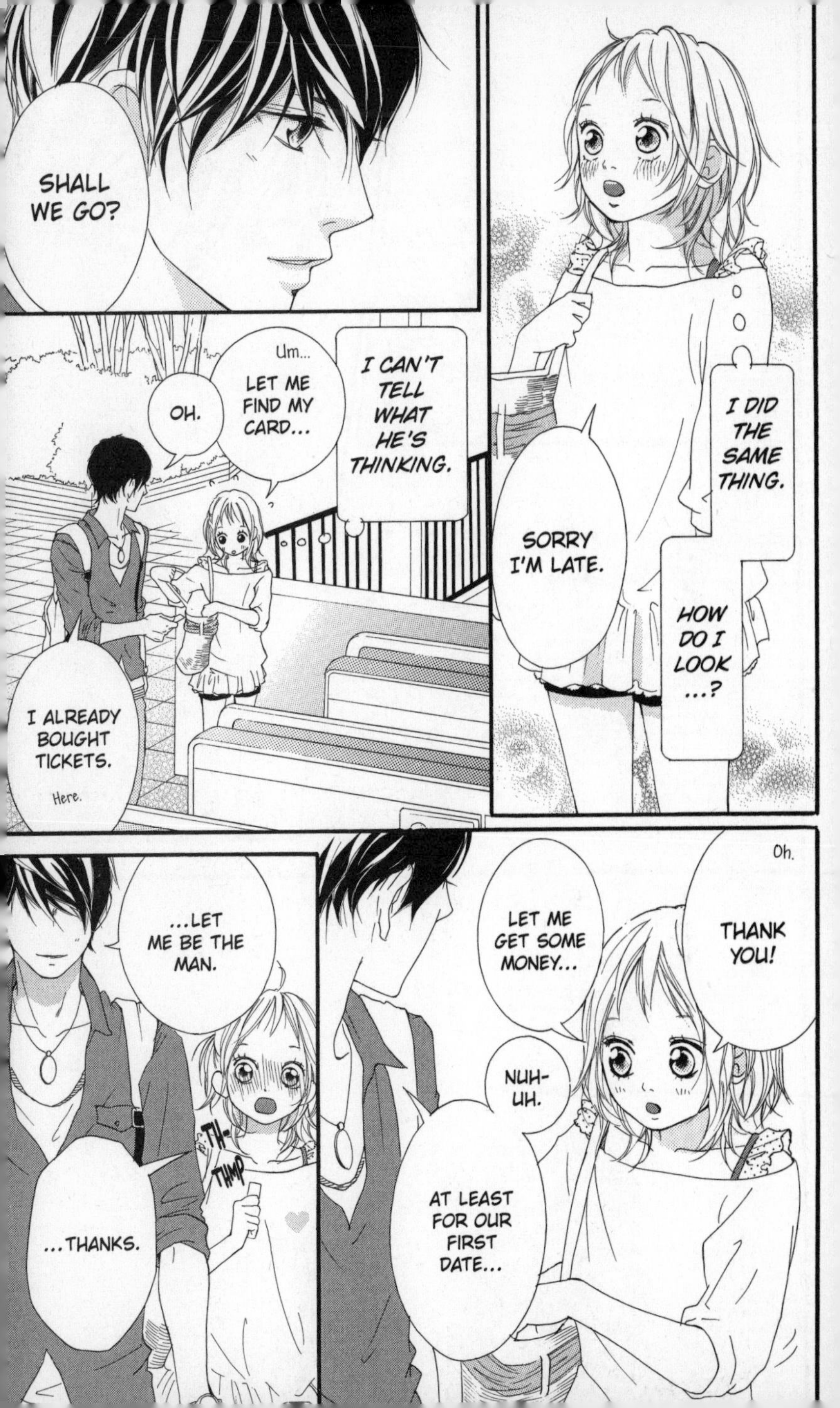
I DID THE SAME THING.
SORRY I'M LATE.
HOW DO I LOOK ...?
SHALL WE GO?
I CAN'T TELL WHAT HE'S THINKING.
Um...
LET ME FIND MY CARD...
OH.
I ALREADY BOUGHT TICKETS.
Here.
Oh.
THANK YOU!
LET ME GET SOME MONEY...
NUH-UH.
AT LEAST FOR OUR FIRST DATE...
...LET ME BE THE MAN.
TH-THMP
...THANKS.

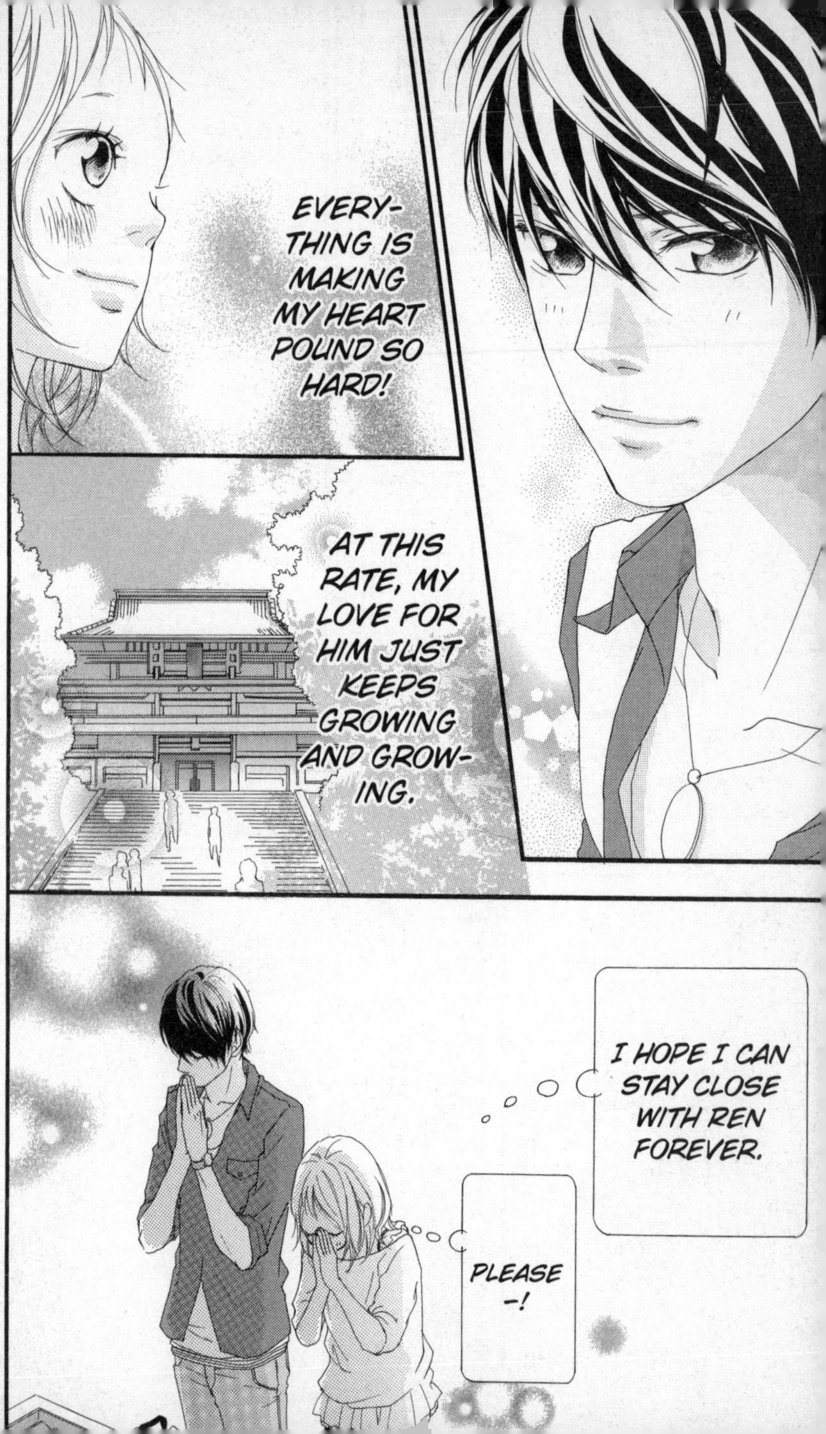
EVERY-THING IS MAKING MY HEART POUND SO HARD!
AT THIS RATE, MY LOVE FOR HIM JUST KEEPS GROWING AND GROW-ING.
I HOPE I CAN STAY CLOSE WITH REN FOREVER.
PLEASE -!

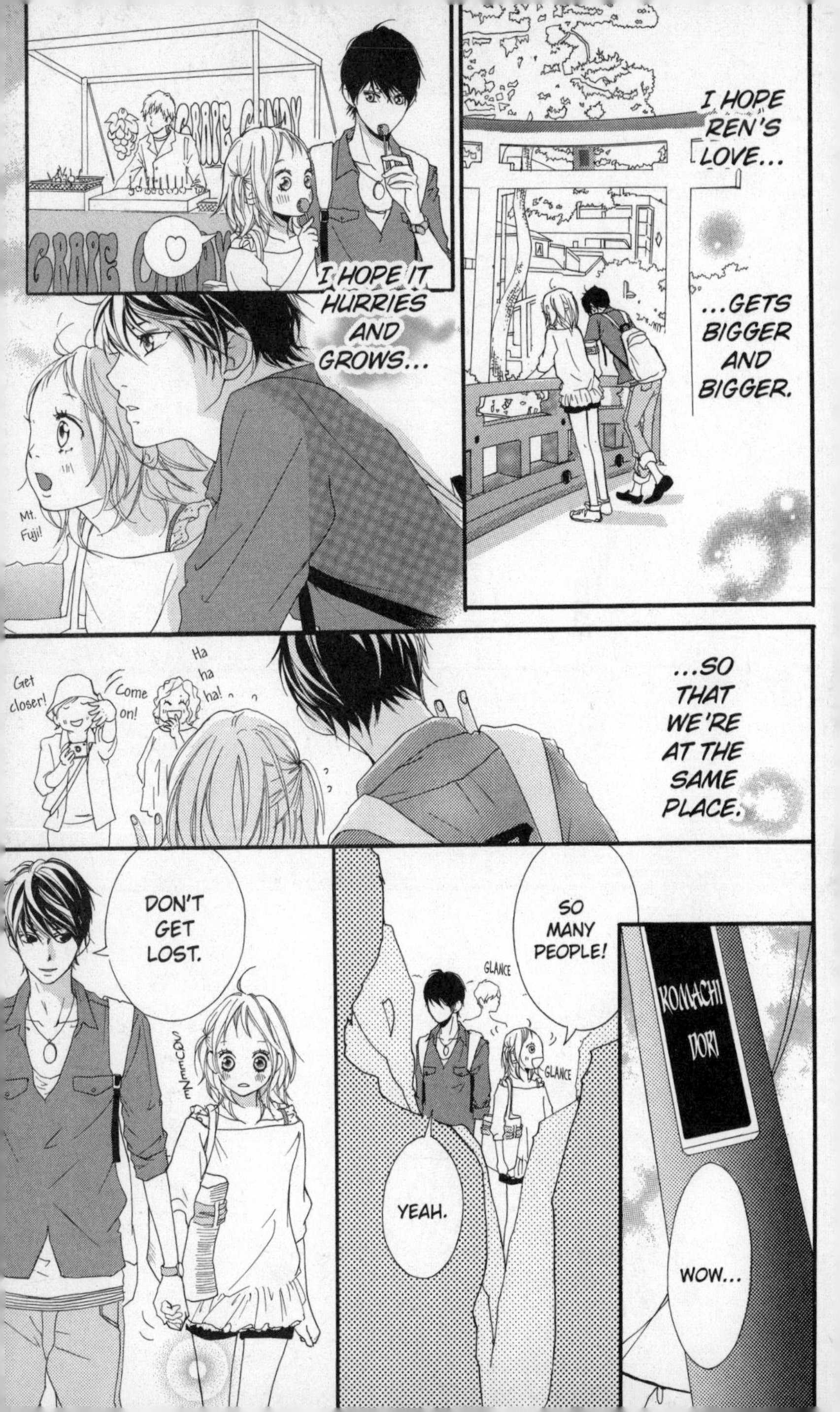

I HOPE REN'S LOVE...
...GETS BIGGER AND BIGGER.
GRAPE CANDY
GRAPE CANDY
I HOPE IT HURRIES AND GROWS...
Mt. Fuji!
...SO THAT WE'RE AT THE SAME PLACE.
Ha ha ha!
Come on!
Get closer!
KOMACHI DORI
WOW...
SO MANY PEOPLE!
GLANCE
GLANCE
YEAH.
DON'T GET LOST.

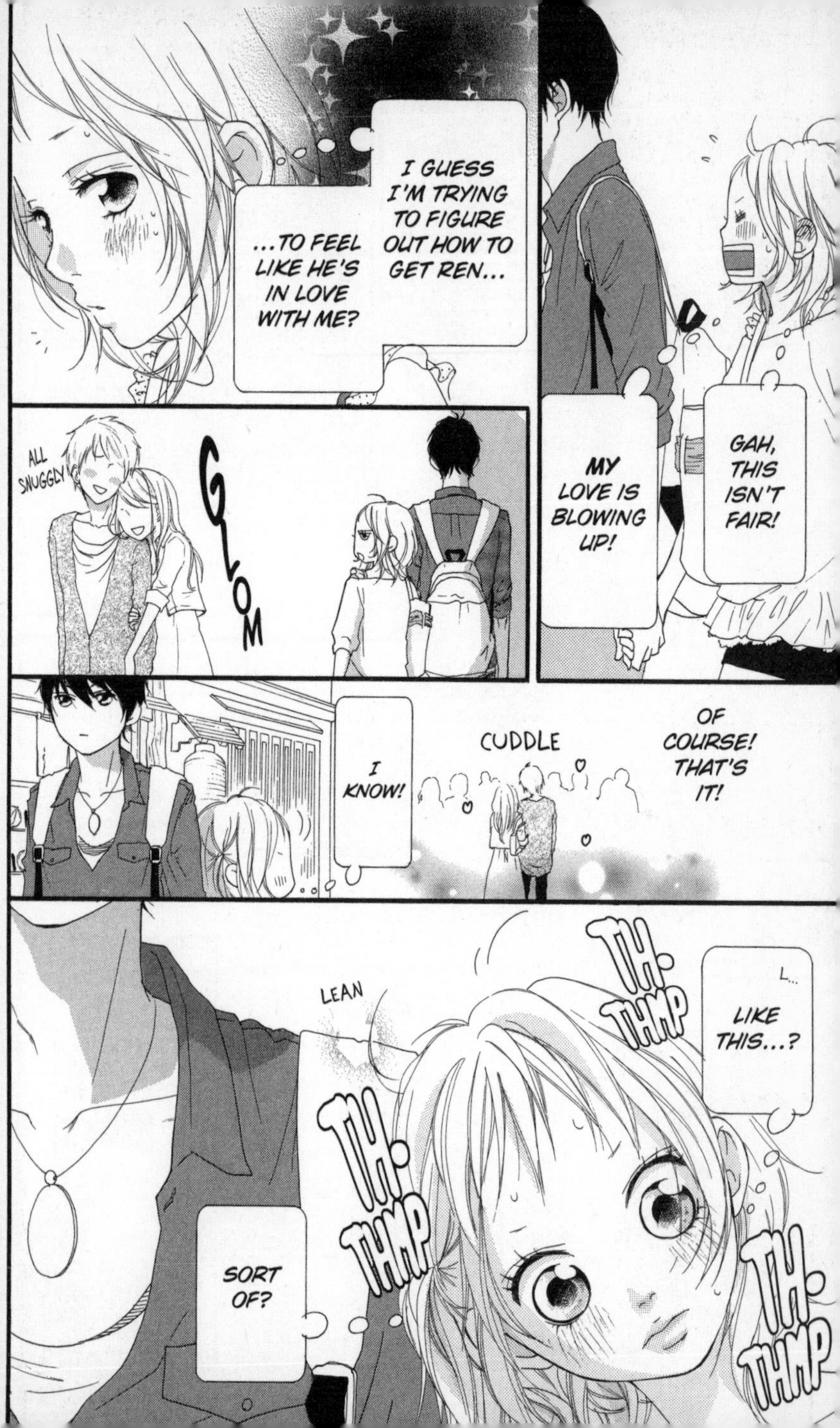
GAH, THIS ISN'T FAIR!
MY LOVE IS BLOWING UP!
I GUESS I'M TRYING TO FIGURE OUT HOW TO GET REN...
...TO FEEL LIKE HE'S IN LOVE WITH ME?
GLOM
ALL SNUGGLY
OF COURSE! THAT'S IT!
CUDDLE
I KNOW!
L... LIKE THIS...?
TH-THMP
TH-THMP
LEAN
TH-THMP
SORT OF?

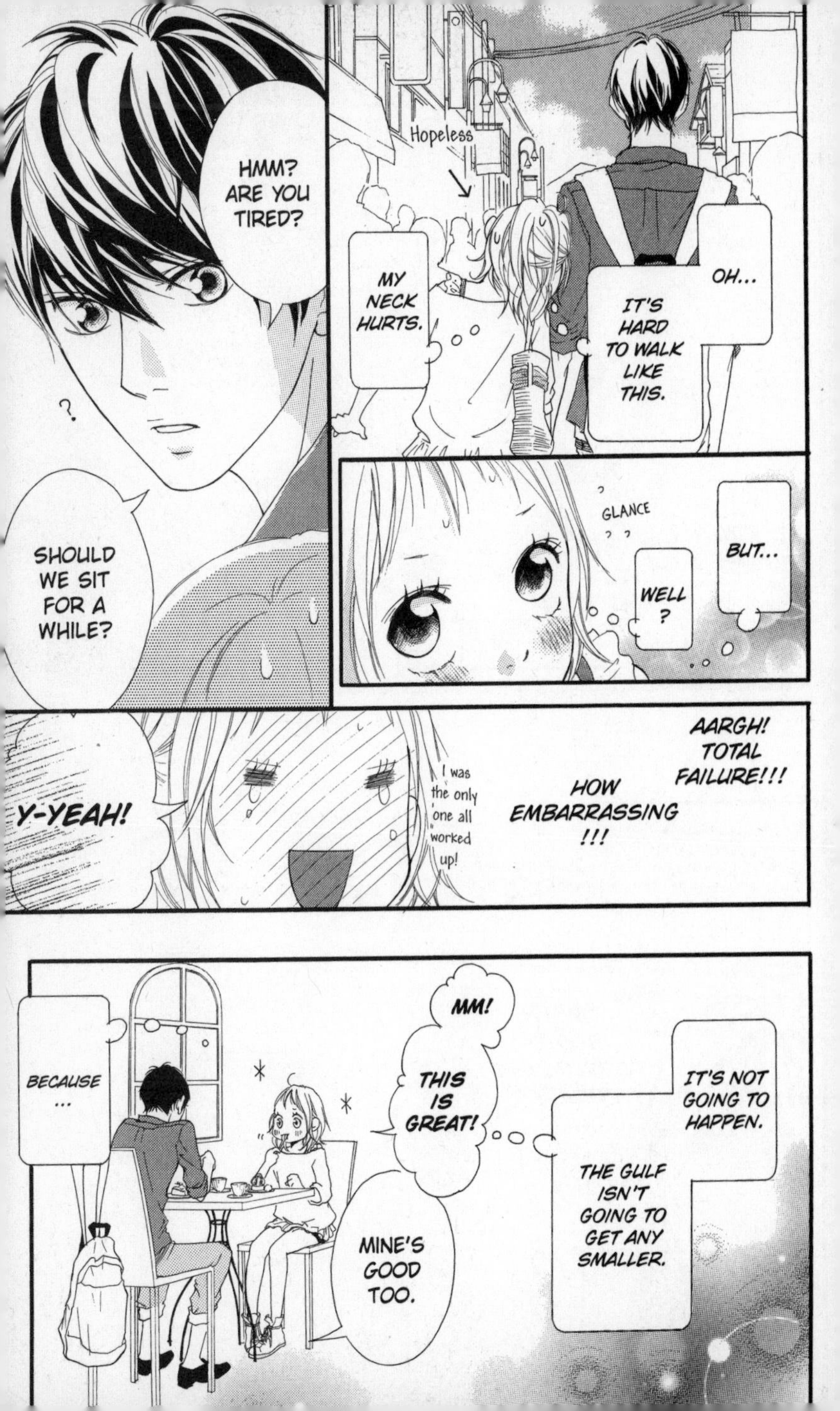

OH...
IT'S HARD TO WALK LIKE THIS.
Hopeless
MY NECK HURTS.
BUT...
GLANCE
WELL ?
HMM? ARE YOU TIRED?
?
SHOULD WE SIT FOR A WHILE?
AARGH! TOTAL FAILURE!!!
HOW EMBARRASSING !!!
I was the only one all worked up!
Y-YEAH!
IT'S NOT GOING TO HAPPEN.
THE GULF ISN'T GOING TO GET ANY SMALLER.
MM!
THIS IS GREAT!
MINE'S GOOD TOO.
BECAUSE ...

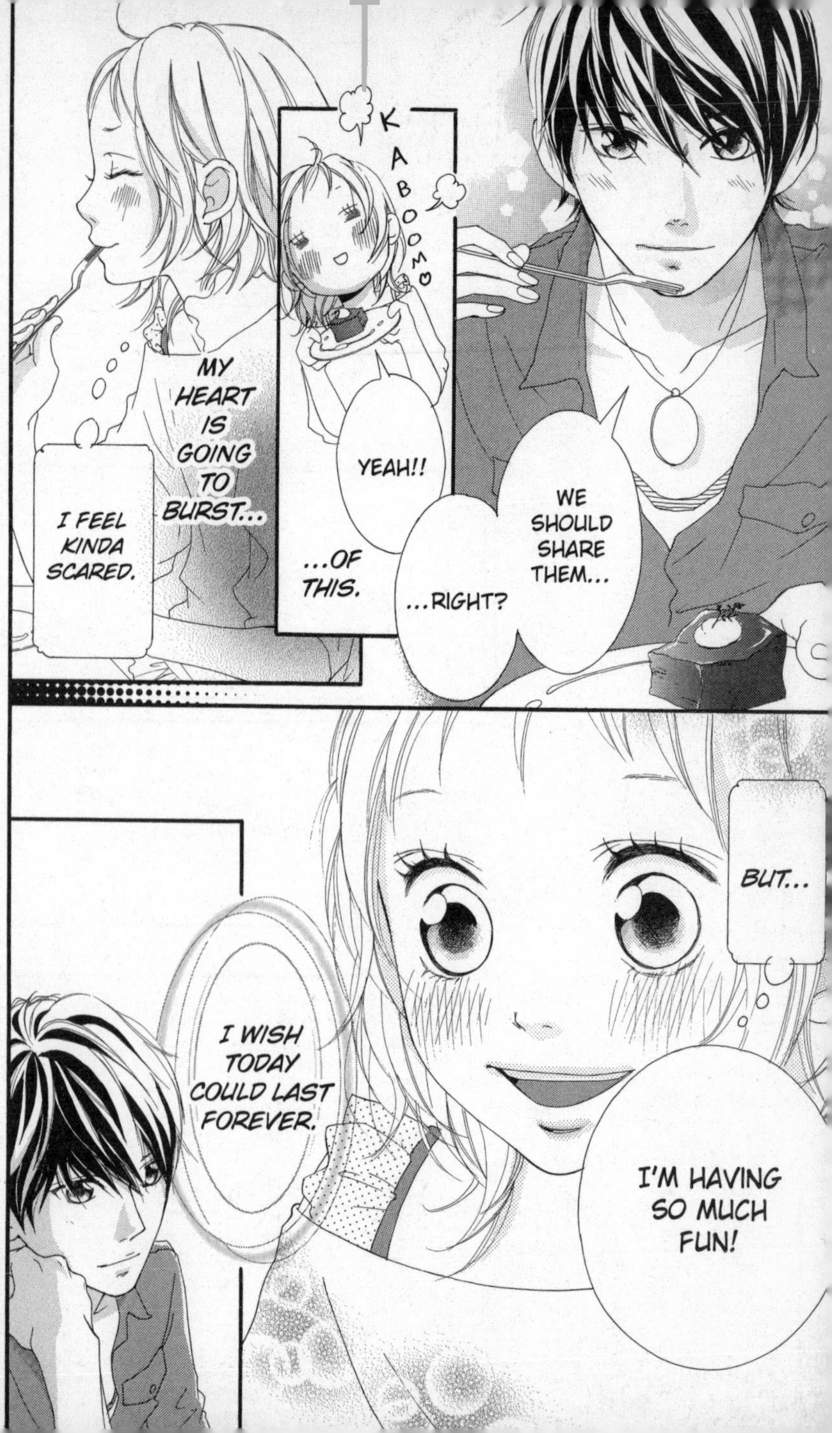
WE SHOULD SHARE THEM...
...RIGHT?
YEAH!!
KABOOM
...OF THIS.
MY HEART IS GOING TO BURST...
I FEEL KINDA SCARED.
BUT...
I'M HAVING SO MUCH FUN!
I WISH TODAY COULD LAST FOREVER.

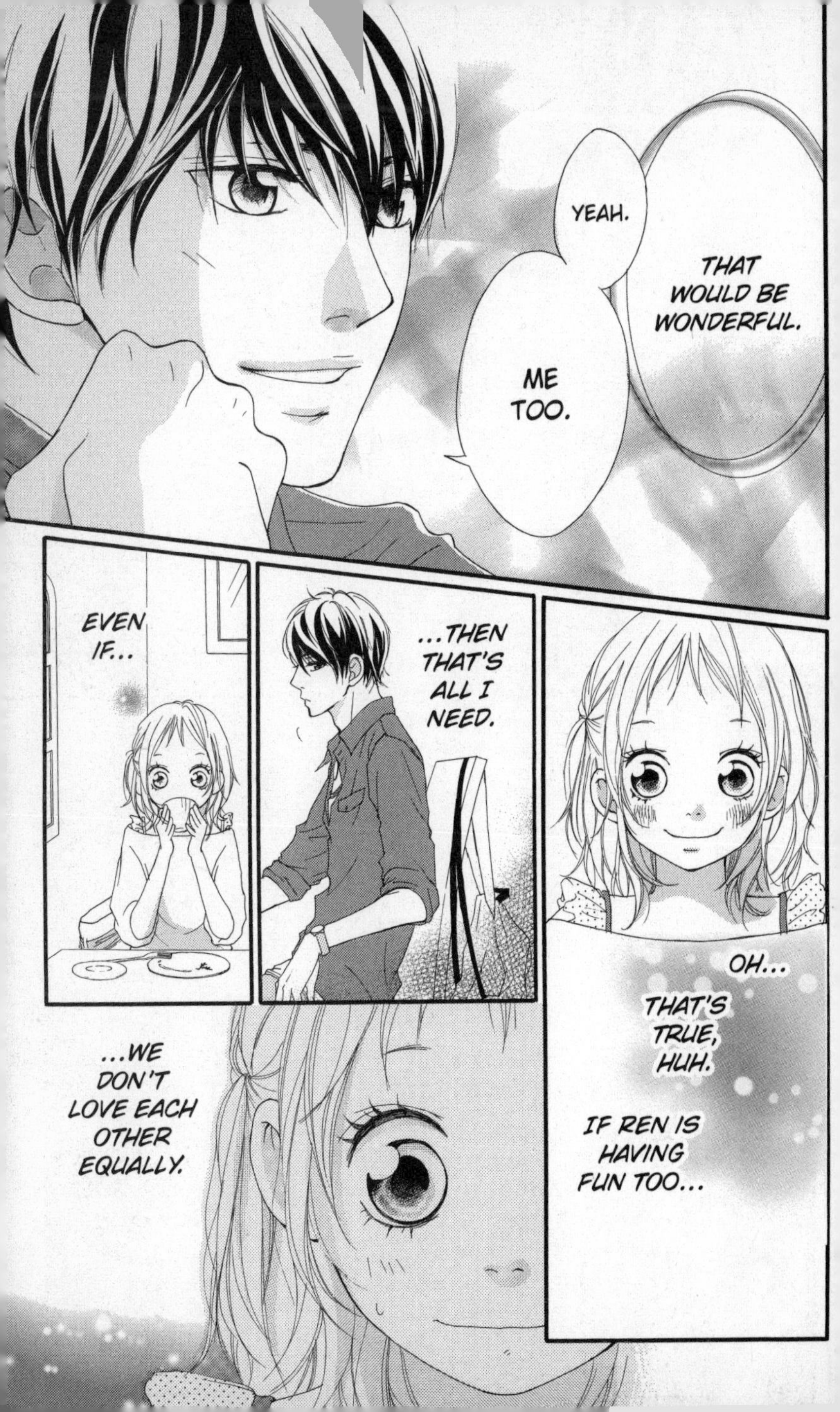
THAT WOULD BE WONDERFUL.
YEAH.
ME TOO.
OH...
THAT'S TRUE, HUH.
IF REN IS HAVING FUN TOO...
...THEN THAT'S ALL I NEED.
EVEN IF...
...WE DON'T LOVE EACH OTHER EQUALLY.

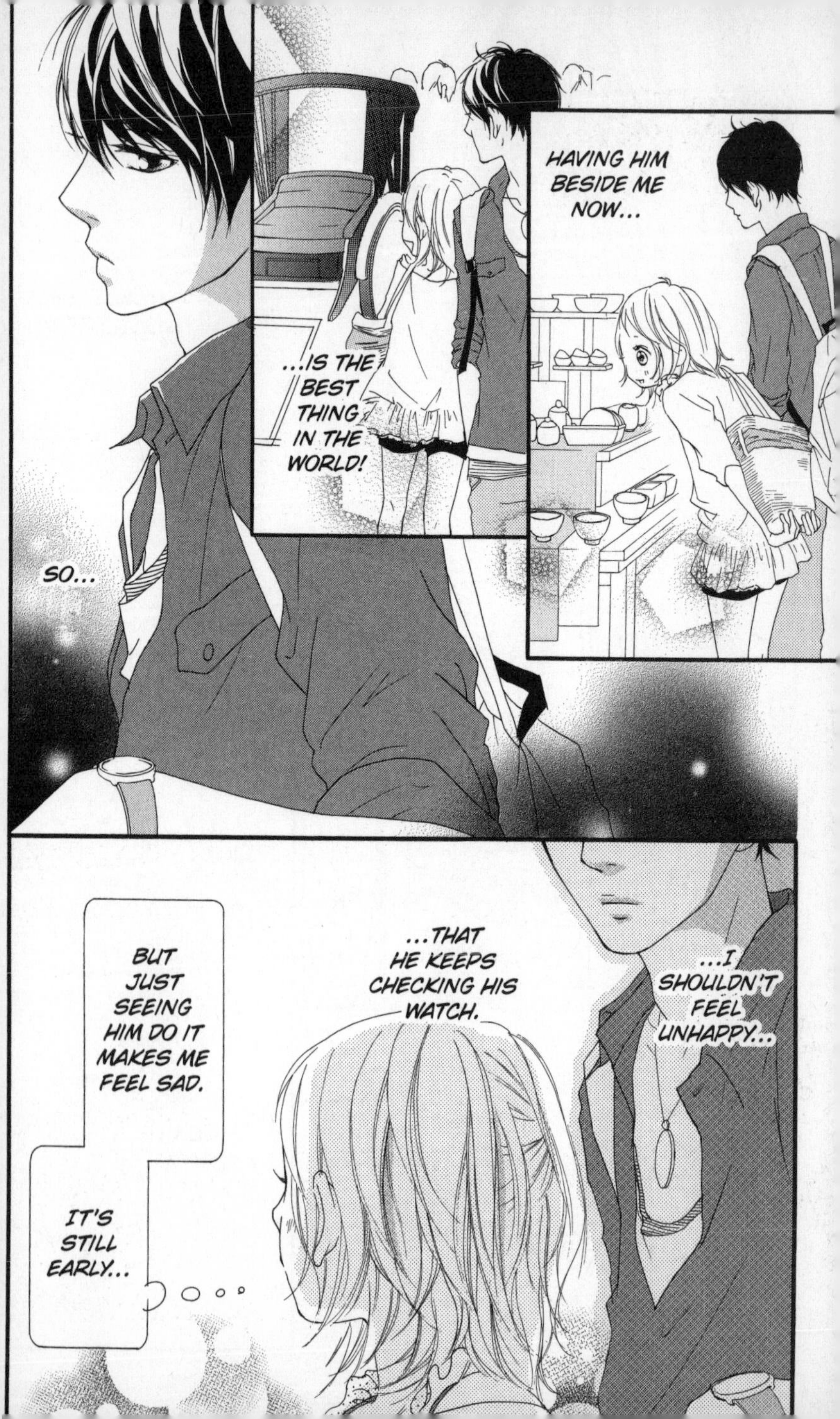
HAVING HIM BESIDE ME NOW...
...IS THE BEST THING IN THE WORLD!
SO...
...I SHOULDN'T FEEL UNHAPPY...
...THAT HE KEEPS CHECKING HIS WATCH.
BUT JUST SEEING HIM DO IT MAKES ME FEEL SAD.
IT'S STILL EARLY...

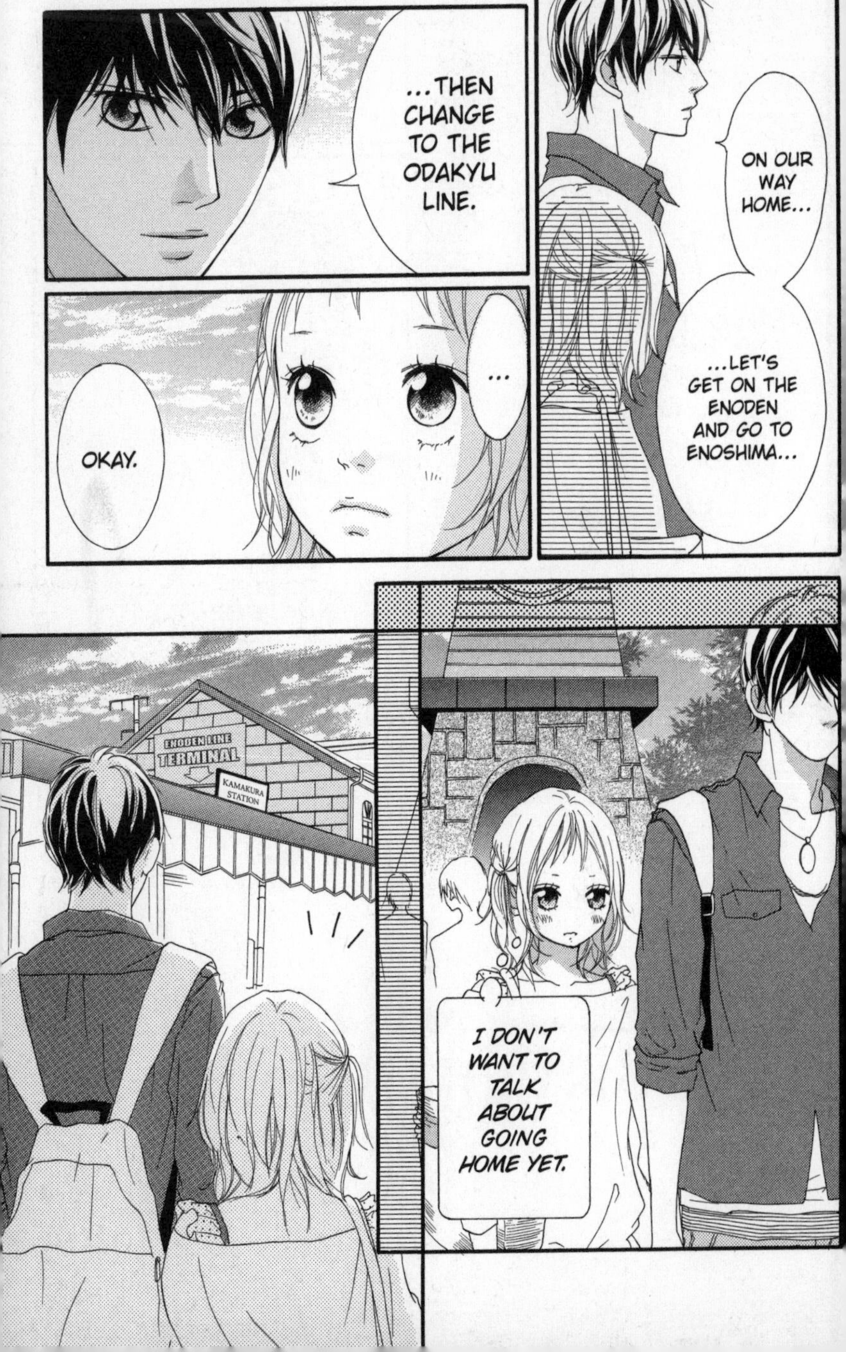
ON OUR WAY HOME...
...LET'S GET ON THE ENODEN AND GO TO ENOSHIMA...
...THEN CHANGE TO THE ODAKYU LINE.
...
OKAY.
I DON'T WANT TO TALK ABOUT GOING HOME YET.
ENODEN LINE TERMINAL
KAMAKURA STATION

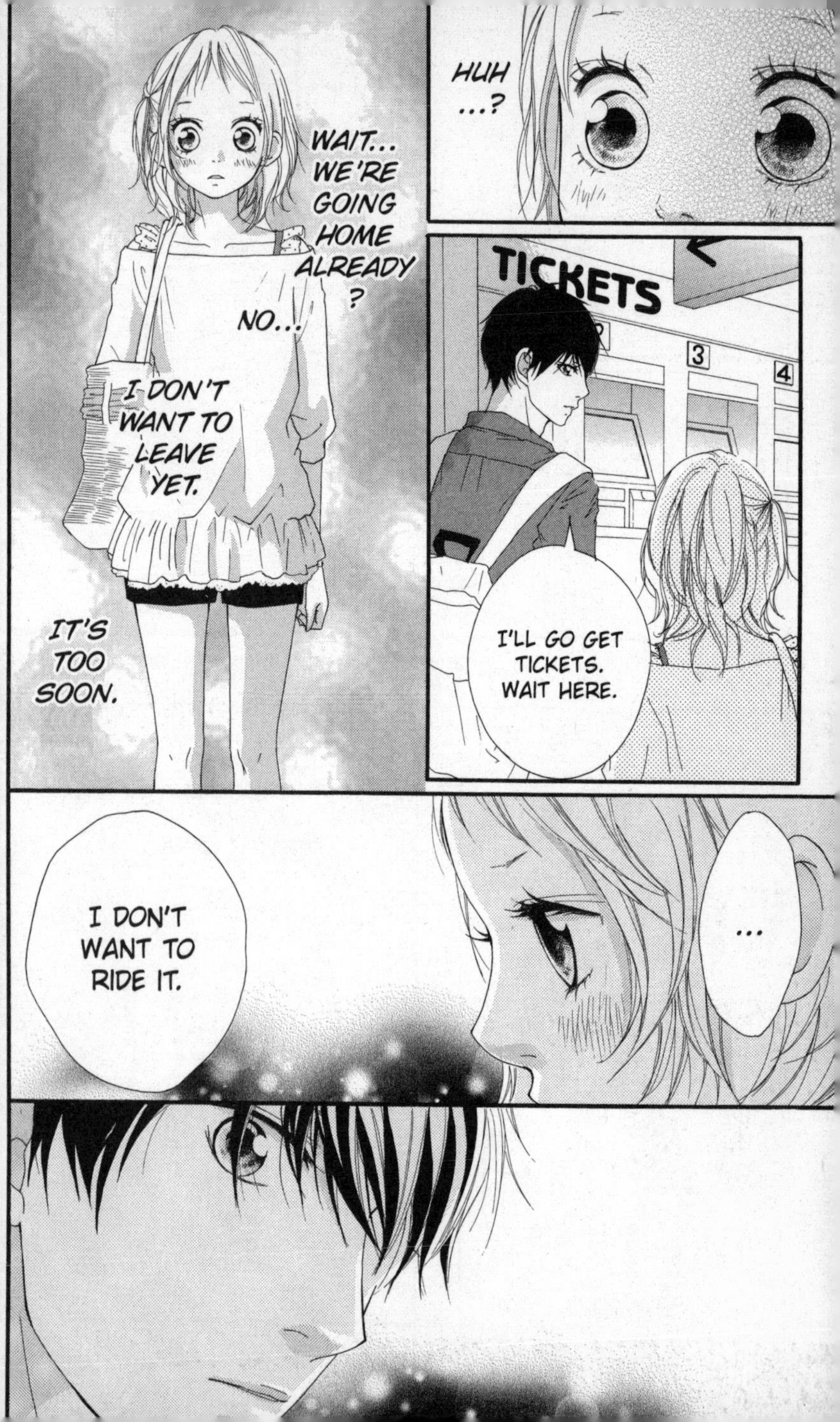
HUH ...?
TICKETS
3
4
I'LL GO GET TICKETS. WAIT HERE.
WAIT... WE'RE GOING HOME ALREADY?
NO...
I DON'T WANT TO LEAVE YET.
IT'S TOO SOON.
...
I DON'T WANT TO RIDE IT.

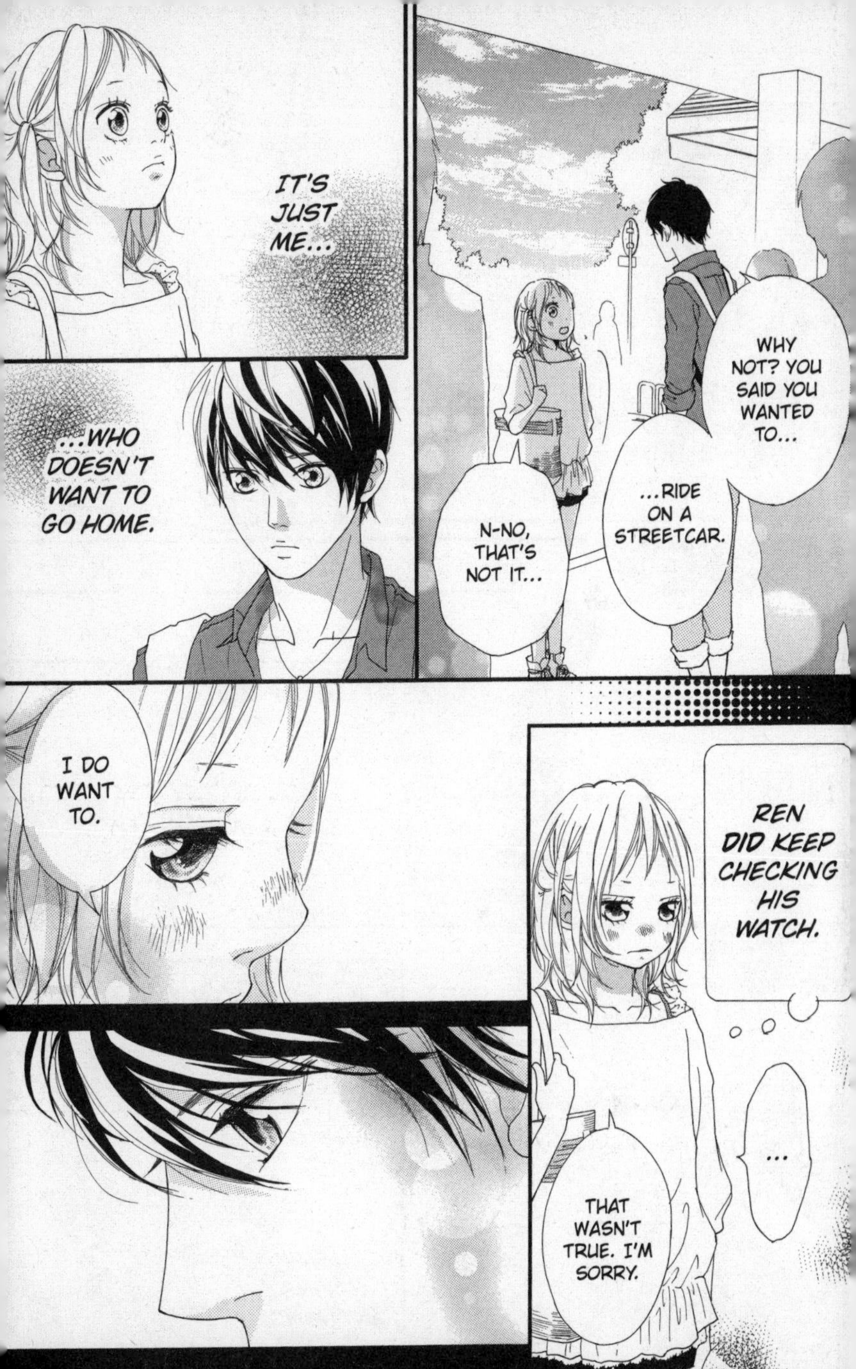
WHY NOT? YOU SAID YOU WANTED TO...
...RIDE ON A STREETCAR.
N-NO, THAT'S NOT IT...
IT'S JUST ME...
...WHO DOESN'T WANT TO GO HOME.
REN DID KEEP CHECKING HIS WATCH.
...
THAT WASN'T TRUE. I'M SORRY.
I DO WANT TO.

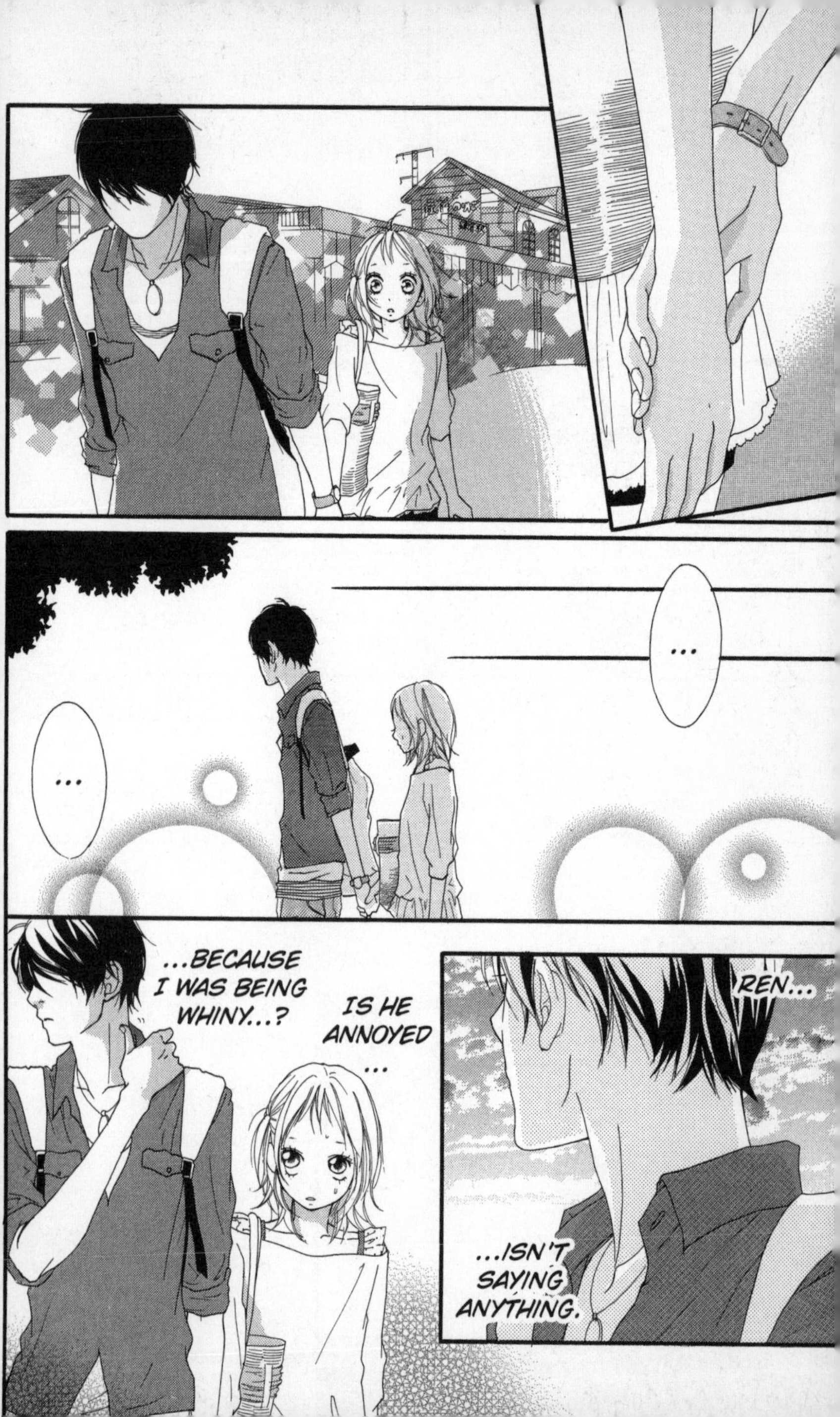
...
...
REN...
...ISN'T SAYING ANYTHING.
IS HE ANNOYED ...
...BECAUSE I WAS BEING WHINY...?

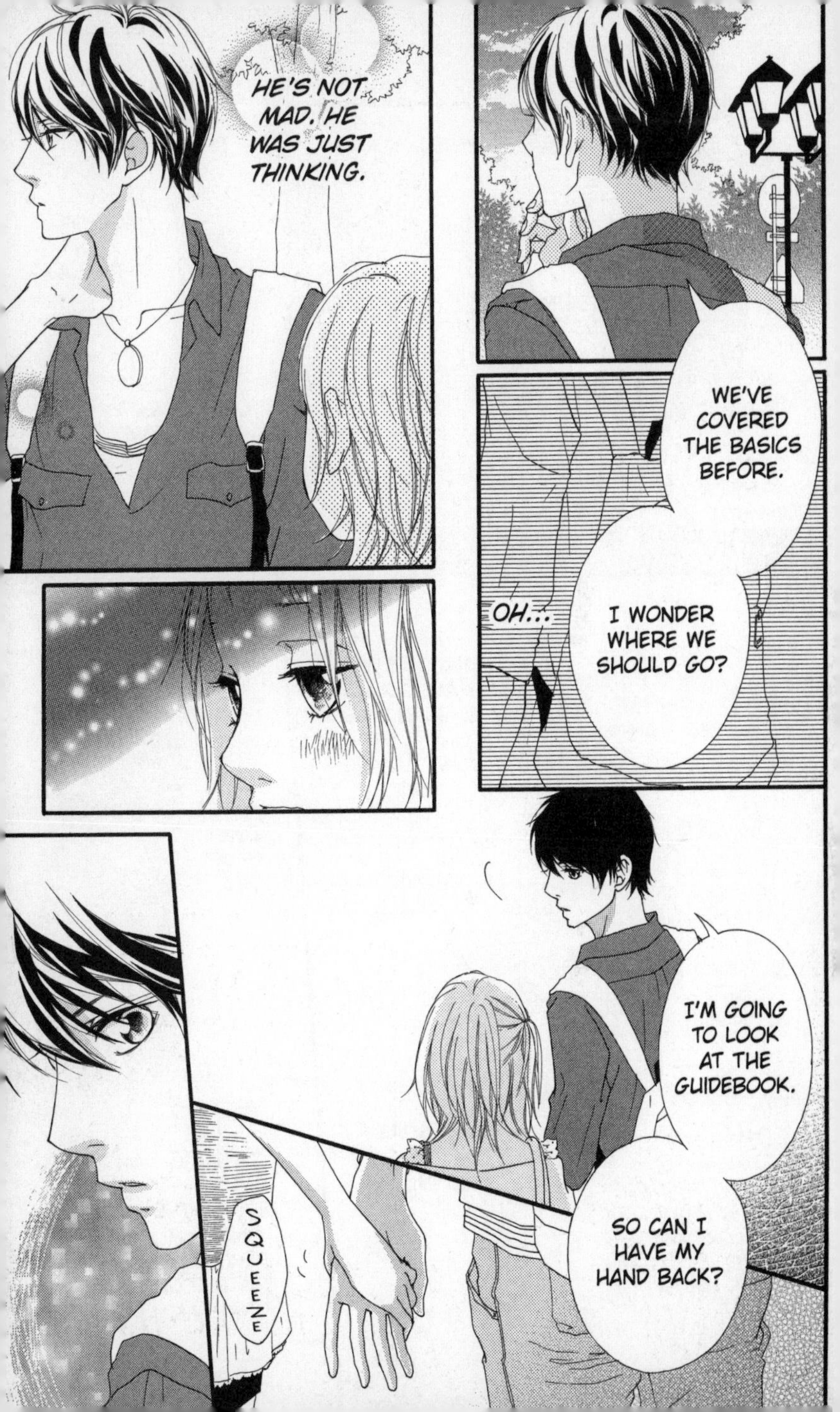
WE'VE COVERED THE BASICS BEFORE.
HE'S NOT MAD. HE WAS JUST THINKING.
I WONDER WHERE WE SHOULD GO?
OH...
I'M GOING TO LOOK AT THE GUIDEBOOK.
SO CAN I HAVE MY HAND BACK?
SQUEEZE

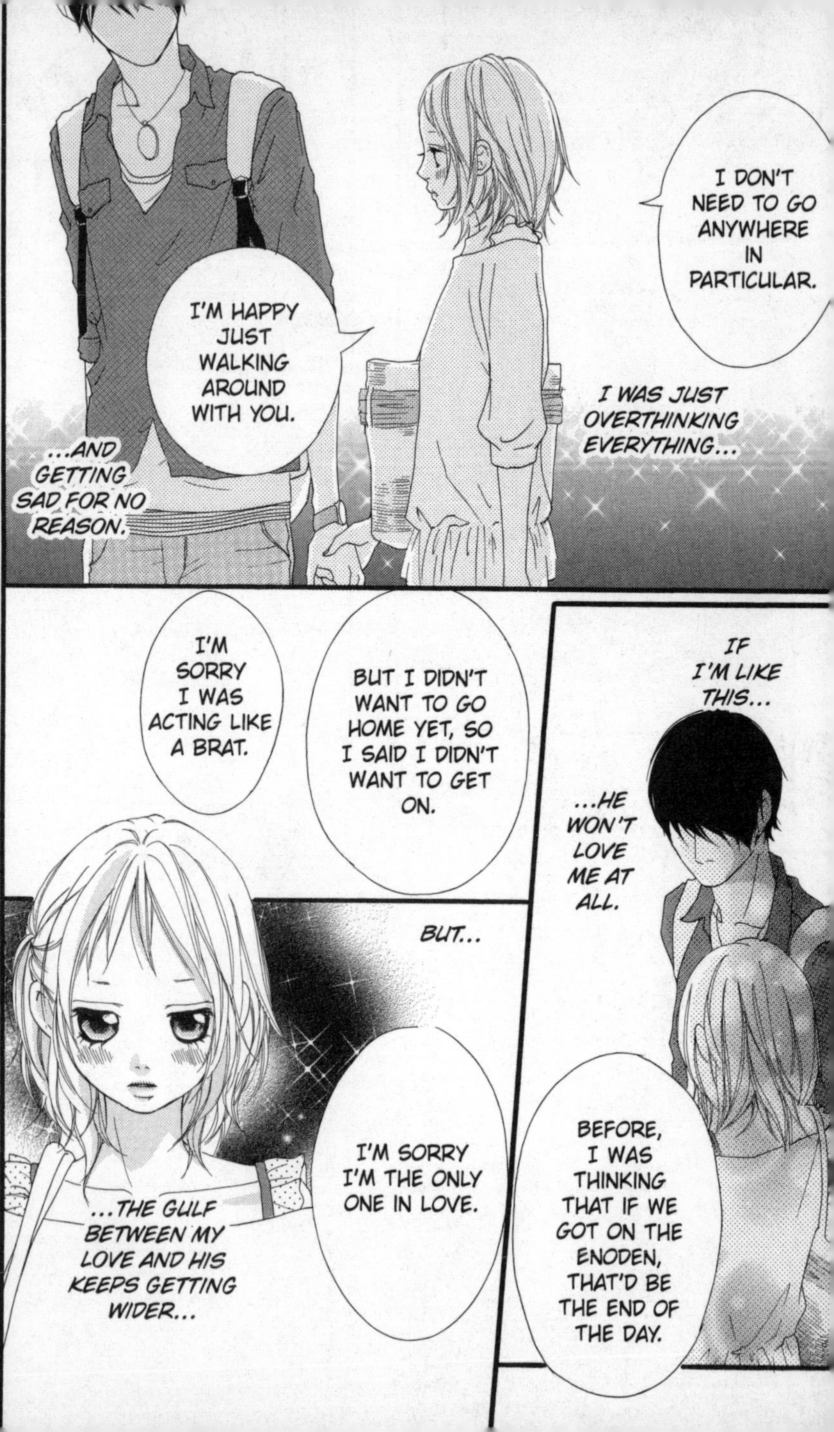
I DON'T NEED TO GO ANYWHERE IN PARTICULAR.
I'M HAPPY JUST WALKING AROUND WITH YOU.
I WAS JUST OVERTHINKING EVERYTHING...
...AND GETTING SAD FOR NO REASON.
IF I'M LIKE THIS...
...HE WON'T LOVE ME AT ALL.
BEFORE, I WAS THINKING THAT IF WE GOT ON THE ENODEN, THAT'D BE THE END OF THE DAY.
BUT I DIDN'T WANT TO GO HOME YET, SO I SAID I DIDN'T WANT TO GET ON.
I'M SORRY I WAS ACTING LIKE A BRAT.
BUT...
I'M SORRY I'M THE ONLY ONE IN LOVE.
...THE GULF BETWEEN MY LOVE AND HIS KEEPS GETTING WIDER...

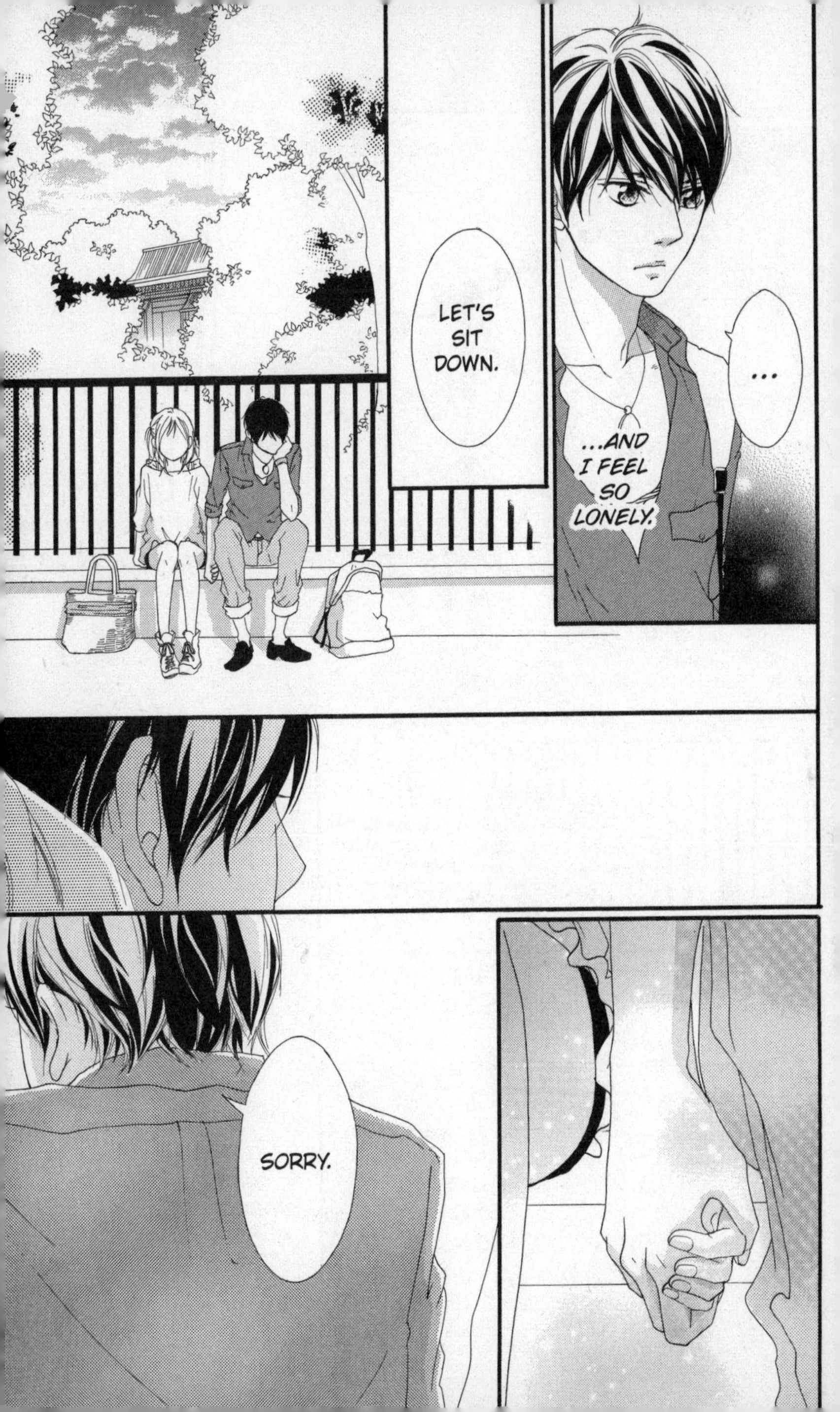
...
...AND I FEEL SO LONELY.
LET'S SIT DOWN.
SORRY.

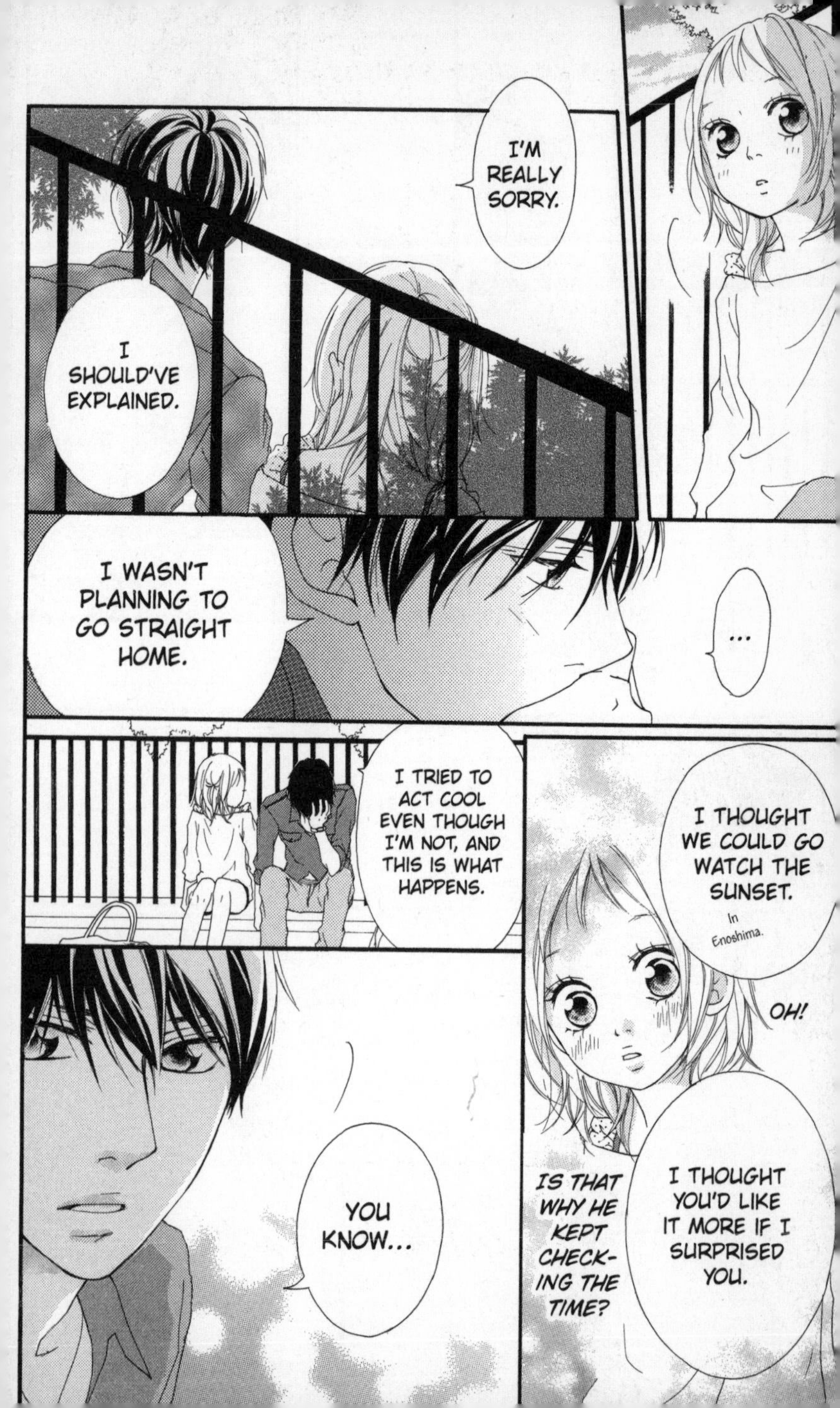
I'M REALLY SORRY.
I SHOULD'VE EXPLAINED.
...
I WASN'T PLANNING TO GO STRAIGHT HOME.
I THOUGHT WE COULD GO WATCH THE SUNSET.
In Enoshima.
OH!
I THOUGHT YOU'D LIKE IT MORE IF I SURPRISED YOU.
IS THAT WHY HE KEPT CHECKING THE TIME?
I TRIED TO ACT COOL EVEN THOUGH I'M NOT, AND THIS IS WHAT HAPPENS.
YOU KNOW...

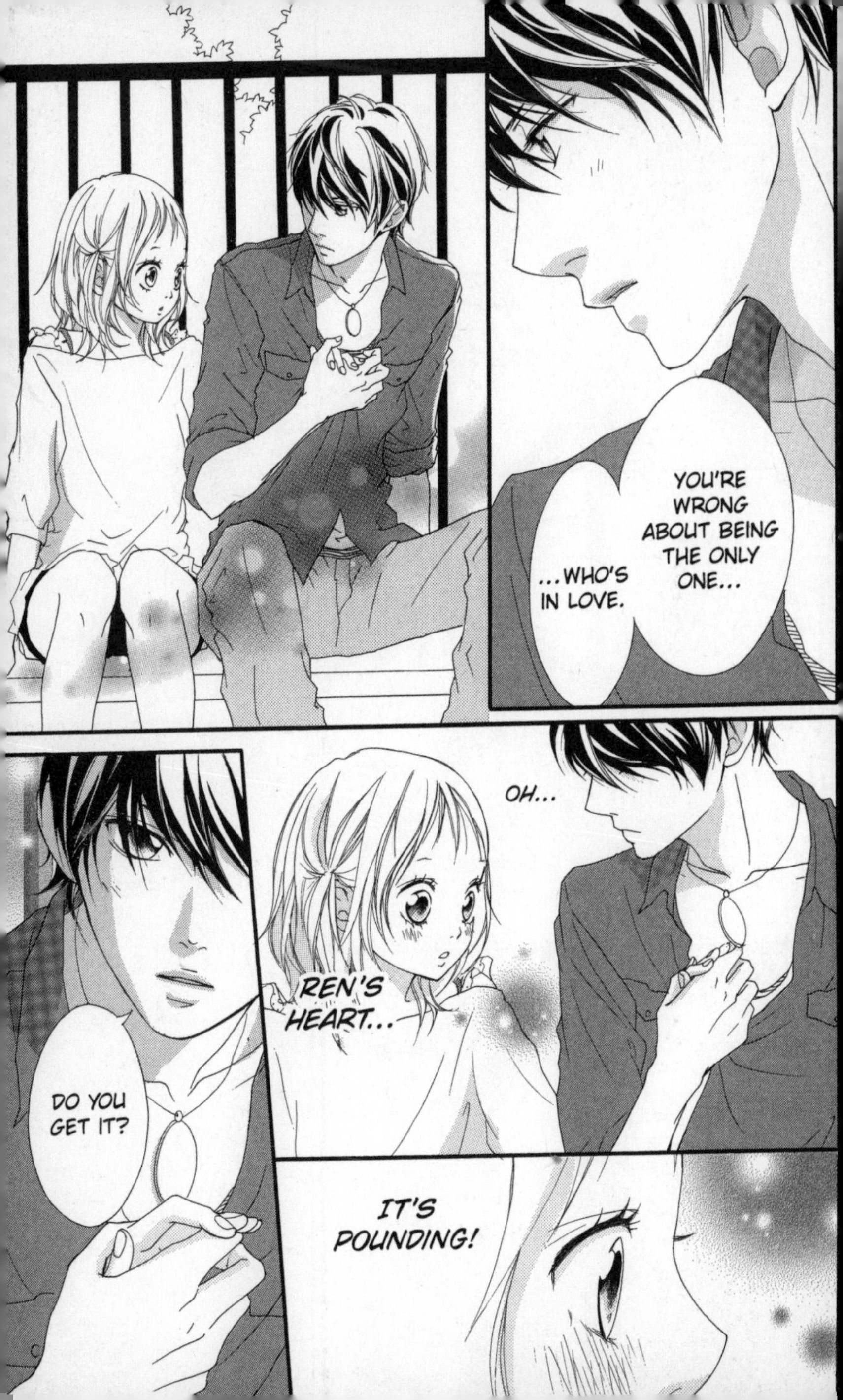
YOU'RE WRONG ABOUT BEING THE ONLY ONE...
...WHO'S IN LOVE.
OH...
REN'S HEART...
IT'S POUNDING!
DO YOU GET IT?

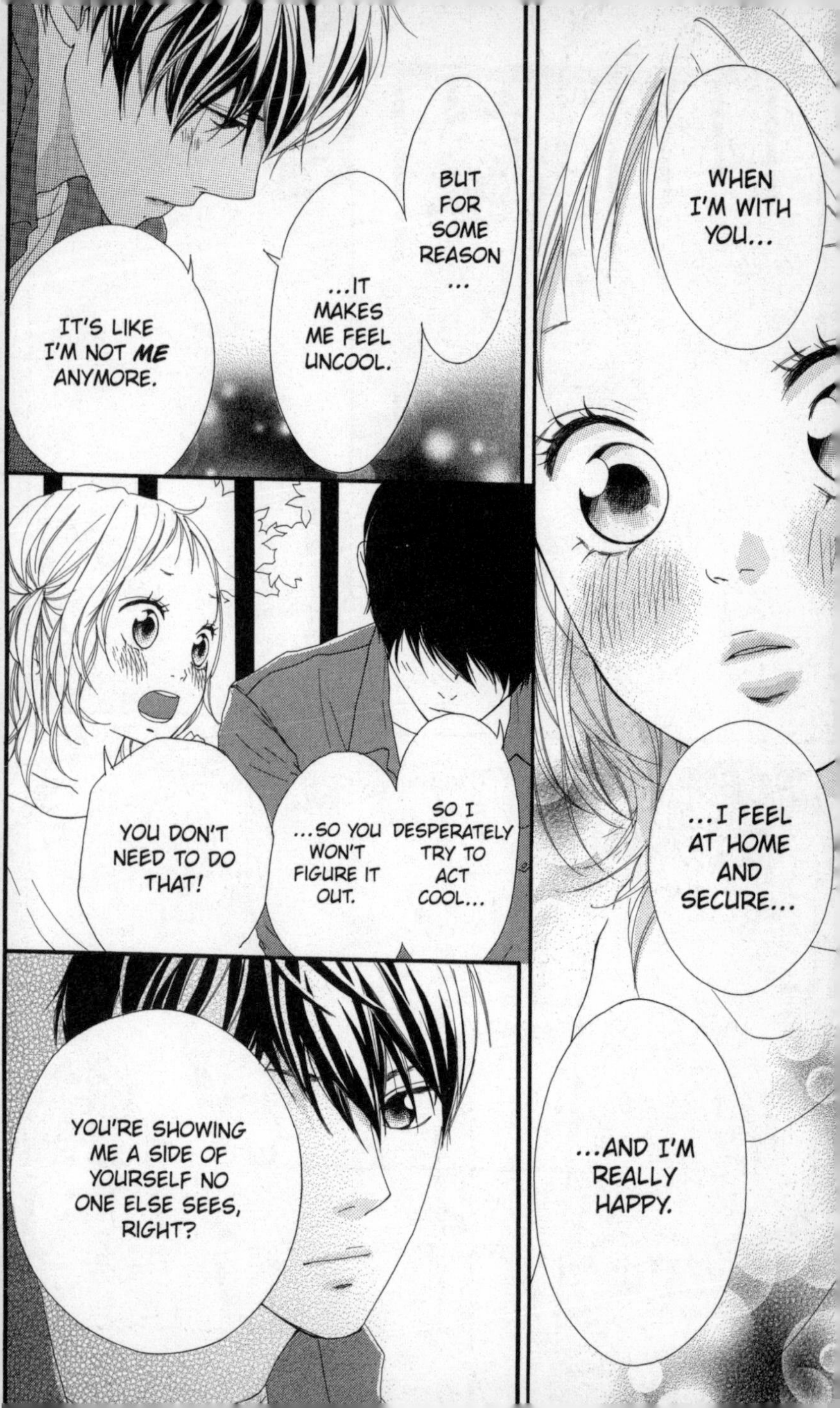
WHEN I'M WITH YOU...
...I FEEL AT HOME AND SECURE...
...AND I'M REALLY HAPPY.
BUT FOR SOME REASON...
...IT MAKES ME FEEL UNCOOL.
IT'S LIKE I'M NOT *ME* ANYMORE.
SO I DESPERATELY TRY TO ACT COOL...
...SO YOU WON'T FIGURE IT OUT.
YOU DON'T NEED TO DO THAT!
YOU'RE SHOWING ME A SIDE OF YOURSELF NO ONE ELSE SEES, RIGHT?

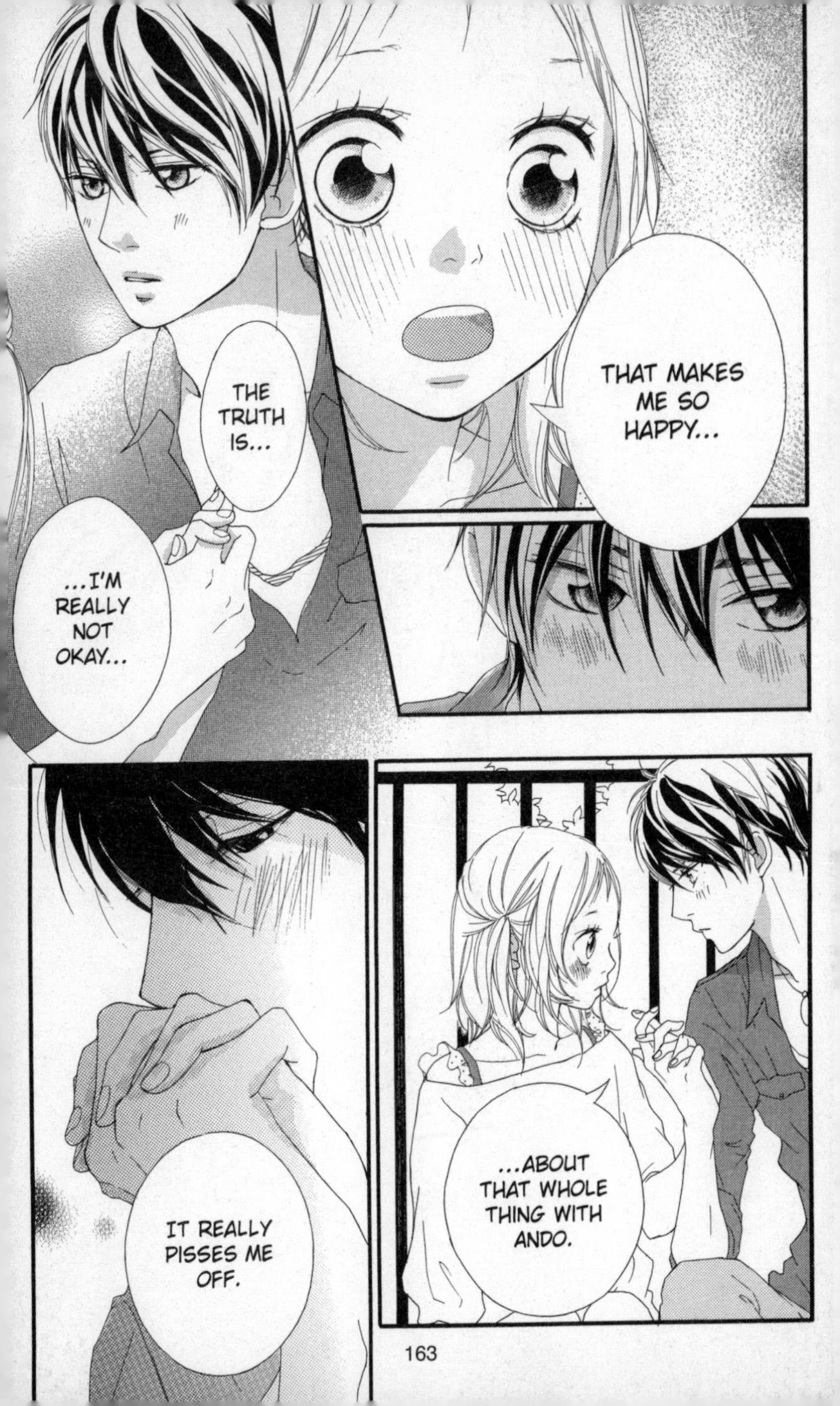
THAT MAKES ME SO HAPPY...
THE TRUTH IS...
...I'M REALLY NOT OKAY...
...ABOUT THAT WHOLE THING WITH ANDO.
IT REALLY PISSES ME OFF.

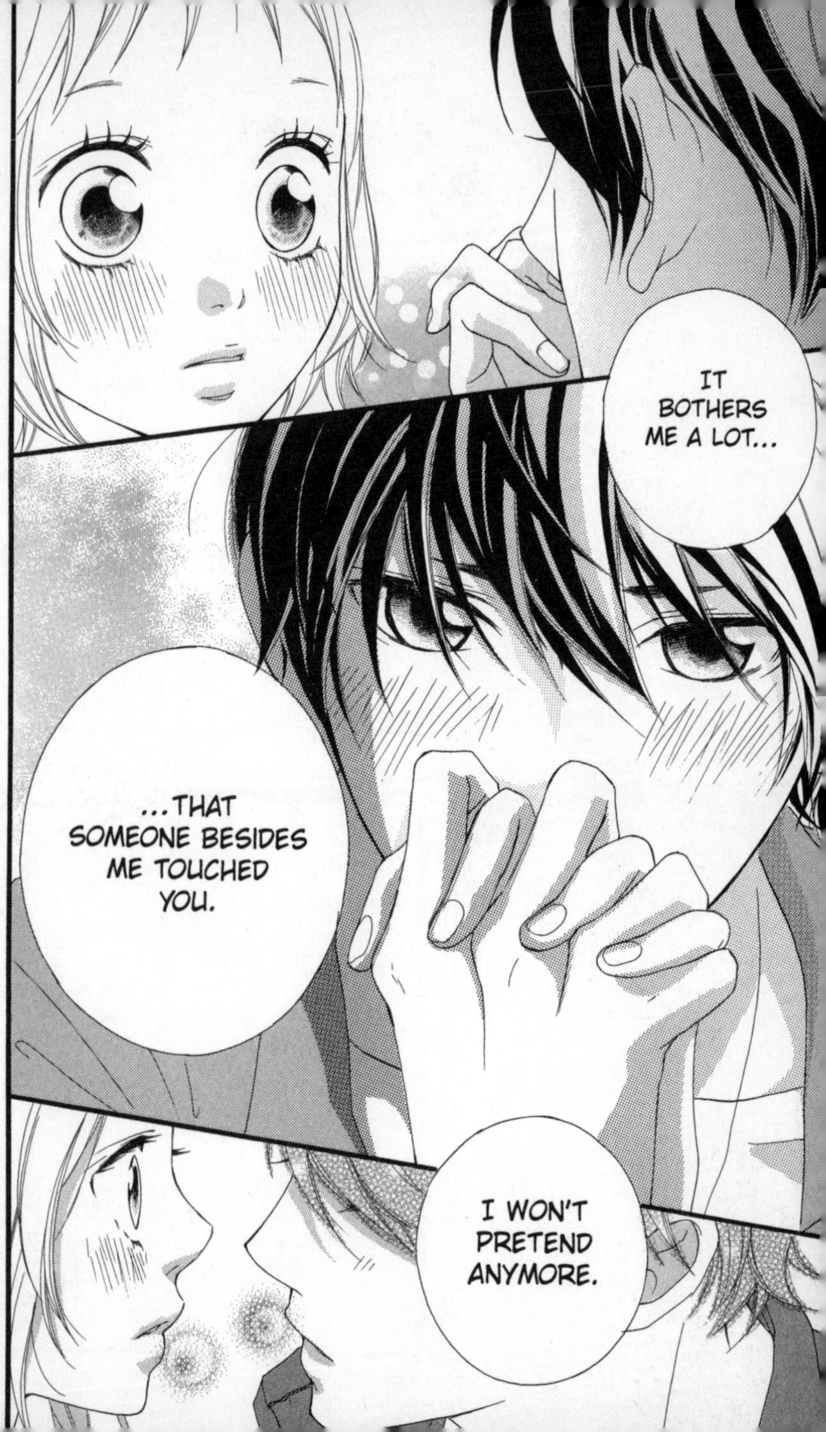
IT BOTHERS ME A LOT...
...THAT SOMEONE BESIDES ME TOUCHED YOU.
I WON'T PRETEND ANYMORE.

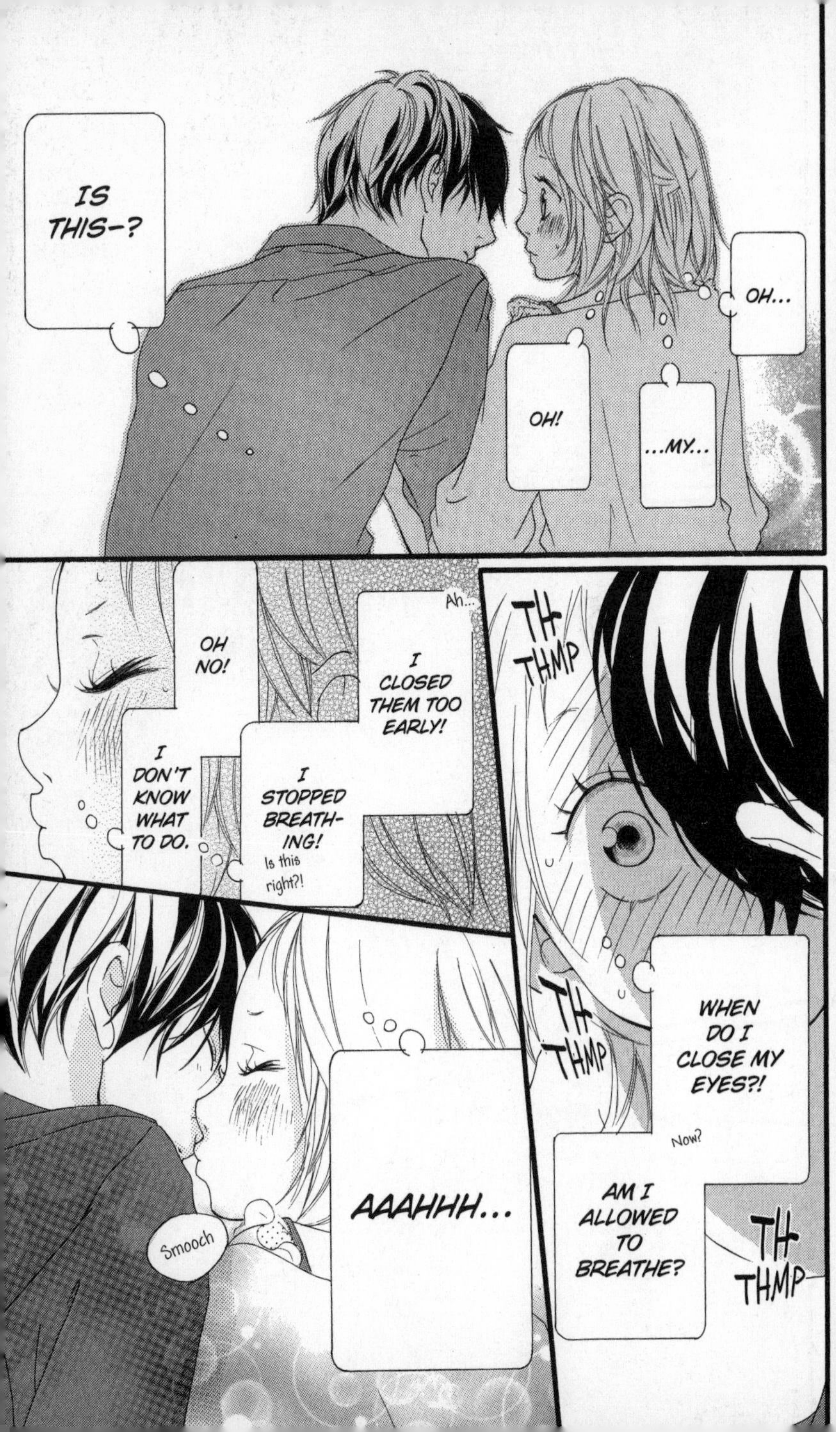
OH...
...MY...
OH!
IS THIS-?
TH THMP
WHEN DO I CLOSE MY EYES?!
Now?
AM I ALLOWED TO BREATHE?
TH THMP
TH THMP
Ah...
I CLOSED THEM TOO EARLY!
OH NO!
I STOPPED BREATHING!
Is this right?!
I DON'T KNOW WHAT TO DO.
AAAHHH...
Smooch

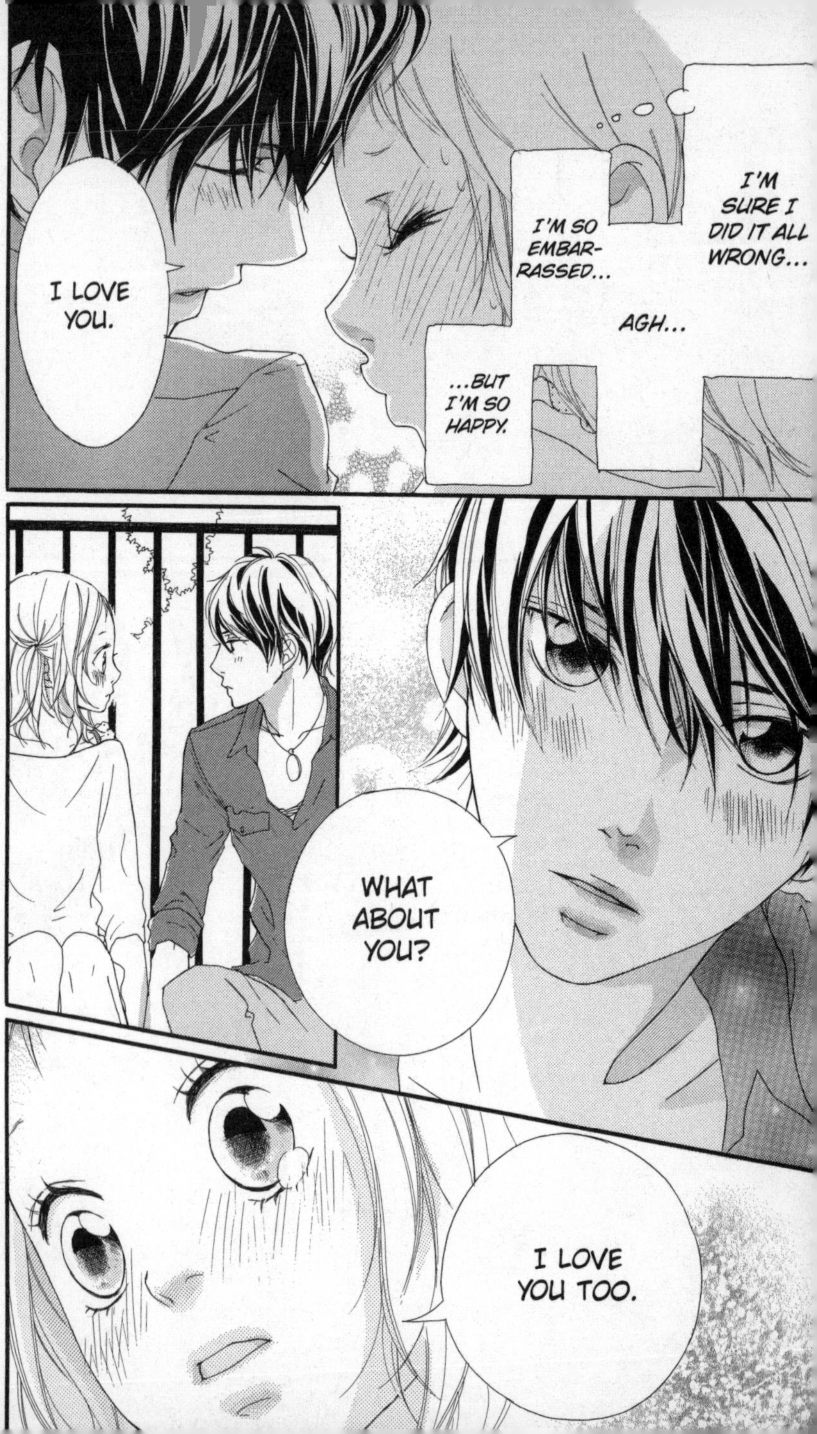
I'M SURE I DID IT ALL WRONG...
I'M SO EMBARRASSED...
AGH...
...BUT I'M SO HAPPY.
I LOVE YOU.
WHAT ABOUT YOU?
I LOVE YOU TOO.

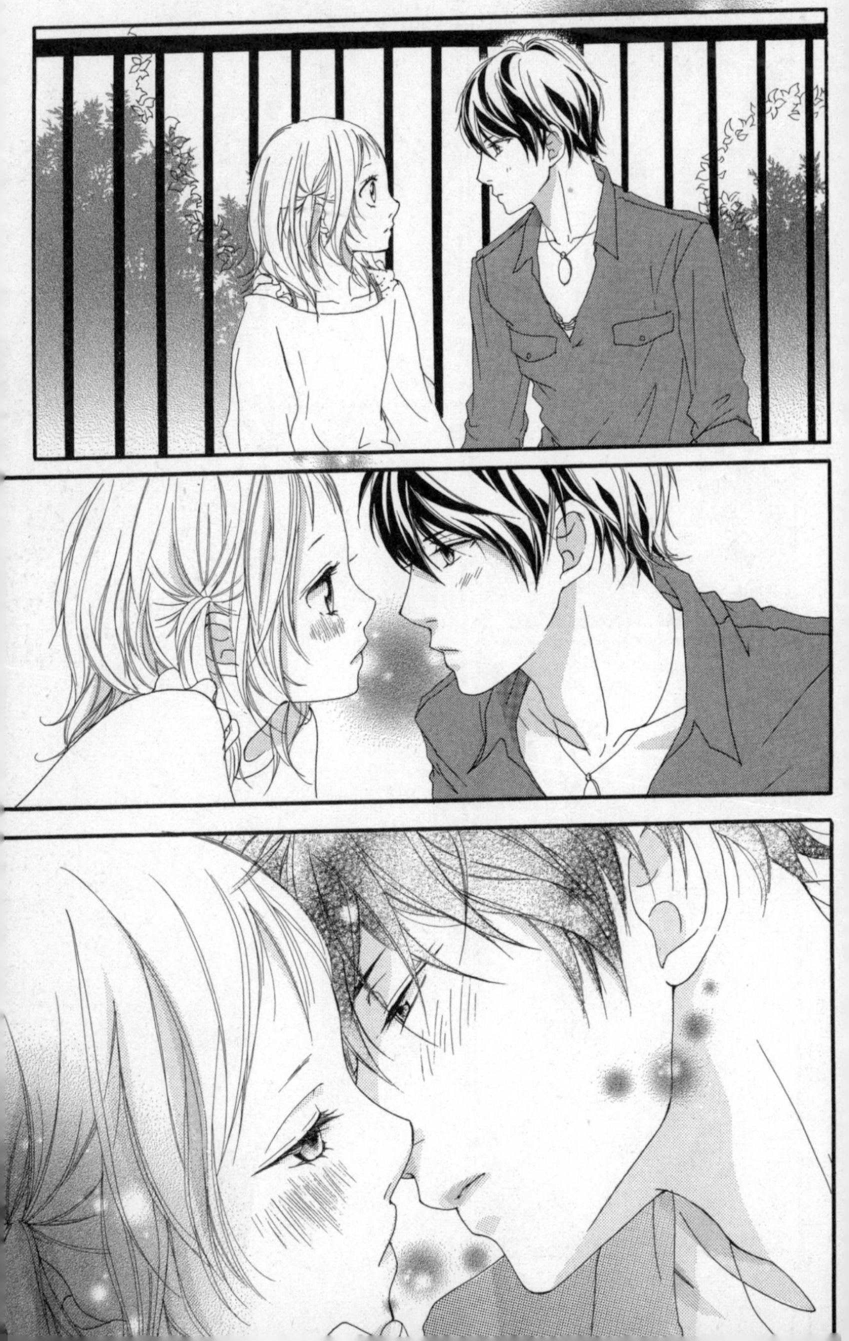

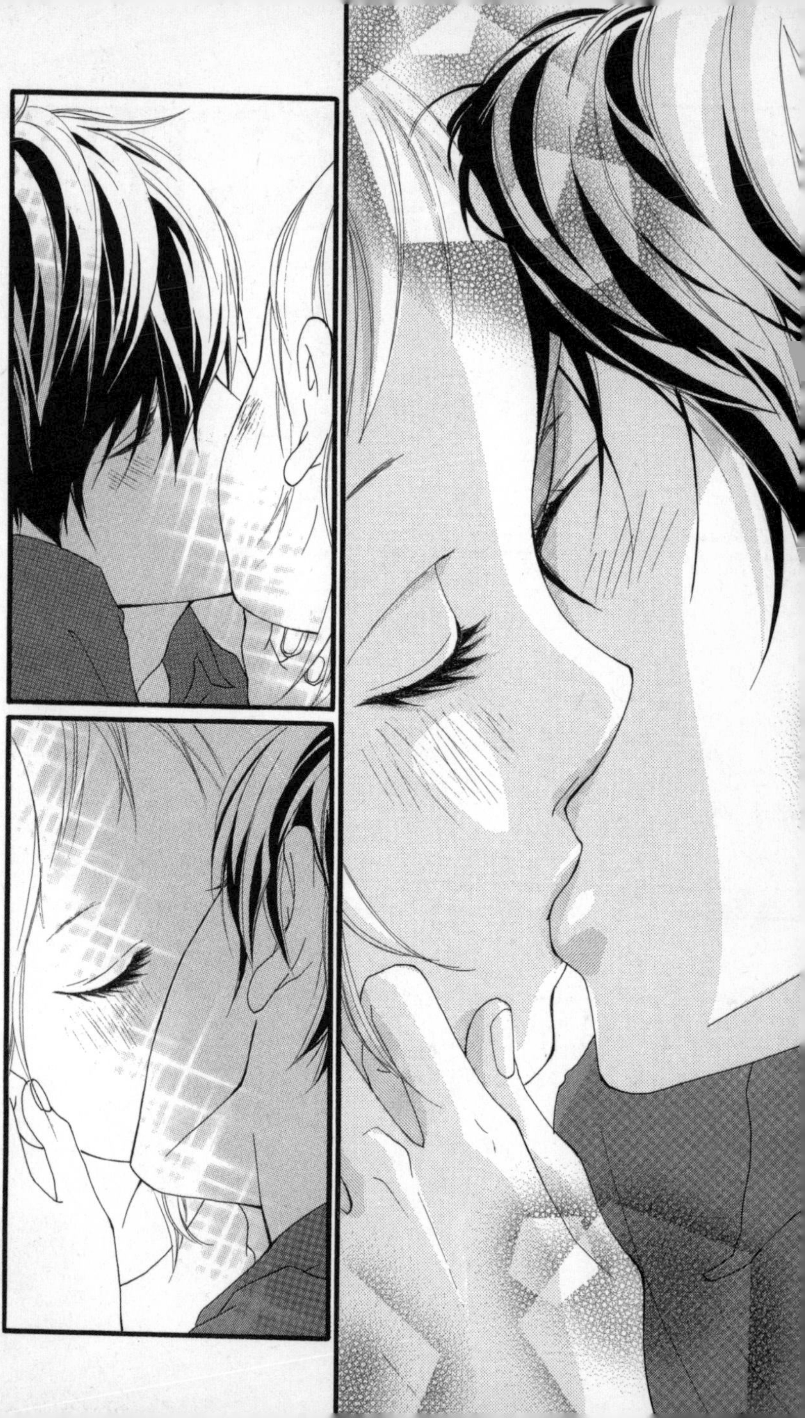

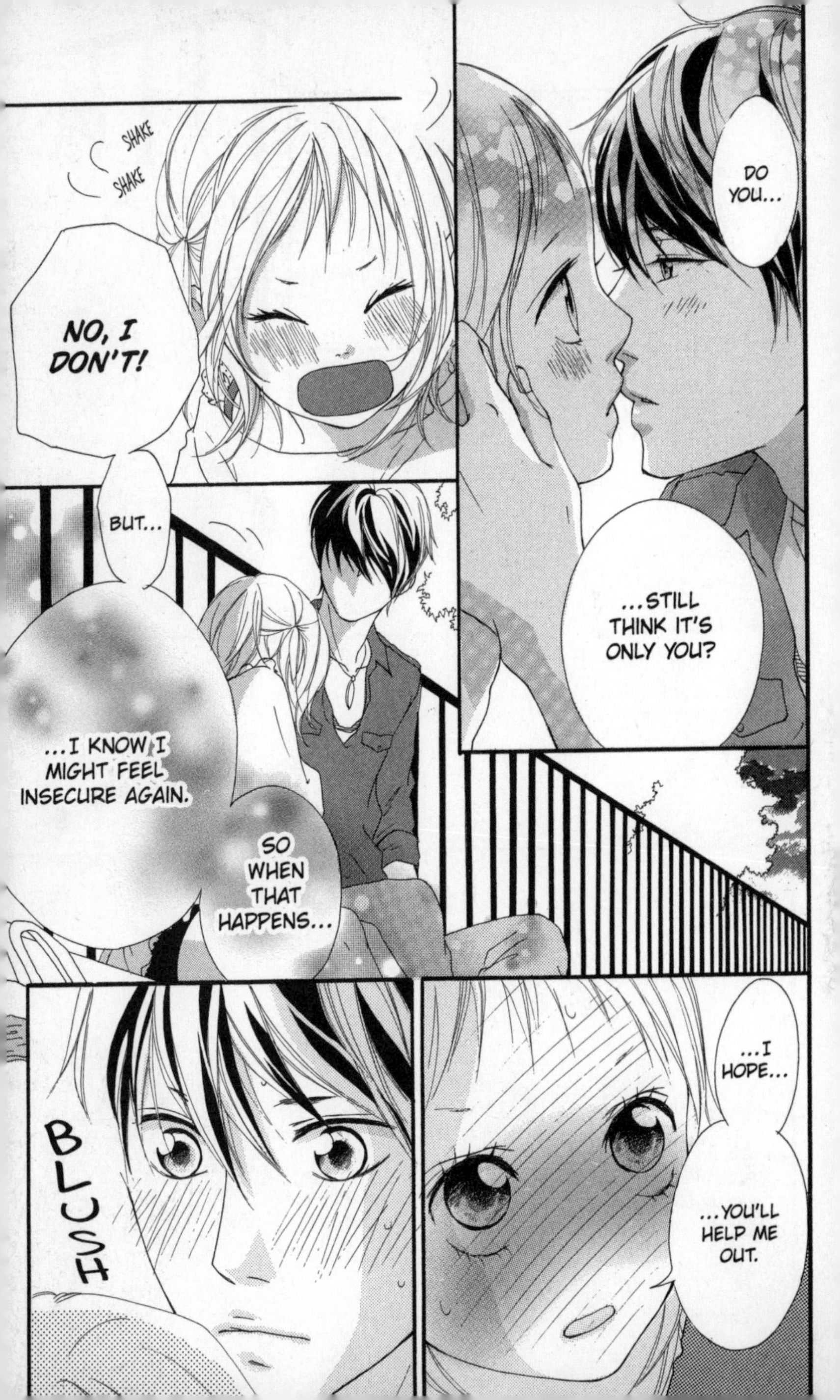
DO YOU...
...STILL THINK IT'S ONLY YOU?
SHAKE
SHAKE
NO, I DON'T!
BUT...
...I KNOW I MIGHT FEEL INSECURE AGAIN.
SO WHEN THAT HAPPENS...
...I HOPE...
...YOU'LL HELP ME OUT.
BLUSH

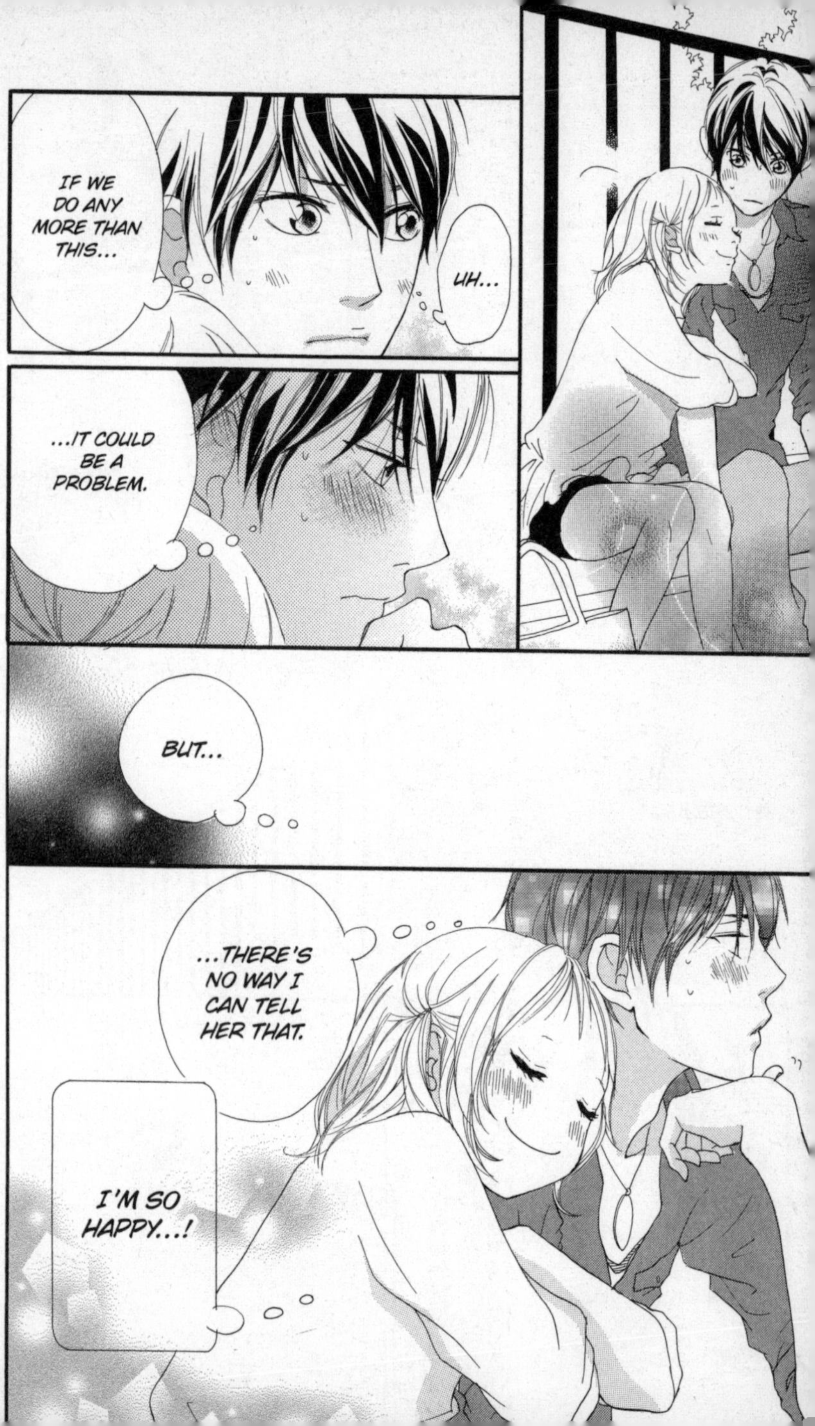
UH...
IF WE DO ANY MORE THAN THIS...
...IT COULD BE A PROBLEM.
BUT...
...THERE'S NO WAY I CAN TELL HER THAT.
I'M SO HAPPY...!

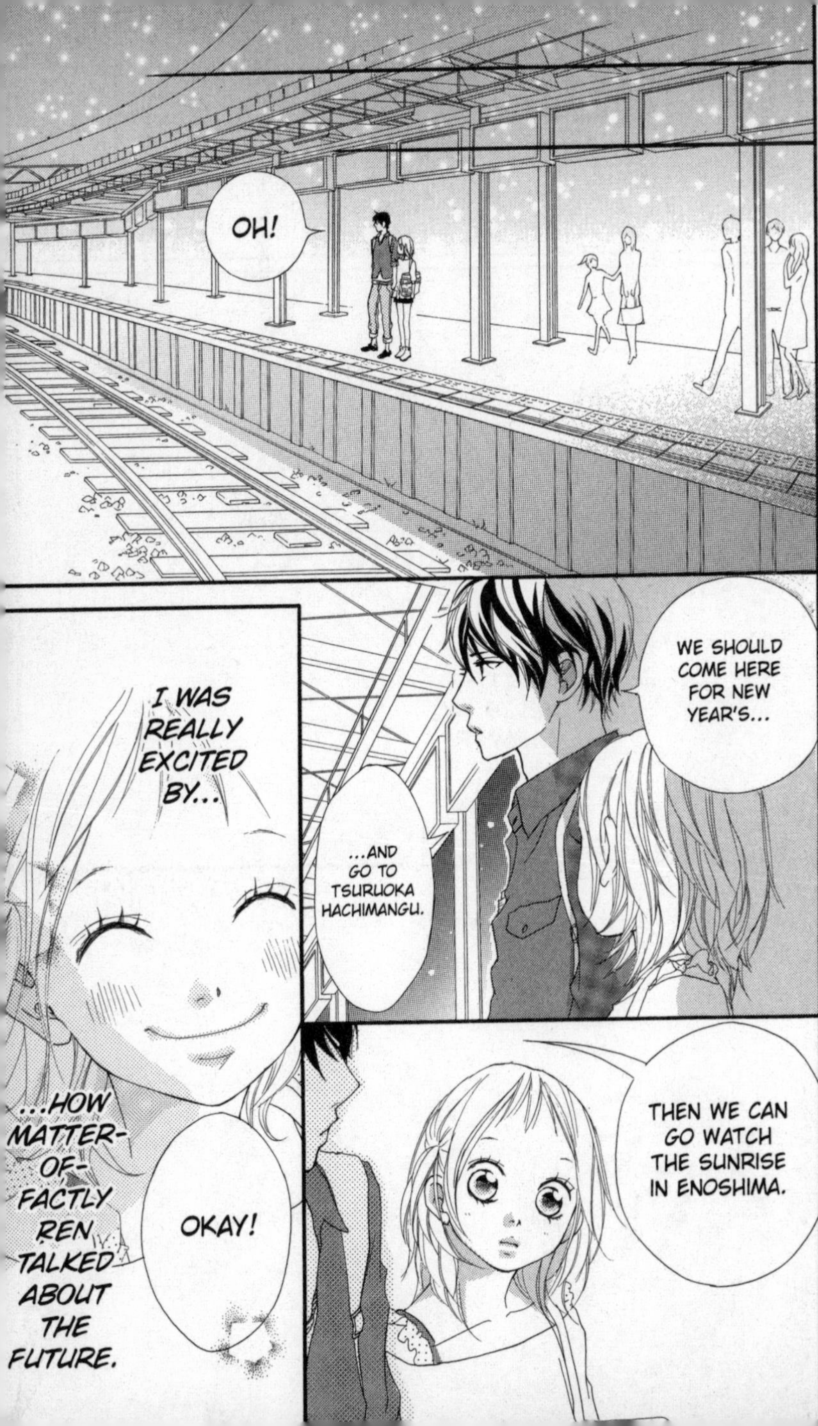
OH!
WE SHOULD COME HERE FOR NEW YEAR'S...
...AND GO TO TSURUOKA HACHIMANGU.
THEN WE CAN GO WATCH THE SUNRISE IN ENOSHIMA.
OKAY!
I WAS REALLY EXCITED BY...
...HOW MATTER-OF-FACTLY REN TALKED ABOUT THE FUTURE.

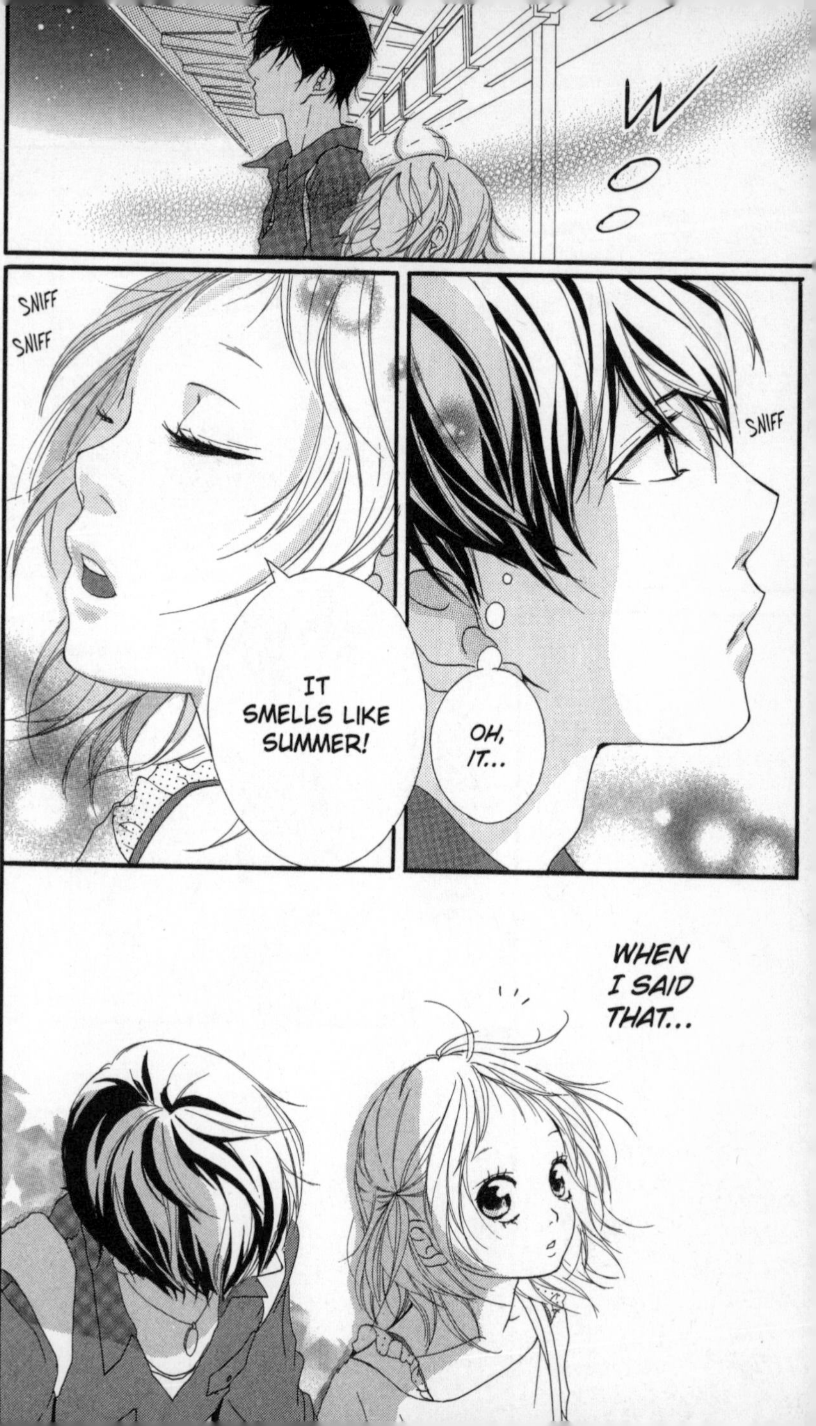
WOO
SNIFF
OH, IT...
SNIFF
SNIFF
IT SMELLS LIKE SUMMER!
WHEN I SAID THAT...

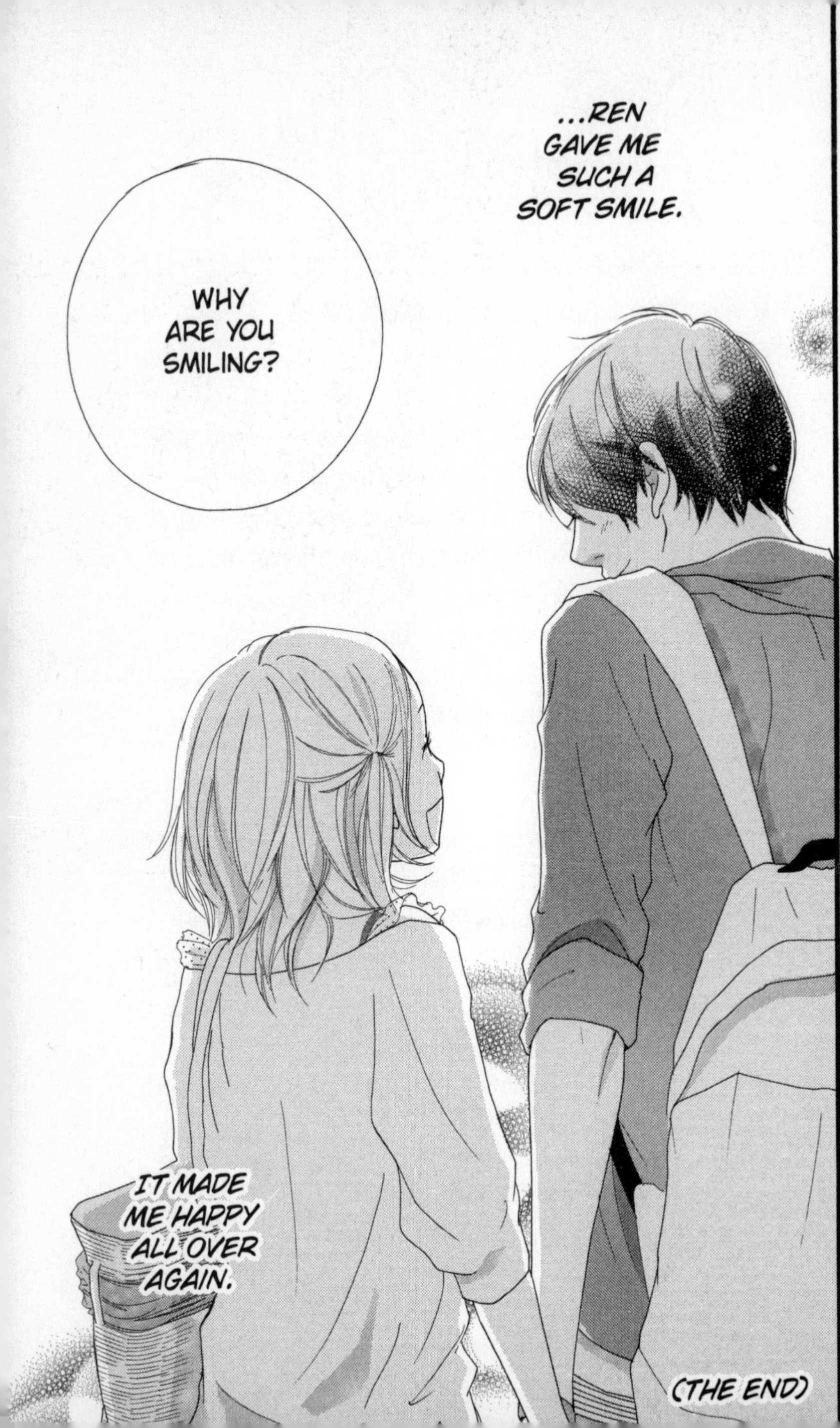
...REN GAVE ME SUCH A SOFT SMILE.
WHY ARE YOU SMILING?
IT MADE ME HAPPY ALL OVER AGAIN.
(THE END)

POSTSCRIPT ★

In the fall of 2009, I decided when to end *Strobe Edge*. This is the last stop. It's exactly the place I imagined when I picked up the series again.

Even though I'm the one who decided to end it, I remember I was very down—even more so than now, when the series has actually ended. Up until now, most of my waking hours were spent thinking about *Strobe Edge*. But I realized that once I start the next story I won't have the time or the need to keep thinking about Ninako, Ren, Ando and the others. It was a real jumble of emotions. But when I finished the last part, I was able to make it exactly the way I had pictured it. I know now that this was the best way for *Strobe Edge* to go.

I would like to use the experiences I gained here and keep moving forward. I'm going to keep working harder and harder! Please support me so I can continue to grow! Thank you so much for reading *Strobe Edge* until the end!!! Let's meet again in another place!!!

There's an extra treat starting on the next page. Take a look!

★　Io Sakisaka　★

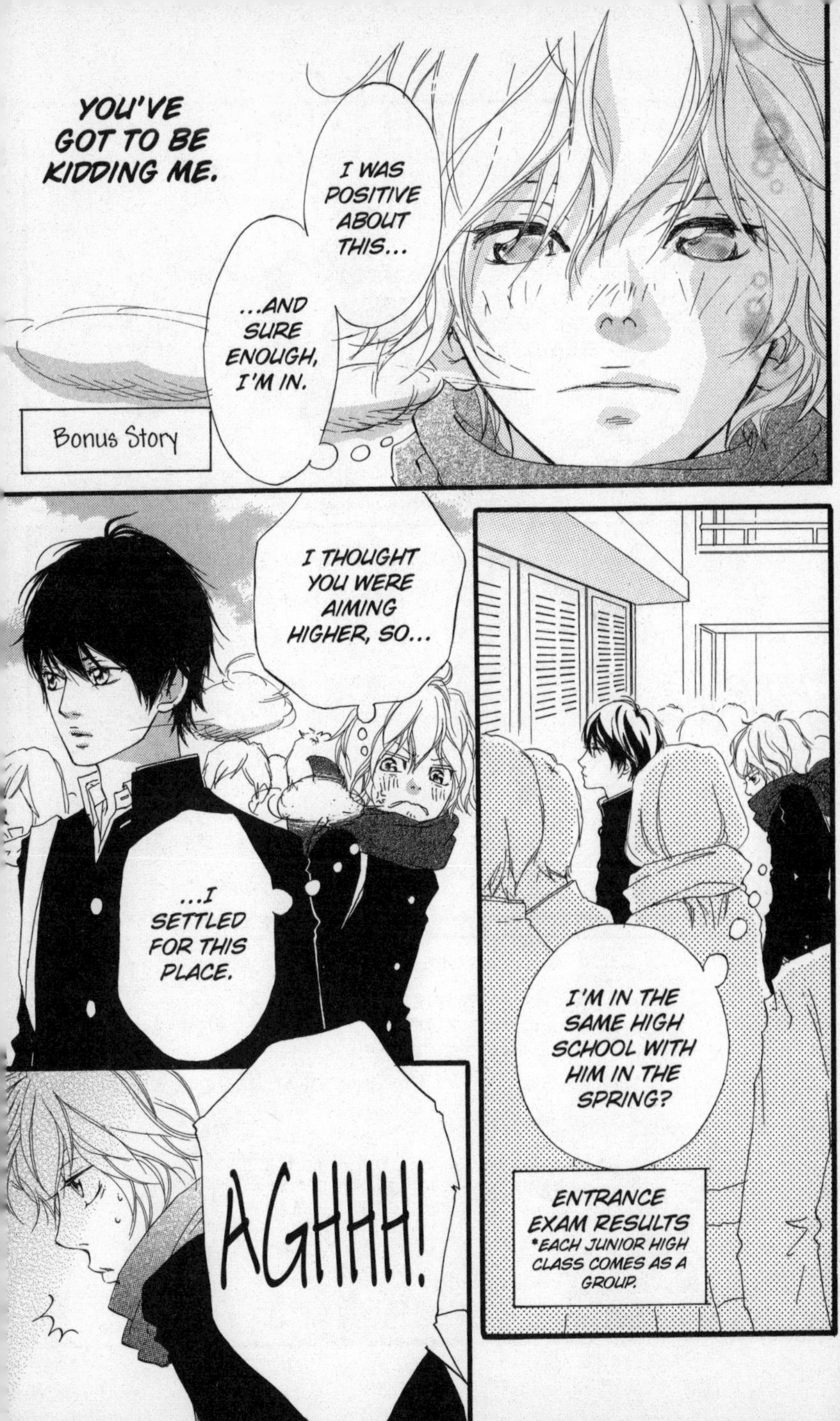
I WAS POSITIVE ABOUT THIS...
...AND SURE ENOUGH, I'M IN.
YOU'VE GOT TO BE KIDDING ME.
Bonus Story
I'M IN THE SAME HIGH SCHOOL WITH HIM IN THE SPRING?
ENTRANCE EXAM RESULTS
*EACH JUNIOR HIGH CLASS COMES AS A GROUP.
I THOUGHT YOU WERE AIMING HIGHER, SO...
...I SETTLED FOR THIS PLACE.
AGHHH!

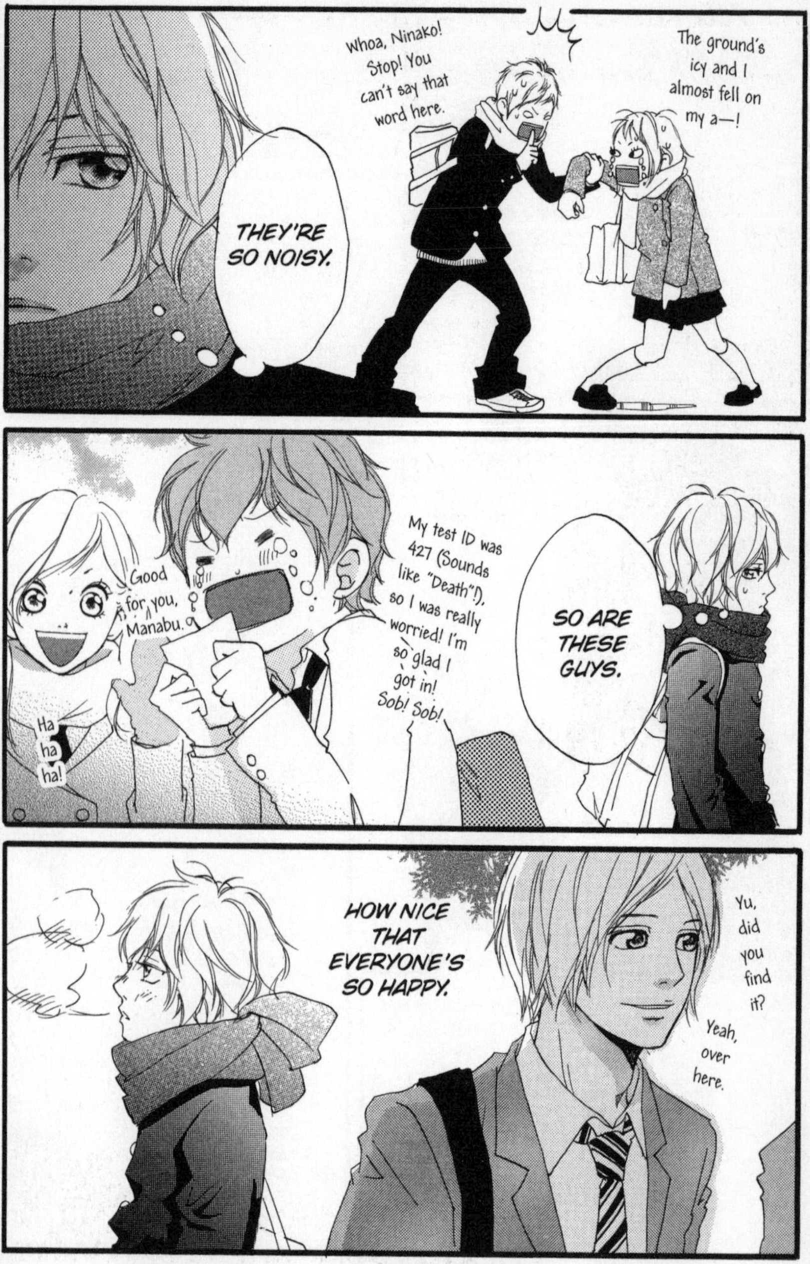
The ground's icy and I almost fell on my a—!
Whoa, Ninako! Stop! You can't say that word here.
THEY'RE SO NOISY.
SO ARE THESE GUYS.
My test ID was 427 (Sounds like "Death"!), so I was really worried! I'm so glad I got in! Sob! Sob!
Good for you, Manabu.
Ha ha ha!
Yu, did you find it?
Yeah, over here.
HOW NICE THAT EVERYONE'S SO HAPPY.

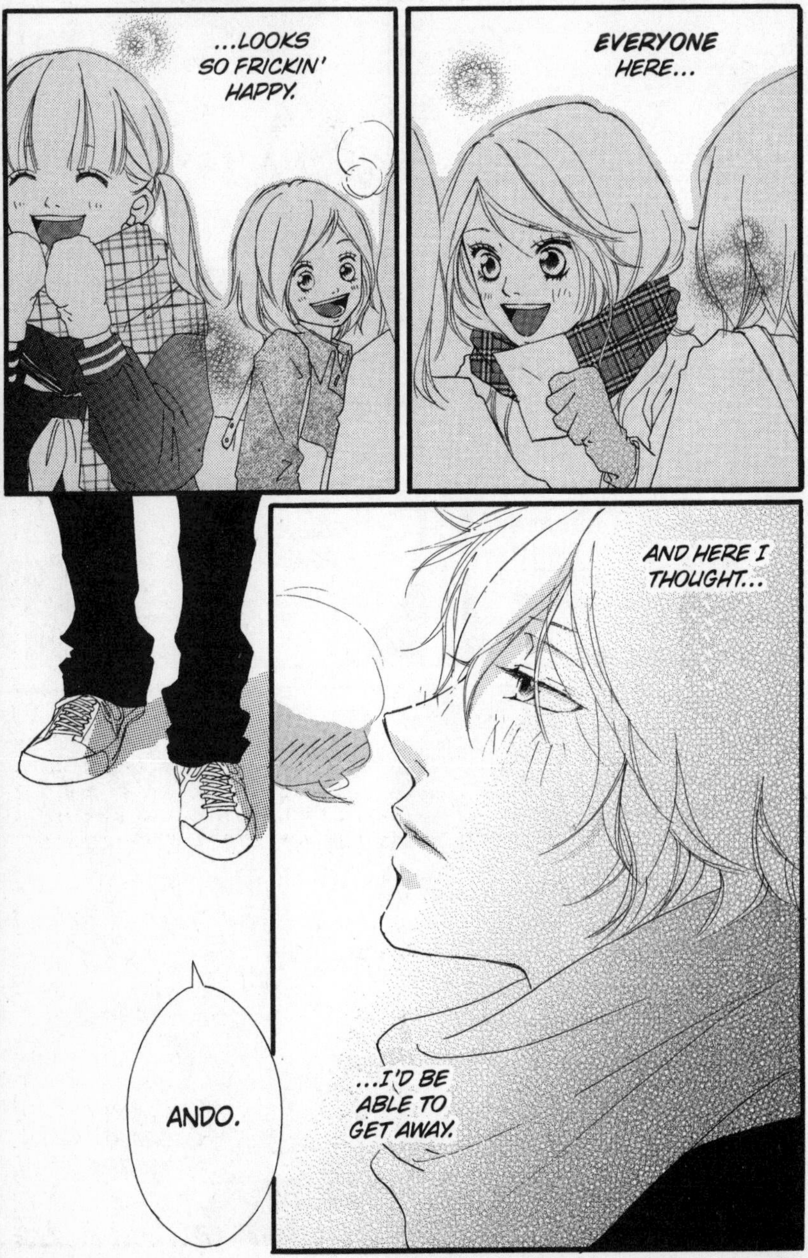
EVERYONE HERE...
...LOOKS SO FRICKIN' HAPPY.
AND HERE I THOUGHT...
...I'D BE ABLE TO GET AWAY.
ANDO.

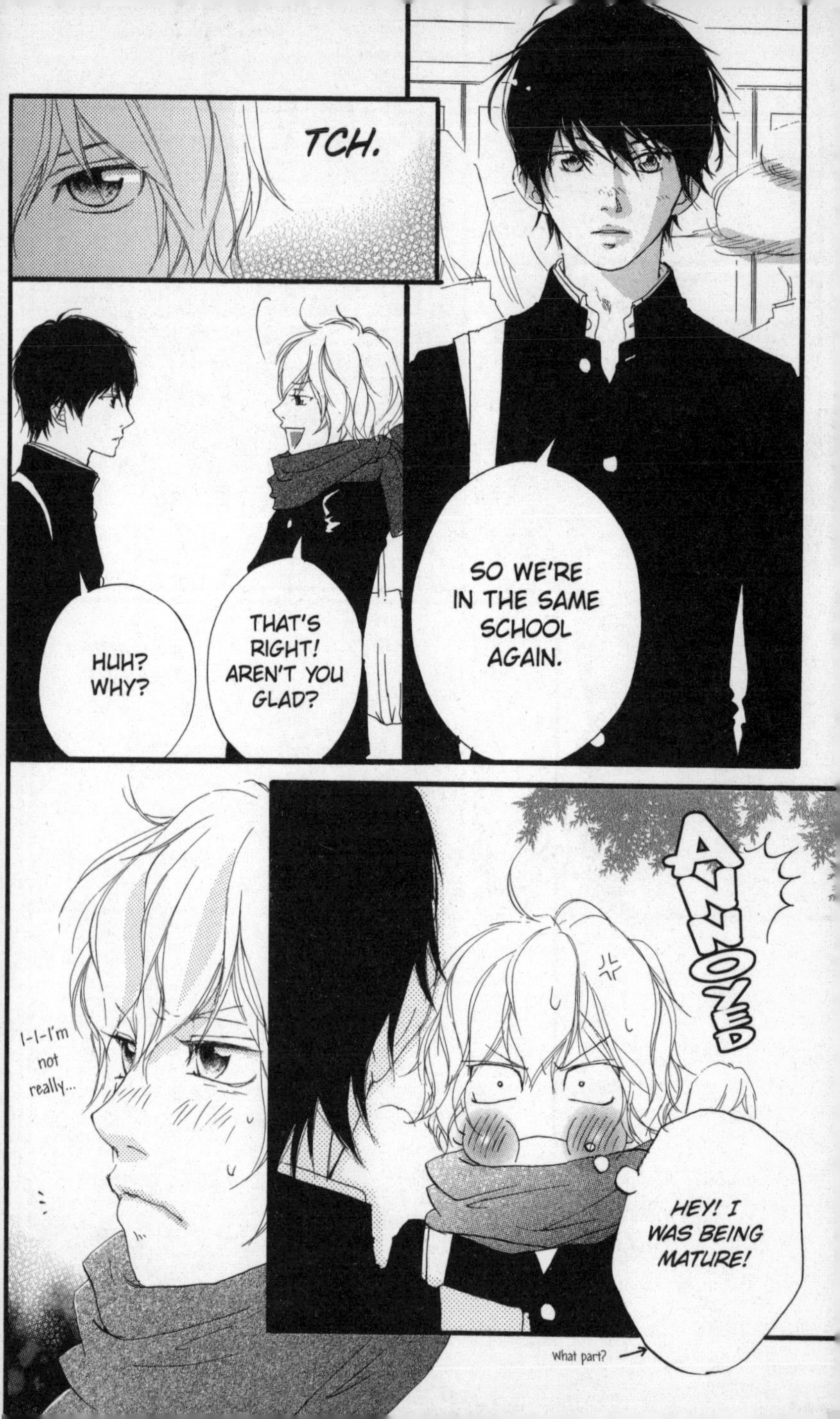
SO WE'RE IN THE SAME SCHOOL AGAIN.
TCH.
THAT'S RIGHT! AREN'T YOU GLAD?
HUH? WHY?
ANNOYED
HEY! I WAS BEING MATURE!
What part?
I-I-I'm not really...

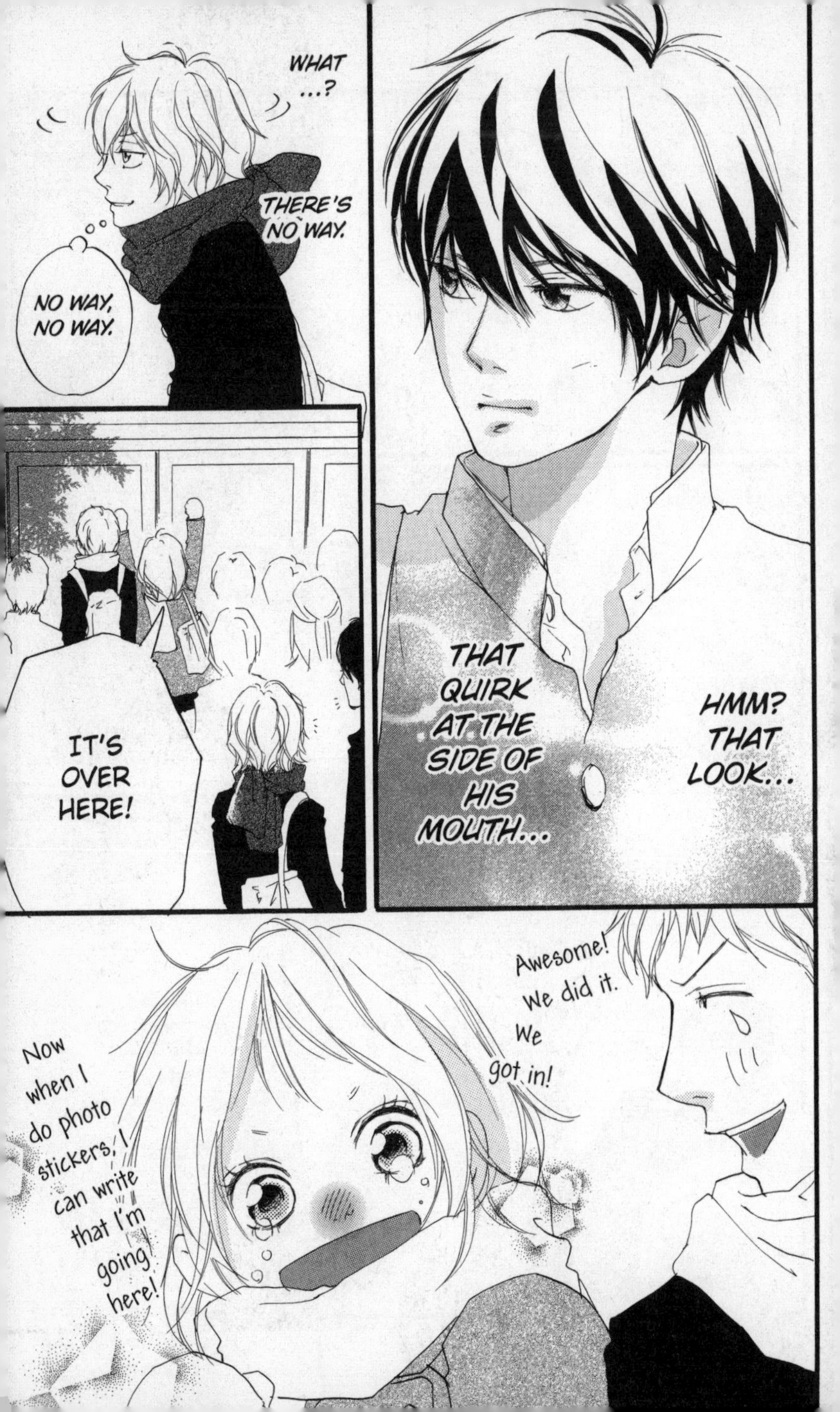
HMM? THAT LOOK...
THAT QUIRK AT THE SIDE OF HIS MOUTH...
WHAT ...?
THERE'S NO WAY.
NO WAY, NO WAY.
IT'S OVER HERE!
Awesome! We did it. We got in!
Now when I do photo stickers, I can write that I'm going here!

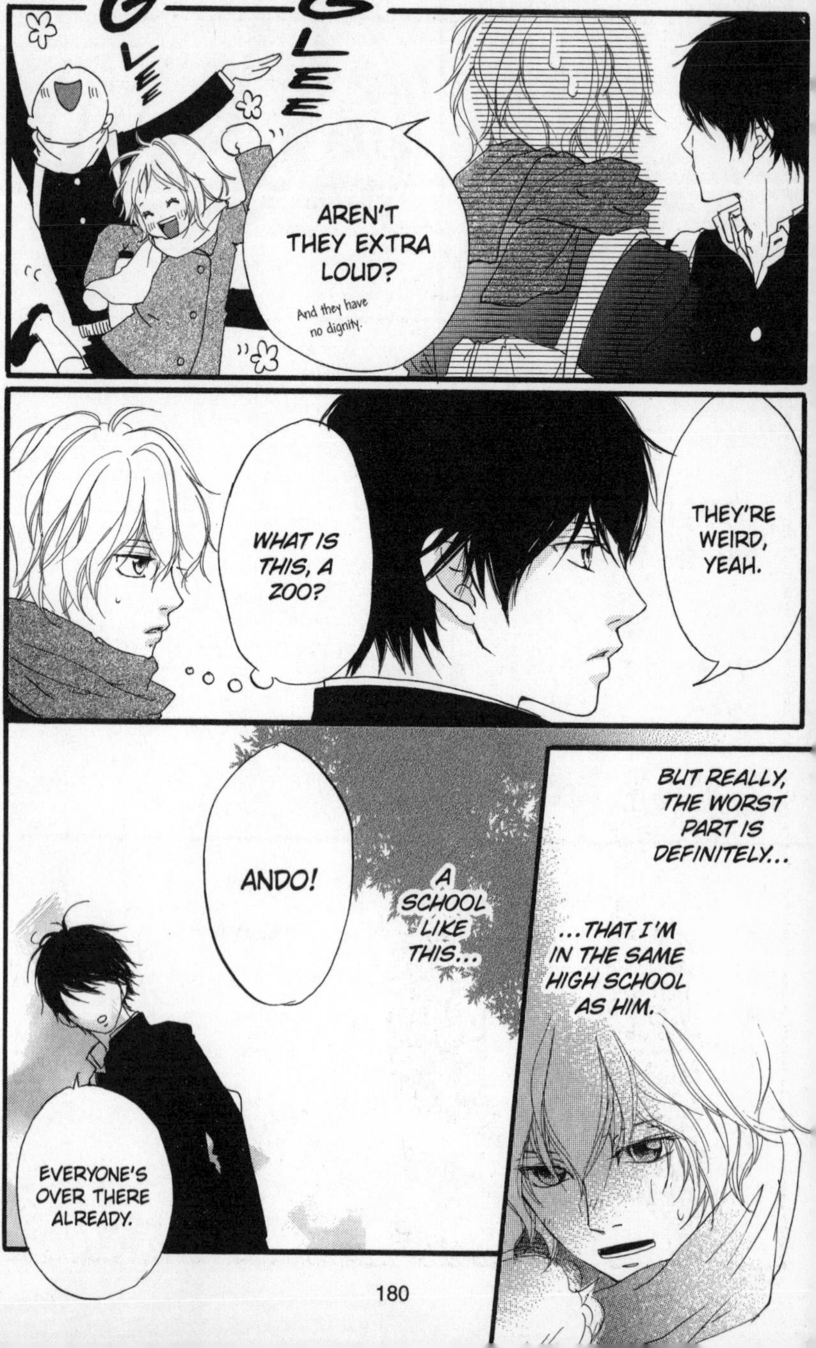
G-LEE
G-LEE
AREN'T THEY EXTRA LOUD?
And they have no dignity.
THEY'RE WEIRD, YEAH.
WHAT IS THIS, A ZOO?
BUT REALLY, THE WORST PART IS DEFINITELY...
...THAT I'M IN THE SAME HIGH SCHOOL AS HIM.
A SCHOOL LIKE THIS...
ANDO!
EVERYONE'S OVER THERE ALREADY.

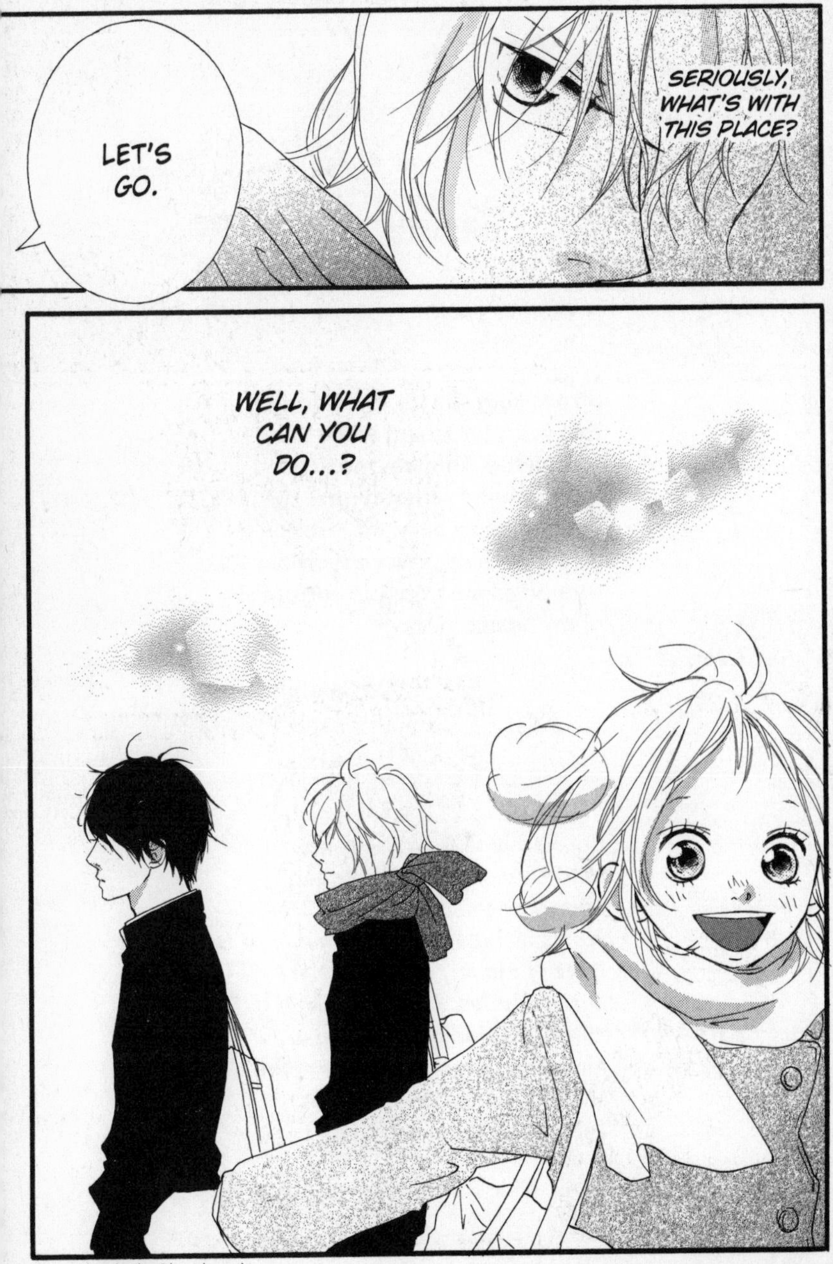
SERIOUSLY, WHAT'S WITH THIS PLACE?
LET'S GO.
WELL, WHAT CAN YOU DO...?

Continued in *Strobe Edge* volume 1!

...so, so much!

Thank you...

Strobe Edge ran for three and a half years [in Japan] and is now completed. This was my first long-running series. It gave me such joy to be busy with work. I want to thank everyone who supported me from the bottom of my heart!

—Io Sakisaka

Born on June 8, Io Sakisaka made her debut as a manga creator with *Sakura, Chiru*. Her works include *Call My Name*, *Gate of Planet*, and *Blue*. Her current series, *Ao Haru Ride*, is currently running in *Bessatsu Margaret* magazine. In her spare time, Sakisaka likes to paint things and sleep.

STROBE EDGE
Vol. 10
Shojo Beat Edition

STORY AND ART BY
IO SAKISAKA

English Adaptation/Ysabet MacFarlane
Translation/JN Productions
Touch-up Art & Lettering/John Hunt
Design/Yukiko Whitley
Editor/Amy Yu

STROBE EDGE © 2007 by Io Sakisaka
All rights reserved.
First published in Japan in 2007 by SHUEISHA Inc., Tokyo.
English translation rights arranged by SHUEISHA Inc.

The stories, characters and incidents mentioned in this publication are
entirely fictional.

Printed in the U.S.A.

Published by VIZ Media, LLC
P.O. Box 77010
San Francisco, CA 94107

10 9 8 7 6 5 4 3 2 1
First printing, May 2014

www.viz.com   www.shojobeat.com

Surprise!

You may be reading the wrong way!

It's true: In keeping with the original Japanese comic format, this book reads from right to left—so action, sound effects, and word balloons are completely reversed. This preserves the orientation of the original artwork—plus, it's fun! Check out the diagram shown here to get the hang of things, and then turn to the other side of the book to get started!

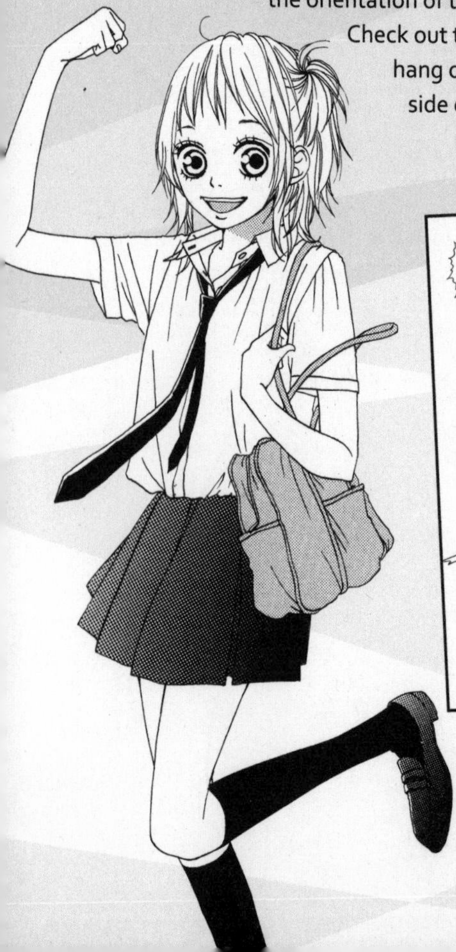

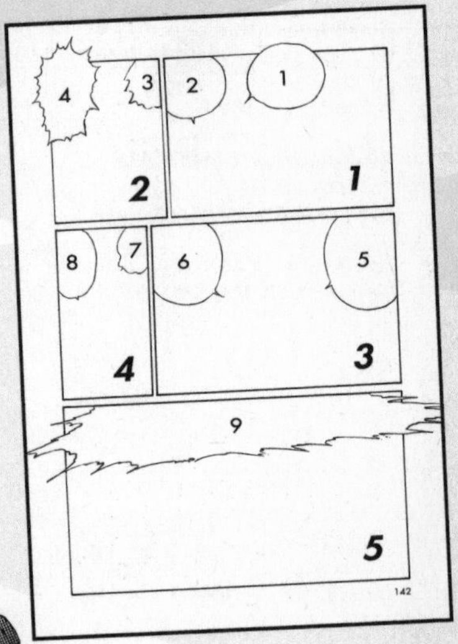
1
2
1
2
3
4
2
5
6
3
7
8
4
9
5
142